Between Mission and Market

Between Mission and Market

The Freshman Year in a Corporate Age

Daniel Rosenberg

LEXINGTON BOOKS
Lanham • Boulder • New York • London

Published by Lexington Books
An imprint of The Rowman & Littlefield Publishing Group, Inc.
4501 Forbes Boulevard, Suite 200, Lanham, Maryland 20706
www.rowman.com

Unit A, Whitacre Mews, 26-34 Stannary Street, London SE11 4AB

British Library Cataloguing in Publication Information Available

Library of Congress Cataloging-in-Publication Data

Names: Rosenberg, Daniel, 1966- author.
Title: Between mission and market : the freshman year in a corporate age / Daniel Rosenberg.
Description: Lanham, Maryland : Lexington Books 2017. | Includes bibliographical references and index.
Indentifieres: LCCN 2017002431 (print) | LCCN 2017016080 (ebook) | ISBN 9781498532679 (Electronic) | ISBN 9781498532662 (cloth : alk. paper)
Subjects: LCSH: Universities and colleges--United States--Finance. | Universities and colleges--United States--Admission--Economic aspects. | Universities and colleges--Curricula--United States. | College freshman--United States. | SAT (Educational test) | Adelphi University--Curricula.
Classification: LCC LB2342 (ebook) | LCC LB2342 .R67 2107 (print) | DDC 378.1/060973--dc23
LC record available at https://lccn.loc.gov/2017002431

∞™ The paper used in this publication meets the minimum requirements of American National Standard for Information Sciences Permanence of Paper for Printed Library Materials, ANSI/NISO Z39.48-1992.

Printed in the United States of America

To Celina, Gabe, and Nora

Contents

Acknowledgments

Taking the measure of the changing nature of the freshman year of college and in this context analyzing a program at one school—Adelphi University—is no easy task. I have the aid of three wonderful editors at Lexington–Rowman & Littlefield, Melissa McLaren, Nicolette Amstutz and James Hamill. I express my gratitude to Marianne Horan for developing what is now the General Studies Collection at Adelphi's University Archives in Swirbul Library. Circles of critics and observers helped to ease the challenge and to shape the present work. I am grateful to all of them for pushing me to consider and revisit the main arguments. In the first place, Peter Katopes, former provost at LaGuardia Community College of the City University of New York and one-time head of General Studies at Adelphi, readily contributed documents, memories, and sharp insights with me. Alan Sadovnik of Rutgers University, a co-founder of General Studies at Adelphi University, made important corrections to the historical record. I am beholden to previous Adelphi president Bob Scott, whose judicious analysis has been patient and unsparing. In long talks, dean Della Hudson of Adelphi shared unique recollections of the relationship between higher administration and General Studies in the 1990s. Regular exchanges with the president of the American Association of University Professors, my friend Rudy Fichtenbaum, shed much light on the conditions of instructors in the business climate of higher education.

I owe a substantial debt to Dee Donat for compiling documentary evidence of General Studies students' academic outcomes. Anthony Dotterman (whose Modern Language Association panels on freshman programs are a meeting place for workers in freshman programs), Sarah Eltabib, John Rizzi, and Carla Deazle have been unstinting in assessing chapters and debating points. Karen Sandoval's reports from conferences have included a host of valuable sources. Carl Mirra readily critiqued the sections on Long Island schools and communities. I have benefited from conversations with Adelphi colleagues Melanie Bush, Devin Thornburg, Traci Levy, Les Baltimore, Deb Little, Marsha Darling, Debbie Cooperstein, Raysa Amador, Esther Goodcuff, Nava Lerer, and Sal Primeggia. Adelphi professor Sergio Argueta graciously invited me to discuss common concerns on his WBAI-FM radio program *Behind the News Long Island*. Dave Parkin donated a study of SAT grades and college chemistry outcomes. Sam Grogg, Jane Fisher, Bill Proto, Gayle Insler, and Tim Burton, among others, afforded me an inner glimpse into the tussles of corporate academia. The pertinent experience of Adelphi during the presidency of the late Peter Diamandopoulos furnished edifying background for my research.

I was able to sound out my cousins David Ost of Hobart and William Smith Colleges and Triin Roosalu of the University of Tallinn on relevant questions. Tatiana B., a former student, allowed me to use a paper she had written about applying to college. General Studies alumni Glenda Athus, Monique Walker, Dr. Mario Tomei, and Asafu Owosu added to my understanding of student experience. Writer and National Public Radio commentator Heather King granted permission to use a substantive piece on the mores of capitalism. Lisa Wolf-Wendel recounted key issues of international student recruitment at the University of Kansas.

My brother Jesse, professor of music at Northwestern, has from the beginning reviewed the entire project, while suggesting changes to sharpen the arguments. My brother Fred, a teacher in his own right, has been steadfast in showing me the impact of high stakes testing on the public schools. The gestation of this book overlaps the college careers of my daughter Celina (whose candid estimates were invaluable), and my son Gabe (whose meticulous editing has civilized a maze). I have lived every detail of this book with my wife Nora for three decades, and I am grateful to her beyond words.

Introduction

Lessons of a Freshman Program

The first year of college is inherently demanding. Thrust into an unfamiliar environment, freshmen must grapple with new responsibilities, social pressures, anxieties, expectations—all while maintaining good academic standing and making the critical decisions that will determine the course of their lives. Today, in the midst of national economic problems, the pressures upon freshmen are greater than ever. Consider this: Just one generation ago, annual tuition for a private four-year college, adjusted for inflation, ran roughly half what it costs today. Factor in the meager job prospects students now face upon graduation and it's enough to make one question the whole notion of higher education at all.[1]

Overwhelmed by numerous social and psychological pressures, freshmen are suffering from alarming rates of emotional, psychological, and mental disorders. Disturbing levels of drug and alcohol use, before and during college, compound the picture. The first semester in college, a scholarly study points out, is "marked by escalated risk-taking, including alcohol consumption." Clearly, "increased use of alcohol is related to adaptations to new social settings and physical environments." A third of college students meet the diagnostic criteria of substance abusers. A researcher reports that first-year students are the most likely to require urgent care treatment for drinking; another relates their stronger likelihood to binge drink.[2]

The American Psychological Association recognizes "a growing crisis" of "depression, anxiety, suicidal ideation, alcohol abuse, eating disorders and self-injury" among American students, a trend confirmed by UCLA's Higher Education Research Institute and college mental health workers around the country. Addictions to stimulants and other drugs characterize many of those entering college for the first time. The fundamental challenges of entering higher education—alone enough to cause debilitating stress and anxiety—are exacerbated now by economic displacement and financial insecurity.[3]

These circumstances demand schools take special measures to ease students' transition from high school into college. Some schools provide built-in counseling and tutoring. Others offer specially designed orientations or structured group experiences for first year peers (a common class, seminar, trip, etc.) that serve to establish social support systems early on. How much universities are willing to invest in such endeavors revolves around the tension between education and profitability. Minimizing class sizes, preserving a cohort, extending mental health services, and providing regular tutoring may all positively serve the educational purpose, but they will go up in smoke if they do not fit lucrative aims.

The present investigation focuses on issues confronting college freshmen in general, and Adelphi University's General Studies Program (now called a Learning Community) in particular. Founded in 1985, General Studies is a specialized one-year program with a fixed core curriculum, faculty mentoring, and academic counseling targeted to freshmen with lower SAT scores and high school GPAs. This critique seeks to present the experience of the program in a rapidly changing national context of how colleges admit freshmen, and how students experience the first year of college.

A school's awareness of the freshman struggle, and the steps it takes with that awareness, is a practical litmus test of its advancement. The particulars of the present study contend upon this platform: how can a college program attempting to meet freshman needs operate and survive amid the onrushing business model in education, the destructive fixation on exams, the denigration of the humanities in college curricula, the desperate competition of colleges for market share, and economic challenges striking the college-age population and their families?

General Studies at Adelphi, like a number of similar programs around the country, is based on the notion that colleges shortchange applicants in relying too heavily on test-based criteria to judge qualifications. Indeed, a new wave of thinking stirs doubt around the academic forecasting ability of the SAT and other standardized tests, while suggesting that higher learning should adopt more enlightened views of what constitutes college potential and recommending a variety of formats for the assessment of students. This reconsideration of student potential naturally pays heed to volumes of scholarly investigations in the fields of sociology, psychology, and history. These inquiries suggest that too many higher education postulates regarding admissions rest upon outworn assumptions concerning intelligence, buttressed by standardized exams and standardized interpretations of what they mean. Legal scholar Lani Guinier calls the exam-centered terrain a "testocracy," a "twenty-first century cult of standardized, quantifiable merit that values perfect test scores but ignores character."[4]

The notion that schools should function like a business has also threatened to consume elementary and secondary education. Continuous testing of children, undergirded by Common Core State Standards, saps the learning process of essential intangibles. Core-resistant English teacher Claire Needell Hollander appreciates when her students "read with solemnity and purpose, when the project of making meaning becomes personal," and maintains that collecting the "itemized skills required for reading and writing at each grade level" into a "checklist" would "border on the absurd." Sadly, "the convenient fiction that yearly language learning can be precisely measured by various 'metrics' is supplanting the importance of literary experience." To be sure, resistance to this practice intrudes upon corporate assumptions of education. According to Harvard Business School research, "educators and businesspeople lack a shared view of the reality of U.S. education." The former believe that the metric-based instruction and outcome assessment preferred in the corporate sector do not apply in the educational sphere, and "have little confidence that business leaders deeply understand education."[5]

Nevertheless, the view prevails among educational policy makers that business people, grounded in the bottom line, are best suited to run all educational systems, from public schools to higher education. As enterprisers and investors who hire employees, they have particular views of the means and ends of education and specific answers to what the job market truly needs college graduates to know.

The ability to think critically and appreciate diversity is served by a liberal arts education. And yet, when asked directly, employers often state very different aims. According to a Hart Research survey, "employers rate proficiency in areas related to awareness of and experience with cultures both inside and outside the United States, staying current on global trends and developments, and staying current on developments in science, as notably less important when compared with the other learning outcomes tested." Employers do not mind if college graduates have been exposed to multicultural subjects, "but clearly do not view them as being critical to career success as cross-cutting skills and other skill and knowledge areas."[6]

Inside Higher Ed reports a study showing that "a liberal arts-style education can be associated with greater odds, compared to others with bachelor's degrees, on such qualities as being a leader, being seen as ethical, appreciating arts and culture and leading a fulfilling and happy life." Broadly educated students, according to the research, noted having to "examine the strengths and weaknesses of their views, and those of others, and whether they spent class time regularly talking about issues for which there was no single correct answer." The latter might buttress genuine critical thinking skills, yet do not seem to be the preferred traits of the marketplace. In fact, *Insider Higher Ed* indicates that college presidents, donors, and trustees increasingly reflect the business sector's doubts about the importance and centrality of liberal arts.[7]

Performance pay, based on stepping up graduation rates, looms as a goal of many universities. Pledging a school's effective delivery of graduates to the job market, meeting numerical test sums, and accelerating degrees assumes that colleges and their constituents do not live in a bigger context. Still, the supposition prevails that universities can whisk their students into the labor force regardless of the state of the economy, if only they try hard, objective reality notwithstanding. Colleges of all types, reports *University Business*, "prove their value by trumpeting high graduation rates," and specifically by guiding students into occupational direction. For "as soon as they enroll as freshmen," registrants must be steered toward competencies in "skills that employers want."[8]

It is assumed that American business efficiency can work the same magic upon social institutions and public services as it has upon the national economy, through time-tested methods of getting more out of less, cutting services, reducing labor, and raising prices. The language and essence increasingly borrow from societal sectors outside the academic tradition, as if the socially beneficial mechanisms of higher education innovation have no effective function within it. Purportedly, hope lies only within corporate sources. As Ariel Diaz writes in *Wired*, "higher education is no different than the automotive industry or healthcare" when you get down to it.[9]

Where did this business model for education originate? Richard Daniels, Lisa Blasch, and Peter Caster explain that governing boards in the late nineteenth century "restructured American universities along the lines of corporate ideals," and since then "the move to business-styled bureaucracies for managing university life has been quite relentless." Institutions became "competitors for the traffic in merchantable instruction," sociologist Thorstein Veblen wrote. Yet many faculty today are unaware of the trend's longevity, though the past century is threaded with similar notations by respected teachers the world over. The late Supreme Court justice William Brennan compared colleges to "big business," with notions to "cut costs and increase efficiencies" commensurate with "any large industrial organization."[10] A 1996 Harvard study put the present crisis in no uncertain terms: "Universities appear less and less as charitable institutions seeking truth and serving students and more as a huge commercial operation."[11]

The tendency penetrates methods to gauge student knowledge. Clearly, accrediting bodies and colleges themselves undertake regular reviews of what is being taught and learned. Yet increasingly the drive for "efficiencies" reduces valuation to strict numbers, even as investigations reveal the complexity of learning and the need for intelligently nuanced appraisal. According to the American Psychological Association magazine *Monitor on Psychology*, the "push for accountability is changing the university accreditation process." Accreditors now ask: how directly is college education tied to employability? Do college students ensure a reliable return on investment to institutions that provide school loans? How do curricula and courses of study fit the concrete measurements of a university's production?[12]

One approaches the questions in light of the contemporary focus on itemized results—the ledger-book reduction of knowledge. Emphasis on "practicality" in calculating both the meaning and the value of a college education leads inevitably, in the words of American sociologist and economist Thorstein Veblen, to "considerations of a pecuniary kind . . . some variant of the quest of gain." Colleges also demonstrate a clear preference for the enlargement of bureaucracies (while maintaining or reducing full-time faculty numbers), a sheer mushrooming of administrative appointments, whose many beneficiaries often have little academic experience. Benjamin Ginsberg's seminal *The Fall of the Faculty* makes it clear: With reduced faculty input, search firms produce "vice-presidents, associate vice-presidents, provosts, associate provosts, vice provosts, assistant provosts, deans, deanlets, deanlings, each commanding staffers and assistants—who more and more, direct the operations of every school." Describing a similar entourage centuries ago, Thomas Paine observed: "It is easy to conceive that a band of interested men, such as Placemen, Pensioners, Lords of the bed-chamber, Lords of the kitchen, Lords of the necessary-house, and the Lord knows what besides, can find as many reasons for monarchy as their salaries, paid at the expense of the country, amount to."[13]

This present study traces the tenuous life of a freshman program in the context of all these questions and developments. The national perspective is first outlined in three dimensions: the economics of college life, the struggle over the SAT and standardized testing, and the terrain of the freshman experience. The research then takes up the origins and growth of Adelphi's General Studies Program or Learning Community, and addresses how General Studies students measure up to those in the university's freshman mainstream, by a close comparison of grades. An investigation follows into how General Studies students have performed in light of two college success forecast tools: high school grade point averages and college entrance exams.

Retention and graduation rates of General Studies students over a span of years are analyzed in detail, as are the demographics of the General Studies constituency. The future of the General Studies Program, and ones like it, is considered. I will project that current broader developments in higher education, unless challenged and reversed, can produce an unhealthy environment for the survival of such programs. The words of Thorstein Veblen will be proven as relevant today as they were when he pronounced them in 1918: "The intrusion of business principles into the universities goes to weaken and retard the pursuit of learning, and therefore to defeat the ends for which a university is maintained."[14]

NOTES

1. College Board, *Tuition and Fees And Room and Board Over Time 1975–76 to 2015–16,* https://trends.collegeboard.org/college-pricing/figures-tables/tuition-and-fe

es-and-room-and-board-over-time-1975-76-2015-16-selected-years. Accessed July 31, 2016.

2. Tamar Lewin, "Record Level of Stress Found in College Freshmen," *New York Times*, January 26, 2011, A1; Mary Beth Marklein, "Colleges Tout Well-Being, Not Just Job Prospects," June 22, 2014, http://www.usatoday.com/story/news/nation/2014/06/22/colleges-looking-to-cultivate-well-being/9731389/. Accessed June 23, 2014; Susan Snyder, "A Rise in Mental-Health Help on Campus: Colleges Respond as More Students Seek Help for Problems Small and Serious," www.allbusiness.com/medicine-health/diseases-disorders-mental/13368747.html. Accessed June 9, 2011; Association for University and College Counseling Center Directors, *2011 AUCCD Survey*, 167; 434; Laura L. Talbott et al., "Drinking Likelihood, Alcohol Problems, and Peer Influence Among First-Year College Students," *The American Journal of Drug and Alcohol Abuse*, Vol. 34, No. 4 (2008), 434; John R. Knight et al., "Alcohol Abuse and Dependence Among U.S. College Students," *Journal of Studies on Alcohol*, Vol. 63, No. 2 (2002), 263–70; Margaret M. Benningfield, Elisa M. Truceo, Paul J. Barreira, and Shelly F. Greenfield, "Treatment of Alcoholic Intoxication at University Health Services: Examining Clinical Characteristics, Drinking Patterns, and Adherence with Referral," *Journal of Alcohol and Drug Education*, Vol. 53, No. (April 2009), 54–69; "College Freshmen Drink at Levels Well Beyond the Binge Threshold," *Brown University Digest of Addiction Theory and Application*, Vol. 26, No. 1 (January 2007), 1.

3. American Psychological Association, The State of Mental Health on College Campuses: A Growing Crisis," www.apa.org/about/gr/education/news/2011/college-campuses.aspx. Accessed June 9, 2011; Michael S. Schmidt, "Student, 20, Jumps to His Death at N.Y.U., *New York Times*, November 4, 2009, A26; Kevin Eagan et al., *The American Freshman: National Norms Fall 2014*, Cooperative Institutional Research Program at the Higher Education Research Institute at UCLA, 2014, 13–15; Carrie Sturrock, "Colleges Reach Out to Prevent Suicides," *San Francisco Chronicle*, February 4, 2007, http://sfgate.com/cgi-bin/article.cgi?files=/c/a/2007/02/04/MNG9ONUKVP1.DTL. Accessed February 7, 2007; Eagan et al., 13–14; Emotional Health Chart, "Backgrounds and Beliefs of College Freshmen," *Chronicle of Higher Education*, February 5, 2015, http://chronicle.com/article/BackgroundsBeliefs-of/145125/. Accessed March 5, 2015; Rose Marie Ward, Barbara B. Oswald, and Maria Galante, "Prescription Stimulant Misuse, Alcohol Abuse, and Disordered Eating Among College Students," *Journal of Alcohol and Drug Education*, Vol. 60, No. 1 (2016), 59–80.

4. Jeff Bryant, "Lani Guinier On Our Ivy League Meritocracy Lie: 'You Don't Want Only Those People Who Do Well on the SAT,'" *Salon*, February 4, 2015, http://www.salon.com/2015/02/04/lani_guinier_on_our_ivy_league_meritocracy_lie_you_dont_want_only_those_people_who_do_well_on_the_sat/. Accessed February 11, 2015.

5. Claire Needell Hollander, "No Learning Without Feeling," *New York Times*, June 9, 2013, SR7; Education by the Numbers, "The Push for Standards is Seeping Into Arts Education," *The Hechinger Report*, http://educationbythenumbers.org/content/arts-education-data_2636/. Accessed January 16, 2015; Michael E. Porter and Jan W. Rivkin, *An Economy Doing Half Its Job*, Harvard Business School, 2014, 18.

6. Hart Research Associates, *Falling Short? College Learning and Career Success*, January 20, 2015, 2–5.

7. Scott Jaschik, "The Proof Liberal Arts Colleges Need?" *Inside Higher Ed*, January 22, 2016, https://www.insidehighered.com/news/2016/01/22/study-traces-characteristics-undergraduate-education-key-measures-success-life?utm_source=Inside+Higher+Ed&utm_campaign=2bec496f31-DNU20160122&utm_medium=email&utm_term=0_1fcbc04421-2bec496f31-199367377. Accessed January 22, 2016; Scott Jaschik, "The 2016 Inside Higher Ed Survey of Chief Academic Officers," *Inside Higher Ed*, January 22, 2016, https://www.insidehighered.com/news/survey/2016-inside-higher-ed-survey-chief-academic-officers?utm_source=Inside+Higher+Ed&utm_campaign=2bec496f31-DNU20160122&utm_medium=email&utm_term=0_1fcbc04421-2bec496f31-199367377. Accessed January 22, 2016.

8. Dawn Papandrea, "Outlook on Enrollment: Perfect Storm of Challenges Ahead," *University Business*, January 2015, Accessed January 15, 2015.

9. Ariel Diaz, "How Technology Will Change Entry-Level Higher Education," *Wired*, June 27, 2013, http://www.wired.com/insights/2013/06/how-technology-will-change-entry-level-higher-education/. Accessed July 2, 2013; Karl Marx, "Economic and Philosophic Manuscripts of 1844," in Karl Marx-Frederick Engels, *Collected Works*, Volume 3, New York, 1975, 272.

10. Richard Daniels, Lisa Blasch, and Peter Caster, "Resisting Corporatization of the University," in Geoffrey D. White and Flannery C. Hauck, eds., *Campus, Inc.: Corporate Power in the Ivory Tower*, Amherst, NY, 2000, 69; Thorstein Veblen, *The Higher Learning in America*, New York, 1957 (1918), 65, 127; *National Labor Relations Board v. Yeshiva University* 444 U.S. 701–4.

11. Eric Gould, *The University in a Corporate Culture*, New Haven, 2003, 30, 89.

12. The Futures Project, *Correcting Course: How We Can Restore the Ideals of Public Higher Education in a Market-Driven Era*, 2005, 1; "A Push for More Accountability is Changing the Accreditation Process," *Monitor on Psychology*, October 2011, 16.

13. Veblen, 44–45; Benjamin Ginsberg, *The Fall of the Faculty: The Rise of the All-Administrative University and Why it Matters*, New York, 2011, 2; Adelphi AAUP, *Fact Sheet #3*, October 28, 2015; Thomas Paine, *Common Sense and Other Writings*, New York, 2005, 150.

14. Veblen, 164.

ONE

College as Big Business

The core belief underlying the General Studies Program, as well as others like it around the country, is that institutions of higher learning must pay special attention to first-year students. Although views about the transition from high school to college have evolved in recent years, their application depends upon the relationship of forces in the field of higher education. The vital issues are related to matters of recruitment and retention, as well as academic success. Admissions officers intensively research and chart rates of freshman acceptance, deposits, enrollments, and "yield" and "melt" over time.[1] (Yield refers to the proportion of accepted students who enroll; melt is the decline, usually in the summer, from the number of students who have made deposits to the number who actually show up in the fall.)

A school's viability hinges on how efficiently it can convert the many thousands of interested prospective students into matriculated ones. The results also affect the school's ability to capture its anticipated and necessary share of a market composed of local or similar competitors. The offering of new majors—such as Emergency Management, Sports Sales, or Casino Studies—might help keep up with changing times, as well as tap into perceived public needs. Politics may also prod academic brainstorming: Indiana University of Pennsylvania provides training for FBI agents in "anti-terrorism and weapons of mass destruction."[2] Revenue-delivering goals can parallel or transcend those of academic innovation and rigor when universities devote special attention to freshmen. Yet the calculations which take so many variables into account—economic, social, political, perceptual, and budgetary—also entail crossed fingers and speculation. Eric Gould, an author and Georgetown professor, writes in *The University in a Corporate Culture* that "whether colleges or universities like it or not, they have had to acquire much talent in betting on student futures."[3] When a gamble, however pegged to actuality, falls short, decision makers may reallocate funds, reduce budgets, opt for alternative forms of instructional staff, or project other savings.

THE BOTTOM LINE

This narrow viewpoint suffuses "a discourse," writes Gould, "derived from finance and accounting, of objectives, accountability, assessment, resources, selling (of credits to customers) and delivery (of instruction to the purchasers of credits and ultimately of the instructed to appropriate work positions." Schools apply cost accounting to the testing of knowledge. Some higher education administrators may insist that high school standardized testing cannot effectively calculate student potential because it does not measure intelligence or intellectual curiosity equally for all test takers. But pressures now operate upon colleges to prove their learning outcomes ever more concretely or lose their status. State bodies likewise posit an "outcomes-based funding system" of public institutions. Academics feel the pressure to think in like terms, as Richard Wolin affirms in *The Nation*: "The university is discussed and justified on economic lines as a 'cost center' or business enterprise, with leading educators proclaiming that the best way to advance the university's standing is by adjusting its pedagogical mission to conform to the commercial and technological imperatives of the global-economic order." Several states base public college funding on the chance of graduates finding employment and earning high salaries, as if no precarious economic milieu complicates and confounds the job search. While denouncing "pressures to commodify higher education," which "turn students into customers," the president of the University of New Hampshire frames the logical extension of the process thusly: "throw everything online" and "substitute call centers for face-to-face interactions." Indeed, executives from outside the academic sphere now view online learning as more useful than the conventional classroom setting, because it may be offered to and taken advantage of by more students at a fraction of the cost of a regular class. Similar cost-cutting impulses within the university system foster sharp dispute over the role and direction of schools.[4]

Public institutions are no less vulnerable to corporate management vision and practice. A *Houston Press* journalist warns: "When the basic functions of government—the penal system, education, etc.—are turned over to private interests, the result is usually not more efficiency, but inequality and scandal." Educator Larry Hanley observes the growth of "market-like practices, roles, and ideologies within the academy." Applying measurements to nearly everything in higher education, "with accompanying material consequences," has taken on new scope and energy, prompting calculations of input and output by departments and disciplines.[5]

While there are major differences between current institutions of higher learning and the American colleges of the period about which Thorstein Veblen wrote in *The Higher Learning in America* (1918), his observations were remarkably prescient. One of the more disturbing patterns he perceived was "a movement in the direction of a closer and more mechanical specification of the terms on which the higher degrees are to be conferred," thus subordinating the pursuit of knowledge to "aggregate quantity" and the "interstitial intervals allowed by a strictly drawn accountancy." He described a college administrator who acted to "standardize and control the work of his staff" by reducing course content to "symmetrical and permanent shape under the form of certified syllabi," thus to be more easily taught by interchangeable faculty. In Veblen's view, such "standard erudition in uniform packages" needed only close following of instructions to transmit: "add hot air and serve."[6]

Schools today more creatively and assiduously establish matrices, benchmarks, or other aims to use as a guide for assessment, but blur the line between academic goals and marching orders. Of special concern is the incorporation of corporate methodologies to calculate faculty "productivity," predicated on the assumption that numbers tell all. Standardization of the outputs of higher education is at odds with the many dimensions of educational experience and instructional labor, but gallops along presently at a steady pace. A company called Academic Analytics, contracted by many schools, tracks college teachers in terms of publications, research, and other indices. Colleges use the data for evaluating the professors. But professorial work, a professor at Rutgers declares, entails "being innovative, being interdisciplinary, taking risks," not simple output. *Inside Higher Education* adds "the productivity algorithm doesn't take into account teaching or service." Moreover, it ignores the many other elements of student growth, including campus and community involvements during the college years. "Metrics have less to do with individual attainment and more to do with capturing data for management," says *The Guardian*.[7]

The journal *Academe* states that "simply asking colleges and universities to provide 'evidence' of student learning outcomes, as accreditors do, does not guarantee that students actually learn." Yet the more meticulously that syllabi project the end results of coursework, the more they are now considered complete. Joel Thomas Tierno, a professor of philosophy at the College of Southern Nevada, criticizes the direction in no uncertain terms: "The curriculum is quantifiable, measurable, and marketable. You can advertise it. You can look at it from the standpoint of numbers, adjust it to maximize FTE [full-time equivalent], use it to bait students/customers. The heart of the university becomes nonhuman."[8]

INSTRUCTIONAL LABOR

A "market-discipline" is observable throughout higher education. It includes transforming instructional labor along the lines of a part-time/off the tenure track instructional force. Though paid less and left unprotected, most new adjunct hires hold respectable credentials. Yet the fact that they may teach many classes in different places, without firm roots, leads critics to fear a resulting loss of faculty input in higher education. "Contingent" professors now make up a majority of faculty at four-year schools and preponderantly work at more than one institution. All too often, a student registers for a course whose instructor is listed as "Staff." As asserted in a 2012 report by the Center for the Future of Higher Education, impermanence impairs the educational experience altogether: "Across the nation, college administrations have institutionalized employment practices that threaten the quality of the education students receive, mismanaging valuable human resources." A German Studies professor notes: "With corporatization came prioritization of the student 'customer experience': climbing walls, luxury dorms, and coursework that is transactional rather than educational. To facilitate the optimal experience for these customers, administrators began to increase oversight of their faculty, which, with an ever-adjunctifying professoriate unable to fight back, became ever easier to do."[9]

Since the 1970s, the corps of tenure-track full-time professors has been transformed into a working population teaching on a shakily conditional basis. The numbers of adjunct professors are in fact rising rapidly. The trend holds across the nation. While some adjuncts hold jobs outside the academy and teach part-time within it (thus bringing professional experience to Nursing, Social Work, Business, Education, and Psychology classes), most are otherwise unemployed. Some equate adjuncts with fast-food workers. In the public sphere, the Institute for Policy Studies has shown that contingent hiring has increased the fastest at universities where administrative salaries have risen the most, and where student debt is most severe. At the same time, administrative positions have proliferated across the board, sufficient to consider them a strong factor in increased tuition. Widening part-time faculty employment naturally lowers institutional expenses, since compensation is low and benefits nonexistent. Yet at the same time executive hires have ballooned at most schools, including Long Island's private colleges and comparable local competitors. Notes the Campaign for the Future of Higher Education, between 1987 and 2012, "while the numbers of temporary faculty mushroomed and the percentage of permanent faculty plummeted, the numbers of administrative staff more than doubled." The financial consultant Bain & Company remarks that "support and administrative costs . . . have grown faster than the cost of instruction across most campuses." Although the evidence of wage inequality in many fields is abundant,

Bain nevertheless declares: "In no other industry would overhead costs be allowed to grow at this rate."[10]

It appears however that the champions of higher ed's corporatization see no conflict in pushing the business model while championing the ethics of higher learning. They may even invite respected social reformers to deliver commencement speeches, while on-campus pay inequalities continue apace. Resorting to contingent (adjunct or non-tenure track fulltime) faculty is in fact a salient hallmark of the contemporary academic economy, not only in the United States. The sporadic and irregular labor of part-time workers in the most advanced economies is characteristic of contemporary income inequality, according to The Organization for Economic Co-operation and Development (OECD). A third of British college instructors are part-timers. The Australian scholar Leanne McRae points out that widespread adjunct employment casts doubt not upon the abilities "of adjunct staff to appropriately instruct university students, or to reflexively deploy expertise," but rather on "the contextual conditions that define adjunct labour and that have resulted in the widespread and long-term adoption of sessional work as appropriate employment at universities." Their exploitation goes unappreciated or is excused, contends McRae, even by tenured faculty. And still, "adjunct academics currently do extraordinary work when faced with these conditions to both create and interface with the critical needs of students." But higher education governing boards and accrediting associations have recently questioned the ability of schools to meet their academic mission unless they significantly upgrade part-timers: raising pay, normalizing procedures for terminating and hiring, guaranteeing renewable contracts, encouraging research, and including them on faculty and planning committees.[11]

Part-timers comprise no less than 75 percent of college faculty in the United States. Regional New York City-area colleges may be cited in evidence of the direction. Hence in 2014, Hofstra had 650 adjuncts and 498 full-timers and St. John's, 838 adjuncts and 614 full-timers. Realizing the immense savings to be had in skirting health or other benefits, most universities see hiring adjuncts as a no-brainer. Some in the academic community openly argue the cheap labor advantages to higher education. An article in the *Journal of Business Ethics* avers that since part-timers are "significantly less expensive than tenure-track faculty, any attempt to improve the pay and conditions of adjunct faculty will encounter unpleasant trade-offs." Thus, it claims, the additional costs of improved working conditions would compel schools to lay off adjunct professors. Student-teacher ratios would then soar. The learning experience would suffer. Human Resources officers argue in like tones about the potential harm to universities of paying clerical and non-academic staff overtime wages: "Institutions would be under pressure to raise tuition, when student debt is at an all-time high, and decrease services to cover the costs of these changes." The College and University Professional Association for

Human Resources, a custodian of higher ed's cheap labor disposition, insists that awarding overtime pay to post-doctoral researchers (who work sixty hour weeks and average $43,000 annually) would leave schools no choice but to reduce services (including health coverage) and personnel across the board. A coalition of schools has in fact argued that awarding overtime pay to employees averaging between $29,000 and $40,000 a year would seriously impair higher education. Close to half the U.S. Senate is on record alleging that overtime supplements for low-paid college workers (including teaching assistants) would ruin all chances of keeping higher ed costs down.[12]

Depending on the region, level, and college, part-time instructors earn between $1,800 and $5,000 per course, and are subject to "termination or nonrenewal without due-process procedures," long considered normal protections "of academic freedom." Contracts for the better-paid full-time nontenure professors generally last a year. The American Association of University Professors finds adjunct labor emblematic of academe, no longer "simply a 'temporary' way station on the road to a tenure-track faculty career." Adjuncts, writes the journal *Hybrid Pedagogy*, are the round pegs who do not fit, lacking supplies and private offices: they must discuss matters with their students in public view. Weather permitting, a bench will do, or one may consider the lobby of a building. Populating the ranks of academia, part-timers are frequently unacknowledged as serious pedagogues. The *St. Louis Post-Dispatch* utters the obvious "Excellence in Higher Education Starts with Better Pay for Instructors," but are administrators listening?[13]

It is no wonder that part-timers or non-tenure track full-timers increasingly seek union affiliation, or that some on the National Labor Relations Board sense that contingent hiring has become an expression of an unwelcome "'corporatization' of higher education." Unions within the educational industry, like the AAUP, or more recently the Service Employees International Union, have attempted to respond to the need. The psychological effects of employment insecurity in education are no less than one would expect in other occupations. In fact, according to scholars Gretchen M. Reevy and Grace Deason, "contingent faculty who have lower family incomes, who have been unable to find a permanent position, who are most committed to their institution, and who use dysfunctional coping mechanisms are most likely to perceive higher levels of workplace stressors and harm and to experience higher levels of depression, anxiety, and stress." Furthermore, warn Reevy and Deason, "harm to the faculty is likely to indirectly cause harm to the students and therefore to the mission of the institution." *Inside Higher Education* says that instructors who work contingently "are among the most vulnerable workers in higher education," subject at earliest pretext to dismissal for sundry reasons. But educational institutions, as the AAUP points out, may deem it "advantageous to have both the flexibility to add and drop teachers to meet instant needs and to retain teachers who are unlikely to risk their unprotected jobs by being troublesome over curricular or administrative matters."[14]

Straying from the anti-union tenor of many administrations, a contributor to *University Business* counsels schools to accept adjunct organization as an intelligent "long-term investment rather than a disruptive short-term cost." But college administrations resist faculty union organizing drives, especially ones devoted to better salaries for low paid instructors. They enjoy the advantage of advisors experienced in negating unionization in other industries. *University Business* supplies strategic advice toward the same end in higher education. It counsels college officials to win the "hearts and minds" of faculty to oppose unions. Administrators should base their pitch on the assertion of a union's disruption of campus culture and unity, says the journal. They should emphasize the deleterious impact upon college budgets: "Cite facts, data and anecdotes to strengthen your message." Moreover, "pick a powerful messenger" to represent the administrative position, perhaps a respected professor arising to administration after long years of teaching and service: "who has the deepest emotional connection to employees and faculty, and who can effectively and passionately make the university's case."[15]

The esteemed former instructor, now become dean or provost, might well expect to be given the benefit of the doubt by erstwhile colleagues in Biology, Film Studies, English or some other discipline. Hence, the double take when a thus ascended administrator begins to advocate managerial prerogatives which as a faculty member he or she had long questioned or never expounded: such as the need to prevent unionization of part-timers.[16]

Besides widespread use of adjuncts, colleges have circumvented job security for full-time instructors who did not belong to conventional departments by holding that they were not in fact teachers, but staff or administrators. Their jobs have been as collapsible as a folding chair. In resistance, campus unions, as at Adelphi, try to win protections for contingent professors. Wright State's (Ohio) bargaining unit now includes "all Senior Lecturers, Lecturers, Instructors, Clinical Assistant Professors, Clinical Instructors, and Visiting faculty employed full-time . . . , hereafter referred to as Non-Tenure Eligible (NTE) Faculty." Hofstra University's contract recognizes "all full-time faculty, those holding special status, those holding the title of assistant or associate chair, all regular adjunct faculty." The University of Oregon's "tenure-related faculty, non-tenure-track faculty, adjunct faculty, post-retired or emeritus faculty, library faculty, and officers of research, including research assistants, research associates, and postdoctoral scholars" belong to the same union. The Professional Staff Congress in the City University of New York has won three-year appointments for adjuncts. In general however, ensuring faculty security in the corporate age remains an increasingly uphill battle.[17]

ENROLLMENT MANAGEMENT

The corporate business model is evident in the operations, promotions, recruitment, and policies of schools. It has entirely transformed the process of admitting students to college. Issues affecting incoming class engagement, persistence, and graduation rates have long been too numerous for traditional admissions offices to handle. As the need for advanced management skills among college administrators became evident, Harvard Business School pioneered appropriate training in the 1970s. It helped lay the basis of today's college management system. Harvard exposed "administrators to the kind of rigorous training that generations of corporate managers have received at the school," precisely because (as the *New York Times* then reported, those "who administer the nation's colleges have generally been ill-equipped to meet the kinds of financial and social pressures that have suddenly descended on them."[18]

Offices of enrollment or enrollment management are foremost examples of college managerial strategies. They coordinate the many-sided elements of student recruitment and consolidation. Traditionally, recruitment, admissions, and institutional aid were separate jurisdictions. Now, however, it is more common for schools to centralize varied and related functions, as well as previously distinct collections of information. Companies can help. At Lane College in Tennessee, for instance, software purchased from Three Rivers Systems' CAMS Enterprise eliminated the split between separate data systems for recruiting and admissions. Generally, the people who recruit draw up strategies conforming to each interval on the continuum of the prospective students' search, with a battery of tactical approaches suited to each. Indeed, the wooing of students is but one component in an optimal "systems model" contouring admissions to each applicant.[19]

Enrollment management requires a high-powered administrative structure and streamlined operation. Assimilating a group of offices and officers working toward a common goal, under the jurisdiction of a vice-president or senior vice-president, is no mean task. With a senior or executive vice-president at the helm, the Office of Enrollment Management would likely embrace or team up with crucial branches, each led by an assistant vice-president, or at least a director. The assistant vice-president for school security (public safety), the director of athletics, the assistant vice-president for financial services, the assistant vice-president for student affairs, and the director for career development might all belong to the circle of enrollment management.

Each bailiwick has its own subdivisions: Student Affairs, for instance, comprises student life, clubs, organizations, Greek life, orientation, dormitories, and commuter services. The Admissions office naturally handles transfer students, applicants to graduate school, and freshmen, with different people in charge of each area, and then in turns broken down by geographic region. Clearly, the Office of Admissions sits at the very heart of enrollment management. Its executive director (often holding the simultaneous title of assistant vice-president) would report to the senior or executive vice-president of enrollment management. A swarm of associate and assistant directors of varying levels of experience, frequently prefixed "senior," often inhabits the Admissions Office.

An unusually wide range of responsibilities may accrue to an institution's enrollment chief, who often serves as senior vice-president. A recent job description gives an enrollment management vice-president oversight over all recruitment and retention strategies, the issuing of relevant reports and analyses, the operation of academic support and retention services, the circulation of all enrollment publications and advertising materials, and the administering of academic scholarships.[20]

To this administrator may fall not only the executive decisions of the high vice-presidency, but also the ultimate determination of a college's food offerings, new construction, parking, or whether to close due to weather emergencies: dressed to the nines, these second-in-commands may carry instruments to measure snow or wind. Indeed, such decisions as the placement of parking facilities underneath athletic fields (as at Adelphi and Worcester Polytechnic) fit relevantly under the enrollment umbrella. Hence, experts suggest that successful enrollment demands not only skilled leadership but also an active hands-on approach: the leadership must have the ability to see the bigger picture, transcend small crises, delegate and develop, and build consensus.[21]

The multiplication of vice-presidents along the management continuum is breathtaking. Some refer to such a large swelling on the collegiate body as "administrative bloat." Overall, it would be difficult to find more "vice" in any comparable college aggregation. Vice-presidents may have advanced degrees in Educational Administration, a discipline pressured to emphasize the second word in its title and to apply business methods to the tasks of higher education. Others have may have trained in a discipline of the liberal arts, but special importance is accorded a nose for business-dipped common sense. While not always at odds with the values of education, work in the enrollment field involves a different dedicated knowledge base. Pooling the systems of student life, financial aid, marketing, and admissions, among others, while respecting their independence, is a tall order. Assuming the optimum case, where harmony reigns among the vice-presidents, unhampered by turf wars, successful enrollment officers must be ruthlessly honest in evaluating the operations. They take steps to prevent role confusion, over-centralization, and lack of coordination.[22]

The focus on enrollment management takes diverse forms, underlined by the need to highlight the relevant functions and substantially elevate the officer in charge. A school in the state university system in New York recently moved enrollment management tasks from an associate vice-president within Business Affairs to a full vice-president holding a seat in the institution's cabinet. Some schools may have neither the experienced personnel nor the resources to upgrade themselves in this way. Or they may wish to organize their activities to a degree their current practicalities cannot encompass. Consequently, numerous institutions have contracted their enrollment management/admissions services to outside companies. Mid-American Christian University in Oklahoma, for example, abolished its enrollment management division entirely and signed on with Hobsons, a Cincinnati-based consulting firm that provides expert assistance in promotions, outreach, and retention. (Among its other partners is the well-regarded California Polytechnic State University.) Some schools pay private contractors to send out letters of acceptance or rejection to applicants, rather than notifying students themselves. Unfortunately, some contractors (such as Student Aid Services, a firm used by Fordham University) have been known to commit embarrassing errors when informing college hopefuls of their official status. But colleges may be quite as culpable in this regard.[23]

Enrollment managers must be adept at determining which relevant operations should be conducted in-house and which should be outsourced. In the business of student recruitment, college managers are trained to rely on the expertise, manpower, and experience of a host of enterprises. The latter analyze data, diagnose problems, and sell solutions. Their services offer many temptations to college administrations attempting to operate on a multitude of fronts. The companies break down the numbers and can calculate the "metrics" of nearly any dimension of the enrollment strategy. Hartwick Day (a division of Royall & Company), for example, "helps colleges and universities optimize price to meet the market efficiently and outperform data-based enrollment expectations." Thus, to aid colleges in balancing the disbursement of merit aid, Hartwick Day can determine whether the SAT score or the high school grade point average better forecast college success. This may lead a school to rethink its aid criteria, and perhaps to consider other revisions.[24]

Astute college enrollment officers will also look at evolving demographics in the chief recruitment locations. Migration patterns, economic trends, and the latest high school graduation trends all require close study and evaluation. Private colleges in particular have sought to chart out the student market in sophisticated, strategic, business-like strokes. Colleges are farming out the recruitment of foreign students to the corporate sphere, usually because their budgets cannot cover in-house outreach. Shorelight and INTO University Partnerships are among the enterprises cooperating with U.S. institutions to draw more students from abroad. Their goal is to assist in creating "pathways" (an oft-used expression among college recruiters).

This area of business endeavor with colleges is in fact known as the "third-party/outsourced pathway market." Shorelight signs contracts with colleges allowing the firm to administer educational programs, hire faculty and administration, and run classes on campus property. Revenues are shared between institution and corporation, with a greater share going to the school. The companies seek out foreign students with the assistance of "agents." When Shorelight and the University of Kansas decided to collaborate, faculty members worried whether the students to be admitted were those who had paid the most to agents. They wondered as well about faculty oversight over the Shorelight courses. Shorelight has been the recipient of substantial largesse from major investor Huron Consulting Group, whose interests run the gamut of American industries, including health and education. According to *Inside Higher Ed*, college administrators who contract out international recruitment "typically say that they lack the expertise and capacity . . . to go it alone." *Inside Higher Ed* also posits that the impetus to "bring more full fee-paying international students to their campuses" is both "noble and financial." But it "reflects some of the most vexing issues in American higher education today, among them issues of readiness and rigor and commercialization and commodification."[25]

Naturally the issue of preparation for American colleges applies to all students, regardless of where they live. But the mode of drawing foreign students has elicited particular concerns, since colleges and recruiters have occasionally resorted to questionable methodologies. An example is the work of Global Tree Overseas Education Consultants with Western Kentucky University. Global Tree's campaign in India has acquired recruits to Western Kentucky with an advertisement urging "Hurry Up" and a promise of letters of acceptance within one day of applying. Such quick appraisal of qualifications is called "Spot Admissions" or "Spot Assessment," an approximation of a fast food drive-thru. (This is not the only parallel with rapid-fire customer assistance: more than one college now has a director of "One Stop Services.") An example of a hard-sell, according to Boston College's Center for International Higher Education, the Global Tree initiative is calculated by "the university and the agent . . . to get warm bodies in the door." But the approach also makes difficult, if not impossible, an assessment of the readiness of applicants.[26]

But the principle also operates on the domestic front. Schools may award certain benefits to applicants who show up to an "Instant Admissions Day." Unity College of Maine and Concordia University in Texas are among the institutions promising to review transcripts, assess credentials, grant admissions, extend financial aid, and facilitate enrollment in quick order. Moreover, the "Day" records a much higher yield of registered students than is evident among regular applicants.[27]

There are few limits to the sphere of college management, and few requirements in terms of broader knowledge. Rudy Fichtenbaum, president of the American Association of University Professors, assesses the character of present-day college administration:

> Decisions over program development and discontinuance, admission standards and tuition hikes are increasingly made unilaterally by an ever-growing army of professional administrators, many of whom have spent little time in the classroom, the lab, or the library. They move from institution to institution, often leaving a mess in their wake, which then needs to be cleaned up by a new administrative team that is hired at even higher salaries than their predecessors. They are often hired with little or no faculty input, to "make hard choices," a euphemism for transferring resources from academic programs to other areas of the "enterprise."

A hundred years ago Thorstein Veblen declared, "no man whose energies are not habitually bent on increasing and proving up the domain of higher learning belongs legitimately on a college staff."[28]

CORPORATE ENROLLMENT STRATEGIES

Concepts from the corporate sphere permeate higher outreach discussions. More than lingo is involved. A noted consultant urges college presidents to listen "to experts from other industries to learn about new market opportunities," and to be bold enough to make "the tough decisions to free up resources, seize opportunities, and challenge long-standing assumptions and practices." The intrepid bold managerial style is presented as a radical break with the timeworn. A change of vocabulary comes along with the new regime. Student information systems acquire the moniker "Customer Service Management," available for institutional purchase in a wide variety of platforms. The fleet of course platforms like Blackboard, Moodle, Canvas, and Follett are collectively called "Learning Management" or "Learning Delivery" systems that companies continuously develop, improve, and sell.[29]

One firm, Academic Impressions, exhorts administrators to pursue "faculty buy-in for student success" and counsels "onboarding" of customer service personnel through careful training. If schools find in-house switchboard hires too expensive, they may want to use a corporation like CMD Outsourcing Solutions, Inc., which caters cheaper options to colleges. The company Echo360, which devises a variety of learning technologies, asserts that higher educators can learn much from the calorie-tracking device "Fitbit." Just as Fitbit aggregates in-process health data that may launch new steps to improvement, "leveraging real-time data on student behaviors to identify where students are struggling and risk falling behind" may accomplish similar aims in the classroom. Indeed, "what gets measured gets improved." Calculation of all learning steps must be mastered for the purpose of transformation, according to Echo360.[30]

Academic Impressions pledges its cooperation not only with the new, but also the more traditional college administrators, like deans. A dean representing a college unit or set of disciplines would ideally handle the "integrating of corporate input into the curriculum," to "more effectively position students for success in the workforce through targeted skills training." Corporations, claims Academic Impressions, have a special role to play in enabling "partnership tailored to student engagement." The corporate world can give recommendations on "measuring, analyzing, and prioritizing," about which conventional deans arising from the faculty are likely to know little. Managing employees presents another area in which a professor transformed into dean or chair may be inexperienced. Again, the corporate model is put forth as the obvious one to follow. According to Academic Impressions, the business world would have much to teach in "creating a performance management process," and "imposing discipline" at the college level. Academic Impressions' conferences around such issues are meaty with detail. Under the firm's tutelage, college administrators may imbibe strategies straight from the canon of business leadership: "leading and influencing," the "leader as diagnostician," "5 paths to leadership," "creative leadership," and "leveraging the knowledge of others," among others.[31]

Enrollment managers turn more and more to "predictive modeling," through which they analyze an extensive body of relevant data on students to ensure maximum accuracy in predicting enrollments. The maximum yield of enrolled students, from the pool of accepted applicants, is paramount. In the end, though, no method is impeccable. Since tuition and tuition-discounting policies also remain vital to a school's ability to foretell enrollment, the think tank Stevens Strategy urges officers to revisit them regularly, reminding colleges that while "higher tuition levels will drive students to find cheaper alternatives," too liberal a discount may trigger a dangerous decline in a school's net tuition intake. In maintaining balance while maximizing returns, Stevens recommends colleges pursue RCM (Responsibility Centered Analysis) and PRO (Programs and Resource Optimization) as soundly business-oriented formulae. Schools may then be able to "get the maximum number of desirable students without going over their financial aid budget."[32]

Naturally, as Stevens Strategy avers, subjective factors may seriously undermine fulfillment of recruitment goals. At Adelphi University in the 1990s, for instance, administrative and trustee misuse of funds (leading to a state hearing and the dismissal of the president and trustees) turned many accepted students away from the school toward other choices. Adelphi's freshman yield declined from 46 percent in 1990–1991 to 24 percent in 1996–1997, a reduction in sharp contrast with the record of neighboring colleges.[33] Such were extraordinary circumstances. But today's colleges lose students all the time. According to a 2012 article in *The New York Times' Education* section, "33 percent of all students transfer; 25 percent transfer more than once; 37 percent transfer in their second year; 22 percent transfer in their fourth or fifth years."[34]

A mistaken projection of how many accepted applicants really show up may lead to budgetary shortfalls with severe repercussions, including the ousting of senior vice-presidents and admissions officers. Consulting enterprises that provide advice on how to win prospective students, recommend a multi-pronged action program. In one strategy, offices of enrollment separate applications into parallel "funnels." Some companies use the term "silo." In any case, one funnel deals with the continuum of applications, check-up, and follow-up. Another funnel handles inquiries, again with spin-off categories. Noel-Levitz, a key advisory group for this strategy, claims that "the funnel captures the rates of movement of prospective students toward enrollment at key intervals" and thus becomes "a predictive set of metrics for forecasting enrollment yields." Firms in the business of assisting recruitment and retention employ the language of putting student needs first, an idea originally conceived by radical educational reformers opposed to the traditional view of students as passive sponges, or mere receptacles of knowledge. For example, Skyfactor, a student retention consulting service, warns its university clientele that retention schemes that "do not include the perceptions of the students themselves" are bound to fail. Schools need instead "a holistic" design and "a continuous cycle of communication across departments," generating "actionable data" furthering retention.[35]

Easy and well-organized access to applicants' records and financial conditions is possible with the right software. Of course, mistakes do happen. Faulty software has been known to alter applicants' names beyond recognition, thereby conjuring nonexistent applicants into life and then deluging them with offers, reminders, and all the temptations normally provided to real-life high school seniors. In addition, colleges may also send letters of acceptance en masse to students who either never applied or were actually rejected, as happened at New Jersey's Kean University in February 2015. Technical errors are so common as to be practically normal. At the same time, when other soon-to-be-graduated high school students receive notices reading "We're missing your application" from schools they did not apply to, it may not be as much a mistake as a deception. No wonder some parents wax bitter at the "cynical gamesmanship of the college application process" or that *Bloomberg News* refers to "the college admissions racket."[36]

Helix Education, a consultant in the field, suggests institutions opt for an "in-house" approach rather than hiring different vendors for separate promotional channels. Colleges should "hire and grow resident experts across all channels," people who would know a school's brand better by being on campus. And then "the data can be more easily centralized for sophisticated attribution, modeling, and channel re-allocation." However, it appears that higher education administrators prefer to deal with different companies on distinct strategic aspects of enrollment, for example advertising or web development. Noel-Levitz consults with more than a thousand higher education institutions about enrollment. By no means are the points of service confined to student recruitment, but extend to retention and all relevant interstices, including the juxtaposition of financial aid and rising tuition. *Forbes Magazine* writes: "When Noel-Levitz takes on a client, it takes the school's admissions and retention data, scrubs it clean and uses the results to tell the school who's coming, who's going and who might be enticed to stay with a few more aid dollars or certain enhancements to student life." Noel-Levitz makes proposals to schools on the basis of specific data: "One of the things that's a hallmark of this company is we don't fly around and give our opinion," explains Noel-Levitz CEO Kevin Crockett. "We always will back that opinion with data points."[37]

The host of silos, funnels, and metrics produced by corporate consultants is a marvel, new models appear as if by magic. But there seems to be less time devoted to estimating bigger factors impacting college attendance: the financial situations of families, the trends of salaries, the costs of health care, the price of housing, the persistence of discrimination. Jon McGee, author of *The Changing Marketplace in Higher Education,* insists that many "institutions get caught up in the present—because they have to be. . . . We have to enroll a new class every single fall. So a lot of energy goes to the immediate rather than what will or might happen five or ten years down the road." There is a tendency among administrators, says McGee, to close their eyes to the larger picture. But a serious enrollment attitude must appreciate the difference between "Wall Street and the macroeconomy" and "Main Street and the personal economy." It must also recognize other factors: "And if you add race and ethnicity to the mix, the median family income for, say, white and Asian families is nearly double the median family income for Black and Hispanic families."[38]

FINANCIAL AID

Financial aid occupies a crucial space within enrollment management. As Eric Gould points out, when an institution has joined the belief that "the degree itself is a commodity item priced according to need and what the market will bear," it must prepare accordingly. Financial aid, he asserts, may be considered "the fine art of the college recruiting profession," entailing "careful massaging of minor differences in offers between student cohorts" and a sure grasp of "statistics and probability theory." The trick, as Gould sees it, "is to offer the least amount of institutional aid that will tip the balance in favor of one's school even while maintaining or improving quality and attracting enough students who can afford to pay . . . so that a reasonable margin of gain from tuition revenues can be shown."[39]

College administrators and admissions directors contend that careful balance must determine enrollment services, like financial assistance. As stated by the journal *University Business,* "We can define enrollment capacity as the maximum enrollment attainable without having to add significant fixed costs (variable costs—such as adjunct faculty—can ebb and flow with enrollment)." Schools may also beckon enrollees by making it easier to fulfill program requirements. *University Business* continues: "This requires continually evaluating and focusing your core curriculum to minimize the number of required courses. It also means providing the best possible advising so that students can better sequence their courses." Institutions and students alike may then keep costs lower. Schools must exercise budgetary balancing, particularly when extending scholarship packages. Highly trained specialists may be called upon for reality-based projections. "Models can be used to examine the price sensitivity of the admit pool and project the impact of changes" advises *University Business,* while due study of "the price elasticity of the admit pool (and major subpopulations within the pool)" will better "anticipate a group's response to a higher or lower net price." The factors can thus be assessed dispassionately.[40]

Assessing student debt demands reflection by wise heads. How much can a student and her family bear? How likely is mounting debt to threaten the school's ability to retain her and thousands of others? Will she leave? To what degree can an institution lure transfer students to make up for those who depart for financial reasons? The bottom line necessitates expert calculations. A high school student's soaring joy upon acceptance to a desired institution may be obliterated by a financial aid package leading straight to debtor's prison. Tuition tends to rise, and not by magic, but rather concerted decision. Grants-in-aid remain in force, but pay for less. Further complicating the picture, according to the *Chronicle of Higher Education,* "Many colleges intentionally give less institutional grant aid to returning students, raising net prices for families by as much or more than they up the sticker price." Tackling such issues embodies only part of the challenges of enrollment management.[41]

DIRECTIONS IN MARKETING

A researcher at the Wharton School asserts that increasingly sophisticated college marketing is driven by "increased competition among privates, publics, community colleges, online programs and even the lure of joining a technology startup straight out of high school." Indeed, higher education institutions, "like other brands, are struggling to differentiate themselves in a more crowded field." She observes that such "competition can push companies to squeeze their profits or even take losses in order to stay in the game" and draws a parallel with competing soda brands. Though on a more diminished scale than beverage firms, colleges also consider mergers in order to continue operating: Clarkson with Union College Graduate School in New York, Jefferson with Philadelphia University in Pennsylvania, Berklee with Boston Conservatory. Before Dowling College in Long Island went extinct, London-based Global University Systems (funding "projects in the Americas, Europe and Asia, building teams and capacity within areas of vocational training, professional education, corporate and executive training, English language training and higher education") tried to come to its rescue in academic bailout mode. One should not confuse mergers with the Five College consortium formed by schools in west central Massachusetts or the Consortium of Colleges on the Creative Coast (Florida's Gulf coast), which are collaborations between independent institutions, facilitating learning in the first place. Bringing libraries into alliance is an example of cooperative sharing of services. In Pennsylvania's Lehigh Valley, six schools (including Muhlenberg and Moravian) have formed a common health plan.[42]

Kimberly R. Cline, the president of Long Island University, while insisting that "branding a university is fundamentally different than branding a product" since a school, after all, is more multifaceted than a company, admits that branding is as essential to education as it is to commerce, for the two worlds pursue the same rules of self-promotion: "Articulate the vision and dare to be bold. Distinguish the brand. . . . Bring the brand to life. Offer salient examples of how people 'live the brand.'" This is why the journals, workshops, researchers, and firms in the areas of technology, recruitment, public relations, and outreach regularly urge the importance of giving each college a unique brand.[43]

Anyone who imagines that a prospective recruit's tour of a school is only generally mapped out, with formal and relatively informal components, including inspection of library, dorms, dining facilities, under the leadership of bouncy student guides walking backwards, must accommodate a new world. A properly led college tour in fact leaves little to chance, according to marketer Marc C. Whitt. Student tour leaders, described by Whitt as the "sales force," must be "well-trained professionals who clearly understand their role. And companies are ready to teach the

"Three Ts of the Admissions Tour": Training, Technology, and Targeting.[44]

In keeping with the emphasis on appearance, colleges conduct "tours that turn heads." Or beginning at the other end, college tours should "sweep them off their feet," counsels *University Business*. Suggested methods embrace the setting up of props on campus for visitors to take "selfies" and creating parking signs with the names of the arriving guests. Colleges may purchase the advice of companies focused on the theory and practice of campus visits. One such firm is VisitDays. As proof of the evolving species of corporate work with higher education, the company mulls and sifts tour types according to a school's culture, traditions, demographics, and goals. It coordinates visits from setting targets to itemizing steps to meeting goals. Every phase can be planned. VisitDays builds on an institution's reputation and brand, and is a repository of ideas on signage, lighting, musical adornment, and program design for student visits.[45]

Outreach must be intensified, revolutionized, entirely recast, say the consultants. To recruit, colleges must fully engage the students through social media. They must dive into all the communication streams in which their constituents swim. Keeping up with ever-changing technology used by young people is a challenge. Applicants to college increasingly rely on mobile devices rather than conventional computers to obtain school information. Institutions respond in kind, but are obliged to gear home pages to different platforms. They will lose customers when they have not conceived an entirely distinct mobile attitude, highlighting brevity, keywords, sound, and color. Similarly, outreach offices have to adapt to the rapidly shifting terrain of youth social media, casting their nets wider than the ever-burgeoning Facebook and Instagram. College web analyst Karine Joly thus recommends that schools learn how to use SnapChat, whose photo and video-adorned messages disappear immediately upon being viewed by recipients. She reports that SnapChat captures the immediacy of actual use intrinsic to youth behavior. To congratulate new admits, snaps provide "a visual and personal touch at this crucial time in the recruiting cycle." Joly's frequent video conferences and online workshops (the advice has a price) provide wide-ranging instruction in institutional social media.[46]

College website development is a popular subject for conferences. Experts tutor admissions officers on "Storytelling, Marketing & Higher Ed," in how to inspire applicants with tales of struggle and success. College use of social media, email, and mobile platforms for contacting applicants presupposes knowing how young people communicate. But competition for students can acquire a hurried character, particularly among private colleges, which prevents truly thorough investigation of deeper issues involved in bringing students to college. Enrollment managers can be quite skilled in meticulous planning and projecting, but to "think deep" is not always possible or necessary. Shallow, cosmetic approaches result. In the meantime, branding packages not only a school's image of itself but also its prospective applicants. Since the latter may be quite varied, outreach efforts go awry when assuming an applicant can be attracted like a moth to a flame. Thus, while colleges develop hip new electronic connections with applicants, a significant number of students in fact prefer to speak on the telephone or even receive letters in the mail: snail mail. While most prospective students use email to contact a school, nearly a quarter would rather make a phone call. Of those whose applications are incomplete, more would prefer to be informed by a missive in a stamped envelope than by email or phone. Several colleges have had great success in getting accepted students to attend by hand-delivering letters of acceptance. But other schools might find this rather costly.[47]

Creative video can implant atmospheric images in the heads of potential students and alumni donors. One may subtly insert anything considered intrinsic to the institution. Academic Impressions counsels colleges to learn from the advertising strategy of Red Bull, the energy drink, especially to grasp how the manufacturer of the highly caffeinated beverage has become a sponsor of televised cliff diving, ice climbing, and snowboarding competitions, thus identifying the product with risk and excitement (rather than severe heart problems in young adults). Sonic Foundry, an especially inventive enterprise consulting with over 1,200 institutions, provides video tips to help schools "Out-recruit, Outperform and Outretain" their competitors. Guiding schools how to "Unleash the Power of Video On Your Campus," Sonic Foundry proclaims that campus video can harness and channel all critical processes into a seamless "Youtube-esque environment" for students, professors, recruiters, and alumni donors. Online classes, professional training, and on-demand lectures can become part of a constantly growing video databank, which can help "increase tuition-based enrollment without building new classrooms." In consequence, Sonic Foundry maintains, the video-enhanced institution may witness the unfolding growth of "student pass rates and grades," "retention and graduation rates," and "improvements in faculty and student efficiency and productivity." But when it comes to video to elicit new student applications, schools err when they generalize the viewing habits of the college-bound. Thus, female applicants are more likely than males to watch online videos when searching for colleges; the same holds true for African Americans and whites, as contrasted with Hispanic applicants.[48]

As fast as the fields of contact multiply, higher institutions have to spearhead and innovate. Gone are handwritten records and scribbled notes reporting encounters with potential applicants. In their place, colleges introduce apps for enrollment managers and outreach counselors. The results of visits to high schools may be efficiently entered in spreadsheets. Using an app, an administrator can post and access all relevant data. Schools are indeed encouraged to cement their brand with upgraded apps, not merely improved websites. Similar invention informs freshman orientation, comments *University Business*:

> A customized online check-in form developed within Oracle's PeopleSoft Campus Solutions pulls information directly from the student information system. . . . Eliminating packets also means less paper, fewer boxes and envelopes, and lower labor costs—for a total annual savings in the neighborhood of $21,000.

Joanna Young, the chief information officer at Michigan State University, expresses it well: "Brands can be made or broken by how an organization establishes itself in the marketplace. Technology establishes its value to an organization, and its customers, in a similar fashion."[49]

Marketing also shapes the newer roles of college bookstores. Barnes & Noble CEO Max Roberts urges administrators to transform college bookstores from "a place to buy affordable textbooks" into "a social hub that celebrates and supports the aspirations of your students, from day one as freshmen to their post-college lives as alumni." Relevant to the project is the clearly reduced use of printed textbooks in courses, though the speed of decline may be more apparent than actual. The tendency is to convert newly available bookstore space, owing to the textbook vacuum, into a "town square marketplace" offering tech support or sales, as well as "healthier food options" than offered in school cafeterias. (Of course, some college food services have leaned away from fast-food supremacy, but these bookstores of the future may even serve wine and beer.)[50]

As predicted by two forward-looking architects, Jay Silverberg and David Glover, the new bookstore will offer tech support and sales, and "more insignia merchandise. It's a revenue stream-with-heart." One should not forget, advise Silverberg and Glover, that "insignia apparel" products "are ways for students to express a connection with their school that will have benefits for student and institution." It helps if a bookstore is located near other key venues, like the building from which campus tours are launched or even better, close to a basketball arena or football stadium, "which gives it enormous game-day foot traffic."[51]

Still, college bookstores confront the behemoth Amazon, the great consolidator of used and new textbooks. In this context, consultants like the Nebraska Book Company sell solutions to campus stores. They appeal to the image of independent entrepreneurship, which must be protected from outsourcing (which ironically goes unchecked in other institutional activity). In fact, too many smaller college stores have thrown in their lot with Amazon in order to survive. But Nebraska can help them acquire "an in-depth understanding of relationships, technology, the dynamic of traffic movement and SEO (search engine optimization), pay-per-click, affiliate, and an understanding of conversion rate, merchandising, product information management, and much more." Moreover, Nebraska will help college booksellers solidify personal relationships with faculty, something the transnational giants are incapable of doing: "The bookstore can increase profits because now it knows earlier than anyone else what books will be needed and they can source those books used and get a larger volume of more affordable product on the shelf for their students. This enriches the faculty experience, the student experience, and the bookstore experience. Everyone wins."[52]

BRANDING

Branding institutions of higher learning borrows heavily from evolving theories of how to promote corporations. The *Harvard Business Review* provides a helpful breakdown of the stages of consumer thinking, which any entity may employ on the road to expansion. The initial move by consumers of products, health care, insurance, higher education, and other services is to consider the options. Once exploration has begun, they next tend to evaluate, compare offers, and do research. Thirdly, they reach the "point of purchase," where "placement, packaging, availability, pricing, and sales interaction" play the decisive role. Lastly, consumers will grow to appreciate the product, to "enjoy, advocate, bond," and then advocate it to others. Successful branding, says the *Review*, does not drop out of the sky, but can only result from a comprehensive "customer experience plan."[53]

Applying the strategy to nonprofit institutions (like hospitals and colleges), or to benevolent associations (like churches) calls for a creative combination of diminishing, while tying in the bedrock principles on which the institutions were founded. For the mission statement gives central credence to the beneficial purpose. To this an administration is verbally sworn. Meanwhile college branders try to make the promotional cap fit the school, altering its width and breadth, but also proposing to reshape the head it is intended to cover. Corporate consultants engaged by universities have no direct authority to carry out the latter act, but it is up to administrators to make the deeper anatomical adjustments.

Branding pervades the assortment of public relations initiatives reaching out to new students and alumni donors. A vice-president of public affairs likely coordinates the work, stretching from overarching strategy to color scheme, from official banner to the almost indecipherable miniaturized logo on a business card. According to Benjamin Ginsberg, publications "might include a 'view book' aimed at attracting new students, dozens of newsletters and periodicals trumpeting the school's achievements, and a glossy alumni magazine designed to evoke feelings of nostalgia and a spirit of generosity among the school's graduates." Luanne M. Lawrence of LML Marketing & Communications emphasizes that a school's brand cannot drop out of the sky or be determined on impulse.

Consultants aid institutions in profound consideration of the intended audiences, framing messages and offshoots with intelligence, and launching test cases before unleashing a campaign in the public eye. Since support from across campus will facilitate brand dissemination, a college can obtain "buy-in" from people who work for it by making sure they are consulted, and then trained. With proper coordination, the institution may expect maximum return on investment, or ROI (the business idiom filling many college plans).[54]

In college branding, ROI is joined by RACI (Responsible. Accountable. Consulted. Informed.). RACI, submits marketing vice-president Deborah Maue of Columbia College (Chicago) embraces the strategy necessary once again to encourage "buy-in." She observes that enrollment managers and college marketing officials, while devoted to the same object, often conflict because they both claim to be the ultimate decision makers. Thoughtful implementation of RACI will preempt the problem, posits Maue. But extension of the ideal of RACI to the practical involvement of faculty in promotional planning is more problematic. Instructors are the most crucial people in higher education for obvious reasons, and their work involves deeper thought than commercial jingles will allow. But branding is often in the hands of people to whom higher learning is a phrase.[55]

Some schools subscribe, at least on paper, to involving faculty, students, and academically minded administrators in branding policy. "Successful branding," observes *University Business*, needs "research and collaboration," for sometimes it takes the average of multiple perspectives to capture a school's essence. Vermont's Marlboro College designated a dining room wall for anyone to write suggestions and criticisms about promotional tone and direction. Photography majors at Philadelphia's University of the Arts compete to portray the virtues of the firm Parkhurst Dining, thus connecting "fine art with fresh food." The University of Denver sought student and faculty input about a new logo. After faculty objections to a promotional campaign launched by the slogan "If," the University of Oregon scaled it back. It chose to suspend its connection with a marketing firm and opted to use in-house expertise more sympathetic to the educational mission. Indeed, the school has sought out faculty opinion. However, more often than not, marketing decisions are hatched by a few and then left to the specialists, whose tone suffuses the results. A firm hired by cash-strapped Wright State (Dayton, Ohio) took $250,000 to design a new logo. The new one deleted the image of namesake Wilbur Wright from the university's symbolism. It also resembled the emblem of a local waste disposal company. Various campus constituencies expressed dismay, leading the university to deem it unsuitable. A faculty member naturally wondered whether the whole investment was worthwhile, or even necessary. Notwithstanding the collaborative ethos of enrollment management theory, the process often lacks start-to-finish inclusive decision making.[56]

College allocations to the firms that do the branding are significant, compared to the cost-cutting measures so often implemented on campus. The University of Vermont's $1.5 million dollar outlay to a well-established agency (titled 160over90) has elicited protests from UVM teachers. The contract with 160over90 operates at the same time as a school policy of sharply reducing the budget for academic departments in the social sciences and humanities. The faculty union leader thus observes: "If the $1.5 million figure is accurate, that certainly raises questions. United Academics includes faculty members who in recent years have had our workloads increased, our staff and teaching assistant support diminished, our income lowered, even our teaching careers brought to an end."[57]

A college brand may tap into a school's other attributes, both big and small. An institution may parlay a high rating (even a dubious one like "Most Polite University") into a selling point. Beyond their traditional mottos, institutions also deploy a catchy phrase to encapsulate the brand, with an outside firm of wordsmiths contributing ideas. Once a slogan is chosen, it may be trademarked. Slogans demand facile two- or three-word spin, far snappier than the old Greek or Latin phrase adorning many an institution's signage. Examples include: "It's time." "Get the point." "Redefining what's possible." "Change the world." "CompleteLife." "It matters." "Experience Amazing." "Think Marist." "ThinkOutside." Juxtaposition of literal and figurative is common: stay close: go far; small school: big dreams. Some slogans are more verbose: "Your Moment. Your Move. Your Simmons: Where leaders make themselves." After weighing multiple variants and issuing a major announcement of the new slogan, an institution can make it integral to the brand and a viable promotional device. With a few more words, sculpted ads can supply apparent depth to a slogan. At Baylor University (which paid admitted students to retake the SATs to increase its average scores in 2008), recruits are lured by these sentence fragments: "It's about a university at the forefront of poverty research. Where social science meets social responsibility. Where learning is magnified by doing. Where fact is energized by faith. And where the words, 'love thy neighbor,' are not just words." Baylor's ads reach consistently for the stars: "A place that is authentic in its beliefs and genuine in its quest for quality." It is "where the pursuit of knowledge is measured in the difference it makes in the lives of the people it touches."[58]

The sparkling catchphrase is the demand of the hour. A brand is supposed to embrace, if not enhance, a school's heritage, meaning, and accomplishments. The brand is a symbol of all that is good and hopefully great about an institution. Boiling this down is a challenge. Being conversant with the brand's essence and higher purpose is increasingly expected of college spokesmen speaking in public, faculty and students included. Agreed-upon imagery and phrasing can create a lasting impact upon those to whom the message is brought. If need be, an admissions or public affairs office can supply faculty members with a "script" when they meet prospective students. It is important, says one school, to "identify institutional ambassadors and provide them with the tools and assets they need to be sure we are 'singing off the same sheet of music' regarding institutional messages."[59]

GLOBAL BRANDING

Harnessing universities to product-selling convictions is international. Colleges in the United Kingdom have for quite some time been transforming themselves into a "quasi-commercial service industry," notes the *International Journal of Public Sector Management*. The *Journal* finds little difference in their struggle for market share with the endeavors in the for-profit world, observing that "image and reputation of some universities have been argued to be more important factors than actual teaching quality." Image has become a crucial instrument in promotion by Lithuania's University of Vilnius, a distinguished school dating to 1579. The school's striking architecture is the stuff of guidebooks and post cards. The administration reasoned during the 1990s that the university's key selling point was the ancient physical structure: magnificent buildings, walkways, courtyards, museums, alleys, the botanical garden. For this reason today, "heritage items are used in corporate design." Tours of university applicants focus upon the institution's visual glory. Vilnius assumes the students see themselves as customers, and takes for granted that visiting "clients are not interested in the success of the institution" in the educational sense.[60]

Colleges in Norway have developed a branding tradition as well. Their administrations have in fact become expert in a business vocabulary, write Arild Wæraas and Marianne Solbakk of the University of Tromsø. In their country, schools have incorporated intangibles into the organizational identity: attitude and spirit. Noting the relative absence of pedagogical message in higher ed branding, professors Solbakk and Wæraas ask "if general academic values have a place in branding processes, and whether such processes would build on the cultural heritage that primarily confirms the University as a *scientific* institution; e.g. freedom of research, objectivity, truth, freedom to teach and to learn, etc." But instead, "branding may have a potential for challenging the institutional integrity of universities."[61]

Israeli sociologist Gili S. Drori is no less concerned. He terms branding a "transformation of universities from professional (and often public) institutions of research and learning into market players." From updating signs, sayings, and symbols, schools move then to trademark them as merchandise: "university icons are no longer mere identity markers of the university as an academic community, but rather they have become commodities that leverage the university's reputation." In all, says Drori, college branding weakens the academic principle, shifting the terrain from the ostensible mission-market balance to a decided avalanche in favor of the latter. The institution now becomes a "promotional university." As a result, marketing and academics interact not as separate or cooperating spheres, but the first commits injury to the second. Therefore, "promotion and marketing change the tone, if not the core, of academic work," Drori adds, sacrificing "knowledge creation, teaching, and study to the logics of marketing and service.[62]

APPEARANCE

While a college's actual or ostensible image becomes a trademark, its physical appearance plays a role in attracting students and can be integrated into the brand itself. The experience at Vilnius is instructive, but using appearance has been done on a simply monumental scale in the United States. "First impressions are critical," writes higher education marketer Marc C. Whitt, "when families are determining whether to invest time and resources." How an institution looks, says Whitt, "speaks volumes to visitors about the quality, sense of care and level of stewardship we seek to present." Although Adelphi University elicits an overwhelmingly local student body, the appearance of its campus has emerged as a striking factor in competition with other institutions like Hofstra University, St. John's University, and Molloy College. Adelphi freshmen commonly rate the campus visit as the most compelling reason in choosing the school. They calculate Adelphi's "attractiveness of campus" as the university's most winning appeal, above academic and learning experience. *MiBiz,* a Michigan business publication, points out that "students hold the overall aesthetic experience of a college experience on par with the quality of education it offers." College marketers clearly are aware of how to tap into every factor of persuasion, mastering all routes to converting applicants into bodies in classrooms.[63]

It is expeditious (Thorstein Veblen pointed out) for a school to spend "the greater proportion of the available income of the university in improving and decorating its real estate," while expanding the ranks of lower-salaried faculty, who are uninsured and expendable, so "notoriously underpaid . . . as seriously to curtail their working capacity." For when it comes to new construction, further institutional reputation is so often at stake. "Architectural vagaries," the "architecture of notoriety" can bring new donors, new titles to buildings, and new selling points.[64]

THE BUSINESS OF FLIPPED CLASSROOMS

Physical transformation of a school involves both mission-based and market-tied elements. Old classrooms are clearly not up to swiftly changing mechanisms of instruction. But upgrading classroom technology tends to have promotional, as well as academic, appeal. Crestron Electronics, a technology company that specializes in automation systems, has been among the pioneers in providing "complete wireless HD presentation from any mobile device and any platform" to college classrooms. Its "AirMedia" platform enables thirty students at once to launch and view a selection of course-based wireless presentations on different screens. Stunning electronic walls convert from writing boards to computer screens as if by magic: each wall in turn metamorphoses into something else at the touch of a finger. A professor can amble from group to group offering feedback, or otherwise watch, comment, and monitor, all from a stance other than the classical conductor presiding over the orchestra. Colleges have accompanied these breakthroughs with massive logistical restructuring, such as gutting a building of its classrooms and standard seats and replacing them with foldable chambers and wheeled tables and chairs, which can be moved silently and smoothly. The instructor and students can thus physically adjust the learning space for individual group projects, or in fact any particular need of the day. Malleable spaces whose walls can flex or disappear are known as "flipped classrooms," because they flip pedagogical and architectural tradition upside down. Desks and tables move on ball bearings, but are collapsible or convertible in purpose, adjustable in height and width.[65]

Technological innovation is as much a talking point as pedagogical tool, if not more so. Promoters portray the new classroom as a studio or a workshop, a place for experimentation, free-wheeling improvisation, and spontaneous exchange. The instructor strolls, listens, provokes, cajoles, and questions, helping the students to think independently. Long-standing shortfalls in learning outcomes seemingly may be reversed through architecture. Designers become partners with colleges in turning teaching on its head. This is represented as a good thing in every sense. Bentley University business dean Chip Wiggins writes in *University Business*: "In this setting, each student becomes a dynamic contributor to the discussion: standing up to debate with classmates, illustrating points on multimedia boards, and continually engaging their smaller team to share perspectives based on collective experiences."[66]

The "collaborative classroom space" industry promises to put the instructor in a different pedagogical role, rather off to the side. The students are to be front and center, a welcome repudiation of archaic teacher centrality and sponge-like methodology. Since instructors might share in the educational process as co-participants with students, in a more collective atmosphere that empowers the latter, the technological enhancements are portrayed as part of democratization of space and class time. So say certain advocates, who also point out that traditional teaching has just about run its course, thus demanding a transformation in professorial role. Enterprises in the field make ample use of "flip" to denote a nearly revolutionary upending of hidebound teacher-based schooling; they invoke the image of creative disruption and subversion of outworn formats. According to *University Business* "increased interaction and engagement in class should be the outcome of a successful and progressive flipped classroom." To be sure, the purported redistribution of authority in the classroom also extends to greater learning outside of it. Ongoing technologies assist the transfer of classroom functions to smaller settings. However democratic it may all seem, the process clearly diminishes the faculty role and the need for full-time instructors. The teaching skill becomes secondary to pushing buttons. *University Business* accordingly urges colleges to "question the need for individual faculty offices, which take up a huge footprint." Remedies might include "consolidating teacher offices into a single cooperative work area." The Campaign for the Future of Higher Education cautions: "Too often, practices promoted as 'innovations' have at their core the goal of minimizing or eliminating direct interaction and the development of relationships between individual faculty and students."[67]

Many enterprises have emerged to promote the new orientation. The Flipped Learning Network (FLN), a company that provides "educators with the knowledge, skills, and resources to successfully implement Flipped Learning," explains "flipping" as the practice which creates "flexible spaces in which students choose when and where they learn," and "deliberately shifts instruction to a learner-centered approach, where in-class time is dedicated to exploring topics in greater depth and creating rich learning opportunities." More than one firm couches the new instructional systems in declarations of student autonomy and faculty independence. The Citrix company gears its technology sales precisely in this vein. By purchasing its products, a college will "embrace mobility," "inspire learning" and allow students to choose "the location where they feel most productive and inspired."[68]

The companies plowing the terrain of higher learning vie with each other as bitterly as the schools they serve. Consequently, they are as subject to the laws of competition as firms in any other industry. Simultaneously, the enterprises in the field germinate and consolidate. The online and distance learning course developer Learning House, which partners with scores of colleges, bought out its rival, Acatar, in 2015, shortly after taking over The Software Guild. Datatel and SunGard Higher Education, student data software management companies, merged in 2011, the better to capture market share from rivals Oracle and Jenzabar. Providence Equity bought out "instructional delivery system" giant Blackboard in 2011 as well. But the rise of other learning system formats makes Blackboard's status insecure and subject to potential resale. The global investment firm KKR & Co., credited with some of the largest buyouts in corporate history, partnered with the former Kaplan Test Prep CEO Jonathan Grayer in 2010 to form an education investment company, Weld-North LLC. RuffaloCody acquired the aforementioned educational consultant Noel-Levitz in 2014. The student success firm Hobsons (which owns the Predictive Analytics Reporting Framework as well as Starfish Retention Solutions) belongs to a British conglomerate, Daily Mail and General Trust PLC.[69]

At every level and recess of the education world, corporations run the show. In *Geek Heresy*, Kentaro Toyama writes that while "tech giants are messianic about their creations," they also greatly oversimplify and exaggerate their products: "America is in an orgy of educational technologies despite scarce evidence that they improve learning."[70] Certain newer technologies, according to researchers, produce at best mixed results for learning outcomes. Colleges may purchase and employ them in any case, for not all protagonists of classroom change are motivated by interest in the learning process—nor are all sellers necessarily interested in revolutionizing education or deepening scholarly engagement.

The foregoing survey of corporate involvement in higher education is far from comprehensive, but demonstrates a trend that dwarfs the correspondence of business interests and college administration in years past. While the exaltation of business sense in the allegedly more efficient method of institutional administration and conduct has remained constant, the proliferation of companies taking on more and more academic, recruitment, and managerial functions on campuses is relatively new. A deeply rooted assumption that business operations must play a decisive role in the world of higher learning has erupted into corporate colonization of college education. Through promoting entrepreneurial success as the lesson for all fields, and the person of wealth as the representative of efficiency in all endeavors, the companies themselves have enjoyed the benefit of their own mythology. Against this backdrop, the apparently mundane benefits of scholarship and learning stand little chance.

CORRUPTION

The more that commercial motives and methods influence academic practice and policy, the more likely that ethical lines may become blurred in several dimensions, with infractions known to other industries oozing into higher education. Large firms, for example in the pharmaceutical industry, can dodge legal standards, while remaining undeterred by sizable fines. At the college level too, writes Tricia Bertram Gallant in *ASHE Higher Education Report*, corporate influences may induce shortcuts, quick fixes, jump-starts, come-ons, and the like. In keeping with inflated school reputations, "students and faculty are increasingly being viewed less as teachers and learners and more as . . . the means for advancing the institution in rankings and prestige," Gallant contends. "Academic capitalism does not create a situation in which academic misconduct is acceptable, but it does complicate notions of academic integrity and cheating."[71]

The propensity to compromise integrity stems from the culture of profiteering, which in a yet thoughtful appraisal, "left no other bond between man and man than naked self-interest, than callous cash payment" while operating "in the icy water of egotistical calculation." When the branding mind-set is applied to education, it likewise fosters an atmosphere conducive to fabrication, evidenced in recent school cheating scandals and ongoing misrepresentations of school credentials. Similarly, the needs of a particularly lucrative college program, like a prodigious football team, replete with boosters, donors, and accolades, can generate a culture of corruption and behavioral double standards. Yet many university decision makers incline to ignore the implications, even in extreme cases, in favor of the fortune earned.[72]

The sway of power and money in college operations is nothing new: colleges have long given preferential admission to the offspring of donors, alumni, and legislators (regardless of qualifications). However, the decidedly more assertive proclamation of "academic capitalism" can probably be dated to the 1980s, when then-president Ronald Reagan initiated an expansive retreat in government monitoring, protection, and policies of social responsibility and gave more freedom to the large enterprise-dominated market forces. Agencies established as watchdogs over business behavior, as cognizant of union rights, or as patrolmen against unethical practices, were weakened. While originally set up in response to public outcry, their functions and purview narrowed toward ineffectiveness or obstruction under Reagan. Simultaneously, tax breaks for the wealthiest 1 percent helped usher in wealth and income inequality more akin to theft. Forty years later, twenty Americans owned as much wealth as the bottom half of the population, 152 million people. Without fear of government oversight, according to David Callahan in *The Cheating Culture,* the corporate world manifested greater indulgence in the "temptations to cheat." In fact, such "temptations . . . are naturally part of capitalism."[73]

Despite the claim that hard work is the guarantor of success, millions can see that it is rarely so. Getting into this or that outstanding public or prep school envisions an end-around into a concentrated hierarchy, which endures beyond high school. Hence the widespread resort to an enervating competitiveness at such secondary institutions as New York's renowned Stuyvesant and Horace Mann, and to cheating. The "surprise" consists not so much in the revelation of widespread dishonesty, but in the decades required for the "cheating culture" to become public knowledge. In all, fair chances appear subordinate to market forces and established influence.[74]

According to veteran education analyst Diane Ravitch, "what we need is not a marketplace, but a coherent curriculum that prepares all students."[75] Such an approach might also embrace going beyond test-based measurements of academic potential (and favoritism toward alumni families, greater attention to advising and counseling freshmen, promotion of exploratory interdisciplinary courses prior broader than a profession, (particularly in the first year), and infusion of college administration with people dedicated to education. Fair labor standards for contingent teachers, more college investment in full time professors, and strengthening tenure would help prioritize and stabilize pedagogy.

Holistic approaches, however, stem from interests that fall outside the contemporary thrust in higher education. Not only is the corporate model unreliable when it comes to pedagogy, but it also spurs the expansion of a part-time instructional labor force and an increasingly indebted student body. These are decisive sectors whose intensifying vulnerabilities are fatal to higher education. Measured and sober estimates of how best to enhance the educational experience of freshmen and others depend on input from faculty, students, families and constituencies which put learning at the forefront, and which would provide necessary counterweight to the onslaught of corporatization in higher education.

NOTES

1. Eric Hoover, "In An Uncertain Summer, Colleges Try to Control Enrollment 'Melt,'" *The Chronicle of Higher Education*, Vol. 55, No. 42, A22; Kate Zernike, "In Shifting Era of Admissions, Colleges Sweat," *New York Times*, March 8, 2009, A1.

2. Lisa Leigh, "Specialty Majors Are The Rage on Some Campuses," Christian Science Monitor, October 5, 2004, www.csmonitor.com/2004/1005/p15s01-legn.html. Accessed October 6, 2004; "Higher Ed Casino Programs Mirror Trend," *University Business*, August 2005, 20; Associated Press, "FBI Offers Anti-Terror Degree at Indian U. of Pa., But Not Everyone Can Enroll," *Patriot-News* (PA), July 17, 2011, http://mobile.pennlive.com/advpenn/pm_103982/contentdetail.htm?contentguid=cj2qrW2m. Accessed August 1, 2011.

3. Eric Gould, *The University in a Corporate Culture*, New Haven, 2003, 70.

4. Gould, 86; Richard Wolin, "Democracy and Education," *The Nation*, May 21, 2012, 31–32; "UNH President: Students Aren't 'Customers,'" *Concord Monitor*, February 18, 2014, http://www.concordmonitor.com/home/10551111-95/unh-president-students-arent-customers. Accessed February 20, 2014.

5. Calvin TerBeek, "Privatization Everywhere: Public Universities Want to Go Private," *Houston Press*, October 29, 2013, http://blogs.houstonpress.com/hairballs/2013/10/privatization_everywhere_publi.php. Accessed October 31, 2013; Larry Hanley, "Academic Capitalism in the New University," *Radical Teacher*, No. 73 (August 2005), 3; Massimo De Angelis and David Harvie, "'Cognitive Capitalism' and the Rat Race: How Capital Measures Immaterial Labour in British Universities," *Historical Materialism*, Vol. 17, No. 3 (2009), 10–12.

6. Thorstein Veblen, *The Higher Learning in America*, New York, 1957 (1918), 93, 82.

7. Ellen Wexler, "Can Data Measure Faculty Productivity? Rutgers Professors Say No," *Chronicle of Higher Education*, December 11, 2015, http://chronicle.com/article/Can-Data-Measure-Faculty/234595?cid=at&utm_source=at&utm_medium=en&elq=34d9f7505bb141d19a7e8a5f92015a24&elqCampaignId=2057&elqaid=7213&elqat=1&elqTrackId=d0c3cc811eef44cc96cf2a2d92f9d1ac. Accessed December 14, 2015; "Rutgers Professors Oppose Academic Analytics," *Inside Higher Education*, December 15, 2015, https://www.insidehighered.com/quicktakes/2015/12/15/rutgers-professors-oppose-academic-analytics?utm_source=Inside+Higher+Ed&utm_campaign=2dc9d50965-DNU20151215&utm_medium=email&utm_term=0_1fcbc04421-2dc9d50965-199367377. Accessed December 15, 2015; "Our Obsession with Metrics Turns Academics into Data Drones," *The Guardian*, November 27, 2015, http://www.theguardian.com/higher-education-network/2015/nov/27/our-obsession-with-metrics-turns-academics-into-data-drones. Accessed December 11, 2015.

8. Miguel Martinez-Saenz and Steven Schooner Jr., "Resisting the 'Student-as-Consumer' Metaphor," *Academe*, November–December 2014, http://www.aaup.org/article/resisting-student-consumer-metaphor#.VJrYcJAJA. Accessed November 18, 2014; Joel Thomas Tierno, "How Many Ways Must We Say It," http://www.aaup.org/article/how-many-ways-must-we-say-it#.VJrYTJAJA. *Academe*, November–December 2014. Accessed November 18, 2014.

9. Steve Street et al, "Who is Professor 'Staff,' *Center for the Future of Higher Education*, August 2012, 1, 2, 4; Rebecca Schuman, "Syllabus Tyrannus," *Slate*, August 26, 2014, http://www.slate.com/articles/life/education/2014/08/college_course_syllabi_they_re_too_long_and_they_re_a_symbol_of_the_decline.html. Accessed September 3, 2014.

10. Institute for Policy Studies, *The One Percent at State U: How Public University Presidents Profit From Rising Student Debt and Low-Wage Faculty Labor*, Washington DC, 2014; Tamar Lewin, "Student Debt Grows Faster at Universities With Highest Paid Leaders, Study Finds," *New York Times*, May 19, 2016, A11; John Branshaw and Samuel Duneitz, "Busting the Myths: The Annual Report on the Economic Status of the Profession, 2014–1015," *Academe*, March–April 2015, 4–18; American Institutes for Research and the New England Center for Investigative Reporting, "U.S. College Staffing Changes, 1987–2011," http://college-table.wgbh.org/_local. Accessed April 27, 2015; Data on Executive, Administrative and Managerial Totals at Adelphi, Fairfield, Fordham, Hofstra, LIU Post, Marist, St. Bonaventure, and St. John's University, courtesy Rudy Fichtenbaum, AAUP, May 4, 2015; Campaign for the Future of Higher Education, *Back to School in Higher Ed: Who Needs Faculty?* September 2015, 6; Jeff Denneen and Tom Dretler, *The Financially Stable University*, Boston, 2012, 5.

11. OECD, *In It Together: Why Less Inequality Benefits All*, Paris, 2015, 29–32; Anna Fazackerly, "Why Are So Many Academics on Short-Term Contracts for Years?" *The Guardian*, February 4, 2013, http://www.guardian.co.uk/education/2013/feb/04/academic-casual-contracts-higher-education. Accessed May 4, 2013; Leanne McRae, "The Exploitation of Expertise: Adjunct Academics and the Commodification of Knowledge," *Fast Capitalism*, Vol. 9, No. 1 (2012), http://www.uta.edu/huma/agger/fastcapitalism/9_1/mcrae9_1.html. Accessed December 30, 2014; Adrianna Kezar and Daniel Maxey, "The Changing Academic Workforce," *Trusteeship Magazine*, Association of Governing Boards, May–June 2013, http://agb.org/trusteeship/2013/5/changing-academic-workforce. Accessed December 30, 2015.

12. Howard Bunsis, *Analysis of the Financial Condition of Adelphi University*, AAUP, November 2015, 56; Karin Kapsidelis, "Report Finds Low Pay, Job Security For College Faculty, *Richmond Times-Dispatch*, April 8, 2013, http://www.timesdispatch.com/news/local/education/college/report-finds-low-pay-job-security-for-college-faculty/article_4fca512c-75db-5f6f-9b04-c28e442ca274.html. Accessed April 9, 2013; Colleen Flaherty, "The Cost of Being Decent to Adjuncts," *Inside Higher Ed*, March 17, 2016, https://www.insidehighered.com/news/2016/03/17/paper-argues-adjuncts-push-better-pay-and-working-conditions-prohibitively-expensive?utm_source=Inside+Higher+Ed&utm_campaign=317bbf5d0f-DNU20160317&utm_medium=email&utm_term=0_

1fcbc04421-317bbf5d0f-199367377. Accessed March 17, 2016; College and University Professional Association for Human Resources, "DOL's Proposed Overtime Rule: Higher Education's Comments & Concerns," September 2015; College and University Professional Association for Human Resources, "Proposed OT Rule Could End Up Hurting Those it Intends to Help," April 29, 2016, http://blog.cupahr.org/2016/04/proposed-ot-rule-could-end-up-hurting-those-it-intends-to-help/. Accessed April 30, 2016; Schuyler Velasco, "How Might Overtime Change Affect Middle Class? Look at Colleges," Christian Science Monitor, May 28, 2016, http://m.csmonitor.com/Business/2016/0518/How-might-overtime-change-affect-middle-class-Look-at-colleges. Accessed May 18, 2016; Ross Eisenbrey, "Universities, Inequality, and the Overtime Rule," *Economic Policy Institute*, April 20, 2016, http://www.epi.org/blog/universities-overtime-rule/. Accessed May 6, 2016; Sean Higgins, "Senate GOP Moves to Counter Overtime Rule," *Washington Examiner*, June 7, 2016, http://www.washingtonexaminer.com/senate-gop-moves-to-counter-overtime-rule/article/2593211?utm_source=Sailthru&utm_medium=email&utm_campaign=Issue%3A%202016-06-08%20Higher%20Ed%20Education%20Dive%20Newsletter%20%5Bissue%3A6160%5D&utm_term=Education%20Dive%3A%20Higher%20Ed. Accessed June 10, 2016.

13. Beryl Lieff Benderly, "Campaign Aims to Unionize Boston's Adjunct Faculty," *Science Careers*, April 15, 2013, http://sciencecareers.sciencemag.org/career_magazine/previous_issues/articles/2013_04_15/caredit.a1300075. Accessed April 16, 2013; Campaign for the Future of Higher Education, "The Cold Facts About Higher Education and Contingent Faculty Appointments," May 6, 2013, http://futureofhighered.org/the-cold-facts-about-higher-education-and-contingent-faculty-appointments/. Accessed May 21, 2013; Erin Hatton, "The Rise of the Permanent Temp Economy," *New York Times*, January 26, 2013, http://opinionator.blogs.nytimes.com/2013/01/26/the-rise-of-the-permanent-temp-economy/. Accessed May 28, 2013; John W. Curtis and Saranna Thornton, "The Annual Report on the Economic Status of the Profession," *Academe*, March–April 2013, 7–13; Keith Johnson, "No Holes for Round Pegs: Why Adjunct Faculty Don't Fit In," *Hybrid Pedagogy*, May 26, 2016, http://www.digitalpedagogylab.com/hybridped/no-holes-us-round-pegs-adjunct-faculty-dont-fit/?utm_source=feedburner&utm_medium=feed&utm_campaign=Feed%3A+HybridPed+%28Hybrid+Pedagogy%3A+a+digital+journal+of+learning%2C+teaching%2C+and+technology%29. Accessed May 31, 2016; "Excellence in Higher Education Starts with Better Pay for Instructors," editorial, *St. Louis Post-Dispatch*, May 29, 2016, http://www.stltoday.com/news/opinion/columns/the-platform/editorial-excellence-in-higher-education-starts-with-better-pay-for/article_19cce031-d66a-559d-94e9-aadca42fc672.html. Accessed May 30, 2016.

14. "Standing Up for Equal Pay for Equal Work: The Current Situation of Contingent Faculty at IC," *The Ithacan*, December 9, 2016, https://theithacan.org/opinion/contingent-faculty-union-releases-paper-on-bargaining-priorities/. Accessed December 16, 2016; Larry Gordon, "California Colleges See Surge in Efforts to Unionize Adjunct Faculty," *Los Angeles Times*, January 3, 2015, http://www.latimes.com/local/california/la-me-unions-colleges-20150104-story.html#page=1. Accessed January 5, 2015; National Labor Relations Board, *Pacific Lutheran University and Service Employees International Union, Local 925, Petitioner*. Case 19–RC–102521, December 16, 2014, 19; Rudy Fichtenbaum, "Protecting Academic Freedom for Faculty Working on Contingent Contracts: Contract Language for Full-Time Faculty at Wright State University," *Journal of Collective Bargaining in the Academy*, Vol. 0, Article 25, 1–10; Brittany Horn, "Adjunct Faculty to Join SEIU," *Albany Times Union*, September 22, 2014, http://www.timesunion.com/local/article/College-of-Saint-Rose-adjunct-faculty-votes-to-5772307.php. Accessed October 17, 2014; Gretchen M. Reevy and Grace Deason, "Predictors of Depression, Stress, and Anxiety Among Non-Tenure Track Faculty," *Frontiers in Psychology*, July 7, 2014, http://journal.frontiersin.org/Journal/10.3389/fpsyg.2014.00701/full. Accessed August 6, 2014; Maria Maisto, "The Adjunct's Moment of Truth," *Inside Higher Ed*, September 10, 2009, http://www.insidehighered.com/views/2009/09/

10/maisto. Accessed May 21, 2013; American Association of University Professors, *Academic Freedom and Tenure: National Louis University (Illinois)*, April 2013, 12.

15. Carol Patton, "Adjuncts Demand to Be Heard," *University Business*, December 2016, 25; Nick Kalm and Courtney Harper, "Stronge Messages Can Defuse Campus Unionizing Campaigns," *University Business*, June 29, 2016, http://www.universitybusiness.com/article/strong-messages-can-defuse-campus-unionizing-campaigns. Accessed June 29, 2016.

16. Hank Reichman, "Columbia Provost Coatsworth Escalates Assault on Grad Student Union Rights," *Academe Blog*, December 2, 2016, https://academeblog.org/2016/12/02/columbia-provost-coatsworth-escalates-assault-on-grad-student-union-rights/. Accessed December 5, 2016.

17. *Agreement between Wright State University and the Wright State University Chapter of the American Association of University Professors*, August 20, 2014–June 30, 2017, Article 2, section 2.3; *Collective Bargaining Agreement by and between Hofstra University and the Hofstra Chapter of the American Association of University Professors*, September 1, 2011–August 31, 2016, Article 2, section 2.2; *Collective Bargaining Agreement between The University of Oregon and United Academics, AAUP/AFT, AFL-CIO*, July 1, 2013 through June 30, 2015, Article 1; David W. Chen, "CUNY Deal on Contract After Threat of Walkout," *New York Times*, June 16, 2016, A24.

18. Rober Reinhold, "College Aids Study Business," *New York Times*, July 22, 1971, 43.

19. Hossler, 10, 25, 85; Stefanie Botelho, "Lane College Selects CAMS Enterprises as its ERP Software," *University Business*, January 21, 2015, http://www.universitybusiness.com/news/lane-college-selects-cams-enterprise-its-erp-software. Accessed January 21, 2015.

20. University of North Alabama, Online Employment System, Associate Vice President for Enrollment Management, https://jobs.una.edu/postings/4064. Accessed February 2, 2016.

21. Mary Piccioli, "Keys to a More Effective Enrollment Strategy," *University Business*, December 2013, http://www.universitybusiness.com/article/keys-more-effective-enrollment-strategy. Accessed December 24, 2013; Lauren Williams, "Location, Variety Take Priority in Meal Planning," *University Business*, September 2013, http://www.universitybusiness.com/article/location-variety-take-priority-meal-planning. Accessed December 24, 2013; Jacqueline Gregory, "Seven Ways Enrollment Managers Can Thrive Today," *University Business*, October 2013, http://www.universitybusiness.com/article/seven-ways-enrollment-managers-can-thrive-today. Accessed December 24, 2013; Dawn Papandrea, "Vehicle Management Moves Forward," *University Business*, November 2015, 31–35.

22. Adelphi University Enrollment Working Group, *Undergraduate Enrollment Management Analysis*, August 26, 2015, 94–95.

23. Ashleigh Livingston, "PSU Working to Boost Enrollment," *Press-Republican* (Plattsburgh, NY), November 20, 2016, http://www.pressrepublican.com/news/local_news/psu-working-to-boost-enrollment/article_d2c17ff9-fdf2-5e1b-afb6-c2e82520afa4.html. Accessed November 23, 2016; Silas Allen, "Mid-America Christian University Outsources Enrollment, Plans Expansion," *The Daily Oklahoman*, July 5, 2012, http://m.newsok.com/mid-america-christian-university-outsources-enrollment-plans-expansion/article/3689775. Accessed July 6, 2012; Hobsons, *Higher Education Professionals, Admissions & Enrollment*, http://www.hobsons.com/education-professionals/higher-education/admissions-enrollment-professionals/. Accessed July 6, 2012; Ashley Southall, "2,500 Applicants Get False News of Acceptance to Fordham," *New York Times*, December 12, 2013, A31.

24. Hardwick Day, *Enrollment Optimized*, https://www.hardwickday.com/. Accessed October 9, 2015; Interview with Kristen Capezza, director of admissions, Adelphi University, October 6, 2015.

25. Shorelight Education, "Adelphi University and Shorelight Education Launch New Program For International Students," October 1, 2015, http://www.shorelight.

com/adelphi-university-and-shorelight-education-launch-new-program-for-internat ional-students. Accessed October 9, 2015; Amy Baker, "Tom Dretler, Shorelight Education, USA," *The PIE News*, December 5, 2014, http://thepienews.com/pie-chat/tom-dretler-shorelight-education-usa/. Accessed October 9, 2015; Ben Unglesbee, "New international recruitment program draws questions from faculty and students," *Lawrence Journal-World*, April 21, 2014, http://www2.ljworld.com/news/2014/apr/21/new-international-recruitment-program-draws-questi/. Accessed October 9, 2015; Interview with Lisa Wolf-Wendel (associate dean for research and graduate studies, University of Kansas), October 15, 2015; "Pathway Provider Wins Injunction Preventing Release of Contract," *Inside Higher Ed*, March 7, 2014, https://www.insidehighered.com/quicktakes/2014/03/07/pathway-provider-wins-injunction-preventing-release-contract. Accessed October 9, 2015; "Huron Consulting Group Announces Strategic Investment in Shorelight Education," *Reuters*, July 9, 2014, http://www.reuters.com/article/2014/07/09/il-huron-consulting-idUSnBw095190a+100+BSW20140709. Accessed October 9, 2015; Elizabeth Redden, "Bridge or Back Door," *Inside Higher Ed*, April 30, 2014, https://www.insidehighered.com/news/2014/04/30/look-landscape-pathway-pro grams-international-students-run-cooperation-profit. Accessed October 9, 2015.

26. Ad, Dir, One Stop Student Services, Kent State University, *University Business*, June 29, 2016, http://careers.universitybusiness.com/jobseeker/job/29235661/Dir%2C%20One%20Stop%20Student%20Services/Kent%20State%20University/?str=1&max=25&vnet=0&long=1. Accessed June 29, 2016; Stephanie Saul, "Recruiting Students Overseas to Fill Seats, Not to Meet Standards," *New York Times*, April 20, 2016, A1.

27. Matt Zalaznick, "Instant Admissions: An Enrollment and Engagement Boost," *University Business*, December 2016, 15.

28. Rudy Fichtenbaum, *Presidential Address*, American Association of University Professors, June 15, 2015, courtesy of Rudy Fichtenbaum; Veblen, 13.

29. Nancy Mann Jackson, "How Colleges Make the Big LMS Switch," *University Business*, February 2015, 39–42; Canvas ad, *University Business*, February 2015, 43; Jenzabar CRM ad, *University Business*, February 2015, 57.

30. *Academic Impressions, Gaining Faculty Buy-In for Student Success Initiatives and Programs*, webcast, January 26, 2016; *Academic Impressions, Improving Customer Service in Higher Education: Second Edition*, September 2014; ad for CMD Outsourcing Solutions, *University Business*, January 2016, 65; Frederick Singer, "What Higher Education Can Learn from Fitbit," *edSurge*, January 4, 2016, https://www.edsurge.com/news/2016-01-04-what-higher-education-can-learn-from-fitbit. Accessed January 6, 2016.

31. *Academic Impressions, Corporate Partnerships for Academic Leaders*, Conference March 23–24,2015, 2, 4; *Academic Impressions, Prioritizing Academic and Administrative Programs*, Conference March 30–31, 2015, 5, 6; *Academic Impressions, Communication and Conflict Management for Department Chairs*, Webcast, February 19, 2015; *Academic Impressions, 7 Strategies for Dealing with Difficult Colleagues*, Webcast, January 27, 2015, 3; *Academic Impressions*, Leading and Influencing as a Department Chair, Conference, June 8–10, 2015, 4, 5; *Academic Impressions*, Collaborative Leadership in Higher Education, Conference, July 27–28, 2015, 2, 3.

32. Amit Mrig, Daniel Fusch, and Patrick Cain, *Small But Mighty: 4 Small Colleges Thriving in a Disruptive Environment*, Denver, June 2015, 8, 14; Bill Berg, "Predictive Modeling: A Tool, Not the Answer," *University Business*, July 18, 2012, www.universitybusiness.com/article/predictive-modeling-tool-not-answer. Accessed August 1, 2012; Stevens Strategy, *Has Tuition Discounting Lost Its Mojo*, Grantham, NH, 2012; Christopher Drew, "Help for the Not So Needy," *New York Times*, July 22, 2012, ED14.

33. Gayle Insler et al., "The Committee to Save Adelphi, Petitioners against Peter Diamandopoulos et al., Respondents," *To the Board of Regents*, 1996, 26.

34. "Student Churn," *New York Times Education Life*, April 15, 2012, 4.

35. Gould, 69; Chris Nicholson, "Enrollment Yields Becoming Ever Harder to Meet," *University Business*, July 2014, http://www.universitybusiness.com/article/enrollment-yields-becoming-ever-harder-meet. Accessed August 6, 2014; Noel-Levitz,

2010 *Admissions Funnel Benchmarks for Four-Year Public and Private Institutions*, Coralville, IA, 2010, 12, 1; Skyfactor, "What's Missing From Your Student Success Initiatives," ad, *University Business*, March 2015, 19.

36. Caryn Meyers Flieger, "Admissions Officers Speak Out," *University Business Magazine*, March 30, 2013, http://www.universitybusiness.com/article/admissions_officers_speak-out. Accessed March 26, 2013; Lori Rozsa, "Colleges, Recruiting Even the Imaginary Students," *New York Times*, December 9, 2014, http://mobile.nytimes.com/blogs/parenting/2014/12/09/colleges-recruiting-even-the-imaginary-students/?_r=1&referrer. Accessed December 11, 2014; Patricia Alex, "Kean University Sends 3,000 Students Acceptance Notices in Error," *Bergen Record*, February 27, 2015, http://www.northjersey.com/news/kean-university-sends-3-000-students-acceptance-notices-in-error-1.1279158. Accessed March 5, 2015; Janet Lorin, "College Admissons Racket: They're Not Going to Let You in Anyway," Bloomberg Business, January 28, 2015, http://www.bloomberg.com/news/articles/2015-01-28/college-admissions-racket-they-re-not-going-to-let-you-in-anyway. Accessed January 28, 2015.

37. Helix Education, *Which Higher Ed Marketing Approach Is Right For Your Institution?* n.d., 5, 7; Maggie McGrath, "The Invisible Force Behind College Admissions," *Forbes*, August 2014, http://www.forbes.com/sites/maggiemcgrath/2014/07/30/the-invisible-force-behind-college-admissions/. Accessed August 6, 2014.

38. Tim Goral," On Topic: Q & A with Jon McGee," *University Business*, April 2016, 8–9.

39. Gould, 29, 69–70.

40. Bill Berg, "The Goldilocks Principle: Ensuring Your Capacity to Meet Demand Is Just Right," *University Business*, December 2014, http://www.universitybusiness.com/article/goldilocks-principle-ensuring-your-capacity-meet-demand-just-right. Accessed December 17, 2014.

41. Ben Miller, "Why Colleges Are Like Cable Companies," *The Chronicle of Higher Education*, January 20, 2015, http://m.chronicle.com/article/Why-Colleges-Are-Like-Cable/151205/. Accessed January 20, 2015.

42. Anya Kamenetz, "How Private Colleges Are Like Cheap Sushi," *NPR*, July 12, 2014, http://www.npr.org/blogs/ed/2014/07/08/329889370/how-private-colleges-are-like-cheap-sushi. Accessed August 4, 2014; "Mergers & Acquisitions: Experts Say 2013 Could Bring a Flurry of M & A Activity in the Beverage Sector," *Beverage World*, January 2013, 46; Kellie Woodhouse, "Anatomy of Failed Merger," *Inside Higher Ed*, August 5, 2015, https://www.insidehighered.com/news/2015/08/05/college-merger-negotiations-are-long-and-complicated. Accessed December 27, 2015; Harold Brubaker and Martha Woodall, "Jefferson, Philadelphia University to Merge," *Philadelphia Inquirer*, December 19, 2015, http://articles.philly.com/2015-12-19/news/69169280_1_institutions-merger-philadelphia-university. Accessed December 27, 2015; Berklee College of Music, "Berklee and The Boston Conservatory Agree to Merger," press release, January 19, 2016, https://www.berklee.edu/news/berklee-and-boston-conservatory-agree-merger. Accessed January 20, 2016; Candice Ferrette, "Dowling College in Oakdale Closes its Doors After 48 Years," *Newsday*, May 31, 2016, http://www.newsday.com/long-island/education/dowling-college-in-oakdale-closes-its-doors-after-48-years-1.11861115?pts=809706. Accessed June 1, 2016; Greg Cergol, "Dowling College Rescinds Decision to Close, Negotiates Deal to Stay Open," *NBC New York*, http://www.nbcnewyork.com/news/local/Dowling-College-Shutdown-Delays-Negotiations-382266911.html. Accessed June 10, 2016; Global University Systems, *Partnership Opportunities*, http://www.globaluniversitysystems.com/partnership-opportunities. Accessed June 10, 2016; Meghan Delaney, "Manatee and Sarasota Colleges Collaborate and Receive Support from Area Foundations," *Bradenton Herald*, January 5, 2016, http://www.bradenton.com/news/local/education/article53085105.html. Accessed January 6, 2016; Sherrie Negrea, "Higher Ed Allies in Efficiency: Colleges and Universities Share Services to Control Costs," *University Business*, April 25, 2016, http://www.universitybusiness.com/article/higher-ed-allies-efficiency. Accessed April 25, 2016.

43. Kimberly R. Cline, "Redefining the Concept of the University Branding," *University Business*, March 2015, http://www.universitybusiness.com/article/redefining-concept-university-branding. Accessed March 5, 2015.

44. Marc C. Whitt, "It's Not All About Digital," *University Business*, April 2015, 20; Lauren Williams, "Higher Ed Recruiters Hesitant to Use Newer Social Media Platforms," http://www.universitybusiness.com/article/higher-ed-recruiters-hesitant-use-newer-social-media-platforms. *University Business*, July 2014. Accessed August 6, 2014.

45. Ioanna Opidee, "Tours That Turn Heads," *University Business*, October 2015, 34–38; VisitDays, "Strategies for Increasing Campus Visits, Registration, and Attendance," http://app.visitdays.com/resources. Accessed October 9, 2015; Stefanie Botelho, "New Cloud-Based Recruiting Platform Debuts," *University Business*, October 5, 2015, http://www.universitybusiness.com/news/new-cloud-based-college-recruiting-platform-debuts. Accessed October 7, 2015.

46. Esther Shein, "Mobile First," *University Business*, March 2015, 39–42; Karine Joly, "Should Your University SnapChat?" *University Business*, March 2015, 22–24; http://collegewebeditor.com/blog/#. Accessed November 25, 2015.

47. *UB Tech 2013: A National Summit on Higher Education Technology and Leadership*, 2013 Sessions-Full Program, http://ubtechconference.com/sessions-2013. Accessed February 20, 2013; Raquel Bermejo, *2015 High School Students' and Parents' Perceptions of and Preferences for Communication with Colleges*, Ruffalo Noel Levitz, Cedar Rapids, 2015, 4–8, 13; Collin Binkley, "To Woo Students, More Colleges Now Hand-Deliver Acceptances," *Associated Press*, March 21, 2016, http://bigstory.ap.org/article/b457a2313b4b4355a67d88720579385d/woo-students-more-colleges-now-hand-deliver-acceptances. Accessed March 21, 2016.

48. Tim Ponisciak, "What Red Bull Can Teach You About Engaging Alumni through Video," *Academic Impressions*, January 20, 2016, http://www.academicimpressions.com/news/what-red-bull-can-teach-you-about-engaging-alumni-through-video?mkt_tok=3RkMMJWWfF9wsRonu67NdO%2FhmjTEU5z16ewkXKexlMI%2F0ER3fOvrPUfGjI4ETsVrI%2BSLDwEYGJlv6SgFS7jFMaxzzLgLXBM%3D. Accessed January 20, 2016; Mediasite by SonicFoundry, "6 Academic Video Tips that Help You Out-Recruit, Outperform and Out-Retain: Strategies From University of Maryland Dental," http://www.sonicfoundry.com/webcast/6-academic-video-tips-help-you-out-recruit-outperform-and-out-retain-strategies-university. Accessed January 16, 2015; Mediasite by SonicFoundry, *Unleash the Power of Video on Your Campus*, White Paper, 2, 3, 5; Raquel Bermejo, *2015 High School Students' and Parents' Perceptions of and Preferences for Communication with Colleges*, Ruffalo Noel Levitz, Cedar Rapids, 2015, 10.

49. Marcia Layton Turner, "Recruitment Goes Mobile," *University Business*, August 2014, http://www.universitybusiness.com/moe/article/recruitment-goes-mobile. Accessed August 6, 2014; Marcia Layton Turner, "Records and Registration," *University Business*, August 2014, http://www.universitybusiness.com/moe/article/orientation-station. Accessed August 6, 2014; Joanna Young, *The Differentiation Scale*, April 24, 2014, University of New Hampshire, http://cio.unh.edu/2014/04/24/the-differentiation-scale/. Accessed August 6, 2014.

50. Barnes & Noble College, "A Message from Max Roberts," http://www.bncollege.com/whatsnext/. Accessed August 4, 2014.

51. Jay Silverberg and David Glover, "The Future College Bookstore: Leave the Books, Take the Panini," *FastCoexist*, October 22, 2014, http://www.fastcoexist.com/3036953/futurist-forum/the-future-college-book-store-leave-the-books-take-the-panini. Accessed October 23, 2014.

52. Nebraska Book Company, *A Brave New World of Retail*, November 12, 2015, http://nebook.com/index.php/a-brave-new-world-of-retail/. Accessed November 18, 2015.

53. David C. Edelman, "Branding in the Digital Age," *Harvard Business Review*, December 2010, 3, 6.

54. Benjamin Ginsberg, *The Fall of the Faculty: The Rise of the All-Administrative University and Why it Matters*, New York, 2011, 53; Luanne M. Lawrence, "7 Steps To

Launch a Robust Brand Strategy," *Academic Impressions*, March 1, 2016, http://www.academicimpressions.com/news/7-steps-launch-robust-brand-strategy?mkt_tok=3RkMMJWWfF9wsRonuqvLeu%2FhmjTEU5z16ewkXKexlMI%2F0ER3fOvrPUfGjI4HRcJlI%2BSLDwEYGJlv6SgFS7jFMaxzzLgLXBM%3D. Accessed March 1, 2016.

55. Deborah Maue, "Sales vs. Marketing in Higher Education," *Inside Higher Ed*, February 25, 2016, https://www.insidehighered.com/blogs/call-action-marketing-and-communications-higher-education/sales-vs-marketing-higher-ed. Accessed February 25, 2016.

56. Dawn Papandrea, "On Board with the Brand in Higher Ed," *University Business*, December 2014, http://www.universitybusiness.com/article/board-brand-higher-ed. Accessed November 20, 2014; Stefanie Botelho, "Parkhurst Partners with UArts Students," *University Business*, May 17, 2016, http://www.universitybusiness.com/news/parkhurst-partners-uarts-students. Accessed May 17, 2016; Jamie Owen Daniel, "One Faculty, Organizing for a Stronger Voice," *Academe*, November–December 2014, http://www.aaup.org/article/one-faculty-organizing-stronger-voice#.VJrysJAJC. Accessed November 18, 2014; Miguel Martinez-Saenz and Steven Schooner Jr., "Resisting the 'Student-as-Consumer' Metaphor," *Academe*, November–December 2014, http://www.aaup.org/article/resisting-student-consumer-metaphor#.VJrYcJAJA. Accessed November 18, 2014; Kellie Woodhouse, "Scaling Back on Branding," *Inside Higher Ed*, January 20, 2016, https://www.insidehighered.com/news/2016/01/20/university-oregon-drops-multimillion-dollar-branding-campaign?utm_source=Inside+Higher+Ed&utm_campaign=ccf46d4be6-DNU20160120&utm_medium=email&utm_term=0_1fcbc04421-ccf46d4be6-199367377. Accessed January 20, 2016; Lance Lambert, "Wright State Rejects New Logo, Keeps Wilbur," *Dayton Daily News*, March 17, 2016, http://www.mydaytondailynews.com/news/news/wright-state-rejects-new-logo-keeps-wilbur/nqnRr/. Accessed March 17, 2016.

57. Molly Walsh, "UVM is Paying a Philly Firm $1.58 Million to 'Rebrand,'" *Seven Days*, February 10, 2016, http://www.sevendaysvt.com/vermont/uvm-is-paying-a-philly-firm-158-million-to-rebrand/Content?oid=3166349. Accessed February 17, 2016.

58. Bryan Grilli, "Adelphi Ranks Number One for Student Politeness, Thank You Very Much," *The Delphian*, September 21, 2015, 1; Steve Kolowich, "Here Are 88 Weird College-Owned Trademarks, Arranged as a Poem," *The Chronicle of Higher Education*, October 17, 2014, http://chronicle.com/article/Here-Are-88-Weird/149415/. Accessed October 20, 2014; Steve Kolowich, "How Universities Turn Slogans Into Cash," *The Chronicle of Higher Education*, October 17, 2014, http://chronicle.com/blogs/wiredcampus/how-universities-turn-slogans-into-cash/54929. Accessed October 22, 2014; Stefanie Botelho, "Simmons College Announces New Website and Brand Messaging," *University Business*, January 23, 2015, http://www.universitybusiness.com/news/simmons-college-announces-new-website-and-brand-messaging. Accessed January 24, 2015; Richard Pérez-Peña and Daniel Slotnik, "Gaming the College Rankings," *New York Times*, January 31, 2012, A14; Baylor University, "It's Not Just About Feeding Every Family in Texas," ad, *University Business*, March 2015, 29; Baylor University, "There is No Neutral in Education," ad, *University Business*, October 2015, 19; Baylor University, "It's Not Just About Identifying Lost Souls," ad, *University Business*, October 2015, 51.

59. Adelphi University, Work Group on Branding, Marketing, and Reputation, *Final Recommendation*, April 1, 2016, 10.

60. Chris Chapleo, "What Defines 'Successful University' Brands," *International Journal of Public Sector Management*, Vol. 23, No. 2 (2010), 169–72; Nijole Bulotaite, "University Heritage: An Institutional Tool for Branding and Marketing," *Higher Education in Europe*, Vol. 28, No. 4 (December 2003), 450–53.

61. Arild Wæraas and Marianne N. Solbakk, "Defining the Essence of a University: Lessons from Higher Education Branding," *Higher Education: The International Journal of Higher Education and Educational Planning*, 57 (2009), 449–53.

62. Gili S. Drori, "Branding of Universities: Trends and Strategies," *International Higher Education*, 71 (Spring 2013), 3–5.

63. Marc C. Whitt, "It's Not All About Digital," *University Business*, April 2015, 20; Adelphi University Office of Research, Assessment, and Planning, *Results of Newly Enrolled Freshmen Survey*, September 2013, 2–3, 5, 13; Nick Manes, "Modernizing, Maintaining Facilities Drives Building Activity for West Michigan Universities, *MiBiz*, June 7, 2015, http://mibiz.com/news/design-build/item/22597-modernizing,-maintaining-facilities-drives-building-activity-for-west-michigan-universities. Accessed June 18, 2015.

64. Veblen, 59–60, 106.

65. Crestron, "AirMedia," ducts/airmedia_mobile_wireless_hd_presentations/index.html. Accessed March 5, 2015; Adelphi University, "Gallagher Lab," http://it.adelphi.edu/catalog/gallagher-lab/. Accessed March 5, 2015; Spectrum Industries, "Stay Ahead of the Curve," ad, *University Business*, October 2015, 39.

66. Chip Wiggins, "Collaborative Learning Space Matters," *University Business*, May 2016, 52.

67. Ryan Derousseau, "Is Technology Actually Making Higher Education Less Efficient?," *The Hechinger Report*, December 12, 2014, http://hechingerreport.org/content/technology-actually-making-higher-education-less-efficient_18416/. Accessed December 16, 2014; Nancy Mann Jackson, "Taking Command of the College Classroom," *University Business*, December 2014, http://www.universitybusiness.com/article/taking-command-college-classroom. Accessed December 22, 2014; Ginsberg, 12–14; Marcia Layton Turner, "New Visions for Campus Space," *University Business*, January 2016, 59; Campaign for the Future of Higher Education, *Back to School in Higher Ed: Who Needs Faculty?* September 2015, 4.

68. Lauren Williams, "Flipped Classrooms 2.0," *University Business*, May 2015, 48; Flipped Learning Network, *What is Flipped Learning?* 2014; Citrix, "Embrace Mobility. Inspire Learning. Optimize IT for Educators and Students," ad, *University Business*, October 2015, 16–17.

69. Tim Goral, "Learning House Acquires Acatar," *University Business*, May 18, 2015, http://www.universitybusiness.com/news/learning-house-acquires-acatar. Accessed May 19, 2015; Steve Kolowich, "A Back Office Deal," *Inside Higher Ed*, August 8, 2011, https://www.insidehighered.com/news/2011/08/08/sungard_and_datatel_announce_merger. Accessed December 23, 2015; Steve Kolowich, "Blackboard Gets Bought," *Inside Higher Ed*, July 1, 2011, https://www.insidehighered.com/news/2011/07/01/blackboard_bought_by_providence_equity_partners. Accessed December 23, 2015; "Blackboard CEO Addresses Sale Rumors," *Insider Higher Ed*, December 17, 2015, https://www.insidehighered.com/quicktakes/2015/12/17/blackboard-ceo-addresses-sale-rumors?utm_source=Inside+Higher+Ed&utm_campaign=42ef953f10-DNU20151217&utm_medium=email&utm_term=0_1fcbc04421-42ef953f10-199367377. Accessed December 17, 2015; *Weld North Portfolio*, http://www.weldnorth.com/?page_id=6. Accessed May 22, 2015; *Jonathan N. Grayer*, http://www.weldnorth.com/?portfolio=jonathan-n-grayer. Accessed May 22, 2015; *About Us*, http://www.weldnorth.com/?page_id=2. Accessed May 22, 2015; *KKR Today*, http://www.kkr.com/our-firm/kkr-today. Accessed May 22, 2015; RuffaloCody Announces Merger With Noel-Levitz, news release, August 14, 2014; Hobsons, *Our Mission*, http://www.hobsons.com/about-hobsons/our-mission/. Accessed June 19, 2015; Ryan Derousseau, "Is Technology Actually Making Higher Education Less Efficient?," *The Hechinger Report*, December 12, 2014, http://hechingerreport.org/content/technology-actually-making-higher-education-less-efficient_18416/. Accessed December 16, 2014; "Hobsons to Buy Analytics Project," *Inside Higher Ed*, January 12, 2015, https://www.insidehighered.com/quicktakes/2016/01/12/hobsons-buy-analytics-project?utm_source=Inside+Higher+Ed&utm_campaign=cf4c931911-DNU20160112&utm_medium=email&utm_term=0_1fcbc04421-cf4c931911-199367377. Accessed January 15, 2016; Carl Straumsheim, "Completing the Student Life Cycle," *Inside Higher Ed*, February 23, 2015, https://www.insidehighered.com/news/2015/02/23/student-success-company-hobsons-acquires-starfish-retention-solutions. Accessed January 15, 2016.

70. Kentaro Toyama, *Geek Heresy: Rescuing Social Change from the Cult of Technology*, New York, 2015, x, 7, 11.

71. Tricia Bertram Gallant, "Twenty-First Century Forces Shaping Academic Integrity," *ASHE Higher Education Report*, Vol. 33, No. 5 (2008), 73–74.

72. Karl Marx and Frederick Engels, *The Communist Manifesto*, New York, 1948, 11; Veblen; Katie Thomas and Michael S. Schmidt, "Drug Firm Guilty in Criminal Case," *New York Times*, July 3, 2012, A1; Ariel Kramer and Randy Leonard, "Reports of Cheating at Barnard College Cause a Stir," *New York Times*, May 8, 2013, A25; Freeh Sporkin & Sullivan, LLP, *Report of the Special Investigative Counsel Regarding the Actions of the Pennsylvania State University Related to the Child Sexual Abuse Committed by Gerald A. Sandusky*, July 12, 2012, 14–17, 129–30, 139; Damon Sayles, "UCLA Offers 8th-Grade Quarterback," *ESPN LA*, June 12, 2013, http://espn.go.com/los-angeles/college-football/story/_/id/9378320/ucla-gives-offer-8th-grade-quarterback-lindell-stone?src=mobile. Accessed June 12, 2013.

73. University of Texas at Austin, *Investigation of Admissions Practices and Allegations of Undue Influence, Summary of Key Findings, Final Report to the Office of the Chancellor of the University of Texas System*, February 6, 2015; Chuck Collins and John Hoxie, *Billionaire Bonanza: The Forbes 400 and the Rest of Us*, Institute for Policy Studies, December 2015; David Callahan, *The Cheating Culture*, Orlando, 2004, 17–45, 138.

74. Callahan, 180–231; Vivian Yee, "Stuyvesant Students Describe the How and Why of Cheating," *New York Times*, September 26, 2012, A1.

75. Diane Ravitch, "Why I Changed My Mind About School Reform," *Wall Street Journal*, March 9, 2010, http://online.wsj.com/article/SB10001424052748704869304575109443305343962.html. Accessed June 24, 2011.

TWO

The Crisis of the SAT

Standardized college entrance exams, particularly the SAT prepared by the College Board (and traditionally referred to as College Board exams), are now too widely disputed to be the last word in evaluating applicants for admission. In fact, many schools across the country have downgraded the marks by listing them somewhere in the middle of the pack of admissions criteria.[1] But far out of proportion to their officially contextualized place, whether listed fifth, seventh, or ninth in the official list of a school's measures, SAT and other exam marks formally and informally impact the views of many in the academy. Indicative is the remark by the superintendent of a school district in Pennsylvania's Schuylkill County, whose students "know the SATs are the tests that really count if they want to go to college." The College Board openly stands by the SAT as the signal forecaster of academic success. The tests continue to carry determinative weight, though many oppose their practical centrality or question whether they belong in the picture at all. In many cases, these exams form crucial parameters of acceptance and of university self-description. They occupy a prominent place on the highlights page of university websites.[2]

While the usefulness of these tests has been called into question since their germination in the mid-twentieth century, recent decades have seen an uptick on the part of many administrators, faculty, and other commentators. As the *New York Times* noted in 1999, test scores generally correlate "with parental education and income," producing a result that "will look awfully aristocratic." Another *Times* article from that year attacks standardized exams from a different angle: "In a culture obsessed with measurement, the SAT has arguably become the single most important test for American high school students—an academic and psychic rite of passage that strongly influences future educational options, prompts fierce anxiety and serves as an almost mystical barometer of self-worth." As the SAT and other standardized exams have been subjected to closer inspection, their connection to college success has become harder to chart.[3]

Secondary school GPAs, on the other hand, have experienced the inverse fate: the more research is conducted on college forecasting tools, the more GPAs rise as a more reliable predictor of first-semester freshman grades. To be sure, high school grades must be examined with care as well. To view them as infallible guides to academic outcomes is to forget that teenagers develop unevenly. Leaving aside for now the issue of how they are graded, students change in many ways throughout high school. A typical Adelphi freshman, Tatiana B., for instance, remembers being habitually late to her first period class when she began high school—"Walking around, talking to friends, wasting my time. I was young and stupid"—but her attendance rose steadily through her remaining high school years.[4]

As a reliable college predictor, high school grades prevail over the SAT. But it's not the only variable that does. Educational background, parental education, extracurricular activities in high school, distance of school commute, and early vs. late filing of financial aid FAFSA (Free Application for Federal Student Aid) forms all portend freshman progress. Gender is also a factor in anticipating college success at the outset: female freshmen do somewhat better than males in college courses, though not as well on the exams for admission. Regular proclamations that the exam "indicates likely success in college" nevertheless emanate from the test's sponsor, the College Board.[5] While more college-bound students take the ACT than the SAT, the present study takes the latter as exemplary for the New York and Northeast regions in which Adelphi University operates. The SAT is the entrance exam through which most of the area's students endeavor to pass, and its primacy is spreading to areas previously dominated by the ACT.[6] It is also more of a lightning rod for debate than the rival ACT. Nevertheless, prognostic models of entering classes that exclude SAT marks compare favorably with those that include them in likely graduation outcomes. Even the extent of a student's immersion in Facebook has been judged a comparable predictor of academic performance to the SAT. But the SAT marches on regardless, chosen by one school district after another to replace the ACT, as if there are no doubts as to its efficacy. Recently revised by the College Board, the very changes themselves generate panic and confusion.[7]

ROOTS OF THE SAT

Nicholas Lemann, an astute scholar of the SAT and standardized testing, traces the college entrance exam (originally the Scholastic Aptitude Test: the "A" later represented "Assessment") to particular currents swirling through higher education before and after World War II. Among them was the notion of intelligence testing. Some educational reformers were concerned about the level of prior knowledge attained by young people entering college. Even with few students attending college in the 1930s, key higher educators believed that half of them were unfit. Their desire to weed out, if not block, the poorer students would later animate their opposition to the GI Bill, by which millions of war veterans might pursue a college education. But at the same time, they did not mind the deferment of military service granted by the government to men going to college, since it would increase the number of test takers. The theory of eugenics, postulating the methodology through which the most intelligent and capable people might be bred, also impacted early reasons for standardized testing. Lemann points out that Henry Chauncey, a pivotal SAT developer, looked into Nazi educational tests as a possible source upon which to draw. What united the various theorists, says Lemann, was the search for the most capable leaders and the need to find a tool that would carefully select the deserving few: "None of them championed the expansion of education."[8]

Even so, other initial proponents of the SAT began to express doubts long before the exam became a powerful force. Carl Brigham, for example, warned in the mid-1930s that the coming phenomenon would be based on "one of the most glorious fallacies in the history of science, namely that the tests measured *native intelligence* purely and simply without regard to training or schooling." Tests, he felt, should rather be considered "a ready method of interview" than "a measure of some mysterious power." The SAT's prediction of college success in the 1950s in fact showed mixed results, accurately anticipating the college grades of only 15 percent of freshmen. But the path toward "the big test" accelerated. Brigham bemoaned what he perceived to be looming on the horizon: "If the unhappy day ever comes when teachers point their students toward these newer examinations, and the present weak and restricted procedures get a grip on education, then we must look for the inevitable distortion of education in terms of tests." And the result would include, as Lemann observes, "a system for serial ranking people by a supposed innate worth" revealed in test results.[9]

The view of the SAT and standardized testing as a national necessity was nevertheless at high tide by the early 1960s. Banesh Hoffman's *The Tyranny of Testing* (1962) anticipated many of today's dissents. He then characterized the College Board's influence over the U.S. educational system as far too intrusive, inviting an approach based on drills and memorization. The SAT, he wrote, had reduced college aptitude to "an ability to answer rather trifling though sometimes tricky arithmetical, algebraic, and geometrical multiple-choice questions," and an adeptness in picking the "best" word fill-ins and verbal analogies, the "correct" answer to which may well be wrong. Test manufacturers built the format for speed:

"A two-hour multiple-choice test may contain some two hundred questions, a fact to which professional testers point with pride rather than consternation." Generating outcomes by machine, the exam invited mechanical thinking. That such exams yielded quick results, along with a package of judgments and policies, explained much of their appeal to educational authorities. Yet the genuine worth of answers chosen at the rate of a hundred per hour was dubious indeed: "How deeply can such questions probe and still be machine-gradable?"[10]

The SAT fomented shallow teaching and learning, added Hoffman. Who tended to do well? Not the "deep student" who is "constructive and creative," but rather one who can quickly adopt "a pre-determined single correct and sometimes quite pedestrian answer." The College Board rewarded the "superficially brilliant," while penalizing students of "depth, subtlety, and critical acumen." Since the entire premise was faulty, revising the SAT would make no difference. It was bound to favor "the quick-reading, . . . cynically test-wise candidate" and undermine "the intellectually honest candidate with a subtle, probing, critical, or creative mind," according to Hoffman. Nevertheless, standardized testing entities structured a way of life: "They . . . assess our scholastic achievement throughout our school days. They stand harsh guard at the gateway to National Merit Scholarships, and they tell admissions officers how many points worth of college aptitude we possess."[11]

By the late twentieth century, the SAT culture prevailed among college applicants. Exam preparation penetrated middle and secondary education. Its psychological impact was profound. Nicholas Lemann comments: "To the taker it was a scientific, numeric assignment of worth which, no matter how skeptical one tried to be about testing, lodged itself firmly in the mind, never to be forgotten." The proliferation of "test prep, the obsessing, the cheating, the fevered late-night freshman-year SAT-score revelation" were all indicative.[12]

DEFENSES OF THE SAT

The SAT today certainly has its ardent defenders, beginning with the College Board itself. In view of recent revisions instituted by the Board, one may expect a flood of new studies. But considering that the Board has undertaken to revamp the exam in the face of broad criticisms of its value, its long-standing assertion of SAT supremacy as success forecaster has been remarkable. Changes in format have induced new fears in the students about to experience it, which may affect confidence and final marks, according to the *New York Times*. There is no reason to suppose that the results of the new SAT will be any less the subject of doubt and criticism. Publications directed to young audiences give expression to new SAT trepidations. Considering that the revised version is more "word-heavy," *Teen Vogue* reports students who took sample tests "finding themselves confused just trying to navigate through all the excess words and focus in on what the real question was actually asking." At the same time, *Seventeen* predicts the SAT will be "more difficult for students who are math-oriented and students who are less exposed to reading, including people who grew up speaking another language at home." Penn State's *Daily Collegian* editorializes: "Everyone's minds [sic] work and learn in different ways, and standardized testing has always been organized in a fashion which ignored this fact. With this latest progression, they are making it even more difficult for certain students to truly convey their intellectual capabilities." A Stanford freshman declares "without SAT scores, higher education could return its focus on identifying true, deep and brilliant thinkers and developing them to their fullest potential instead of rewarding the most 'excellent sheep.'" The *Washington Post* regrets that the reach and clout of the SAT's "hairy hand" will not recede.[13]

Nonetheless, the College Board and its advocates stand by the exam and standardized testing in general. Michigan State psychology professor David Z. Hambrick thus declared in 2011 that while not perfect, the SAT remains a good prophet of college outcomes, including in junior and senior years. Furthermore, it previews "life outcomes well beyond the college years, including income and occupational achievements." While he granted that the SAT cannot possibly measure a student's every attribute, "relatively speaking" it remains an effective measure of the higher education career. He paralleled test marks with IQ scores, finding both stable and reliable over time. Hambrick bluntly acknowledges that if people find it dismaying that an intelligence test remains instrumental in college admissions, "that's just too bad." His viewpoint coincides with the mammoth "meta-analysis" commissioned by the College Board itself in 2001, which sustained other voices supporting the SAT at the turn of the twenty-first century. Conducted at the University of Minnesota, the investigation collected the records of a million test takers between the 1940s and 1999. It "culled its results from more than 1,700 previous analyses," noted the journal *Black Issues in Higher Education*. It concluded, like Hambrick ten years later, that the SAT nicely anticipated college grades, graduation rates, and future endeavors. The Board paid the university a quarter of a million dollars for the research.[14]

Accordingly, *Education Week* reported "SAT Said to be Reliable Predictor of College Success." In 2009, *U.S. News & World Report* endorsed the SAT, "in combination with other data." It termed the exam a "valid, fair, and reliable data tool for college admissions. All of the available research supports this point." Since high test scores are key to the magazine's touted annual college rankings, the positive evaluation held no mystery. Warning colleges against being deluded by inflated high school grades, it deemed the SAT a superior college entry filter, though again as one of several criteria. The exam offered "a standardized, level playing field in the admissions process," equal for all, in the College Board's quest "to connect students to college success, with a commitment to equality and equity."[15]

CRITIQUES OF THE SAT

However, criticisms of the SAT, in both old and new incarnations, have mounted. That the single one-shot exam cannot be seriously accepted as a guide to student success has become a cornerstone of the attack. The emphasis on testing extends to business-oriented education systems around the world. Hence, one cannot be surprised by the unfavorable reactions to it in other countries, exemplified for instance in Lucy Clark's book about Australia, *Beautiful Failures.*[16] Critics charge that the battery of college-bound learning styles cannot be homogenized in the high-stakes testing arena. Moreover, researchers have found that the SAT's verbal and math components are of widely varying relevance in anticipating success in certain majors, including those which may feature both skills. Their conclusions pool in the finding that high school grades are a better instrument, since they reflect the entire record of secondary schoolwork.

The performance of female SAT takers in science majors is discussed more fully below. But scholars at Ball State University have examined the applicability of College Board scores to Psychology majors. Psychology grade point averages in college correlate strongly with the number of courses the student took in high school in English, Science, Math, Social Science, and foreign language. Doing well on the SAT math section augured well for Psychology majors, but good math grades in high school were just as likely to facilitate success in the major. Leading students in Ball State's Psychology department were far more likely to have done well in secondary school English than to have scored high on the SAT verbal. Naturally, the researchers report variation between different schools. For example, math SAT grades were not as significant an indicator for Psychology majors at Holy Cross College. Another project monitored students taking Computer Science and Bacteriology courses at Old Dominion University. High school grade point average led SAT scores as prognostic indicator in both courses, but not by as much in Computer Science as in Bacteriology. Lectures and laboratory work typified both courses. But the authors of the study propose that the Bacteriology course included a hands-on emphasis the other class lacked.[17]

High school average is a consistently better predictor, submits Doris Zahner of the Council for Aid to Education. Compared to all others, it correlates more with both freshman and college grades. The secondary school average is more responsible for how a college student will do than anything else. A 2012 study, based on a survey of freshmen who were then tracked through graduation, raises an entire set of factors not ordinarily considered in how students do in college or when they graduate. Discounting the traditional IQ implications of the SAT, it demonstrates that "emotional intelligence," which embraces empathy, social responsibility, flexibility, and impulse control, is a significant predictor of college performance.[18]

Scholars have suggested that a student's "self-efficacy," by which is meant adeptness at performing tasks, asking for help, and handling social situations, offers a reasonable preview of college success. A study at the University of Utah posits that "self-efficacy" is "associated with significantly higher odds of persisting from semester 2 to semester 3 and achieving a higher GPA: even after controlling for gender, race/ethnicity, HS GPA, ACT score." Robert J. Sternberg of the University of Wyoming points out "tests of general academic aptitudes only account, at most, for 25 percent of the variation in academic success in college." Students may test well, yet lack the "self-regulation skills" essential to good college grades. Having been pushed too hard by one's parents does not augur well for college achievement either. Sternberg adds, "Self-efficacy is one of the best positive predictors of success in any working environment." It includes the ability to form a perspective and maintain an ethical stance.[19]

Factors taking primacy over standardized exams help account for so many of the withering judgments of the SAT. Still within the debate over blockbuster tests, new data proposes that once students are admitted to college, their performance on regular quizzes is a better indicator of learning than midterm and final exams. Other decent gauges include independent research, group work, and similar concrete activities. Experience in college internships anticipates academic accomplishment more than standardized test scores, choice of major, student generational status, or extracurricular involvement. Leading academics have proposed ditching national entrance exams entirely or reducing their role in college admissions in favor of a more comprehensive approach to applicants' profiles. The head of the University of California once asserted that the exams themselves constitute a profitable industry, and sadly drive high school curricula. Students "spend hours each month—directly and indirectly—preparing for the SAT, studying long lists of verbal analogies such as 'untruthful is to mendaciousness' as 'circumspect is to caution. . . . ' all "taking valuable class time away from reading, writing and arithmetic." In many cases, the only concrete outcome of these ineffective exercises is the development of one's test-taking skills.[20]

Noted educator Diane Ravitch explains:

> [W]e were able to retreat, as a nation, into this notion that good education was just a test score, a test score on a standardized test where all the kids needed to do was to look at four boxes and say, "Oh, if I

> eliminate A and B, then I only have to have a guess between C and D." And then you have a whole system across the United States where kids are doing these four boxes, making a good guess, and then if enough of them know how to make the good guess, we say we've improved achievement. We haven't improved achievement. We haven't improved performance. We've achieved—we've improved test scores. And the test scores may be, in fact, representative of very little other than the ability to take a test. And I ask you, if you finish high school, and you've got a test-taking skill, what can you do with it?

A California panel concluded a study with the pronouncement that "the advantage that the SAT . . . is often assumed to possess—that it is largely effective at identifying students with strong potential who have not yet been able to demonstrate that potential—is largely a phantom." Nationwide research by the Century Foundation drew the same conclusion. Broader critiques of true-false and multiple choice tests (which "turn the examination into a guessing-game that stresses knowledge of minutiae rather than understanding of fundamental concepts and principles") accompany the doubts of standardized veracity. The arguments of critic Jacques Barzun continue to echo: "The multiple choice test. . . . is harmful to learning and teaching." It engenders "passive-recognition knowledge, not active usable knowledge." Such tests "break up the unity of knowledge and isolate the pieces," he maintained in 1988.[21]

Challengers to the college entrance exams perceive practical and wide-ranging problems. The SAT and the ACT sell students' personal information (gathered during exam registration) to colleges which advertise themselves according to targeted profiles. Hyping the numbers seems to flow from the business model of education. The producers of entrance tests (such as the Pearson PLC publishing company, which allegedly bribed New York state officials in exchange for testing contracts) appear to be among their strongest backers, continuing to contend that marks foretell college performance, notwithstanding a spate of refutations.[22]

Scoring problems surface periodically, profoundly shaking the test takers, for as one admissions aide put it, "scores are absurdly important." Misconceived questions parallel those witnessed on statewide secondary and primary school exams. The issue is not new: one recalls a test taker who gave identical answers on two identical reading comprehension tests, but received two different grades. The College Board has confessed to incorrect time allotments for different SAT sections, yet obliges students to take the test over. The Board's electronic system of reporting test results to colleges does not always work: early admission applicants are thereby impeded because deadlines are missed. Revised SAT and Preliminary SAT (PSAT) formats seem to make no difference: the issues recur. Millions of nerve-wracked students search in vain for the online posting of exam results. Test scanning and grading services belong to corporate entities, whose errors have necessitated recounts. But glitches are not the only problem. Theft of answers is both informal and organized. SAT-prep companies in Asia offer students practice with the actual test they eventually take. Scandalous activities sprout from test mania.[23]

Test prep feeds on the dread of students and their families. Huntington, one of thousands of tutoring firms, casually informs a parent that the college entrance exam "is one of the most demanding tests your child will take in his or her life-time." The tone is a persuasive lead-in to "commercially driven admission practices" at the college level, says critic Lloyd Thacker, as those who strive for status in dubious ratings submit to "a rising obsession with quantification, which skews everything from college search to benchmarks of success, and the nature of learning and decision making." Thacker indicts the "influence of anxiety selling by industries such as test prep, scholarship search, and athletic agents." They create "an overstressed, sleep-deprived, performance-driven generation of students who view acceptance into a name-brand college as a prize to be won."[24]

The College Board, writes James Murphy in *The Atlantic,* is pushing hard to make exam prep part and parcel of the high school curriculum. The obsession with standardization, states a New York City high school principal, hails from "a world where data and numbers are used to evaluate everything, including our children and our school." He prefers "a far more substantive assessment," for grades alone "provide limited information, are often demeaning and serve to highlight the evaluator's limited tools, and often limited vision." But James Murphy fears the SAT's persistence. Its newly revised format will spawn still more test prep companies and classes, raising the anxieties of students and parents higher still. The Princeton Review SAT courses begin at $600 for fifteen hours of instruction in a large setting to at least $1500 for twenty-five hours in a class of four. The College Board thus creates a continuously festering sore: keep it as is and it hurts. Revise it, and it hurts more. But out of the wound profits flow.[25]

Writing in *Educational Leadership,* NYU professor Susan Neuman recoils from the data-adulterated spectacle that is "sucking the life out of meaningful, content-rich education for young learners." It similarly impacts teachers, who are mandated to devise spreadsheets with innumerable columns to track the trajectory of children from the earliest grades. Rubrics for every assignment enrich the charted measurements. With small respite, regularly scheduled tests wrest valuable time from genuine instruction. Staking so much on standardized examinations, complains a school principal, "inevitably conflict[s] with authentic educational practice," especially when such tests are used to evaluate public school teachers. It is precisely this data-driven evaluation that sometimes drives students, teachers, and administrators alike to cheat, for they are made to feel that high test scores foretell security and a bright future. Theft of answers, misrepresentation of results, and crooked test preps belong to one game, here and abroad. Scandal (recent elementary school tests were leaked online in the United Kingdom on two occasions) is inevitable. The nationally applied Common Core, complete with numerous standardized tests from elementary through secondary levels, presents more of the same in the purported interest of establishing minimum standards. A veteran secondary school teacher asks, "What, we will all wonder, is the correct number of standardized tests necessary for every student to experience in a year, or in an entire school career? Here's the correct answer. None." Nearly half of Common Core's twenty-five drafters were associated with the producers of the ACT or SAT. Diane Ravitch declares that "if the sanctions and punishments tied to test scores are wrong now—promoting teaching to the test, narrowing the curriculum and gaming the system—the sanctions and punishments will still be wrong two years from now."[26]

In a study of college readiness, the ACT itself appears to accept the national conversation about standardized exams by advocating "a more holistic picture of students" that embraces "behavioral domains" to gauge potential success. It counsels admissions officers to seek out such applicant traits as motivation, engagement, extracurricular involvement, and discipline. It is high time, agrees David Holmes in *The Journal of College Admission,* for schools to include student traits like perseverance and honesty among criteria for acceptance. Students without such characteristics, albeit with higher college entrance scores, are more likely to drop out, Holmes notes. Interestingly, these observations coincide with the fleeting insight of the exam-focused college rankers at *U.S. News & World Report,* who point out that while "criticism of current admissions practices such as standardized tests increases, promising new alternatives are emerging."[27]

THE SAT AND GENDER DISCRIMINATION

Despite these more telling indicators of college success, stigma marks the multitude whose abilities the SAT obscures. Thus, an investigation directed by McKinsey & Company blames the low quality of U.S. public school instruction upon the teachers' own poor performance on the SAT. Better to recruit today's teachers from the higher scorers, it reasons. Such correlative results become causative "evidence" and then generic excuses, which reaffirm doubts about future achievement. This casts aspersion on women, who make up 84 percent of public school teachers. Scholars Michael Inzlicht and Catherine Good contend that female students, whose purportedly weaker math skills have produced a stereotype of deficiencies (including on the SAT), have "felt less accepted, felt that others had lower expectations for them, felt a greater desire to fade into the woodwork, felt less trust of their learning environment, and had lower confidence in their abilities." Psychologists Diane M. Quinn and Steven J. Spencer believe that a girl taking the SAT "has an extra worry to contend with that a boy does not: A stereotype that she, as a girl, has inferior math skills." University of California psychology professor Rebecca Zwick observes that The SAT, the ACT, and most of the SAT Subject Tests have been found to under-predict women's college grades. The same holds for a number of other standardized tests taken while still in secondary school, even though female students do as well as or outperform males "on an array of other academic benchmarks in high school and college."[28]

Numerous investigations verify that girls and women are discouraged at the outset from considering scientific careers, whether by general prejudice, faculty bias, or opposition from those around them. According to a UNESCO report, a high school girl who excels equally with a male counterpart in science courses "is three times less likely than a high school boy to earn a doctorate in science." The report declares: "In secondary school, with little or no choice about the subjects they study, girls perform as well as boys in science courses. . . . Why, after having done well in science in secondary school, do so many young women turn away from the field? Much of the blame lies with stereotypes." The sentiments of Nobel laureate biochemist Sir Tim Hunt confirm UNESCO's findings. In his view, women are too emotional to work in science labs, too prone to cry, and too likely to fall in love with fellow researchers: all such tendencies detract from "getting at the truth" of science. Prevailing skepticism about their place in the sciences have induced among many female and African-American scientists what the American Institute of Physics terms the "imposter syndrome," feeling they are not welcome in scientific professions.[29]

According to veteran political scientist Andrew Hacker, female students tend to do better in class, but "worse" on tests like the SAT, especially the math component. He suggests that females do better in complex math class assignments because they tend to analyze more carefully or think things through. Yet this works against them in the pressurized atmosphere of the SAT examination room. Says Hacker, "pausing to ponder can spell death in multiple-choice testing, since speed is crucial for a high score." He observes, "the importance we assign to standardized tests is eclipsing that of assessments by sentient teachers," while protesting that "our testing imperium . . . blatantly slights the talents of half our society, just when girls and women are revealing abilities that match or surpass those of boys and men." Interestingly, male and female averages earned in college courses do not diverge as widely as their SAT scores. (Freshmen women *do* spend more time studying than their male counterparts, however.) Nonetheless, lower test scores stigmatize, and the consequent shadow on academic possibilities leads some to view the academic ability of many student demographics as inherently cursed. Groups thus labeled, as reported by the Brookings Institution's Brown Center on Education Policy, include not only women, but also students of color and those of lower socioeconomic status.[30]

Others still adamantly insist that the quantitative element in college entrance exams directly prophesizes success in the sciences. For instance, close to half of students obtaining SAT math scores above 660 achieve "As" in a sample university's General Chemistry courses, while only 12 percent of those between 340 and 550 achieve the ultimate grade. Arguments hold that lower-scoring standardized test takers, like those admitted to General Studies programs at Northeastern or Adelphi, are unsuited to be science majors, or at least require more preparation. A study of college courses by the *Journal of Chemical Education* finds "that mathematical skill measured by SAT-M [math] scores is an important factor in determining grades," and posits that math scores, more than any other variable, accurately foretell how students do in the sciences.[31]

The sample findings, however, treat the SAT data as proof of the incongruity of low test scorers with science majors, without questioning societal practice or exam legitimacy. The National Science Foundation states bluntly: "The science and engineering workforce is largely white and male" and "women's participation in science and engineering occupations is lower than it is in the U.S. workforce as a whole," but women are "the vast majority of those employed in traditionally female occupations, such as nursing."[32] A report on health majors by the *Journal of Blacks In Higher Education* points out: "health professions schools that use a holistic admissions process that takes into account more than an applicant's grades and test scores, achieve an entering class that is more diverse and in most cases there is no change in measures of academic quality, student academic performance, or student retention. . . . Being a good health professional is about more than scientific knowledge. It also requires an understanding of people."[33]

More legitimate indicators of a student's science potential might comprise his or her general views about scientific study, previous exposure to the subject, and the type of pedagogy previously experienced. According to a report from the Center for Public Education, taking rigorous math classes in high school, "no matter prior academic achievement," better foreshadows college success. Thus, high school students "taking more challenging courses have better chances of success in their first year of college." These findings once again raise questions about the standardized test measures. Advanced placement courses may also augur college prowess better than national entrance exams, but one should resist granting them too much sway. Former college advisor John E. Stafford warns that AP classes can perpetuate a narrow definition of college eligibility, while stressing out the students enrolled. Ironically, while high school AP classes can foster college skills, they are less available at high schools where minority youth predominate (despite the presence of eligible students). On the whole, fewer opportunities exist for minority students to take science AP classes, while female students in general are discouraged from taking them when they are offered. In the lower grades moreover, African-American children are commonly bypassed for selection to gifted programs. The myth that certain student constituencies are inevitably lower achieving is thus perpetuated.[34]

At the graduate school level, the Graduate Record Exam generally required for admission to master's and doctoral science programs is no more trustworthy than the SAT, according to physicists Casey Miller and Keivan Stassun. "In simple terms," they write, "The GRE is a better indicator of sex and skin colour than of ability and ultimate success." It also says more about the socioeconomic status of applicants than about their acumen for science careers. Miller and Stassun submit that over-reliance on GRE results leads admissions committees to create graduate student bodies in which minorities and women are underrepresented. It would be preferable at the very least to supplement the GRE with scrutiny of applicants' "drive, diligence and the willingness to take scientific risks," or else the STEM (science, technology, engineering, and math) professions will continue to exhibit a low level of diversity.[35]

POVERTY AND RACE

Scorning the "nearly iconic status in America" of the ACT and SAT, the National Association for College Admission Counseling (NACAC) recommends that college guidebooks "eliminate test scores as a measure of institutional quality." NACAC research shows that test score differences mirror wealth and parental level of education, but not scholarly acumen. The data is quite clear in this respect, with students splitting chiefly along class lines above and below the SAT mean. The *New York Times* charted the exam results by income levels in 2009: "Generally speaking, the wealthier a student's family is, the higher the SAT score." The Jack Kent Cooke Foundation finds that both ACT and SAT scores of lower-income students produce a "false negative," which suggests lack of capability. Of course, test results can reveal inequities going back further than high school, mirroring societal biases of race, gender, and class. For example, Harold Berlak found that in statewide exams "minor differences in the number of correct answers on a multiple-choice test create grossly inflated failure rates for persons of color." Berlak attributed this to "the way the tests are normed and cut scores set," leading to a profound misreading of many talented students. The problem, he felt, was "systemic and structural," rooted in "the way the tests are constructed and administered, the way results are reported, and in the organizational structure and administrative rules of the accountability system itself."[36]

Poverty, limiting access to such an important experience as preschool, wreaks havoc on educational outcomes initially and throughout the school experience. Truly, posits the Economic Policy Institute, educational progress for all must be accomplished as part of a policy of creating more jobs, better funding of public institutions, raising wages, sustaining safety net programs, and combating housing discrimination. Disparities in test marks at all pre-college levels emerge in every nook and cranny of the country. In Schuylkill County, Pennsylvania, for example, the wealthiest districts show the highest scores, as contrasted with the city of Hazleton, with a much greater population in poverty. (A local school official nevertheless attributes the lower scores to character flaws: "low-income homes are less likely to have the stable home life that contributes to doing well in school . . . and having parents who pay attention to a student's performance in school.") A 2015 Johns Hopkins University study of high school dropout rates (sponsored by AT&T and Target and backed by Colin Powell) points out that low-income school districts (measured by eligibility for free or discounted lunches) now encompass the majority of public high school students.[37]

Recent findings confirm racial disparities in exam results. Appearing to recognize this fact in the aforementioned report on college readiness, the ACT's producers blithely suggest that African-Americans have lower aspirations. Yet the *Journal of Blacks in Higher Education* points out that ACT findings that black students score well below whites, particularly on the verbal component, sidestep the quality of public education prior to college. The same publication considers the SAT nothing less than "a major roadblock to Black students' aspirations to higher education." In larger perspective, a 2014 Columbia University assessment of segregated schools confirms that poorly funded and inadequate public instruction "forces educators in 'low-achieving' schools serving mostly low-income black and Hispanic students to fixate on raising test scores" by gearing teaching to testing. This runs directly counter to effective pedagogies, producing a situation in which "students in less affluent and less white and/or Asian schools often lose more instructional time to mundane and test-prep oriented curriculum."[38]

Stanford's Denise Clark Pope doubts whether "you can design a test that fairly assesses what students learn in high school," asserting that test preparation "has become a time-consuming distraction." Student portfolios and narrative evaluations by high school teachers would provide more appropriate measures, for "by devaluing test scores and by emphasizing more qualitative review methods, colleges may be able to assess more effectively the traits that help students succeed in college, especially traits that are difficult to measure on standardized tests: problem-solving skills, creativity and motivation." *The New York Times* reports that even law school deans are "questioning the wisdom of relying on a single written test as the gateway to legal practice." Perhaps they see that "the obsession with admissions tests is damaging education."[39]

This has become a commonplace affirmation in national studies and local reports. An Indiana newspaper noted in 2014, "Higher education officials said it is actually a student's high school grade point average, not a standardized test score that is the best predictor of how that student will perform in college." Their critique applies also to the ACT. For instance, a survey of two thousand University of Illinois freshmen concludes that first-semester college average more ably predicts graduation rates of minority students than that exam. The SAT has been found especially deficient in gauging the aptitude of bilingual students, however fluent. The tendency of bilingual students under the time stress of the exam is to revert to thinking in their first language, fostering "error-laden negativity," according to the *North American Journal of Psychology*. The math component of the SAT is particularly problematic under the circumstances for bilingual test takers, observes the journal. Of course, students whose first language is English may also feel the effects of such pressures. Yet "the reduced performance of the bilingual students under a time limit may be due to an overload of the working memory capacity system."[40]

PLAYING THE NUMBERS

In practice, the college entrance tests exercise an admissions clout entirely disproportionate to their predictive failure. Tests figure more prominently than admissions offices may let on. California's Claremont-McKenna lists them third from the bottom in qualifications for freshman entry, but from 2004 to 2011 the school went out of its way to falsely report the SAT scores of its first-year students to college rankers. As the *New York Times* put it, the "ninth-best liberal arts college in the country" inflated the results to "influence the rankings, and the deception underscores the importance those rankings have taken on, as colleges fret over the loss of even a notch or two against their competitors." An admissions dean of a rival institution pointed out, "The pressure is real. . . . God forbid you go down in those numbers."[41]

Claremont-McKenna is not alone in fudging the numbers. In 2011, George Washington University was caught exaggerating the proportion of freshmen drawn from the top tier of secondary school graduates, a practice it had been getting away with for years. Three years earlier, church-affiliated Baylor paid admitted students to retake the SATs to increase its average scores. From 2010 through 2013, Flagler College doctored test scores, freshman class rankings, and high school GPAs. Emory University submitted falsified student data to rankings magazines for more than a decade beginning in 2000. Indeed, misrepresentation for the sake of higher evaluation by *U.S. News and World Report* and *The Princeton Review* is especially noted among private colleges battling for position. But New Jersey's *Bergen Record* reports that even public universities, like Kean, Ramapo, and Rowan, have overstated the wave of applications received so they can boast a lower acceptance rate—a feather in the cap of any would-be rigorous institution. A college that rejects more applicants may be considered to have higher standards, no matter how low it stoops to make it appear so. Admissions offices have leeway to manipulate data, since no true monitoring operates for accuracy. In another deplorable practice, perhaps more common than we know, George Washington University also confessed to covering up the rejections of qualified students who could not afford full tuition. False data reporting, and further disadvantaging the already disadvantaged, is only to be expected in America's corporate-driven college system.[42]

RESISTANCE TO CHANGE

The authority of the ACT and SAT remains strong, although studies continue to puncture holes in their anticipatory power. Indeed, the exams continue to factor into the hiring process on Wall Street, where the obsession is to enlist alumni of Ivy League institutions. But the *Wall Street Journal* declares "those best schools do not teach kids anything different from what the average colleges do. They do not prepare them better for the day-to-day work of Wall Street." A growing number of institutions have become SAT-optional, a certain comfort to applicants who did less well on the entrance test. Illustrative is the decision by Hofstra University, which "allows each individual student to decide whether or not the standardized test results accurately reflect his or her academic ability and potential."[43]

Do students applying to SAT-optional schools who do not submit their SAT results do as well in college as those who submit the scores? They do indeed, according to the National Association for College Admission Counseling, because college performance more directly "tracks HSGPA [High School Grade Point Average], even with wide variations in testing." Minority and female students, along with first-generation applicants, are more heavily represented among those opting not to submit SAT marks (which fall an average of 149 points below their fellow students). Is there any difference in graduation rates between the two categories? Virtually none. In fact, says the NACAC, "non-submitters with strong HSGPAs normally graduate at higher rates than students with weaker HSGPAs but much stronger testing." Therefore, "we find high school GPA . . . to be a broadly reliable predictor of college performance, and standardized testing to be very far from 'standardized' in its predictive value." Then of what value is the test? Quite simply and despite the evidence, "test scores contribute to college guidebook rankings." Hamilton College president Joan Hinde Stewart opines: "What has disturbed us about rankings is the embedded notion that you can capture the complexity of higher education in a single number." Yet the sway of test scores over ranking, and ranking (especially set by *US News & World Report*) over reputation, persists in the corridors of higher education.[44]

The College Board, publisher of the SAT, has resisted the condemnations for decades. However, as *The New York Times* reported, the College Board announced in 2014 "a fundamental rethinking of the SAT, ending the longstanding penalty for guessing wrong, cutting obscure vocabulary words and making the essay optional." The Board's head admitted that the SAT and competitor ACT were "disconnected from the work of our high schools." After two years of reflection, he promised to institute a revised test in 2016, along with free online practice and videos. (He might also have admitted that the impractical mechanism had long misrepresented the skills of generations of students). SAT revisions notwithstanding, Washington State's vice-president for student affairs and enrollment maintains that the exam "is inherently biased against women, the poor, minorities, and older students. Revamping is not enough." *The New York Times* reported that the College Board hopes to remedy the now admittedly ill-conceived concept and format, which for decades has unfairly favored those "with wealth, education, access to good schools or all three."[45]

The continuation of the SAT in new form is one of the College Board's strongest forms of resistance to change. The SAT and ACT have succeeded in building a test-giving base in American high schools. Journalist Kate Zernike points out the paradox: "as more colleges and universities moved away from requiring standardized test scores for admission," test producers are "offering the SAT and the ACT even to students who do not plan to go to college." They are pushing the exams in secondary schools. Through agreements with local school boards, students may take the new SAT free of charge or at low cost. In Connecticut, the College Board has succeeded in making the SAT an official replacement for statewide exams in the eleventh grade. The same effort is underway in other states. Bob Schaefer, one of the spearheads of the "Fairtest" movement to make colleges "test-optional" as far as the SAT is concerned, believes that the College Board is "more interested in trying to slow the test-optional movement than improving the test's measurement precision." He doubts whether the updated SAT will reflect the academic predilections of black and female students, as well as working class students overall, any better than its forerunner. By developing an SAT with a different appearance, the College Board has produced "marketing bells and whistles," but not a fairer test.[46]

Even so, neo-conservative scholar Charles Murray warns the College Board not to discard the original assumption that there is a link between social class and inborn brains. For "the most important academic advantage many wealthy families have is intelligence, not wealth." Along these lines, an article in *Intelligence* indeed situates college-educated Fortune 500 CEOs at the very top for intelligence and cognitive ability. Including CEOs without college diplomas, the entire group is deemed brighter than the general population. However, that intellect begets financial success is a traditional rationale for the domination of human affairs by wealthy people, who are "naturally" more advanced. False measurements of the capacity to think have always been bound up with the reputation of the SAT. Nor are they merely historical. Business and political leaders are assumed to be innately brighter. High SAT scorers are considered destined for greatness. No wonder that sixteen- and seventeen-year-olds broadcast or conceal their test marks with exuberance or terrible shame, respectively.[47]

Nevertheless, the preeminence of high school work over a one-shot test as college prognosticator is acknowledged by thousands of educators. But the student's secondary school record may be affected by the nature of local school policies, union and parental input, staffing, funding, facilities, and equipment, all of which go to shape a high school education. Inadequate advising at the secondary level impedes outcomes as well. As long as high schools are unequal in services, equipment, teacher training, and counseling provisions, the test scores will serve as a point of reference for income, not brains. Whatever the redesign, "it is time we say a prayer, throw dirt on the grave and bury the SAT." A writer in the *Chronicle of Higher Education* is equally dubious about retaining the SAT in any form. He urges that "we . . . move away from the notion of a standard, one-size-fits-all high school curriculum leading to a single test" in favor of high school exams more closely connected to what is taught. "Their tests would not drive the curricula—they would be the tail on the dog." Abandoning the SAT, he predicts, would not be quick and painless, but rather "like leaving a bad relationship: unthinkable at first, and then painful, but soon enough, you wonder why you stuck around as long as you did."[48]

Even the SAT's revisions fail to recognize the test's misrepresentation of the college readiness of important student categories. In the wake of SAT amendment proclamations, the movement to repudiate the standardized premise continues. Thus, Hampshire College in Massachusetts will not look at applicants' SAT scores at all. While Hampshire is a maverick, schools not known for experimentation are also part of this process. Kalamazoo College in Michigan plainly states that the entrance exams "say more about an applicant's economic advantages—or disadvantages—than about academic potential." George Washington University has become test-optional as well. Thirty schools in Massachusetts have made the submission of SAT grades a matter of applicant prerogative. Wells College in Auburn, New York has done likewise. "We . . . don't want standardized test scores to be a barrier to acceptance," states Wells' admission director. A president of an SAT-optional college blasts the entire SAT apparatus, redesigned or not, for the exam can never match the prophetic import of high school work. There should be "fewer such exam schemes. They damage the high school curriculum and terrify both students and parents." The multiple choice styling, he continues, "is a bizarre relic of long-outdated twentieth-century social-scientific assumptions and strategies," which "trivialize complexity and ambiguity."[49]

While some test-optional schools make brief announcements to that effect, a Willamette University (Salem, Oregon) faculty report went into great detail: the SAT "over- and under-predicts for a significant number of students in demographically patterned ways," mirrors "unequal encouragement and access" to AP and Honors classes in high school, and impairs college admissions offices with "the effects of stereotype threat." Test scores can mask more valuable college skills, said the professors, for "various character qualities, including diligence and creativity, significantly impact educational attainment and subsequent success." Indeed, more comprehensive methods of evaluating college suitability have been developed. A 2015 report (originating at Harvard Graduate School of Education) calls upon colleges to raise students' community involvement and extracurricular activity to crucial importance in evaluating them for admission. When circumstances make such commitments harder for some students, schools should read applicant essays closely for signs of social awareness. In terms of college potential, some level of community understanding is superior to the number of Advanced Placement courses the student has taken. The report contends: "For too long we have wrung our hands—and pointed our fingers—about a college admissions system that, despite the good intentions of almost all admissions officers, parents, and guidance counselors, increasingly seems to reinforce the wrong messages to our children." And thus, beyond creating an industry based on fallacy and deception, the SAT is useless. Yet every year, without fail, it wreaks havoc upon the lives of tens of millions of aspiring college students.[50]

NOTES

1. Michael Palumbo, Tom Meltzer, and Eric Owens, *The Best Northeastern Colleges 2010: 218 Select Schools to Consider*, New York, 2009.

2. Rebecca Zwick, *College Admission Testing*, National Association for College Admission Counseling, 2007, 10; Tamar Levin, "Slight Dip in SAT Scores for the Class of 2012," *New York Times*, September 24, 2012, A14; Mark Gilger, Jr., "School Analysis Shows Link between Poverty, Academic Performance in Schuylkill County," *Republican Herald* (Pottsville, PA), July 26, 2015, http://republicanherald.com/news/school-analysis-shows-link-between-poverty-academic-performance-in-schuylkill-county-1.1918045. Accessed July 31, 2015; Adelphi University Office of Research, Assessment,

and Planning, "First-time Freshmen Enrollment and Mean SAT Scores," *ORAP Research Bulletin*, May 2014, 1.

3. Nicholas Lemann, "Tinkering with the Test," *New York Times*, September 19, 1999, A19; Stacy Teicher Khadaroo, "Focus Less on the S.A.T., Study Tells Colleges," *Christian Science Monitor*, September 24, 2008, www.csmonitor.com/2008/0924/p03s03-usgn.html. Accessed October 6, 2008; Tony Schwartz, "The Test Under Stress," *New York Times Magazine*, January 10, 1999, 6.

4. Tatiana B., "Independence," by permission of Tatiana B., Adelphi University, 2015.

5. *Understanding Retention: An Analytical Review*, Scannell & Kurz, Inc., March 28, 2008, 18; John Hildebrand, "More Blacks, Hispanics Meet SAT Benchmark," *Newsday*, September 26, 2013, A13.

6. Tamar Lewin, "Testing, Testing," *New York Times*, August 4, 2013, ED14; Nick Anderson, "The SAT, now the No. 2 College Test Pushes to Reclaim Supremacy," *Washington Post*, December 24, 2015, https://www.washingtonpost.com/news/grade-point/wp/2015/12/24/the-sat-now-the-no-2-college-test-pushes-to-reclaim-supremacy/. Accessed December 29, 2015.

7. Linda DeAngelo, Ray Franke, Sylvia Hurtado, John H. Pryor, and Serge Tran, *Completing College: Assessing Graduation Rates at Four-Year Institutions*, Higher Education Research Institute at UCLA, 2011, 22–24; Zwick, 18; National Survey of Student Engagement, *Promoting Student Learning and Institutional Improvement: Lesson from NSSE at 13*, Bloomington, IN: Indiana University Center for Post-Secondary Research, 2012, 19, 26; Reynol Junco, "Student Class Standing, Facebook Use, and Academic Performance," *Journal of Applied Developmental Psychology*, 36 (January–February 2015), 18–29; Suzanne Baker, "Students and Tutors Face ACT/SAT College Exam Dilemma," *Chicago Tribune*, January 10, 2016, http://www.chicagotribune.com/suburbs/naperville-sun/news/ct-nvs-naperville-sat-testing-debate-st-0110-20160110-story.html. Accessed January 11, 2016.

8. Nicholas Lemann, *The Big Test: The Secret History of the American Meritocracy*, New York, 1999, 5, 43, 22–23, 30, 88, 24.

9. Lemann, 33–34, 86, 65.

10. Banesh Hoffman, *The Tyranny of Testing*, New York, 1962, 121, 87, 113, 57, 91, 89.

11. Hoffmann, 98, 101, 94, 137, 20–21.

12. Lemann, 273–74.

13. Anemona Hartocollis, "New SAT Has More Reading (Even in Math) and More Fretting," *New York Times*, February 9, 2016, A1; Katherine Amey, "Why the Newly Redesigned SAT Is Stressing Out Some Students," *Teen Vogue*, February 9, 2016, http://www.teenvogue.com/story/2016-sat-redesign-disadvantages. Accessed February 12, 2016; Hannah Orenstein, "The SAT Is Getting Its Biggest Redesign in a Decade . . . and You Might Not Like It," *Seventeen*, February 10, 2016, http://www.seventeen.com/life/school/news/a37992/the-sat-is-getting-its-biggest-redesign-in-a-decade-and-you-might-not-like-it/. Accessed February 12, 2016; "SAT Changes Further Divide Between Non-traditional Students," *Daily Collegian*, editorial, February 12, 2016, http://www.collegian.psu.edu/opinion/editorials/article_6433f574-d122-11e5-b2e6-ff88f0be4e6d.html. Accessed February 12, 2016; Kelsey Page, "I Am More Than a Number: The Case Against SAT Scores in College Admissions," *Stanford Daily*, December 2, 2014, http://www.stanforddaily.com/2014/12/02/i-am-more-than-a-number-the-case-against-sat-scores-in-college-admissions/. Accessed February 12, 2016; Valerie Strauss, "The Hairy Hand of the SAT Reaches Far into Your Future," *Washington Post*, January 31, 2016, https://www.washingtonpost.com/news/answer-sheet/wp/2016/01/31/the-hairy-hand-of-the-sat-reaches-far-into-your-future/. Accessed February 5, 2016.

14. David Z. Hambrick, "The SAT Is a Good Intelligence Test," New York Times, December 16, 2011, http://www.nytimes.com/roomfordebate/2011/12/04/why-should-sats-matter/the-sat-is-a-good-intelligence-test. Accessed February 12, 2016; "College Board-Sponsored Study Claims SAT is Good Predictor of Grades, Graduation," *Black Issues in Higher Education*, Vol. 18, No. 7 (May 24, 2011), 11.

15. John Gehring, "SAT Said to be Reliable Predictor of College Success," *Education Week*, May 9, 2011, 3; Gaston Caperton, "Test Data Allow Better Decisions," *U.S. News & World Report*, September 2009, 24.

16. Lucy Clark, *Beautiful Failures: How the Quest for Success is Harming Our Kids*, Melbourne, 2016.

17. Frank Meeker, Daniel Fox, and Bernard Whitney, "Predictors of Academic Success in the Undergraduate Psychology Major," *Teaching of Psychology*, Vol. 21, No. 3 (December 1994), 239–40; Larry A. Sparkman, Wanda S. Mauling, and Jalynn G. Roberts, "Non-Cognitive Predictors of Student Success in College," *College Student Journal*, Vol. 46, No. 3, (September 2012); Gary L. Allen et al., "Measures of Learning Rate and Scholastic Aptitude as Predictors of Performance in Training-Oriented Academic Courses," *The Journal of General Psychology*, Vol. 117, No. 3, 279, 280, 285, 291.

18. Doris Zahner, Lisa M. Ramsaran, and Jeffrey T. Steedle, *Comparing Alternatives in the Prediction of College Success*, Council for Aid to Education, 2014; Larry A. Sparkman, Wanda S. Mauling, and Jalynn G. Roberts, "Non-Cognitive Predictors of Student Success in College," *College Student Journal*, Vol. 46, No. 3, (September 2012); Gary L. Allen et al., "Measures of Learning Rate and Scholastic Aptitude as Predictors of Performance in Training-Oriented Academic Courses," *The Journal of General Psychology*, Vol. 117, No. 3, 279, 280, 285, 291.

19. Salvia Artman et al., *The Role of Self-Efficacy Beliefs in College Student Performance & Persistence*, University of Utah Department of Experimental Psychology, 2015, 13; Robert J. Sternberg, "Research to Improve Retention," in *Inside Higher Ed, The Retention Agenda*, 2013, 21–23.

20. Benedict Carey, "Frequent Tests Can Enhance College Learning, Survey Finds," *New York Times*, November 20, 2013, A18; Gould, 47–48; Julian E. Barnes, "The SAT Revolution," *U.S. News & World Report*, November 11, 2002, 50; Cindy A. Kalgo, Eugene T. Parker, III, Jessica K. Ezell Sheets, and Ernest T. Pascarella, *The Differential Effects of Internship Participation on End-of-Fourth-Year GPA By Demographic and Institutional Characteristics*, The University of Iowa, 2013, 12; Kenneth R. Weiss, "UC Chief Seeks to Drop SAT Use in Admissions," *Los Angeles Times*, February 17, 2001, http://pzacad.pitzer.edu/~hfairchi/SAT/LATonSAT021701.html. Accessed June 14, 2011.

21. Democracy Now, *Part II: Leading Education Scholar Diane Ravitch on "The Death and Life of the Great American School System,"* March 8, 2010, http://m.democracynow.org/web_exclusives/572. Accessed June 24, 2011; Barbara Whitaker, "University of California Panel Suggests Abandoning SAT," *New York Times*, January 31, 2002, A22; Monica Potts, "Getting Low-Income Students to Graduate," *The American Prospect*, June 30, 2010, http://prospect.org/cs/articles?article=getting_low_income_students_to_graduate. Accessed July 6, 2010; Peter J. Markie, *Professor's Duties: Ethical Considerations in College Teaching*, Lanham, MD, 1994, 185; Jacques Barzun, "Multiple Choice Flunks Out," *New York Times*, October 11, 1988, A31.

22. Emily Babay, "College Board, ACT Sued Over Sale of Student Information," *Philadelphia Inquirer*, October 31, 2013, http://www.philly.com/philly/news/College_Board_ACT_sued_over_sale_of_student_information.html#WsFRDe6v0JcdWFJs.01. Accessed June 18, 2015. Winnie Hu, "Testing Firm Faces Inquiry on Free Trips for Officials," *New York Times*, December 21, 2011, A29; Anna M. Phillips, "State Officials Throw Out Another Pearson Test Question," *New York Times*, May 2, 2012, http://www.nytimes.com/schoolbook/2012/05/02/state-officials-throw-out-another-pearson-test-question. Accessed May 21, 2012; "Is the SAT Creating A Generation of Bad Writers?" NPR, October 26, 2013, http://www.npr.org/templates/story/story.php?storyId=240954501. Accessed October 28, 2013; Tamar Lewin, "Average Scores Slip on SAT," *New York Times*, September 15, 2011, A20.

23. Hoffmann, 9; John Hildebrand, "A Test of Time," *Newsday*, August 29, 2007, A4; Scott Jaschik, "The SAT's 5-Minute Mess-Up," *Inside Higher Ed*, June 9, 2015, https://www.insidehighered.com/news/2015/06/09/college-board-wont-score-two-sections-sat. Accessed June 18, 2015; Karen W. Arenson, "Officials Say Scoring Errors for SAT Were Understated," *New York Times*, March 9, 2006, A18; Ben Chapman, "Fuzzy Math

on Regents Exam May Have Affected State Results, Teachers Say," *New York Daily News*, July 7, 2011, http://www.nydailynews.com/ny_local/2011/07/07/2011-07-07_fuzzy_math_on_the_regents.html. Accessed July 7, 2011; Karen W. Arenson and Diana B. Henriques, "Company's Errors on SAT Scores Raise New Qualms About Testing," *New York Times*, March 10, 2006, A1; Karen W. Arenson, "1,600 SAT Tests Escaped Check for Scoring Errors," *New York Times*, March 14, 2006, A21; Karen W. Arenson, "SAT Problems Even Larger Than Reported," *New York Times*, March 23, 2006, A21; Jillian Berman, "SAT Snafu Could Leave Many College Applications Incomplete," *MarketWatch*, November 3, 2015, http://www.marketwatch.com/story/your-early-decision-college-application-may-be-missing-something-very-important-2015-11-03. Accessed November 5, 2015; Anemona Hartocollis, "When Pineapple Races Hare, Students Lose, Critics of Standardized Tests Say," *New York Times*, April 20, 2012, A18; Valerie Strauss, "Problems with PSAT Score Delivery Sparks Anger at College Board," *Washington Post*, https://www.washingtonpost.com/news/answer-sheet/wp/2016/01/17/problems-with-psat-score-delivery-sparks-anger-at-college-board/. Accessed January 19, 2016; Renee Dudley et al., "Special Report: How Asian Test-Prep Companies Exposed the New SAT," *St. Louis Post-Dispatch*, March 28, 2016, http://www.stltoday.com/business/local/special-report-how-asian-test-prep-companies-exposed-the-new/article_fcbbcc44-d310-5097-a765-f4c4fd28802d.html. Accessed March 28, 2016.

24. Huntington: Your Tutoring Solution, "Dear Parent," letter to author, January 2015; Lloyd Thacker, "Confronting the Commercialization of College Admissions Leadership Opportunities," *New Directions for Student Services*, No. 118 (Summer 2007), 72-73.

25. James S. Murphy, "The SAT: A New Core Subject in Schools? *The Atlantic*, June 9, 2015, http://www.theatlantic.com/education/archive/2015/06/should-the-sat-be-part-of-school/395417/. Accessed June 18, 2015; Howard K. Suzuki, "A Message to the I.C.E. Community from John Pettinato, January 11, 2012, E-mail, courtesy of John Pettinato; James S. Murphy, "The SAT-Prep Industry Isn't Going Anywhere," *The Atlantic*, March 15, 2014, http://www.theatlantic.com/education/archive/2014/03/the-sat-prep-industry-isnt-going-anywhere/284430/. Accessed February 12, 2016; *Princeton Review SAT Course Price Schedule*, http://www.princetonreview.com/college/sat-test-prep. Accessed February 16, 2016.

26. Susan B. Neuman, "Code Red: The Danger of Data-Driven Instruction," *Educational Leadership*, Vol. 74, No. 3 (November 2016), 24–29; Donald Sternberg, "Dear Parents," September 4, 2012, E-mail, courtesy of Sarah Eltabib; Matt Borden, Letter to the Editor, "The Cheating at a Leading High School," *New York Times*, July 13, 2012, A16; Richard Adams and Sally Weale, "Fresh Humiliation as SATs Answers Published Online for Second Time," *The Guardian*, May 9, 2016; http://www.theguardian.com/education/2016/may/10/fresh-humiliation-as-sats-answers-published-online-for-second-time. Accessed May 27, 2016; Stanley Karp, "The Problems with the Common Core," *Rethinking Schools*, Vol. 28, No. 2 (Winter 2013/14), http://www.rethinkingschools.org/archive/28_02/28_02_karp.shtml. Accessed January 28, 2014; Peter Greene, "The Correct Number of Standardized Tests," *Curmudgucation*, October 26, 2015, http://curmudgucation.blogspot.com/2015/10/the-correct-number-of-standardized-tests.html. Accessed October 29, 2015; Motoko Rich, "Delay Urged on Actions Tied to Tests By Schools," *New York Times*, June 11, 2014, A12.

27. ACT, *The Condition of College and Career Readiness 2013*, Iowa City, 2013, iv, 2, 22–23; David Holmes, "Overdue Revolution: Character Strengths in the Admission Equation," *The Journal of College Admission*, No. 227 (Spring 2015), 46–47; Caroline Duda, January 5, 2015, "3 Holistic College Admissions Trends to Watch," http://www.usnews.com/education/blogs/college-admissions-playbook/2015/01/05/3-holistic-college-admissions-trends-to-watch. Accessed January 7, 2015.

28. Byron Auguste et al, *Closing the Talent Gap: Attracting and Retaining Top-Third Graduates to Careers in Teaching*, McKinsey & Company, September 2010, 14–15; C. Emily Feistritzer, *Profile of Teachers in the U.S. 2011*, National Center for Educational Information, 2011, 12; Michael Inzlicht and Catherine Good, "How Environments Can

Threaten Academic Performance, Self-Knowledge, and Sense of Belonging," in Shana Levin and Colette Van Laar, eds., *Stigma and Group Inequality: Social Psychological Perspectives*, Mahwah, NJ, 2006, 142; Diane Quinn and Steven J. Spencer, "The Interference of Stereotype Threat With Women's Generation of Mathematical Problem-Solving Strategies," *Journal of Social Issues*, Vol. 57, No. 1 (2001), 57; Zwick, 25; Al Baker, "Lots of A's But Fewer Spots for Girls at City's Elite Schools," *New York Times*, March 22, 2013, A1.

29. Corinne A. Moss-Racusin et al., "Science Faculty's Subtle Gender Biases Favor Male Students," *Proceedings of the National Academy of Sciences*, October 9, 2012, Vol. 109, No. 41, 16474–79; Victor Lavy and Edith Sand, "On the Origins of Human Capital Gaps: Short and Long Term Consequences of Teachers' Stereotypical Biases," National Bureau of Economic Research, *NBER Working Paper No. 20209*, January 2015; Kathryn L. Boucher et al., "Forecasting the Experience of Stereotype Threat for Others," *Journal of Experimental Psychology*, Vol. 58 (2015), 56–62; Kimberle Williams Crenshaw et al., *Black Girls Matter: Pushed Out, Overpoliced and Underprotected*, African American Policy Forum, Center for Intersectionality and Social Policy Studies, Columbia University Law School, 2015, 4–5; L'Oreal-UNESCO, *For Women in Science*, 2014, 4, 7, 8; "Sir Tim Hunt 'Sorry' Over 'Trouble with Girls' Comments," *BBC News*, June 10, 2015, http://www.bbc.com/news/uk-33077107. Accessed May 26, 2016; Rachel Ivie and Arnell Ephraim, "Women and the Imposter Syndrome in Astronomy," *AAS Status Report on Women in Astronomy*, January 2011, 7; Jedidah C. Isler, "Being Black in Physics Class," *New York Times*, December 17, 2015, A39.

30. Andrew Hacker, "Standardized Tests Are a New Glass Ceiling," *The Nation*, March 1, 2016, http://www.thenation.com/article/standardized-tests-are-a-new-glass-ceiling/. Accessed March 1, 2016; National Survey of Student Engagement, *Promoting Student Learning and Institutional Improvement: Lesson from NSSE at 13*, 11; Russell Benford and Julie Gess-Newsome, *Factors Affecting Student Academic Success in Gateway Courses at Northern Arizona University*, 2006, 26; Peter Sacks, "Meritocracy's Crooked Yardstick," August 21, 2007, www.fairtest.org/k12/psacks.html. Accessed July 9, 2012; Gregory M. Walton et al., "Psychological Threats Bias Measures of Academic Performance," *Affirmative Meritocracy*, 2011, 7; Tom Loveless, *How Well Are American Students Learning*, Brookings Institution, The Brown Center Report on American Education, Vol. 3, No. 1 (February 2012), 17–18.

31. Adelphi University Office of Research, Assessment and Planning, "Five-Year Trends of Grades in Chem 111 by Math SAT (C- with D)," September 14, 2012, courtesy David Parkin, Department of Chemistry; Harry E. Spencer, "Mathematical SAT Test Scores and College Chemistry Grades," *Journal of Chemical Education*, Vol. 73, No. 12 (December 1996), 1152–53; Benford and Gess-Newsome, 21; Robert H. Tai, Philip M. Sadler, and John F. Loehr, "Factors Influencing Success in Introductory College Chemistry," *Journal of Research in Science Teaching*, Vol. 42, No. 9 (2005), 990. On this score, the author has profited from extensive discussions with Adelphi chemists Steve Goldberg, Dave Parkin, and Joe Landesberg.

32. "The Gender Gap in SAT Scores," *WIA Report*, October 10, 2014, http://www.wiareport.com/2014/10/the-gender-gap-in-sat-scores-3/?utm_source=Women+In+Academia+Report&utm_campaign=c5b808f8f7-Women_in_Academia_Report_6_14_116_13_2011&utm_medium=email&utm_term=0_83e3ee48f9-c5b808f8f7-232756905. Accessed October 17, 2014; National Science Foundation, *Women, Minorities, and Persons with Disabilities in Science and Engineering: 2013*, 2013, 7.

33. "A Holistic Admission Process Produces Better Results for Health Profession Schools," *Journal of Blacks in Higher Education*, October 13, 2013, http://www.jbhe.com/2014/10/a-holistic-admission-process-produces-better-results-for-health-profession-schools/. Accessed October 17, 2014.

34. Charles M. Blow, "A Future Segregated by Science?" *New York Times*, February 2, 2015, A19; Benford and Gess-Newsome, 21; Robert H. Tai, Philip M. Sadler, and John F. Loehr, "Factors Influencing Success in Introductory College Chemistry," *Journal of Research in Science Teaching*, Vol. 42, No. 9 (2005), 990; The Center for Public

Education, *High School Rigor and Good Advice: Setting Up Students to Succeed,"* October 2012, 6–8; John E. Stafford to *New York Times*, "Reducing the Stresses Students Face," *New York Times*, December 31, 2015, A22; College Board, *The 10th Annual AP Report to the Nation*, February 11, 2014, 28; Richard Pérez-Peña, "Active Role in Class Helps Black and First-Generation College Students, Study Says," *New York Times*, September 3, 2014, A14; "The Racial Gap in Advancement Placement Test Scores," *The Journal of Blacks in Higher Education*, November 16, 2015, https://www.jbhe.com/2015/11/the-racial-gap-in-advancement-placement-test-scores/. Accessed November 18, 2015; Jason A. Grissom and Christopher Redding, "Discretion and Disproportionality: Explaining the Underrepresentation of High-Achieving Students of Color in Gifted Programs," *AERA Open*, Vol. 2, No. 1 (January-March 2016), 1–25.

35. Casey Miller and Keivan Stassun, "A Test That Fails," *Nature*, 12 June 2014 (Vol. 510), 303–4.

36. National Association for College Admission Counseling, *Report of the Commission on the Use of Standardized Tests in Undergraduate Admissions*, 2008, 20, 11, 9, 40; Catherine Rampell, "SAT Scores and Family Income," *New York Times*, August 27, 2009, http://economix.blogs.nytimes.com/2009/08/27/sat-scores-and-family-income/?_r=1. Accessed July 4, 2016; Jennifer Giancola and Richard D. Kahlenberg, *True Merit: Ensuring Our Brightest Students Have Access to Our Best Colleges and Universities*, Jack Kent Cooke Foundation, 2016, 21; Harold Berlak, "Race and the Achievement Gap," in Wayne Au, ed., *Rethinking Multicultural Education*, Milwaukee, 2009, 68–69.

37. Emma Garcia and Elaine Weiss, *Early Education Gaps by Social Class and Race Start U.S. Children out on Unequal Footing: A Summary of the Major Findings in Inequalities at the Starting Gate*, Economic Policy Institute, Washington, 2015; Mark Gilger, Jr., "School Analysis Shows Link between Poverty, Academic Performance in Schuylkill County," *Republican Herald* (Pottsville, PA), July 26, 2015, http://republicanherald.com/news/school-analysis-shows-link-between-poverty-academic-performance-in-schuylkill-county-1.1918045. Accessed July 31, 2015; Everyone Graduates Center at the School of Education at Johns Hopkins University, *Building a Grad Nation: Progress and Challenge in Ending the High School Dropout Epidemic*, 2015.

38. ACT, *The Condition of College & Career Readiness 2013*, Iowa City, 2013, 5, 9; "The Widening Racial Gap in ACT Scores," *Journal of Blacks in Higher Education*, September 1, 2011; "New ACT Results Show Very Few Black Student Are Prepared for College," *Journal of Blacks in Higher Education*, August 25, 2014; "The SAT as a Major Roadblock to Black Students' Aspirations to Higher Education," *Journal of Blacks in Higher Education*, Autumn 2000, 85–88; Amy Stuart Wells et al., *Divided We Fall: The Story of Unequal Suburban Schools 60 Years After Brown v. Board of Education*, The Center for Understanding Race and Education, Teachers College, Columbia University, May 2, 2014, 25–26.

39. Denise Clark Pope, "The College Admissions Derby," *New York Times*, April 13, 2002, A17; Elizabeth Olson, "Law Schools Weigh Alternatives to Bar Exam," *New York Times*, March 19, 2015, B1; Brent Staples, "A Broader Definition of Merit: The Trouble With College Entry Exams," *New York Times*, October 2, 2008.

40. Jennifer Edwards, "Higher Education Officials Say That High School GPAs May Be Better Sign of College Success," *Daily Journal* (Franklin, IN), March 23, 2014, http://www.dailyjournal.net/view/story/474c2e40deba4333a11a3147ea37f3a9/AL--Academic-Achievement/#.UzGKzvldUsp. Accessed March 25, 2014; 482-486; Susan Gershenfeld et al., "The Role of First-Semester GPA in Predicting Graduation Rates of Underrepresented Students," *Journal of College Student Retention: Research, Theory, & Practice*, Vol. 17, No.4 (2016), 482–86; Michael A. DeDonno and Karla Rivera-Torres, "The Influence of Time Limit and Bilingualism on Scholastic Assessment Test Performance," *North American Journal of Psychology*, Vol. 16, No. 2 (2014), 214, 218, 220.

41. Claremont McKenna College, "Criteria for Freshman Admission," *Catalog*, 2006–2007, 14; Daniel E. Slotnik and Richard Pérez-Peña, "College Says it Exaggerated SAT Figures for Ratings," *New York Times*, January 30, 2012, A12.

42. Nick Anderson, "Data Errors Could Mean 'Slight Change' in GWU Ranking," *Washington Post*, November 9, 2012, http://www.washingtonpost.com/local/education/

data-errors-could-spell-slight-change-for-gwu-ranking/2012/11/09/04acb40c-2aad-11e2-bab2-eda299503684_story.html. Accessed November 12, 2012; Richard Pérez-Peña and Daniel Slotnik, "Gaming the College Rankings," *New York Times*, January 31, 2012, A14; Emory News Center, "Emory Announces Findings in Data Review," http://news.emory.edu/special/data_review/index.html. Accessed August 20, 2012; "Emory University Sent False Data to Rankings Groups, School Discloses," *New Orleans Times-Picayune*, August 17, 2012, http://www.nola.com/education/index.ssf/2012/08/emory_university_sent_false_da.html. Accessed August 20, 2012; Marcia Lane, "Flagler College Regroups After Test-Score Flap," *St. Augustine Record*, February 18, 2014, http://staugustine.com/news/local-news/2014-02-18/flagler-regroups-after-test-score-flap-0#.U398ohzi0dc. Accessed February 20, 2014; Bob Morse, "Updates to 2 Schools' 2015 Best Colleges Rankings Data," *U.S. News and World Report*, October 8, 2014, http://www.usnews.com/education/blogs/college-rankings-blog/2014/10/08/updates-to-2-schools-2015-best-colleges-rankings-data. Accessed October 17, 2014; Patricia Alex, "Altered Acceptance Rates: Ramapo Among 3 N.J. Colleges Boosting Prestige with Inflated Applicant Pool," *Bergen Record*, May 16, 2015, http://www.northjersey.com/news/altered-acceptance-rates-ramapo-among-3-n-j-colleges-boosting-prestige-with-inflated-applicant-pool-1.1336310. Accessed May 18, 2015; Jeremy Diamond, "GW Misrepresented Admissions and Financial Aid Policy for Years," *The GW Hatchet*, October 21, 2013, http://www.gwhatchet.com/2013/10/21/gw-misrepresented-admissions-and-financial-aid-policy-for-years/. Accessed October 23, 2013.

43. Melissa Korn, "Job Hunt? Dig Up Those SAT Scores," *Wall Street Journal*, February 26, 2014, B1; "Virginia and North Carolina Colleges to Lower Admission Requirements," *WTKR NewsChannel 3*, February 4, 2015, http://wtkr.com/2015/02/04/virginia-and-north-carolina-colleges-to-lower-admission-requirements/. Accessed February 4, 2015; Chris Arnade, "College Costs Expose The False Meritocracy of the American Dream," *The Guardian*, June 18, 2014, http://www.theguardian.com/money/2014/jun/18/college-cost-false-meritocracy-jobs-wealth-education. Accessed June 19, 2014; Heather Doyle, "Hofstra Axes SATs for Undergrad Applicants," *Massapequa Patch*, June 26, 2014, http://massapequa.patch.com/groups/schools/p/hofstra-axes-sats-for-undergrad-applicants668147. Accessed June 30, 2014. See the comprehensive list of SAT-optional colleges at fairtest.org.

44. William C. Hiss and Valerie W. Franks, *Defining Promise: Optional Standardized Testing Policies in American Culture and University Admissions*, National Association for College Admission Counseling, February 5, 2014, 13, 14, 22, 5, 2; Mathew Zalaznick, "Rankled by College Rankings," *University Business*, May 23, 2016, http://www.universitybusiness.com/article/rankled-college-rankings. Accessed May 23, 2016; Adelphi University, *Momentum: The Strategic Plan for Adelphi University 2015–2021*, 18.

45. Jim Paterson, "Case Loaded," *The Journal of College Admissions*, No. 227 (Spring 2015), 35–36; Tamar Lewin, "A New SAT Aims to Realign With Schoolwork," *New York Times*, March 6, 2014, A1; John Fraire, "Why Your College Should Dump the SAT," *Chronicle of Higher Education*, May 5, 2014, A44; Todd Balfmarch, "The Story Behind the SAT Overhaul," *New York Times Magazine*, March 9, 2014, MM26; Richard Pérez-Peña, "Then and Now, A Test That Aims to Neutralize Advantages of the Privileged," *New York Times*, March 7, 2014, A11.

46. Kate Zernike, "Rejected by Colleges, SAT and ACT Gain High School Acceptance," *New York Times*, April 6, 2016, A1; Kate Taylor, "As City Offers Free SATs, Questions About Student Preparation," *New York Times*, March 2, 2016, A25; Wendy Lecker, "The Lies in the New SAT," *Stamford (CT) Advocate*, January 23, 2016, http://www.stamfordadvocate.com/news/article/Wendy-Lecker-The-lies-in-the-new-SAT-6777613.php. Accessed February 22, 2016; Diane Ravitch, "FairTest: The 'New' SAT Is No Better than the 'Old' SAT," *Diane Ravitch's Blog*, February 22, 2016, http://dianeravitch.net/2016/02/22/fairtest-the-new-sat-is-no-better-than-the-old-sat/. Accessed February 22, 2016.

47. Richard Pérez-Peña, "Then and Now, A Test That Aims to Neutralize Advantages of the Privileged," *New York Times*, March 7, 2014, A11; Jonathan Wai and Heiner

Rindermann, "The Path and Performance of a Company Leader: A Historical Examination of the Education and Cognitive Ability of Fortune 500 CEOs," *Intelligence*, Vol. 53 (November-December 2015), 102–7; Erika Oppenhemier, "*Gilmore Girls*: A Case Study in Discussing Your PSAT, SAT and ACT Scores With Classmates," *Huffington Post*, November 23, 2015, http://www.huffingtonpost.com/erika-oppenheimer/gilmore-girls-a-case-stud_b_8547282.html. Accessed December 11, 2015.

48. Lewin, "A New SAT . . . "; John Katzman, "A Better SAT Starts With a Better College Board," *New England Journal of Higher Education*, April 17, 2014, 1.

49. Eric Hoover, "Plans for New SAT Spark Mixed Reviews," *Chronicle of Higher Education*, March 14, 2014, 11; Hampshire College, *No to SATs/ACTs: Not Even Optional at Hampshire College*, June 18, 2014, https://www.hampshire.edu/news/2014/06/18/no-to-satsacts-not-even-optional-at-hampshire-college. Accessed August 4, 2014; Emily Monacelli, "Kalamazoo College Goes 'Test Optional,' Won't Require ACT or SAT Scores for Admission," *MLive*, http://www.mlive.com/news/kalamazoo/index.ssf/2015/03/kalamazoo_college_goes_test_op.html. Accessed March 25, 2015; Diane Ravitch, "Fairtest: George Washington University Drops SAT-ACT Requirement," *Diane Ravitch's Blog*, July 27, 2015, http://dianeravitch.net/2015/07/27/fairtest-george-washington-university-drops-sat-act-requirement/. Accessed July 27, 2015; "Plymouth State University Will No Longer Require SAT/ACT Scores," Plymouth State University, http://www.plymouth.edu/news/plymouth-n-h-state-university-will-no-longer-require-satact-test-scores/. Accessed September 3, 2014; Gerry Tuoti and Edward Donga, "Thirty Massachusetts Colleges Drop SAT Requirement," *Taunton Gazette*, October 21, 2014, http://www.tauntongazette.com/article/20141021/News/310229991. Accessed October 24, 2014; Mike Stoianoff, "Wells College Admissions Now Test-Optional," *The Citizen* (Auburn, NY), March 12, 2016, http://auburnpub.com/news/local/wells-college-admissions-now-test-optional/article_7d730727-7401-5d25-bcad-9db4d12e314e.html. Accessed March 28, 2016; Leon Botstein, "The SAT Is Part Hoax, Part Fraud," *Time International* (Atlantic Edition), March 24, 2014, 17.

50. Willamette University Faculty Admission Committee, "2016 Test-Optional Admissions for the WU CLA," March 21, 2016, http://willamette.edu/news/images/2016/03/test-optional/WU_2016_Test_OptionalFinRec.pdf. Accessed March 28, 2016; Richard Weissbourd, "College Admission 2.0: Service Over Self," *Education Week*, January 20, 2016, http://www.edweek.org/ew/articles/2016/01/20/college-admission-20-service-over-self.html. Accessed January 20, 2016.

THREE

The Freshman Landscape

Freshman anxiety is among the most frequently observed phenomena among people working in higher education. Breakdowns, insomnia, panic attacks, outbreaks of violence, and suicide transpire often enough to constitute a contemporary pattern of mental distress among college students, yet one that often begins when applying to college. Some high schoolers lose their hair in the process.[1] High school juniors and seniors resort to Adderall, an amphetamine normally prescribed for Attention Deficit Hyperactivity Disorder to improve concentration for the SAT. Among the "most addictive substances that have a medical use" and previously "a staple in some college and graduate school circles," it has found a place in secondary schools. Indeed, one dose can provide the "energy and focus to push through all-night homework binges and stay awake during exams afterward." Often abusers of such drugs, many freshmen also enter college with "ulcers, anxiety disorders and control disorders such as cutting and anorexia." The route to higher education, with its attendant frenzy, financial worry, and weighty tests "is making our children sick," insists an MIT administrator.[2]

In fact, college-like stress may begin much earlier. A growing number of middle schools provide college guidance for children as young as eleven. Even first-graders receive career counseling in some New York City public schools, while taking virtual and real college tours. The *Toledo Blade* reports that middle schoolers are among the thirty thousand participants in college-level courses through "College Credit Plus," an Ohio state program. According to *University Business*, college admissions officers are starting to include visits to middle schools in their itineraries. Meanwhile, rising emphasis on testing permeates elementary education, generating resistance. Darla Miller, a third grade teacher in Mississippi, reports that her pupils suffer Common Core-induced ailments: "They cry. They get sick at their stomachs. They spontaneously start running fevers." A Florida law requires students to declare a major while still in high school, despite the criticism it would compound student worry.[3]

A UCLA survey of American freshmen points out that huge numbers report feeling overwhelmed or depressed from the outset. Adelphi University psychologist Jonathan Jackson's insights into freshman difficulties are as perceptive now as when he first made them in 1985. The first year of college automatically poses serious challenges: "What is it about Freshman year that might put college students at greater risk for stress reactions?" First-year students go through "new experiences of freedom, loss, and discovery." One encounters a fresh set of "peers and advisors" and "new intellectual challenges." In dorms, family curfews and restrictions carry no weight. Family ties and off-campus friendships change. New networks unfold. In fact, "conflicts and disagreements with family members are experienced more intensely at this time of transition." Freshman year produces the most basic questions: "Will I fit in?" "Will I be able to cut it?" "Do I have the right clothes?" "What will my roommate be like?" "How will I manage without my family?" Reflecting the weight of these concerns among their readers, magazines geared toward the college-bound fill their pages with counsel.[4]

Aradhana Bela Sood, professor of psychiatry at Virginia Commonwealth University's School of Medicine, astutely points out that freshmen "are suddenly taken from highly sheltered environments and put into campus life. They have to think for themselves and be responsible for their own well-being. Stress and insomnia are major problems." Indeed, Sood comments that the time of life in which most students begin college coincides with the age at which psychotic illnesses first emerge. Her findings coincide with the proposition that college-age youth are transitioning into "emerging adulthood," in which residence, college education, work, and relationships are experienced in flux. Moreover, "risk behaviors" appear to peak in the late teens. Thus, college leadership must guarantee widely available mental health services.[5]

THE TOLL OF STRESS

For too long, writes former dean and professor of education Henry Brzycki, the academic community has wrongly assumed that "that if college students do well academically—and take advantage of internships and student activities or develop a scholarly relationship with a close faculty mentor—then they will also be happy, healthy and flourishing in higher education and life." In fact, adds Brzycki, "well-being encompasses, among other things, emotional health, vitality and satisfaction, life direction and ability to make a difference, the quality of one's relationships, and living a good life." He insists that occasional college workshops and mental health fairs do not meet the gravity of the circumstances. To truly help students "meet the increased psychological demands required in modern life" faculty members must become involved. This may however risk boundary violations in class situations.[6]

Aradhana Bela Sood finds that "there are often very few providers to help a person in crisis. These kids are on waiting lists and they can't get in to see anyone." In the absence of institutional counseling provisions, faculty who witness first-year transitional pressures among students may feel induced toward actions of support for which they may not be qualified, which can fall outside professional propriety. Writing in *Academe*, Rebecca Jordan maintains that previous turning points in young people's lives, such as the first days of grade school, middle school, and high school "were given support. It would be inappropriate and developmentally unfair to move middle schoolers into high school without it. Why do we not provide rules of engagement, training, and metaphorical crutches to our incoming college students?" Colleges that expand or even mandate counseling programs, tutoring assistance, focus groups, and other resources in fact demonstrate social responsibility. Moreover, "There is clear evidence that freshmen who use counseling services are more likely to succeed in college than those who do not." When said services become integrated "into the fabric of the freshman experience," improvements result.[7]

Boston College psychologist Peter Gray reports a spike in calls from students in crisis in recent years, "mainly for problems kids used to solve on their own," such as how to handle an insult: "Students are prepared academically, but they're not prepared to deal with day-to-day life, which comes from a lack of opportunity to deal with ordinary problems." The *New York Times* emphasizes, "because of escalating pressures during high school . . . students arrive at college preloaded with stress." Colleges race to provide services but worry about the expense. In a pinch, they may use undercompensated graduate students, in stark contrast with freshman needs and the escalating salaries at the top of the academic pyramid. While a growing number of college students suffer from mental illness, higher education institutions have not markedly increased the number of professionals serving mental health needs on campus. Inadequacy of counseling staffing and funding influence the student persistence and graduation rates. Students are commonly compelled to wait a month for an initial meeting with a counselor. Even on campuses better known for supporting psychological needs, an urgent case may still take three weeks before intake. To supplement the university's counseling service (where "Buckeye students may be hit with up to a six week waiting period in order to get access to treatment"), Ohio State students initiated a Wellness Center, reports social worker Deona Hooper. Improvising to meet the growing challenges, schools have set up "stress-busting stations" (with video games), introduced pet therapy sessions, and distributed coloring books to alleviate pressure.[8]

Scholars observe stress-related difficulties among freshmen in general, but note particular evidence for students of color. Racism fosters stress, particularly in schools where the numbers emphatically bear out minority status, though it exerts force even when students of color form a bigger part of the student body. This would suggest another reason to sew advising and counseling into the very fabric of a college's freshman services as if intrinsic to college life. When counseling is off to the side, stigma may attach to those who pursue it. Strong evidence in fact describes higher stress levels among working and middle class families in general. To imagine that dauntingly high tuition does not exacerbate the pressures felt by the students of these families is unrealistic indeed. The Brookings Institution finds that "stress related to constant daily struggles and uncertainty results in short time horizons and difficulty investing in the future." Income inequality abets anxiety. Thus the task of alleviating financial burdens while meeting the mental needs of all first-year students is incumbent upon institutions of higher learning.[9]

The experience of applying to college, reports *The Oklahoman* newspaper, "is twisting American high school students into moral and intellectual pretzels." High school seniors tend to apply to more colleges than before. Adelphi University freshmen report having applied to seven colleges, and being accepted to six, before making their choice. Buoyed by the ease of transmitting "electronic documents and driven by the competitive anxiety that plummeting admission rates produce, . . . some students are applying to 20 or more schools," according to the *New York Times*. This induces "a vicious cycle, causing . . . students to become more anxious, and the number of applications per student to grow even more." The *Times* describes a "saturation" of the admissions market. Paradoxically, while fighting to attract the multi-applying aspirants, colleges simultaneously use the deluge to reject more, thereby showing "rigor," as the *Hechinger Report* illustrates.[10]

Most students complete their college applications online. But the convenience of the widely used Common Application website is undermined by frequent malfunctions, which induce chaos and hysteria. In fact, accepted students who applied online are less likely to complete their applications or attend a school than those who applied by mail. It is unclear whether more numerous applications signify student confidence or pessimism. Concerns over qualifications, exam scores, prep courses, early decisions, and financial aid suffuse the application experience.[11]

ARE FRESHMEN PREPARED?

It is not the rare student who wonders if she or he will get in to a particular school. But college educators harbor rising doubts about the readiness of high school graduates for college work, to survive beyond the first year, and to graduate. A Colorado-Boulder professor feels her school's 87 percent acceptance rate takes in many who are unprepared. *Marketwatch* observes "the average GPA for high school seniors rose from 2.64 in 1996 to 2.90 in 2006." Nearly two-thirds of freshmen entered Adelphi University in 2014 with a high school average of "A." Yet findings show a wide divergence between "how high school teachers perceive the college readiness of high school graduates and how college instructors perceive the inclination of their incoming first-year students." [12]

Nervous as they are, high school seniors may have a limited view of their weaknesses and strengths. Millions lack certain basic skills, owing to inadequate high school preparation trickling from eroded education budgets or poor teacher training, not to mention mandated "teaching to the test." Professors assert that even students from reputedly "A-tier" high schools are not as ready as they should be. Many do not have a grasp of what plagiarism is and why it is wrong, thanks to insufficient encouragement in developing their own voices and exposure to principles of academic honesty, as well as from poor models of integrity in the surrounding corporate-political model. There can be no doubt: both students and professors face genuine challenges. [13]

School systems that rank institutions, teachers, and principals according to how students fare on standardized exams do not enhance college readiness. Rather, they introduce huge distortions into the evaluation of students. They make it difficult to gauge what students comprehend. Test grades become the essence of the educational experience, governing everything in between, as we have witnessed in the previous chapter. Whether results are low or high, the preoccupation with them undercuts genuine education.

Inflation of grades in high school is only part of the problem. In other ways, societal forces bend pre-college grades further out of shape. Several studies for example indicate that white teachers often do not assess classroom behavior of different race students on the same plane. Members of minority groups altogether compose the majority of public school children, but 80 percent of teachers are white. Citations for subjective violations, like "defiance," are more often issued to African American than white students. A Johns Hopkins study also notes that high school students of color are more susceptible to administrative disciplinary action than white students. Research at Columbia University Law School demonstrates that African-American girls are much more likely to be suspended or expelled for actions that receive no punishment when committed by white girls. Scholars point out that feelings of being treated unfairly may produce "lower levels of academic engagement, and less academic curiosity and persistence." Discrimination can only compound students' worry about their prospects. When there are more African American teachers in schools with large numbers of black students, reading grades and particularly math grades are positively affected, according to economist Adam C. Wright.[14]

The "blessings" of grade inflation do not shine equally. Just as grade inflation warps the foundation in so many instances, so does the practice of under-grading in high school. There are talented students who in fact never finish high school. Adelphi University's home county of Nassau boasts a strong overall high school completion record, but also includes troubling graduation results in Hempstead, Roosevelt, Amityville, Freeport, and Uniondale. Nearly 40 percent of students do not finish coursework at Hempstead High School. Underequipped and understaffed schools in Wyandanch, Riverhead, and Brentwood in neighboring Suffolk County also have high dropout rates. High school graduation figures of African-American students in New York City, New York State, and the nation at large resemble the Hempstead figure above. Poverty and discrimination impact student outcomes, including grades. One must craft a portrait of college readiness with comprehensive care, eschewing the one-size-fit-all notion, "all things being equal": conditions are not equal.[15]

Ideally when all factors are taken into account, today's first-year students possess academic potential, however imperfect. They can bring evolving skills to the table. But they supplement it with possible overestimation of their abilities on the one hand, and fear of testing, the effects of having been overlooked or disregarded, and clearly rising self-doubt on the other. All produce lack of perspective. And they have grown up in a school system beset with lockstep practice and stat-oriented policy. The question of whether they are ready for college is linked to another: are colleges ready for them?

LEARNING COMMUNITIES

The battery of forces affecting freshman readiness and adjustment lead colleges to consider alternative strategies for creating a student comfort zone, such as introducing freshmen to college life in small clusters or other such "learning communities" with elements of internal support that remain intact during at least the first year. These operate in any number of ways. Learning communities may encompass an entire freshman class, divided into groups according to theme or interest. Other schools gear communities toward particular types of first-year students, such as those who are the first generation of their families to attend college, or students initially deemed "at-risk." A designated learning community will include at least one common course for students belonging to it, often called the first-year or freshman seminar. This can have disciplinary or interdisciplinary foundations. New students at Dubuque in Iowa attend the same lecture series, whose content they discuss in smaller seminars. Alabama's Samford University holds "Focus Learning Communities," each composed of twenty students: they take three common classes in the first year. Florida Gulf Coast University conducts a "Learning Through Service Living-Learning Community," with a strong community service component. An example of a thematic first-year seminar is Brenau University's (Georgia), which highlights the theme of the civil rights movement. One may also cite the global issues suffusing the seminars at Kennesaw State in Georgia.[16]

Hampden-Sydney in Virginia has conducted as many as ten freshman learning communities at a time, each with a designated dormitory, a peer advisor, and a theme: leadership, sports, cinema, science. Moreover, all learning communities take a common course. At the University of North Carolina-Greensboro, groups of Nursing and Business majors have formed communities taking several courses in common, whose instructors collaborate. There are specific communities for residential students. Beyond coursework, UNC-Greensboro maintains that the goals are "creating life-long learning skills and fostering a desire for critical inquiry centered on real problems and challenges." Georgia State University organizes groups of twenty-five freshmen into communities as well. The members share four or five of the same courses, of which one is a class to orient them to college. Over two-thirds of the university's freshmen belong to such communities.[17]

Freshman seminars have long been deemed essential in linking social, integrative, and educational purposes. Many consider them vital to retention. In a program for freshmen with lower SAT scores, Alvernia University forms a "learning community" by linking a first-year seminar to a collectively taken pair of courses in Communications and Theology, all accompanied by focused advising and peer mentoring.[18] Adelphi's semester-long linked Freshman Seminar and First Year Orientation Experience (FOrE) courses have been representative of many efforts at consolidation. The State University of New York's New Paltz campus is hardly alone in assimilating freshmen into small clusters with related courses: First-Year Interest Groups (FIGS).[19]

To the extent that institutions of higher learning grasp the decisive nature of the freshman year, because of the difficulty of student transition and due to the need to heighten retention, they augment learning communities, first-year seminars, and other targeted formats with related services. Rarely do these embrace an intrinsic counseling component, but usually include mentoring. In general practice, mentoring means that older students provide counsel, support, and tutoring. One finds peer far more often than faculty mentoring at the freshman level nationwide.

Florida Atlantic University features it in the learning community it employs to "enhance the student experience." Peer mentoring appears in the University of Maryland's "Gemstone Honors Program" and in Georgia State's first-year seminar. Schools where faculty mentor freshmen include Adelphi (where General Studies helped develop the practice), Purdue (where learning communities are run by faculty), the University of Florida's community for at-risk students (which draws mentors from different departments), and George Williams College of Aurora University (Wisconsin), whose instructors in first-year seminars collaborate on common assignments. (The latter's seminars contain an outside "lab experience" ranging from community service to sailing to horseback riding.)[20]

The degree of organization and implementation of dedicated first-year classes, clusters, cohorts, and auxiliary support varies considerably. That schools of all types and sizes nevertheless have singled out the first-year student as a special case with special requirements is true. But colleges diverge in the most concrete prioritization when it comes to hiring and training faculty and staff assigned to seminars and communities, since as shown above the main trend is toward casualization of the labor force. Hence, the temptation of employing student peer mentors instead of professionals and using adjuncts in place of full-timers to teach freshman seminars. When regular faculty mentor students, colleges may demonstrate that the aim of engaging freshmen is worth a greater investment, not only of money but professionalism. Denison (Ohio), the University of Kansas, the University of Tennessee and Indiana Wesleyan are among the institutions that assign regular faculty to first-year seminars and undertake to help them in how to approach freshmen, what to expect, and skills to use. Indiana Wesleyan maintains that it trains its freshman faculty to bring something special to the classroom, an "awesome sauce" of technique.[21]

GENERAL STUDIES

The term "General Studies" itself is a widely used title for targeted freshman programs. It may also refer to special two-year programs of study that lengthen the transition period before entering a major. North Carolina's Appalachian State University used to have an Office of General Studies, which "operated within Academic Affairs, and coordinated efforts of ASU for orientation and advising of new students as well as general curriculum for all students." A few current General Studies programs admit freshmen whose prior academic record falls below the overall standard. The University of Illinois, the University of Idaho, and the University of Alaska-Fairbanks employ the same phrase to title catch-all programs for undeclared students, freshmen and sophomores. It is another way of saying "undecided." Northeastern University's General

Studies Program instead entails a one-year, freshman experience for students whose prior scholastic achievements might not have yet borne out their potential. Northeastern places General Studies students earning below a certain GPA on probation and may eventually dismiss them. Northeastern provides peer tutoring for General Studies students as well. Boston University's General Studies and New York University's Liberal [formally General] Studies Programs comprise the first two college years. The same holds in Emory's Oxford College.[22]

Boston assigns full-time faculty—who also act as mentors—to its program. But while full-time, Boston University's General Studies instructors have been of two types: tenured professors and lecturers, who are "subject to dismissal or termination at the end of their contract." Some find the latter condition "detrimental to faculty cooperation and good will." Northeastern's General Studies faculty includes part-timers and full-timers. Most of NYU's designated Liberal Studies instructors are part-timers. In some form, Boston and NYU, like Northeastern, regard the students in the programs as a learning community, seeking to encourage a cohort feeling. To be sure, it is not necessary to call a program that functions in this way a "learning community." The General Studies Program at Adelphi changed its name to Learning Community to correspond to what it had become. In the broad picture, however, colleges may also alter program and department titles to make them sound better. When a concept becomes "flavor of the month," name changes may follow.[23]

DIRECTIONS IN FRESHMEN ENGAGEMENT

In aid of the goal of freshman retention, numerous private and public institutions have contracted out tutoring services with companies like InsideTrack in San Francisco, which make coaches available to students for a fee paid per student by the school. Though the cost is low, the goal is "to keep freshmen from dropping out." Many formats, diversely titled, have emerged to bring in freshmen whom the college guides term "improved students," "students needing a second chance," "students with average scores," "late bloomers," and "underachievers." Similar in intent, the programs are by no means identical. Most recruit from secondary schools known for college-bound constituencies. Others, like Loyola of Chicago's LEAP (Learning Environment Enrichment Program), draw students from high schools not necessarily reputed for sending grads to college. In New York, the State University at Buffalo runs ACE (Access to College Excellence Program) for skilled first-year students who may not meet one of the key admissions standards, simultaneously providing regular advising, tutoring, and peer mentoring.[24]

With the help of federal grants, a number of states sponsor college enrollment gateways encouraging foster children enrollment. Some institutions support services for accepted students, some quite broad, as at Sam Houston State, Western Michigan, and the City College of San Francisco. Some provide tutoring and counseling. Program titles signify the outlook: Great Expectations, Passport to College Promise, Fostering Success, Guardian Scholars, and Reach. Graduation rates compare favorably with national trends for low-income students.[25]

The span of freshman program titles is vast. The imagery of focus and support remains, but programs actually come and go. As shown above, the term "General Studies" at Appalachian State no longer applies. Changes are not merely titular. Longevity is hard to achieve, when the sands seem to be shifting under the feet of higher education. Greater concern emerges over whether an academically valid initiative pays dividends in dollars and cents, attracts popularity, and fits "the brand." Hampden-Sydney College's Learning Community budget is quite low, facilitating "value-added" gains through retention. Fort Valley State (Georgia) has run an Early Alert Program for New Freshman since the early 1990s, featuring especially close scrutiny and tracking of early faltering, complete with forms of tutoring and counseling. In the 1990s as well, Jacksonville State in Michigan originated a pathway for students entering with ACT or SAT scores below the institutional criteria, ExSEL (Experiencing Success in Education and Life): a concentrated summer program with a good deal of individual attention. Johnson C. Smith University (North Carolina) started a Freshman Studies Program in the late 1980s, with heavy input from regular faculty and a methodological preference for "directed inquiry as opposed to lecture."[26]

Mississippi State launched a Pathfinder Program to follow up with freshmen missing too many classes by the time of fall midterms. Instructors were encouraged to report absences, while residence hall staff visited the students in question. It was headed by a veteran professor with a record of teaching and scholarship, rather refreshing in circumstances too often resolved by disciplinary measures. The State University at New Paltz first targeted "underrepresented" freshmen for the Educational Opportunity Program Freshman Year Experience in the 90s. By this it meant minority students. Study groups, a first-year seminar, and close monitoring served to improve the students' continuation as upperclassmen. Penn State's Comprehensive Studies Program, for "low-income students who normally would not be admitted because of their low predictions for academic success," dates back to 1989. It too offered tutoring (by students) and access to counseling services. The University of Georgia's Division of Developmental Studies, founded in the same period, assisted freshmen "who narrowly miss regular admission to the University" with a focus on math and English, along with a counseling component. "General College" of the University of Minnesota worked on much the same basis. Gateway at the University of Texas provided entrants with below-average high school grades with smaller classes, weekly meetings with a "coordinator," specially designated advisors, and peer mentors.[27]

EXPLORATORY PROGRAMS AND THE "UNDECIDED"

Concerned about the rising tide of "undecided" first-year students, a number of higher institutions may pressure students to select majors early.[28] On the other hand, many institutions try to alleviate student apprehensions over a field of study. A number have made overtures to first-year enrollees who would like to keep an open mind about majors. Like many, the College at Brockport of the State University of New York obliges freshmen to take a course to encourage major choice. One may surmise that high school seniors who really know exactly what they wish to do for the next fifty years are increasingly rare, even when they immediately opt for a major. Thus, greater awareness of the abstraction of many early career decisions fills public statements from the academy. Wilkes University in Pennsylvania lampoons as "myths" the beliefs that "making a career decision is simple," that concentrating on "classes that relate to your major" is priority, and that narrowing options is advantageous. Small and medium-sized private colleges often have gateways for the "undecided."[29]

Several programs bear the name "Exploratory," including those at Ohio's McMicken and Marietta Colleges, and Ithaca College in New York. Such institutions suggest that taking one's time in determining concentration is intelligent and understandable. "Exploratory students" work with specially trained faculty advisors at Ithaca. For two years, they can "take courses in a variety of fields, not only in the liberal arts but in our professional schools as well." Imagery of freedom accompanies the appeal: "You'll follow your interests, learn more about yourself, find new enthusiasms—and discover the major that's right for you." Students entering Marietta "can declare a major or come in as Exploratory with interest areas." Not surprisingly, the courses to be explored in the latter instance also meet general distribution requirements, thus projecting a roughly equivalent graduation time-frame. Marietta also urges Exploratory enrollees to take a course sponsored by the Career Center, perhaps to dispel insecurities about making a living. Providing additional advising, McMicken proudly embraces the "truly undecided," a valued category because "college is a time for self-discovery and exploration."[30]

State schools take their own initiatives. At Southern Illinois University, "Exploratory" is similarly a euphemism for "undecided." The University of Vermont urges freshmen to "Take Time to Explore." Vermont reassures them that one-third will enter without a major, while another third will surely change theirs. It is wise indeed "to explore different disciplines before selecting a field of study that fits best." And for those entering as "undecided" Vermont offers a first-year seminar and a faculty mentor. However, other Exploratory settings eschew the virtues of being uncertain about a major, which students and families may hear as permission to be dissolute. Some schools more openly identifying students with the term "undecided" confine them to a narrow set of courses (something which the aforementioned Exploratory programs apparently avoid) meeting basic requirements for all majors. How to pose the search for options remains more than a semantic challenge.[31]

In keeping with acceptance of indecision, worry about college affordability, or caution at the academic outset, astute observers reason that taking a "gap year" may serve emotional, maturational, and financial needs of students overburdened with imposed expectations. Many students are drawing such conclusions themselves. Relevantly, a number of schools extend financial aid to accepted students who take a year off before starting college, perhaps to work or do community service. Behind it is the premise that the experience will mature them and clear their heads. Tufts University calls the assisted interval "the bridge year." Nationally, admissions officials in the know understand that postponing the point at which students may enter the ranks of higher education could strengthen their commitment and bolster retention. While acknowledging students who opt for college when they feel more ready, this realization also supports their need to earn money prior to matriculating, if they can find work. But while certain admissions directors may grasp the trend, most cannot afford to do so, because immediate returns are priority.[32]

Another way of assuaging freshman concerns about career is to offer a "fifth year" master's degree. Hence, one would join an educational experience providing a higher credential at an accelerated pace. Granted that more baccalaureate students graduate in six than in four years, which tends to make the idea of a fifth (and final) master's annum problematic. However, schools find that the "4 + 1" concept may enhance retention and student adherence to a particular field. Adelphi University has applied the concept in the fields of Education and Social Work. Massachusetts institutions Clark, Assumption, and Worcester State are among the many working in this direction. Clark University has several "4 + 1" majors. Assumption College has agreements with other institutions for the additional master's year. Recruitment lures revolve around several acknowledged facts: a bachelor's degree is generally insufficient for higher compensation; and job opportunities expand with greater educational certifications. Employers tend to prefer master's degree recipients. Thus, "4 + 1" seeks to rebut the notion that college is a waste of time and money: here instead is a track apparently leading straight to an occupation.[33]

But some occupations are less "useful," high credentials notwithstanding. Elimination from the work force of capable members of the helping professions and of teachers, for instance, flows from shifting federal and state priorities away from social programs. If the trajectory of college teaching persists, recent graduates with doctorates may be fortunate to find full-time work. At some point, the beneficiaries of "4 + 1" will have to pay off their loans.

It is no wonder that students and families try to pursue smart shopping in the search for colleges. Their socioeconomic location, paired with the business imperatives of college operations, remains intrinsic to understanding the entry process into higher education. Psychologists Jean Twenge and Kristin Donnelly relate that societal income inequality has spurred "millennial" college students (born between 1982 and 1999) to become more concerned than previous generations about future employment: "Millennial students' focus on making more money may be a practical consideration."[34]

ORIENTATION

U.S. colleges give great emphasis to orientations. A common summer reading, talent shows, dividing incoming students into compact groups and workshops that may reunite in a particular class when the semester begins, are all intended to carry over into freshman year. Students belonging to a specific summer orientation group may well find themselves enrolled together in the same freshman seminar. To convert the essence of orientation into the academic year can enhance retention. In contrast with the likelihood that "many institutions think orientation ends when classes begin," Muhlenberg College declares "orientation is a year-long process, beginning with June Advising and culminating in the end of the first academic year . . . " Florida's Eckerd College holds a freshman-only three-week-long credit-bearing "Autumn Term" before the start of the regular school year: "Although schoolwork is the main thrust of Autumn Term, with papers to write, presentations to give, and examinations to pass, there is still a major component that emphasizes the traditional orientation activities like "making friends, having fun and getting your fill of fresh squeezed orange juice in the cafeteria."[35]

First-year planners have designated special overtures to first-generation college students, concretized in pre-college summer initiatives geared particularly toward this group. The programs, some credit-bearing, are often called "Bridge" programs: the one at Roosevelt University in Chicago is a good example. It contends that exposure of "at-risk" recent high school grads to college faculty and peer mentors over the summer benefits first-year adjustment and schoolwork. Washburn University in Topeka, Kansas also provides peer mentoring to students in its Ichabod Success Institute, along with a uniform program of courses. Michigan's Northwood University's bridge initiative features a twelve-day immersion for freshmen who did not do particularly well in high school: here too, student mentors assist the program members throughout the year. The New Jersey Institute of Technology has treated the summer endeavor with first-generation freshmen from inner city high schools as a "boot camp" and has run it in the spirit of military training to focus work discipline and group feeling. Said methods, says a NJIT spokesman, help in "tearing down preconceived ideas about college and replacing them with a strong sense of the unknown." This would be quite an accomplishment, but the camp belongs to the common freshman cohort idea, albeit one that takes an unusually severe tack. It is interesting that learning communities encompassing students who scored high on the SAT do not envision boot camps.[36]

Colleges may view the day of freshman matriculation or convocation as another sort of orientation, for students and families alike. Kennesaw State begins a major build-up toward convocation as soon as summer orientation is over. It distributes "induction pins," presents attendees with giveaways, and even offers incentives for first-year students to attend. The entering class may hold a march through campus, or at least be induced to do so. The school band is on board. An aerial photo of students and their families highlights the day. The school has documented the usefulness of convocation to student retention. Polk State College (Florida) also considers freshman convocation a key to student commitment. Polk's "First Flight Student Convocation" kicks off a group of spirited arrangements. Every freshman in the aerospace-spirited institution then receives a "Flight Plan for Engagement" and is assigned to a personal "Flight Leader" or peer mentor. The Leader communicates with the student a week before the big day with a reminder of the event and a promise to meet. On the wings of the moment, each first-year student signs a Pledge to Completion and begins a project of community aid known as "Soar Through Service."[37]

Orientations involve theories of group dynamics, interaction of personnel trained in relevant disciplines, including psychology, and well-planned exercises intended to win over freshmen while dissipating their worries. Nor are freshmen alone with their fears, as many institutions now orient parents, allaying essential concerns. In fact, orientations for parents work to reassure them that their children and money are in safe hands. Similarly, Family or Parents Weekends can produce positive vibes and donations to outlast the reunions. Usually six to eight weeks into the fall, family events show widening range to keep parents, as well as their financial commitments, in a school's portfolio: here a dinner cruise, there a jazz concert: maybe a concert, picnic, or even a faculty panel "lite." The ubiquitous Midnight Madness opening the basketball season may also nicely coincide with a later Family Weekend. As for the students, well-documented and carefully tracked orientation experiences are reported to boost retention and carry over in a relative sense to academic stability.[38]

Colleges have been forced to move beyond helping new students break the ice before their first semester, to a specially organized series of steps to cement their enrollment from the start. Orientations generally tackle vital issues in a compressed several-day span, covering sexual identity, harassment, academic advising, financial aid, multicultural understanding, social relationships, library resources, residential life, and the dangers of drug and alcohol abuse. These are dealt with in rapid succession. The coordinated plans, including talent shows, have witnessed seemingly spontaneous celebratory dances that apparently spur emotional ties to a school. Whether orchestrated or spur-of-the-moment, freshman encounters prior to the academic year may be steered to resemble the feeling of a movement. Colleges monitor and control every aspect of orientation, from the apparently unrehearsed to the openly deliberate, for it can be crucial to enrollment and retention.[39]

THE DECLINE OF THE YIELD

Freshman yield—the percentage of accepted students who actually attend—affects everything. Over the last decade, universities have also had to contend with increasing summer "melt"—the percentage of accepted freshmen who have shown intent to attend a school by depositing, but then go elsewhere—making accurate freshman enrollment predictions even more essential to these institutions. Studies reveal that many find great difficulty in putting tuition together during the summer beyond the initial deposit, leading directly to the "melt." Since high school grads no longer have the benefit of their secondary school counselors who may have helped them get into college, colleges have launched massive text message campaigns in the summer months prior to fall semester to bolster the yield of accepted freshmen who enroll. This has been shown to improve turnout, and, if repeated later, to improve college retention. But even before things get to that point, a large number of high schools offer little concrete college guidance: with a national student-to-counselor ratio of 500:1, and 20 percent of U.S. high schools not even providing a single counselor, many students are lost before they've even seen the path.[40]

Cuts in high school counseling staffs abet the situation. While a classical education textbook posited the need for secondary school counselors to identify college-bound students right after middle school, while helping other students to reach college potential or consider their interests, elimination of qualified personnel by public education budget reductions makes guidance all the more difficult. Of course, better-funded districts can provide hands-on and individualized counseling. On the other hand, as the Jack Kent Cooke Foundation points out in a recent survey, high-achieving, low-income secondary school students generally "don't receive accurate, individualized guidance."[41]

Naturally, the freshman yields are higher at places like Harvard, which have a lower acceptance rate, but whose accepted applicants are more likely to enroll. The same holds for schools with a unique niche, such as Juilliard, Stanford, and the University of Chicago. But first-year yield rates nationwide stand below 50 percent, indicating that students are applying to and being accepted by more schools. *The New York Times* reports that schools may use "the admission game" to "make their yields, and themselves, look good." If not wait-listing them, they can "defer students who they believe are likely to enroll elsewhere." Thus, "the institution is able to appear more selective, report a higher yield, and perhaps, increase its ranking in some publications and its aura of prestige among prospective students."[42]

Yield downturn nevertheless typifies the picture, exacerbated by a decline in the high-school-age population and the increasing number of college applications filed by high school seniors. Moody's Investor Service projects that the number of high school graduates will not rise until 2020. Freshman admissions, graduation rates, trends in student persistence, and issues of retention—along with measures to resolve or control them—still operate within a bigger crisis. Smaller private institutions are particularly affected, says Moody's, because of economic hardship and "fragile consumer confidence." Protests and political argument have focused the college affordability debate on skyrocketing student debt and inadequate job prospects. Circumstances push tuition matters to "a tipping point," making "the cost of college . . . a critical credit factor," according to Moody's. The resulting awareness heightens the scrutiny with which first-year applicants view their prospects. Moody's consequently reports widespread falloff in revenue and enrollments especially at "small, lower-rated universities." Private colleges, observes the *Philadelphia Inquirer*, are dependent "on tuition dollars; for smaller schools, enrollment can vary wildly and is never guaranteed."[43]

Moody's makes a good point by illustrating the link between freshman yield and the economy. Enrollment rates within a school's admitted freshman class vary according to the job picture, tilting away from professions deemed insecure. This leaves fields like teaching increasingly barren. Anticipating no answer to declining freshman yield rates in a clouded economic climate, Moody's still feels that "the traditional higher education business model is generally sound and long-lasting." But to remedy yield shortfall, the service recommends savings through consolidation of offices and departments, "increased use of adjunct faculty," "outsourcing certain administrative or auxiliary functions," a step-up in "online course delivery," and "increased cost-sharing with employees of existing retirement and health benefits." Without these strategies,

Moody's adds "the outlook for the U.S. Higher Education sector is negative." Viewing freshman enrollment through the leaner and meaner corporate prism resonates with many higher education policy makers. Eric Gould writes that alongside highly professional marketing, cost-effective instruction, and adoption of business models, stands "the redistribution of labor . . . away from tenured to part-time and adjunct faculty."[44]

THE PURSUIT OF STUDENT RETENTION

Retention is the other half of yield. College administrations, higher education think tanks, corporate planners, and consultants burn the midnight oil to heighten retention. All of the foregoing endeavors, learning communities, orientation plans, convocation projections, and freshman seminars move toward this goal, an utter necessity. All actions provide testable experience, conclusions to draw, revisions to make. The volume of statistical material is immeasurable. No centimeter of retention inquiry is wasted. Updated annually if not hourly, the data animate the discussions, strategic aims, and day-to-day activity of college directors.

Colleges pay corporations to design retention perspectives. Companies possess greater resources for the generation of statistics and analysis of patterns, and are able to sell uniquely tuned strategies. Educational Testing Service (ETS) and Noel-Levitz are only the tip of the iceberg in a burgeoning enterprise. ETS has developed the "Success Navigator" to factor in every variable of the individual student. It rates the persistence potential by academic skill, commitment, self-organization, and support network. ETS pairs the consequent "Academic Success Index" with a "Retention Success Index," meticulously drawn up for each student. Schools may then use the data to render assistance and provide mentoring, but more importantly calculate the trend of enrollment. ETS maintains in the process that it perceives "the WHOLE STUDENT," giving the college "a holistic view of the critical factors" and facilitating an "ACTION PLAN" for every matriculate.[45]

The John N. Gardner Institute for Excellence in Undergraduate Education holds seminars, workshops, forums, retreats, and conferences on retention issues, in addition to issuing relevant reports. Nautilus Publishing produces a book for students titled *The A Game: Nine Steps To Better Grades*, which can fit different schools into its template. Hence, there are distinct editions for enrollees at the University of Mississippi and Washington State University. The volumes run to type: don't cut class, don't sit in the back of the room, ask questions, be prepared.[46]

Schools agree that "freshman engagement" is a primary step to retention: get first-year students to feel comfortable, and they'll stay. The phrase of course conveys a multitude of goals: easing the transition from high school; eliciting student commitment to remain beyond the first year; encouraging college-level reading, work habits, and writing; offering forms of assistance, from counseling to tutoring to financial advice; and building a culture of togetherness among freshmen. As seen before, this is where learning communities come in. To the extent that they act accordingly, institutions may look upon the retention of each incoming class with relatively enhanced hopes. The point is to provide services conducive to students remaining at the institution. Hence the recognition that freshman year is key.[47]

Many institutions have set up specific structures for freshman retention: an office, or officers, or designated professionals and faculty. If not, then relevant steps proceed from already existing larger frameworks. Illustrative is the University of Texas at San Antonio, which administers freshman-targeted retention initiatives from within the "Center" responsible for the academic services of the entire student body. However, first-year targets there remain distinct, while designed by the same office otherwise assisting non-freshmen. Thus, it "provides programs specific to first-year students," including learning communities, the summer common reading, an early academic warning system, freshman seminars facilitated by older "peer leaders," and general and career counseling. The University College division of Virginia Commonwealth University functions similarly. It administers freshman orientation, the core curriculum, student advising on a mass scale, and learning/writing support services. Academic services offices help students register for classes alongside, instead of, or as a more rapid response to scheduling needs than faculty advising. The University of South Carolina's Student Success Center provides freshmen with success coaches "who reach out to their assigned students even before classes begin to introduce themselves and answer questions. The goal is to start building a relationship."[48]

By the same token, the Office of Academic Excellence, the main engine of academic services, administers SUNY Buffalo's aforementioned ACE Program for freshmen. Auburn University's goal of improved student persistence into sophomore year and beyond has reportedly benefited by a group of freshman-centered steps: assignment of an array of brief papers; greater attention to reading materials, particularly books; and promotion of "high order thinking skills of analysis, evaluation, and application." In general however, it is more difficult for larger universities with academic advising centers, especially public ones, to provide the sort of advising deemed necessary for retention of freshmen or in fact the students of any other baccalaureate stage. While they too struggle to expand advising services, smaller private institutions may not have the extreme advisor-advisee ratio witnessed at a school like Brooklyn College. With funds for additional hires in short supply, Brooklyn's eight academic advisors assist fourteen thousand students with their class schedules, as practical supplement to faculty advisors.[49]

INTERACTION AS SUPPORT

Advising is a widely recognized retention asset in the first year of college. Gallup researchers discovered in 2014 that graduates who received one-on-one mentoring and counseling achieve better academic outcomes. Yet too few schools take this as seriously as constructing hotel-like dorms, state-of-the-art athletic facilities, electric walls, and learning delivery systems. But a Gallup survey reveals that the quality of a student's personal interactions with an educator shapes retention and college career more than the type of school she or he attends. In fact, "where graduates went to college—public or private, small or large, very selective or not selective—hardly matters at all to their current well-being," according to Gallup.[50]

More personal and verbal classroom interactions, not necessarily online or technological, may accomplish more to keep students at a school than the marvelous flipped classrooms in chapter 1. The involvement of students in open class discussion, even in big format introductory courses, strengthens retention. Direct faculty intervention, where instructors ask more questions and provoke exchange, also bears fruit. Conversation between student and instructor facilitates student understanding of course content that might otherwise foster rote memorization. This finding pertains particularly to large lecture classes and their accompanying texts, exams, and quizzes, though most arguments favor smaller classes in the first place. But in general, one-on-one contact generates positive returns in student comprehension and retention.[51]

ECONOMIC CONTEXTS

The motivated, talented, hardworking freshman does not live in a vacuum. The relationship between the college aspirations of students and the living and working conditions of their families is close. Class affects the time parents are able to spend with children in rendering concrete support over the span of educational experience. It influences all the practicalities of life preparation. When the Pew Research Center reports in December 2015 that half of "lower-income parents worry that their children might be shot at some point, more than double the share among higher-income parents," one may perceive that educational paths do not unfold in the abstract. Yet such parents strongly desire that their children go to college. In particular, says the center, "mothers and non-white and lower income parents place more importance on college degrees" than higher-income parents. Mothers recognize the significance of college to a greater degree than fathers, according to Pew. Nevertheless, the progress of the college bound is indissolubly tied to family, class, race, and income.[52]

Economic distress plays an increasing role in students' college decisions. As the Economic Policy Institute implies, it is not far-fetched to speculate on the number of qualified college matriculates from families whose workplace compensation is insufficient to reliably pay bills. Harvard's Institute of Politics reports a "majority concerned about keeping their heads above water," with "nearly half of undergraduates concerned about staying in college." A Public Agenda survey demonstrates that more than half of community college and just under half of four-year college students work twenty hours a week minimum. Holding a job while attending school also factors into the timing of graduation, as for example in the University of Wisconsin's branch campuses where only 20 percent of students graduate in four years. The need to work more hours or full-time is the main reason students leave college. Moreover, writes Tamar Lewin in the *New York Times*, "for every borrower who defaults, at least two more fall behind in payments." Private colleges clustered in Long Island, New York, find themselves induced to struggle for every applicant and continuing student. They endeavor to recruit from a community whose incomes have frozen, whose teen demographics have receded, and whose skepticism about the worth of college programs has mounted.[53]

A preponderance of Americans, according to the Pew Research Center, consider college unaffordable or not worth the investment, returning little for the expense. The troubling levels of new graduate unemployment also sustain current skepticism. Parenthetically, the soaring price of textbooks does not help the material security of current students, although alerting matriculates to a predatory industry. As more college students report concerns about costs, the number unable to purchase textbooks also rises. Higher ed financial analysts forecast the rise of "auxiliary" expenses, like room and board, along with tuition: but college endowments and financial aid grant funds will stagnate.[54]

Practical issues during and after college impel students to serious questions in retrospect. Half the recent alumni of four-year schools claim to have found work that does not require a college diploma. Half regret the chosen college or major. Forty percent could not obtain employment in the field of training. A 2013 analysis titled *Voice of the Graduate* indicates that liberal arts majors "fare the worst across every measure: they tend to be lower paid, deeper in debt, less happily employed, and slightly more likely to wish they'd done things differently." Economists refer to graduates laboring in jobs not requiring a college degree as "mal-employed." While a college degree is necessary for future advancement, states the *New York Times*, "the past decade has not been kind to young people venturing into the working world, even those with newly minted degrees."[55]

At the same time, each completed year of college, even when the student does not graduate, appears to translate into relatively better chances at employment, better pay, and higher total income over the years in the work force. In this light, one may answer "Is college worth it?" in the affirmative. But while the annual incomes for those never completing college exceed the intakes of those who never began it, the employment picture for both graduates and nongraduates remains bleak. Striving to meet basic priorities complicates the ability of a young adult to become self-supporting, impacting whether or when he or she moves out of the family home, "settles down," or considers serious life commitments. More Americans (32 percent) between the ages of eighteen and thirty-four live with their parents than in other arrangement (cohabiting, married, living alone) than at any other point since 1960. Thus, "trends in both employment status and wages have likely contributed to the growing share of young adults who are living in the home of their parent(s)," according to the Pew Research Center. The number of new households created annually has declined. The National Commission on Higher Education Attainment finds that economic factors induce elongated rates of graduation. In fact, the six-year graduation rate is only 59 percent. A majority of the state of Washington's college enrollees do not graduate: its higher ed graduation rates "track almost directly with the socioeconomics of each high school's zip code."[56]

THE NOOSE OF STUDENT DEBT

For many, debt begins before college. Lower income students for example find themselves at a disadvantage if they commit to a school for Early Admissions. The *Huffington Post* explains that this option may "boost their odds of admission by as much as 30 percent by locking into a school if accepted. The catch? You need to be affluent enough to commit to a school without first seeing its financial aid offer and savvy enough to know that the early option exists in the first place." In beginning college, the freshman student enters the dimension of liability. Debt impinges on where students live, what they eat: the *Tampa Bay Times* asserts that the image of college students surviving on cheap instant noodles is not a myth. Indeed, four hundred colleges, including in the New York City area, operate food banks. Historically, extensive student debt does not simply linger, but rather strangles future endeavors. College loan payments hold hostage the battery of future mortgages, car purchases, and credit cards. Unpaid loan debt now exceeds a trillion dollars, more than the total of all U.S. credit card debt. This is an ever-tightening noose. As tuition increases began to surpass income rates in the 1980s, student loans rose accordingly, while lenders were less than forthright with applicants about the implications. In turn, government financing declined. Student payments on loan balances alone fell further behind, weighted by interest. Defaults have emerged as a crucial trend in the realm of higher education. As schools woo students, offering tuition discounts where possible, they strive to avoid words like "cost," "buy," "pay," and "contract." Of course, the level of discounts varies considerably at private schools: where tuition is highest, discounts may increase, as at New York University.[57]

The stress of loan payments correlates with depression, suicidal tendencies, and other mental problems. Increasingly, workshops for student debtors grapple not only with dollars and cents, but misery. But debt is one thing, "excessive debt" another. A 2015 report by Student Aid Policy defines it as a sum a student cannot repay within ten years of graduation; furthermore, the outstanding loans exceed the graduate's expected starting salary. Between one-quarter and one-third of new graduates find themselves in this position. Particularly susceptible are those who majored in Humanities, Education, and Communications as undergraduates. On the other hand, Engineering and Computer Science majors are relatively better secured from excessive debt. However, the proportion of excessive debtors among all students repaying college loans is increasing steadily. Naturally, the weight of loans grows heavier as the first decade after graduation stretches into the second.[58]

Forbes Magazine reports student financial obligations to be so intense that a third of recent graduates regret going to college. Indebtedness, *Forbes* indicates, spills over into declining rates of home ownership among people in their twenties and thirties. The Federal Reserve Bank buttresses the point on the housing market, and shows that high money-owing rates also reduce graduate purchases of new cars. In both cases, "[C]onsumers with substantial student debt may not be able to meet the stricter debt income (DTI) ratio standards that are now being applied by lenders." A purportedly alternative student loan proposal, by which an alumnus would finance a student's tuition and thereafter receive a share of the student's income, offers no solution, but resembles a throwback to feudalism. In any case, researcher Kevin Carey of the New America Foundation's Education Policy Program notes starkly that we are witnessing "a big social experiment": "Let's send a whole class of people out into their professional lives with a negative net worth. Not starting at zero, but starting at a minus that is often measured in the tens of thousands of dollars." The results impinge, writes the *New York Times*, on bigger investments like homes and new cars, but also on going to restaurants or purchasing clothes. When they are able to help their children through college, parents and family members also undertake significant sacrifices: postponing retirement, deferring home maintenance, cancelling vacations, and delaying car repairs.[59]

Meanwhile the poverty level of eighteen to twenty-four-year-olds has grown since 1970. The same holds for unemployment of college graduates between twenty-one and twenty-four over the time period, as well as for underemployment—"which includes those who are officially unemployed, those who want to work but haven't looked recently for a job and those stuck in part-time jobs—of the same population sector." Once again, the declining rate of home purchases by college graduates in debt has been marked. College debt, with clouded job prospects, has meant that millions have been "unable to take even baby steps toward real estate maturity," as the *New York Times* put it. Harvard Business School economists report a halt in real hourly wages among college grads, exempting only those with advanced degrees: the trend is attributable to "structural, not cyclical" weaknesses that "show up in a host of disturbing long-run trends." Among the foremost worries is a nationwide "aversion to full-time hires" in an expanding number of professions, not only in higher education.[60]

Noteworthy is the greater presence of females among student borrowers. A higher percentage of female than male students from low-income and less-educated families complete college, according to the Pew Research Center. Tatiana B., a first-generation college student at Adelphi, aptly reflects, "my parents don't have enough money to lend me for college. What am I going to do? Is this it for me?" The numbers of female grads from the bottom income quartile are disproportionately higher than for male graduates, says Pew: "This contributes to why females have a higher borrowing rate." Debt analyst Mark Kantrowitz points out an additional reason for the greater financial burden carried by female graduates: lower pay when employed. No wonder that UCLA's *American Freshman* survey finds: "While nearly two-thirds of all incoming first-year students have at least "some" or "major" concerns about their ability to finance college, (64.6 percent), women tend to express much greater concern for this issue than their male counterparts."[61]

Student debt also affects African-American college students with greater force. The amounts they owe are greater than owed by college students generally. Inequality of wealth overall, and ongoing racial disparities in pay, ensure the serious nature of the problem. The percentage of both African-American and Hispanic students suffering college debt exceeds the percentage of white students. The percentage of growth in the average student loan debt facing Hispanic and African-American students is also greater than the burdens confronting white students. After examining loan burdens borne by white and black graduates from the same socioeconomic stratum (low-and-moderate income, or LMI), the Brookings Institution found greater debt among African-Americans. In general, student debt is widespread and a sign of new economic gaps on top of old ones in the United States. For as the Pew Research Center has found, there has been a downward dispersion of Americans "out of the middle."[62]

As underemployment threatens repayment of loans by all students, the insufficiency of job opportunity is more severe for African-American college graduates. Abundant research reveals that African-American job applicants with college diplomas are less likely to get called back for second interviews, even than whites with criminal records; likewise, black applicants with "high quality" resumes are only slightly more likely to be brought in for a second round than blacks with "low quality" resumes. The experience is widely shared even by graduates in the more marketable STEM majors: science, technology, engineering, and mathematics. Upholding the importance of college education to African-Americans, which "improves the relative situation of any black American compared with any other black American," Duke University economist William A. Darity, Jr. nonetheless concludes: "But it does not significantly reduce racial disparity. We've got to do something else to really have an effect on that."[63]

The Georgetown Center on Education and the Workforce reports that black students are "under-represented in the number of degree holders in college majors associated with the fastest-growing, highest-paying occupations—STEM, health, and business." Instead they "are highly concentrated in lower-paying majors." But even more successful African-American alumni suffer serious student debt, according to the journal *Race and Social Problems*. "Even in the highest slice of the income spectrum, the families of African-American college students have a lower average net worth, with less home equity, retirement savings and other assets."[64]

The seriousness of African-American student debt is brought into perspective when one realizes that in 2016 "forty-eight percent of all Americans aged 18 to 30 have zero in retirement savings and no access to a traditional pension," as the University of Chicago reports. Thus, one should not underestimate the daunting prospects facing students as a whole. Forty percent of college graduates owe sums greater than the value of their assets. In contrast, the net worth of debt-free college graduates is far greater than that of their liable fellow alumni. The canyon between the categories mirrors parallel wealth gaps in the United States. Student debt induces greater difficulty in making ends meet, deferring necessary purchases, having to work in a field in which one is not trained or may not feel fulfilled, needing to work more hours or more than one job, all of which naturally impact personal and family life. To be sure, student debt is the gift that keeps on taking.[65]

THE CONTRADICTION AT THE CORE

The opportunities to bring new students into higher education ought to provide fruitful collaborative endeavor for generations of college professionals. But even when colleges implement the many positive initiatives described in this chapter, the programs are vulnerable. No guarantees exist that educationally based decisions will guide future moves. There is a clash between the short-term views and long-term strategies of the business and educational sectors of higher education. The pecuniary and educative wings of higher education institutions rarely beat in unison. Consequently, adoption of special approaches to freshmen necessitates persistent advocacy. Only through great effort do pedagogical primacy and consistent support obtain recognition. Corporate-coated templates move far too easily into college helms, translating into "efficiency" across the board in courses offered, salaries paid, programs cut, money spent. People who work with students struggle to be heard. It is increasingly common, reports the *Hechinger Report,* that new college presidents have no academic experience.[66] But their outlook is the main problem.

How does the pervasive business ethos, which penetrates more than method, impact the educational experience of students, the labor of faculty, the level of student debt, the competitive success of schools, the freshman yield rate, and the ability to retain students? How are the various stances to be resolved? What is the bottom line in higher education?

NOTES

1. Jacques Steinberg, Goal is College: Hurdle is Finding Financial Aid," *New York Times,* May 1, 2009, A17.

2. Alan Schwarz, "Risky Rise of the Good-Grade Pill," *New York Times,* June 10, 2012, A1, A22, A23; Rose Marie Ward, Barbara B. Oswald, and Maria Galante, "Prescription Stimulant Misuse, Alcohol Abuse, and Disordered Eating Among College Students," *Journal of Alcohol and Drug Education,* Vol. 60, No. 1 (2016), 59-80; Justin Pope, "Taking Aim at Admissions Anxiety," *Seattle Times,* September 17, 2006, http://seattletimes.nwsource.com/html/education/2003262396_admissions17.html. Accessed June 9, 2011.

3. Don Hossler, *Creating Effective Enrollment Management Systems,* New York, 1986, 22; Howard and Mathew Greene, "Admissions Anguish," *University Business,* June 2005, http://www.universitybusiness.com/toc/default.aspx?issuedate=6/1/2005. Accessed June 19, 2006; Amy Padnani, "At. P.S. 41, College Planning Begins in Pre-K," *New York Times,* January 18, 2012, www.nytimes.com/schoolbook/2012/01/18/at-p-s-41-college-planning-begins-in-pre-k/. Accessed January 23, 2012; Laura Pappano, "Is Your First-Grader College Ready," *New York Times,* February 4, 2015, http://www.nytimes.com/2015/02/08/education/edlife/is-your-first-grader-college-ready.html. Accessed February 4, 2015; Javier C. Hernandez and Al Baker, "A Tough New Test Spurs Protest and Fears, *New York Times,* April 19, 2013, A24; "Mary Mogan Edwards, Ohio College Program Sees Student Enrollment Double," *Toledo Blade,* January 3, 2016, http://www.toledoblade.com/Education/2016/01/03/Ohio-college-program-sees-student-enrollment-double.html. Accessed January 3, 2016; Dawn Papandrea, "Proving Higher Education's Value," *University Business,* January 2016, 29; Jackie Mader, "Testing Gives Third-graders Upset Stomachs, Tears and Even Fevers," *Hechinger Report,* May 1, 2015, http://hechingerreport.org/tests-plus-more-tests-equal-stress-tears-and-fevers/. Accessed May 3, 2015; "Florida Bill Asks High Schoolers to Declare Major," *Associated Press,* March 26, 2005.

4. "2015 Freshmen," Higher Education Research Institute at UCLA, CIRP Freshman Survey 2015, poster; Higher Education Research Institute at UCLA, Research Brief, *The American Freshman: National Norms Fall 2015,* February 2016, 3; Dr. Jonathan Jackson, "For Freshmen Only," *The Delphian,* November 29, 1985, 3; Robert M. Sheffield, Rhonda J. Montgomery, and Patricia G. Moody, *Case Studies for the First Year,*

Upper Saddle River, NJ, 171; Andrea Stanley, "Finding the Perfect Roomie," *Seventeen*, June–July 2016, 102–3.

5. Tim Goval, On Topic: Q & A with Arudhana Bela Sood, *University Business*, April 2015, 12; Jeffrey Jensen Arnett, "Emerging Adulthood: A Theory of Development From the Late Teens Through the Twenties," *American Psychologist*, Vol. 55, No. 5 (May 2000), 469–80.

6. Henry Brzycki, "Faculty Members Must Play a Role," *Inside Higher Ed*, January 5, 2016, https://www.insidehighered.com/views/2016/01/05/helping-faculty-members-help-improve-students-mental-health-essay. Accessed January 5, 2016.

7. Rebecca Jordan, "But I Am Their Professor," *Academe*, November–December 2014, https://academeblog.org/2014/11/18/but-i-am-their-professor/. Accessed November 18, 2014; Jack R. Rayman and Jeffrey W. Garris, "Counseling," in M. Lee Upcraft, John Gardner, and Associates, *The Freshman Year Experience*, San Francisco, 1989, 129, 137.

8. Peter Gray, quoted in Jane Brody, "Giving Children Roots, and Wings," *New York Times*, January 20, 2015, D7; Jan Hoffman, "Anxious Students Strain College Mental Health Centers," *New York Times*, May 27, 2015, http://well.blogs.nytimes.com/2015/05/27/anxious-students-strain-college-mental-health-centers/?_r=0 Accessed May 28, 2015; Kristen Domonell, "Sound Mind, Sound Student Body," *University Business*, March 19, 2013, http://www.universitybusiness.com/article/sound-mind-sound-student-body. Accessed March 20, 2013; Eliza Shapiro, "Mental-Health Breakdown: When Harvard Fails Its Students," *The Daily Beast*, March 18, 2013, http://www.thedailybeast.com/articles/2013/03/18/mental-health-breakdown-when-harvard-fails-its-students.html. Accessed March 19, 2013; Deona Hooper, "Mental Health Matters But What Happens When You Are Waitlisted?," *Social Work Helper*, May 5, 2016, https://www.socialworkhelper.com/2016/05/05/mental-health-matters-happens-waitlisted/. Accessed May 5, 2016; Matt Zalaznick, "Coloring Books, Comfort Dogs and More Help Students Shed Stress," *University Business*, December 23, 2015, http://www.universitybusiness.com/article/coloring-books-comfort-dogs-and-more-help-students-shed-stress. Accessed December 23, 2015.

9. Kellie M. Smith, Megan S. Chesin, and Elizabeth L. Jeglic, "Minority Student College Health: Does Majority Status Matter? Implications for College Counseling Services," *Journal of Multicultural Counseling and Development*, Vol. 42 (April 2014), 78–79, 85–88; Sarah Brown, "Many Black Students Don't Seek Help for Mental-Health Concerns, Survey Finds," *The Chronicle of Higher Education*, January 13, 2016, http://chronicle.com/article/Many-Black-Students-Don-t/234892?cid=at&utm_source=at&utm_medium=en&elq=51cfe8c060724bf0831e84c0cbdeabf2&elqCampaignId=2218&elqaid=7518&elqat=1&elqTrackId=5b462850d4f4438ebf459a7c6b4e7d2a. Accessed January 13, 2016; Carol Graham, Sergio Pinto, and Julia Ruiz, *Stress, Worry, and Social Support: Inequality in America's Cities*, Brookings Institution, November 5, 2015, http://www.brookings.edu/blogs/social-mobility-memos/posts/2015/11/05-stress-worry-support-inequality-cities-graham#.Vjy26SN3g2Q.facebook. Accessed November 7, 2015; Tim Goval, "On Topic: Q & A with Arudhana Bela Sood," *University Business*, April 2015, 12.

10. Eric Schulzke, "College Admissions Race is Distorting the Behavior and Character of High Schoolers, Say Reform Advocates," *The Oklahoman*, February 26, 2016, http://newsok.com/college-admissions-race-is-distorting-the-behavior-and-character-of-high-schoolers-say-reform-advocates/article/5481138?custom_click=rss&utm_source=feedburner&utm_medium=feed&utm_campaign=Feed%3A+Newsok%2FNews+%28NewsOK.com+RSS+-+news%29. Accessed February 28, 2016; Raquel Bermejo, *2015 High School Students' and Parents' Perceptions of and Preferences for Communication with Colleges*, Ruffalo Noel Levitz, Cedar Rapids, 2015, 16; Adelphi University Office of Research, Assessment, and Planning, *Results of Newly Admitted Freshmen Survey*, September 2013, 1; Kevin Carey, "The Truth Behind College Admission," *New York Times*, November 29, 2014, SR2; Mike McPhate, "Common Application Saturates the College Admissions Market, Critics Say," *New York Times*, April 11, 2016, http://www.nytimes.

com/2016/04/12/us/common-application-saturates-the-college-admissions-market-critics-say.html?smid=nytcore-iphone-share&smprod=nytcore-iphone. Accessed April 22, 2106; Laura M. Colarusso, "Colleges Ratchet Up Recruiting of Applicants, Just to Turn Them Down," *The Hechinger Report*, January 12, 2015, http://hechingerreport.org/content/colleges-ratchet-recruiting-applicants-just-turn_18742/. Accessed January 15, 2015.

11. Richard Pérez-Peña, "Online Application Woes Make Students Anxious and Put Colleges Behind Schedule," *New York Times*, October 12, 2013, A14; Elizabeth A. Harris, "Urging Students to Apply for College, City Will Make SAT Free for Juniors," *New York Times*, October 27, 2015, A21; Diane Rado, "Illinois Shifts Gears on College Entrance Exams, Chooses SAT over ACT," *Chicago Tribune*, December 21, 2015, http://www.chicagotribune.com/news/ct-illinois-sat-met-20151221-story.html. Accessed December 21, 2015.

12. Sharon Otterman, "37% of State Graduates College-Ready, Data Show," *New York Times*, June 14, 2011, A23; Daniel Goldstein, "10 Things the College Admissions Office Won't Tell You," *Marketwatch*, December 30, 2015, http://www.marketwatch.com/story/10-things-the-college-admissions-office-wont-tell-you-2014-10-03?page=1. Accessed December 30, 2015; Adelphi University Office of Research, Assessment, and Planning, *Results of the Cooperative Institutional Research Program (CIRP) Survey Fall 2004 to Fall 2014*, 6; Brittany Anas, "Faculty Rep Blasts CU-Boulder's 87% Acceptance Rate, Says Students Not Prepared," *Daily Camera*, February 20, 2013, http://www.dailycamera.com/cu-news/ci_22629042/faculty-rep-blasts-cu-boulders-87-acceptance-rate. Accessed February 25, 2013; Sam Dillon, "U.S. Students Remain Poor At History, Tests Show," *New York Times*, June 14, 2011, A19; *ACT National Curriculum Survey 2012, Policy Implications on Preparing for Higher Standards*, 4; Debra Erdley, "Many College Freshmen Need Remedial Work, Often Delaying Graduation, Increasing Costs," *Pittsburgh Tribune-Review*, July 12, 2014, http://triblive.com/mobile/6376740-96/remedial-students-college. Accessed August 6, 2014.

13. Noel-Levitz, Inc., *2008 National Freshman Attitudes Report*, 4, 6; Noel-Levitz, Inc., *2012 National Freshman Attitudes Report*, 7; Sherry Saavedra, "College Freshmen Not Ready, Study Says," *San Diego Union-Tribune*, April 10, 2007, http://www.signonsandiego.com/uniontrib/20070410/news_1n10college.html. Accessed June 9, 2011; Anna M. Phillips and Robert Gebeloff, "In Data, 'A' Schools Leave Many Not Ready For CUNY," *New York Times*, June 22, 2011, A18; AFL-CIO, *Executive Paywatch: High-Paid CEOs and the Low-Wage Economy*, 2014, http://www.aflcio.org/Corporate-Watch/Paywatch-2014. Accessed January 5, 2015.

14. Motoko Rich, "Where are the Teachers of Color," *New York Times*, April 12, 2015, SR3; Everyone Graduates Center at the School of Education at Johns Hopkins University, *Building a Grad Nation: Progress and Challenge in Ending the High School Dropout Epidemic*, 2015; Kimberle Williams Crenshaw et al., *Black Girls Matter: Pushed Out, Overpoliced and Underprotected*, African American Policy Forum, Center for Intersectionality and Social Policy Studies, Columbia University Law School, 2015, 4–5; Adam C. Wright, "Teachers' Perceptions of Students' Disruptive Behavior: The Effect of Racial Congruence and Consequences for School Suspension," seminar paper, November 2015, 24–25.

15. "Long Island High School Graduation Rates 2015," *Newsday*, http://data.newsday.com/long-island/data/education/graduation-rates-2015/. Accessed June 23, 2016; New York City Department of Education, *New York City Graduation Rates Class of 2016 (2011 Cohort)*, January 2016, 6; National Center for Education Statistics, *The Condition of Education 2016*, May 2016, 187.

16. National Resource Center, First Year Experience and Students in Transition, 35th Annual Conference on the First-Year Experience, *Annual Program*, 2016, 24, 30, 62, 63, 75.

17. Jennifer Vitale, Hampden-Sydney College, "Low-Cost, High Impact: Learning Communities at a Residential College," presentation to FYE 2016 Annual Meeting;

Hanover Research, *Strategies for Improving Retention,* Arlington, VA, November 2015, 26–27, 29–30.

18. Alvernia University, "Freshman Foundations," http://www.alvernia.edu/student-life/student-success/foundations/features.html. Accessed September 18, 2012.

19. Tracy Harris, "Influence of Orientation Coursework on Enrollment Persistence," *Enrollment Management Journal,* Summer 2009, 10–25; Adelphi University, "Learning Communities," http://students.adelphi.edu/gettingstarted/communities.php. Accessed September 9, 2011; Donald J. Perigo and M. Lee Upcraft, "Orientation Programs," in Upcraft, Gardner, and Associates, 93; State University of New York at New Paltz, "First-Year Interest Groups," http://www.newpaltz.edu/firstyearprograms/. Accessed September 9, 2011

20. National Resource Center, First Year Experience and Students in Transition, 35th Annual Conference on the First-Year Experience, *Annual Program,* 2016, 21, 26, 27, 67, 78.

21. National Resource Center, First Year Experience and Students in Transition, 35th Annual Conference on the First-Year Experience, *Annual Program,* 2016, 18, 23, 28, 21.

22. "Appalachian State University: Freshman Learning Communities in General Studies," Ruffalo Noel Levitz, *A Compendium of Successful, Innovative Retention Programs and Practices,* Coralville, IA, 2015, 10; University of Illinois, *The Division of General Studies,* www.dgs.illinois.edu/. Accessed July 28, 2010; University of Alaska Fairbanks, *General Studies,* www.uaf.edu/gs/. Accessed July 28, 2010; Northeastern University, *General Studies Program,* www.gsp.neu.edu/. Accessed July 20, 2010; Oxford College: A Distinctive Place, http://oxford.emory.edu/a_distinctive_place/index.dot. Accessed June 7, 2013.

23. Boston University, *Frequently Asked Questions About CGS,* www.bu.edu/cgs/about/faq/. Accessed July 27, 2010; Anthony Dotterman, *Executive Summary: General Studies Program Panel,* Northeast Modern Language Association 44th Annual Convention, March 22, 2013; Eric Platt, "From the Margins to the Mainstream," *New York Times,* January 20, 2012, ED6; Samuel Weiss, "The Added Option of General Studies," *New York Times,* December 26, 2001, D9; New York University, *The Liberal Studies Program: Vision and Identity,* http://ls.nyu.edu/page/mission. Accessed July 20, 2010.

24. Mathew W. Bowers, "To Keep Freshmen, Colleges Get Creative," *The Virginian-Pilot,* August 30, 2006, http://findarticles.com/p/news-articles/virginian-pilot-ledger-star-norfolk/mi_8014/is_20060830/freshmen-colleges-creative/ai_n41319479/. Accessed September 2, 2006; "At College, Coaching Isn't Just for Athletes Anymore," *Bloomberg Business Journal,* April 23, 2012, 49; Mary Duenwald, "The Consumer: The Dorms May Be Great, But How's the Counseling," *New York Times,* October 4, 2006, F1; Jay Mathews, "Colleges Sharpen Focus on Freshmen," *Washington Post,* April 5, 2005, A12; Kelly Simmons, "Budget Cuts Take Tolls on Georgia Universities," *Atlanta Journal-Constitution,* March 3, 2004, www.ajc.com/wednesday/content/epaper/editions/wednesday/metro_04543816b526c1d0. Accessed March 4, 2004; *Report from John Gardner on His Visit to Adelphi University, March 5, 2003: Regarding the Current Status of the First-Year Experience at Adelphi,* March 19, 2003, 6; Inside College, *Colleges for B Students, Late Bloomers, and Underachievers,* http://www.insidecollege.com/reno/Colleges-For-B-Students-Late-Bloomers-And-Underachievers/239/section.do. Accessed July 11, 2011; Mary Keenan, "Required Learning Communities for Undecided Freshmen," *Enrollment Management Journal,* Winter 2008, 78–115; University at Buffalo, The State University of New York, "Access to College Excellence Program," http://cpmc.buffalo.edu/ace/index.php. Accessed January 13, 2015.

25. Michael Winerip, "Children of the State, Students on Their Own," *New York Times,* October 30, 2013, ED20.

26. Jennifer Vitale, Hampden-Sydney College, "Low-Cost, High Impact: Learning Communities at a Residential College," presentation to FYE 2016 Annual Meeting; Ruffalo Noel Levitz, *A Compendium of Successful, Innovative Retention Programs and Practices,* Coralville, IA, 2016, 51, 66, 67.

27. Ruffalo Noel Levitz, *A Compendium of Successful, Innovative Retention Programs and Practices*, Coralville, IA, 2016, 87, 125, 138, 150, 157, 166.

28. James Hannah, "Colleges Zero in on Students' Majors," *Associated Press*, December 20, 2006.

29. The College at Brockport, State University of New York, *The First-Year Experience*, brochure, n.d.; Wilkes University, "Mistakes and Myths," http://www.wilkes.edu/pages/1182.asp. Accessed September 16, 2011.

30. Ithaca College, "Exploratory Program," http://www.ithaca.edu/hs/exploratory/programs/exploratory/. Accessed September 9, 2011; Marietta College, "Entering as an Exploratory Student," http://www.marietta.edu/first_year/for_undecided_students.html. Accessed September 9, 2011; McMicken College, "Exploratory," http://www.artsci.uc.edu/programs/program_detail.aspx?ID=15BX-EXPL. Accessed September 9, 2011.

31. Southern Illinois University, "Exploratory Students," http://pmac.siu.edu/. Accessed October 9, 2012; University of Vermont, College of Arts and Sciences, *Undecided?*, brochure, n.d.; University of Vermont, College of Arts and Sciences, *The First-Year Experience*, brochure, 2012–2013; University of Scranton, "Options for Undeclared Freshmen," http://catalog.scranton.edu/preview_program.php?catoid=10&poid=892&hl=%22Exploratory%22&returnto=search. Accessed September 9, 2011.

32. Uyanga Tamir, *"A Major in Engineering, With a Minor in 'Keeping an Open Mind,'" New York Times*, December 30, 2011, http://thechoice.blogs.nytimes.com/2010/12/30/cherry-creek-uyanga-tamir-2/?scp=1&sq=A%20Major%20in%20Engineering,%20With%20a%20Minor&st=cse. Accessed January 3, 2012; Robert Clagett, "As Jan. 1 Application Deadline Nears, An Argument for a Year-long Breather," *New York Times*, December 27, 2011, http://thechoice.blogs.nytimes.com/2011/12/27/clagett-gap-year/?ref=us. Accessed December 27, 2011; Alex Williams, "The Old College Try? No Way," *New York Times*, December 2, 2012, ST1; "Tufts University Offers Financial Aid for Students' Year Off," *Reuters*, March 14, 2014, http://www.reuters.com/article/2014/03/14/us-usa-tufts-gapyear-idUSBREA2D1HP20140314. Accessed March 17, 2014.

33. "Schools Using 4 + 1 Programs To Lure Students," *Worcester Business Journal*, May 23, 2016, http://m.wbjournal.com/article/20160523/PRINTEDITION/305209984/schools-using-4+1-programs-to-lure-students. Accessed May 23, 2016.

34. Bourree Lam, "The Most Career-Minded Generation," *The Atlantic*, April 28, 2016, http://www.theatlantic.com/business/archive/2016/04/motivation-college/480342/. Accessed May 3, 2016.

35. Muhlenberg College, "First Year Experience," http://muhlenberg.edu/main/aboutus/dean-academic/fye/. Accessed September 9, 2011; Eckerd College, "Autumn Term," http://www.eckerd.edu/academics/gened/at/index.php. Accessed June 21, 2012.

36. Amanda Worhoff and Cathy Evins, Roosevelt University, "At-Risk Academic Impacts: Studying Bridge and Non-Bridge Student Experiences," presentation to FYE 2016 Annual Meeting; "Building Bridges to Student Success," *University Business*, December 2016, 31–37; Ioanna Opidee, "Supporting First-Gen Students," *University Business*, March 2015, 33–34.

37. N. L. Habers et al., Kennesaw State University, "First-Year Convocation: A Data-driven Approach to Enhancing the Experience," presentation to FYE 2016 Annual Meeting; Cate Igo and Melvin Thompson, Polk State College, "Retention Through First-Flight Student Convocation and Peer Mentoring," presentation to FYE 2016 Annual Meeting.

38. Susan Kinzie, "Orientation 101 for Parents and Freshmen: Letting Go," *Washington Post*, August 26, 2007, C3; G. Jeffrey MacDonald, "Parents of College Freshmen Feel Separation Anxiety," *USA Today*, September 11, 2007, www.usatoday.com/news/education/2007-09-11-long-goodbye_N.htm?csp=34. Accessed September 17, 2007; Brittany Anas, "At CU-Boulder, Orientation is As Much for Parents As their Kids," *Boulder Daily Camera*, June 18, 2011, http://www.dailycamera.com/cu-news/ci_18306530. Accessed June 22, 2011; Matt Rocheleau, "College Orientations for Parents Help

Ease Separation Pains," *Boston Globe*, June 30, 2014, http://www.bostonglobe.com/metro/2014/06/29/college-orientations-for-parents-help-ease-separation-pains/DJUwgU2q56R0bskJhhZ7xM/story.html. Accessed July 3, 2014; Eileen Interiano, "Bonding and Fun Highlight Family Weekend 2014," *The Delphian*, November 3, 2014, 1; Thomas N. Hollins, Jr., "Examining the Impact of a Comprehensive Approach to Student Orientation," *Inquiry*, Vol. 14, No. 1 (Spring 2009), 15–27; K. Booker, "Building the Connection: An Evaluation of New Student Orientation at a Women's College," *The Journal of Orientation and College Transition*, Vol. 13, No. 2 (2006), 5–9.

39. Mathew R. Shupp, *Rethinking New Student Orientation*, 2006, http://www.newfoundations.com/OrgTheory/Shupp721Sp06.htm. Accessed July 30, 2010; Brittany Anas, "Marijuana Hearings at CU-Boulder on Decline after Orientation Does More to Address Pot," *Boulder Daily Camera*, August 8, 2011, http://www.dailycamera.com/cu-news/ci_18630496. Accessed August 9, 2011; Tamar Lewin, "College Flash Mobs Become Pep Rallies Made for YouTube," *New York Times*, October 3, 2011, A12.

40. Larry Gordon, "Advisors Work to Freeze 'Summer Melt,'" *Los Angeles Times*, October 19, 2014, http://touch.latimes.com/#section/-1/article/p2p-81724951/. Accessed October 21, 2014; Susan Dynarski, "The Power of a Simple Nudge," *New York Times*, January 18, 2015, BU6; Elizabeth A. Harris, "Little Guidance: 500 Students Per Counselor," *New York Times*, December 26, 2014, A1; Noel-Levitz, *2010 Admissions Funnel Benchmarks* . . . 3, 6, 7.

41. Edgar L. Morphet et al., *Educational Organization and Administration*, Englewood Cliffs, NJ, 1967, 396; Jennifer Giancola and Richard D. Kahlenberg, *True Merit: Ensuring Our Brightest Students Have Access to Our Best Colleges and Universities*, Jack Kent Cooke Foundation, 2016, 16.

42. Tanya Cardwell, "More on 2012 College Admissions Yields and Wait-List Offers," *New York Times*, May 29, 2012, http://thechoice.blogs.nytimes.com/2012/05/29/more-on-2012-college-admission-yields-and-wait-list-offers/. Accessed May 30, 2012; Tanya Abrams, "Colleges Report 2013 Admission Yields and Wait-List Offers," *New York Times*, May 30, 2013, http://thechoice.blogs.nytimes.com/2013/05/30/college-admits-2013/. Accessed May 30, 2013.

43. Howard Bunsis, *Analysis of the Financial Condition of Adelphi University*, AAUP, November 2015, 31; Chris Nicholson, "Enrollment Yields Becoming Ever Harder to Meet," *University Business*, July 2014, http://www.universitybusiness.com/article/enrollment-yields-becoming-ever-harder-meet. Accessed August 6, 2014; Adelphi University Office of Research, Assessment and Planning, "Fall 2014 First-Time Freshmen Admissions," *Data Snapshot*, Fall 2014; Moody's Investors Service, *Industry Outlook: U.S. Higher Education Outlook Mixed in 2012*, January 20, 2012, 4, 6, 7, 8, 11; Andrew Martin, "Downturn Still Squeezes Colleges and Universities," *New York Times*, January 11, 2013, B3; Jonathan Lai, "For Small Schools, Big Enrollment Problems," *Philadelphia Inquirer*, November 16, 2015, http://mobile.philly.com/news/?wss=/philly/education&id=350303581#PSQpUxYWgY1wz0ly.99. Accessed November 17, 2015.

44. Office of Research, Assessment & Planning, Adelphi University, *New Freshmen by Major Within School*, Fall 2014, September 23, 2014; Moody's, 11; Moody's Investor's Service, *Negative Outlook for US Higher Education Continues, Even as Green Shoots of Stability Emerge*, July 11, 2014, 1; Zinie Chen Sampson, "College Boards Turn to Business Style Approaches," *Detroit News*, June 27, 2012, http://www.detroitnews.com/article/20120627/SCHOOLS/206270376/1026/. Accessed June 28, 2012; American Council of Trustees and Alumni, *Governance for a New Era: A Blueprint for Higher Education Trustees*, 2014, 2, 9, 11; John K. Wilson, Interview with Rudy Fichtenbaum, *Academe Blog*, May 11, 2012, http://academeblog.org/2012/05/11/interview-with-rudy-fichtenbaum/. Accessed June 26, 2012; Jonathan Rees, "Guest Commentary: Adjunct Professors Are Hiding in Plain Sight," *Denver Post*, April 29, 2012, http://www.denverpost.com/headlines/ci_20490316/guest-commentary-adjunct-professors-are-hiding-plain-sight. Accessed April 30, 2012; Gould, 31.

45. Ross Markle and Steve Robbins, *The SuccessNavigator Assessment: A Holistic Approach to Predicting Academic and Retention Success*, Educational Testing Service, 2013, 2, 3; Educational Testing Service, *Influence Student Success*, 2014, 2–4.

46. John N. Gardner Institute, *Expert Consultation and Proven Processes: Student Learning, Success, Retention and Completion*, n.d.; Kenneth J. Sufka, *The A Game: Nine Steps to Better Grades*, The Nautilus Publishing Company, 2011.

47. R. Michael Haynes and T. Wayne Atchley, "The Impact of a Camp Orientation Program on First-Year Academic Engagement and Persistence," *The Journal of College Orientation and Transition*, Vol. 20, No. 2 (Spring 2004), 79, 87, 88.

48. *Report of the Freshman Academic Experience Task Force 2010-2011*, The University of Texas at San Antonio, 23; *Enhancing Student Success*, brochure, Virginia Commonwealth University; University of South Carolina Success Connect, *University Business*, April 2015, 32.

49. University at Buffalo, The State University of New York, "Office of Academic Excellence," http://cpmc.buffalo.edu/oae/index.php. Accessed January 13, 2015; Auburn University Office of Institutional Research and Assessment, *The Impact of First-Year Engagement on Retention to the Second Year*, December 2009, 7–9; Robert Booras, "Speed Advising?" *The Chronicle of Higher Education*, March 18, 2015, http://m.chronicle.com/article/Speed-Advising-/228527/?cid=at&utm_source=at&utm_medium=en. Accessed March 19, 2015.

50. Brandon Busteed, "The Biggest Blown Opportunity in Higher Ed History," *Gallup Business Journal*, October 7, 2014, http://businessjournal.gallup.com/content/178082/biggest-blown-opportunity-higher-history.aspx. Accessed October 17, 2014; *Great Jobs, Great Lives: The 2014 Gallup-Purdue Index Report*, Gallup-Purdue University, 2014, 5, 6, 9.

51. Dan Berrett, "Professor's Place in the Classroom is Shifting to the Side," *The Chronicle of Higher Education*, November 13, 2014, http://chronicle.com/article/Professors-Place-in-the/149975/. Accessed November 13, 2014; Richard Pérez-Peña, "Colleges Reinvent Classes to Keep More Students in Science," *New York Times*, December 27, 2014, A10; Benjamin S. Bloom, "The Search for Methods of Group Instruction as Effective as One-to-One Tutoring," *Educational Leadership*, Vol. 41, No. 8 (May 1984), 6, 14, 15.

52. Pew Research Center, *Parenting in America*, Washington, DC, December 2015, 5, 48, 58.

53. David Cooper and Lawrence Mishel, *The Erosion of Collective Bargaining Has Widened the Gap Between Productivity and Pay*, Economic Policy Institute, January 5, 2015; The Institute of Politics, Harvard University, *Survey of Young Americans' Attitudes Toward Politics and Public Service: 17th Edition*, Cambridge, 2010, 9; Public Agenda, *With Their Whole Lives Ahead of Them: Myths and Realities About Why So Many Students Fail to Finish College*, 2010, 4, 6–7; College Board, *Trends in College Pricing*, 2007; Tara Siegel Bernard, "In Grim Job Market, Student Loans Are A Costly Burden," *New York Times*, April 18, 2009, B6; Arthur Thomas, "UW System Students Under Pressure to Graduate in Four Years," *Milwaukee Journal-Sentinel*, July 11, 2012, http://m.jsonline.com/news/education/uw-system-students-under-pressure-to-graduate-in-four-years-jb5titt-162123005.html. Accessed July 17, 2012; Tamar Lewin, "Student Loan Default Rates Rise Sharply in Past Year, *New York Times*, September 12, 2011, A14; Candice Ferrette, "LI's Private Colleges Face Declining Revenue," *Newsday*, February 8, 2014, http://www.newsday.com/long-island/li-s-private-colleges-face-declining-revenue-1.6997984. Accessed February 10, 2014.

54. Hechinger Report, "As Grads Seek Jobs, Universities Cut Career Services," January 29, 2013, http://hechingerreport.org/content/as-grads-seek-jobs-universities-cut-career-services_10932/. Accessed February 20, 2013; Pew Research Center, *Is College Worth It?*, 2011, 31, 34; Catherine Rampell, "Many With New College Degree Find the Job Market Humbling," *New York Times*, May 19, 2011, A1; Brittany Anas, "Survey: 70 Percent of Students Skip Out on Some Textbook Purchases," *Boulder Daily Camera*, August 22, 2011, http://www.dailycamera.com/cu-news/ci_18723969. Accessed Au-

gust 24, 2011; Julie Mack, "Venting About College Textbook Costs," *Kalamazoo Gazette*, August 31, 2011, http://mobile.mlive.com/advannarbor/pm_103353/contentdetail.htm?contentguid=dkzp50kW. Accessed September 2, 2011; National Survey of Student Engagement, *Promoting Student Learning and Institutional Improvement: Lesson from NSSE at 13*, 17; Hilary Daninhirsch, "Spending, Saving, and Securing Funds," *University Business*, January 2016, 52–53.

55. McKinsey & Company, in collaboration with Chegg, Inc., *Voice of the Graduate*, May 2013, 6, 8, 10, 15, 17–18; Tami Luhby, "Recent College Grads Face 36% 'Mal-Employment Rate," *CNN Money*, June 25, 2013, http://money.cnn.com/2013/06/25/news/economy/malemployment-rate/. Accessed June 26, 2013; Rachel L. Swarns, "Degree? Check. Enthusiasm? Check. Job? Not so Fast," *New York Times*, June 9, 2014, A12.

56. Michael Greenstone and Adam Looney, *Is Starting College and Not Finishing Really That Bad?*, The Hamilton Project, June 7, 2013, 1–4; U.S. Bureau of the Census, *Table MS-2. Estimated Median Age at First Marriage, by Sex: 1890 to Present*, September 15, 2004; Patricia Cohen, "Long Road to Adulthood Is Growing Even Longer," *New York Times*, June 11, 2010, A26; Sam Roberts, "Facing a Financial Pinch, and Moving in With Mom and Dad," *New York Times*, March 21, 2010, A20; Catherine Rampell, "As New Graduates Return to Nest, Economy Also Feels the Pain," *New York Times*, November 17, 2011, A1; Adam Davidson, "Hi Mom, I'm Home," *New York Times Magazine*, June 20, 2014, MM22; Richard Fry, *For First Time in Modern Era, Living with Parents Edges Out Other Living Arrangements for 18 to 34-Year Olds*, Pew Research Center, 2016, 4–6; Tamar Levin, "To Raise Graduation Rates, Colleges Are Urged to Help a Changing Student Body," *New York Times*, January 24, 2013, A15; National Center for Educational Statistics, *Institutional Retention and Graduation Rates for Undergraduate Students*, May 2015, 2015, 1–4; National Commission on Higher Education Attainment, *An Open Letter to College and University Leaders: College Completion Must Become Priority*, January 2013; Jody Lawrence-Turner, "Most Washington Students Starting College Don't Finish," *The Spokesman Review* (Spokane), August 11, 2013, http://m.spokesman.com/stories/2013/aug/11/most-washington-students-starting-college-dont/. Accessed August 13, 2013.

57. Henry O. Levy, "College Admissions Odds Are Stacked Against High Achieving Low-Income Students," *Huffington Post*, November 20, 2015, www.huffingtonpost.com/harold-o-levy/college-admissions-odds-a_b_8575684.html. Accessed November 24, 2015; Lisa Gartner, "That Line About College Students Surviving on Ramen? No Longer Funny at Many Florida Schools," *Tampa Bay Times*, May 27, 2016, http://www.tampabay.com/news/education/college/that-line-about-college-kids-surviving-on-ramen-no-longer-funny-at-many/2279265. Accessed May 29, 2016; College and University Food Bank Alliance, CUFBA Hits 400 Members," December 9, 2016, http://www.cufba.org/. Accessed December 16, 2016; "Vickie Elmer, "Dealing with Student Debt," *New York Times*, April 26, 2012, RE6; Andrew Martin and Andrew W. Lehren, "A Generation Hobbled by College Debt," *New York Times*, May 13, 2012, A1, A20, A21; Howard Bunsis, *Analysis of the Financial Condition of Adelphi University*, AAUP, November 2015, 44, 46.

58. Elizabeth Sweet et al., "The High Price of Debt: Household Financial Debt and Its Impact on Mental and Physical Health," *Social Science & Medicine*, Vol. 91 (August 2013), 94–100; Chad Merta, "College Debt Workshop Urges Participants to Write Suicide Notes," *Chicago Sun-Times*, March 17, 2016, http://national.suntimes.com/national-world-news/7/72/2772778/student-debt-suicide-letters. Accessed March 17, 2016; Mark Kantrowitz, *Who Graduates with Excessive Student Loan Debt?*, Student Aid Policy Analysis Papers, December 14, 2015, 1, 6–13.

59. Halah Touryalai, "Student Loan Problems: One Third of Millenials Regret Going to College," *Forbes Magazine*, May 22, 2013, http://www.forbes.com/sites/halahtouryalai/2013/05/22/student-loan-problems-one-third-of-millennials-regret-going-to-college/. Accessed May 23, 2013; Maureen Groppe, "Mitch Daniels Pushes New Plan to Pay for College," *Indianapolis Star*, March 18, 2015, http://www.indystar.com/story/news/2015/03/17/daniels-asks-congress-try-alternative-student-loan/24911835/. Ac-

cessed March 19, 2015; Meta Brown and Sydnee Caldwell, "Young Student Borrowers Retreat From Housing and Auto Markets," Federal Reserve Bank of New York, April 17, 2013, http://libertystreeteconomics.newyorkfed.org/2013/04/young-student-loan-borrowers-retreat-from-housing-and-auto-markets.html. Accessed May 28, 2013; Annie Lowrey, "Heavy Load of Student Debt Is Weighing on the Economy, Too," *New York Times*, May 11, 2013, B1; Kim Clark, "What Parents Will Give Up for Kids' College," *Money*, November 18, 2015, http://time.com/money/4114995/parents-kids-college-costs-kaplan-survey/. Accessed November 19, 2015.

60. "Starting Out Behind," *New York Times*, editorial, June 8, 2014, SR10; Natalie Kitroeff, "Young and In Debt," *New York Times*, June 8, 2014, RE1; Michael E. Porter and Jan W. Rivkin, *An Economy Doing Half Its Job*, Harvard Business School, 2014, 3, 22.

61. Richard Fry et al., *The Changing Profile of Student Borrowers*, October 7, 2014, 13-14; Tatiana B., "Impressions," 2014, by permission of Tatiana B., Adelphi University, 2015; Mark Kantrowitz, *Who Graduates with Excessive Student Loan Debt?*, Student Aid Policy Analysis Papers, December 14, 2015, 7; Kevin Egan et al., *The American Freshman: National Norms 2015*, Cooperative Institutional Research Program at the Higher Education Research Institute at UCLA, 14.

62. National Center for Education Statistics, "Percentage of undergraduate students ages 18 to 24 in their 4th (senior) year or above who had ever received federal loans, nonfederal loans, or Parent Loans for Undergraduates (PLUS), and the average cumulative amount borrowed, by selected student characteristics and control and level of institution: 1989–1990, 1999–2000, and 2011–2012," https://nces.ed.gov/programs/digest/d13/tables/dt13_331.95.asp. Accessed March 4, 2016; Michal Grinstein-Weiss et al., "Racial Disparities in Education Debt Burden Among Low-and-Moderate-Income Households," *Children and Youth Services Review*, Volume 65 (June 2016), 166-174; Pew Research Center, *The American Middle Class is Losing Ground*, December 9, 2015, 35.

63. Janelle Jones and John Schmitt, *A College Degree is No Guarantee*, Center for Economic and Policy Research, May 2014, 1, 3, 10–12; Patricia Cohen, "Arduous Job Path for Black Grads," *New York Times*, December 25, 2014, B1.

64. Anthony Carnevale et al., *African Americans: College Majors and Earnings*, Georgetown University Center on Education and the Workforce, 2016, 3, 5, 9, 11; Fenaba R. Addo et al., "Young, Black, and (Still) in the Red: Parental Wealth, Race, and Student Loan Debt," *Race and Social Problems* Vol. 8, No. 1 (2016), 64–76; Martha C. White, "Even Well-Off Black Students Carry More Loan Debt: Study," *NBC News*, March 12, 2016, http://www.nbcnews.com/business/personal-finance/even-well-black-students-carry-more-loan-debt-study-n536751. Accessed March 15, 2016.

65. Stan Choe, "Millenials Lack Savings," *U.S. News & World Report*, October 14, 2016, http://www.usnews.com/news/business/articles/2016-10-14/nearly-half-of-young-adults-lack-retirement-savings-pension. Accessed October 14, 2016; Richard Fry, *Young Adults, Student Debt and Economic Well-being*, Pew Research Center, 2014, Washington, DC, 4, 6, 7, 9, 15; Mark Kantrowitz, *Who Graduates with Excessive Student Loan Debt?*, Student Aid Policy Analysis Papers, December 14, 2015, 10.

66. Matt Krupnick, "As Times Get Tough, Colleges Turn to Nonacademics to Lead," *The Hechinger Report*, December 25, 2015, http://hechingerreport.org/as-times-get-tough-colleges-turn-to-nonacademics-to-lead/. Accessed January 5, 2016.

FOUR

Roots of the General Studies Program at Adelphi

Adelphi University is a Long Island school drawing a primarily local student body, with a minority of students coming from adjacent New York City. The historical context of its location has shaped the university and its General Studies Program or Learning Community (as it is now called). Combined with passive or active acceptance of the SAT's intelligence-based stigma, a view arose among some at Adelphi of what and whom low test scores represented. When expressed, opposition to the program employed a jaundiced imagery. General Studies survived despite this resistance, as shall be demonstrated in this and the following two chapters.

Throughout the 1980s, the white population percentage in Long Island shrank as African-American, Latino, and other minorities moved from the cities to the suburbs.[1] Despite the growing diversification, residential segregation persisted in the form of exclusively white high-income enclaves and remarkably creative carving up of school districts into racial reserves. Of course, the local context reflected an ongoing national trend, including denial of mortgages to blacks at twice the rate for whites. But realtor-based "redlining," undergirded by subprime lending by such banks as Wells Fargo, caused the Census Bureau to place Nassau and Suffolk counties among the top 10 most segregated areas in the country. Consequently, school districts show apartheid symptoms through the present day.[2]

SEGREGATION IN LONG ISLAND

The Long Island counties owed a great part of their post–World War II population growth to "white flight" from New York City. One cannot separate Adelphi from its surroundings. The reputation of Nassau and Suffolk for deep-rooted forms of racial segregation is well earned. Community distinctions common to most metropolitan areas have been starker in suburban Long Island. Despite its reputation as a prosperous suburban area, Long Island was not impervious to economic change. Housing and school ghettoization, asserts Long Island's ERASE Racism Initiative, "did not arise solely through economic forces," but with a more purposeful confinement to a few specific areas. Nevertheless, the global wealth and income differentiations witnessed in modern nations from the 1980s onward (which were "most pronounced in the United States" and evoked parallels with "some of the world's less-developed economies") reverberated locally, where middle and lower incomes tended to stagnate. The region had owed much to Cold War defense manufacturing, which was already in a state of decline in the 1980s. The *Long Island Index* placed a number of problems in context in 2010:

> There was a serpent in this garden: a narrowness of vision. . . . In the postwar boom, Long Island grew one community, one school district, one enterprise at a time—each one focused on its own needs. That worked all right when the economy was expanding and land was plentiful and cheap. But when times and conditions changed, we responded less nimbly and aggressively than other regions. As the defense industry shrank, and well-paying manufacturing jobs moved offshore, we had no regional strategy to replace them.[3]

Other key demographic changes occurred in the latter half of the twentieth century in the areas from which Adelphi University customarily drew most of its students. The region's foreign-born population rose from 7.6 to 14.4 percent between 1970 and 2000. That many of these newcomers were Latinos also contributed to the continuing prevalence of Catholicism among all denominations in Long Island. In East Hampton Township, the Latino population increased from five percent in 1990, to 15 percent in 2000, to 26 percent in 2010. Latino and African-American Long Islanders also impacted the political front, by helping to weaken the region's traditional Republican power. While slower and more limited, the region's other transformations paralleled certain long-term national population and economic trends: decline of the manufacturing sector; swaths of once vibrant downtowns unoccupied; slowing wage growth, if not stagnation; and an increase in food stamp recipients due to a greater number falling below the poverty line.[4]

The *New York Times* found "vicious anti-immigrant attitudes and violence" all too common in Long Island. Moreover, added the paper, "Long

Island's toxic reputation goes far beyond one village beset by racist gangs and corrupt policing." Lest it be thought that bias has been spontaneous, the Southern Poverty Law Center would charge the Suffolk County Police Department with a pattern of anti-Latino treatment, including targeting and harassing community members. While Latinos compose only 14 percent of Suffolk's population, they make up 50 percent of driving violation defendants. Long Island Latinos have been kidnapped by neo-Nazis and chased by vigilantes. Far right militia groups have been present and accounted for in local anti-Latino actions.[5]

Long Island began to witness spread-out residential poverty zones, with mounting evidence of a stark hunger problem. By 2010, fully a third of metropolitan New Yorkers under the poverty line (about $23,350 for a family of four at the time) resided in the suburbs around the city. Towns representing the widening sphere of people living below federal standards for a family of four included Nassau's Glen Cove and Suffolk's Brookhaven. These localities witnessed tenants squeezed into illegal and overcrowded apartments, laboring in the low-wage economy where jobs appear sporadically, seasonally, and temporarily. Wantagh, Seaford, Riverhead, New Cassel, and Long Island's well-vacationed East End all reported steady long-term increases in homelessness and hunger. Between 25 and 50 percent of high schoolers in East Hampton and Southampton qualified for discounted or free school lunches. Half the recipients of food aid on Long Island were employed, but unable to afford food without assistance. Of the latter, Tatiana, an Adelphi student born in Ecuador and living in Suffolk County, reflects: "We don't live in poverty and we don't live spectacularly. We live in between. . . . Honestly, we have just enough money to buy the groceries and pay the bills."[6]

Long Island's impoverished communities were hardly inert in the 1960s and 1970s. Rather they launched anti-segregation and anti-poverty efforts at the same time that civil rights movements expanded and spread through the South and the rest of the country. Many local demonstrations of support for Southern voting and integration campaigns took place. Nassau and Suffolk County endeavors included struggles to integrate volunteer fire departments and public schools, eradicate job discrimination, and combat police brutality. Many white high school students actively supported these activities. Locales in which people of color were numerous or a majority—Roosevelt, Hempstead, Freeport, Wyandanch, Central Islip, and Freeport—witnessed some of the most bitterly waged battles against inequalities. Demands to integrate Amityville, Massapequa, and Glen Cove schools were determined but unsuccessful.[7]

PRECURSORS OF GENERAL STUDIES

When Adelphi University began its General Studies Program in the 1980s, the contextual developments outlined above, and consequent discussions about relevant challenges in higher education, were already in progress. Some schools were already engaged in considering admission of students previously deemed unqualified or "at-risk freshmen." Hofstra's contemporaneous New College Division of Special Studies welcomed students whose "educational backgrounds require a more personalized approach to introductory college work," with combined verbal and math SAT marks between 800 and 900. Northeastern's Alternative Freshman-Year Program accepted applicants whose scores averaged a hundred points lower than Hofstra's freshmen.[8] Adelphi however stood by traditional exam benchmarks. But contrasted with first-year students at peer institutions, a university study noted in the 1990s, "a larger proportion of Adelphi freshmen came from working class, blue-collar backgrounds. The proportion of fathers who worked as skilled workers was higher at Adelphi, while the proportion of fathers working as business professionals, lawyers and physicians was higher nationally." Nearly half of Adelphi students were Catholic, though the majority had attended public high schools.[9]

As early as 1966, Adelphi showed signs of innovative thinking concerning the need of the academy to recognize and adapt to contextual change. It was in that year that professor of education Charles Raebeck argued to replace "traditional grading, marking, and testing practices" with "self-evaluation, self-planning, and independently arrived at individual and group projects." It was the first seed of General Studies.[10]

In 1973, Adelphi faculty members took another step by inaugurating the two-semester Program for the Independent Development through Education (PRIDE) for Adelphi freshmen. PRIDE sought students "who may not have necessarily met . . . the academic standards established by the university," and admitted them "on the basis of their potentiality for learning, regardless of their past academic histories." PRIDE admits ran the gamut of SAT scores and high school GPAs. Never a large program, it hosted a score of students each year during its brief existence in the mid-1970s. Young professors spearheaded the program, conducting four related courses in-house for PRIDE students, who were allowed a fifth class outside the fixed curriculum. Sociology, History, English, and Physics comprised the core, since these were the subjects taught by the most committed professors. Several of these elements would influence General Studies.[11]

PRIDE envisioned a "common bond of students and faculty in the program." After a year together, the students entered their majors. One faculty member described the students as "a kind of family," for "we try to keep them together to prevent a sudden disorientation." At several points, the teaching staff openly identified PRIDE as "an alternative to the present structured form of education." In fact, Adelphi offered the core classes solely on a pass/fail basis, ostensibly free of conventional measurements. "The competitive restraints of examinations and grading have been replaced by written evaluations," noted the university's *Delphian* newspaper. Such practices were already the norm at such schools as Ohio's Antioch and New York's Purchase campus, but assumed maverick dimensions at Adelphi. Professors endeavored to show PRIDE's affinity with other mind-opening movements of the time, particularly the women's movement. PRIDE's instructors drew a contrast with the rest of the university. "We're less concerned with what a student can verbalize or repeat on an exam, than with what as a person, they become," said one instructor. According to the student paper, PRIDE replaced "passive non-involvement" of students with "an active way of approaching knowledge." As late as 1984, an Adelphi vice-president mentioned PRIDE as an example of university support for "progressive forms of education," although the program was long gone by then.[12]

THE GERMINATION OF GENERAL STUDIES

PRIDE aside, Adelphi had traditionally featured college entrance examinations in its admissions criteria. But by the mid-1980s, some faculty members (not only those who had taught in PRIDE) had begun to raise questions about the use of the SAT. At a 1984 faculty meeting devoted to attrition and retention, professors indicated that high test scores did not necessarily presage scholarly prowess, suggesting that exam marks were inadequate criteria. Several instructors urged broader consideration of lower-scoring applicants who were deemed otherwise eligible, supplementing a small number of "experimental" admits. Such students might be provided tutoring, and their prospects evaluated at mid-semester. In evaluating entrants, "don't concentrate so much on SATs," said one professor—"look at overall performance." Another veteran instructor commented that, in calculating academic success, the test "doesn't help much"—in fact, "some schools are not even using SATs anymore." A handful of other Adelphi academics expressed these same sentiments.[13]

During the early to mid-1980s, Adelphi experienced a sharp drop in enrollment, losing many potential students to Hofstra, St. John's, Long Island University, and other similar-sized nearby private schools. In early 1985, provost Gerald Heeger came before the Faculty Senate citing evidence that "the enrollment is declining more rapidly than we can deal with," which he attributed to demographic and economic factors (the latter led to more students attending part-time). Determined to increase the university's numbers, he proposed establishing a General Studies Program to enlist freshmen ordinarily rejected under the school's traditional criteria. The ensuing discussion carefully assessed the risks, parameters, and conditions of matriculation for such a group.[14]

To be sure, the initiative to establish General Studies had originated not with Heeger, but with the branch of Adelphi known as University College, designed mainly for adult students taking evening courses. As Adelphi's most experimental school, University College had developed a number of interesting and unique formats, including business courses aimed at adults commuting to work on the Long Island Railroad. Heeger had been dean of University College. Now as provost, he moved to consult with new University College dean Glenn Zeitzer and Zeitzer's lieutenants (Alan Sadovnik, Dominick Cavallo, and Peter Katopes) before he addressed the faculty. Katopes recalls "we were not only mavericks at Adelphi; we were outliers generally." As administrators who did not belong to the regular faculty, they sought to make their mark. Collectively, General Studies was their idea. With this in hand, Heeger made his pitch.[15]

The decision to admit previously excluded freshmen raised many philosophical, social, and practical questions. Would programmatically accepting several hundred "experimental admits" have negative repercussions? Would the group be formally delineated from the other freshmen? Indeed, believing that SAT scores showed true college validity, some at Adelphi urged that lower scorers be segregated from the rest, if not banned as usual. They strongly believed that college entrance tests were the strongest indication of intelligence and, moreover, mental fitness. Behavioral difficulties, indiscipline, and unpredictability were thought to accompany, and be latent in, lower marks. Such concerns immediately rose to the surface in the introductory meetings, emphasizing potential damage to the university's academic culture. The provost first clarified the academic proximity of General Studies freshmen to the others: the university would isolate them from Adelphi's other units. The initial discussions proposed keeping General Studies students apart for two years. The students would not begin their majors or enter mainstream courses until they finished the program, and would essentially have nothing to do with the rest of the student body. In further deliberations, the faculty and administration roughly and quickly sketched a structure in provision of support services, first of all counseling, later twinned with tutoring.[16]

What kind of counselors would students, whose most common denominator was poor SAT scores, need? The first answer was to hire graduate students from Adelphi's Gordon F. Derner Institute for Advanced Psychological Studies to serve as counselors. This may well have indicated an assumption that lower testing connoted something emotionally distinct about the proposed new admits. Given the Derner students' career goals, it appeared to some that General Studies counseling would share a thin borderline with psychoanalysis. But the Faculty Senate was persuaded that otherwise the university would be prone to lower standards of conduct.[17]

The gestation of General Studies took only six weeks. The Admissions Office initially recommended a high school average of 77 and an average verbal-math total SAT score of 800 for potential students, hoping for 200 beneficiaries for the first entrance class, in the fall of 1985.[18] Ultimately, a faculty committee revised the minimum admission criteria to 600 on the SAT and a 75 high school average. In addition, the committee produced a program model, adopted in essence by the Faculty Senate, which stressed the priority of counseling. At all times, the committee recommended, "faculty and said students [should] be aware of their status." To boot, there would be "no institutional funding for these students." Minus the latter, the committee felt it essential that the new program include "the necessary support systems that have proven to be a necessity in the past to the success of students with special needs." The committee proposed one counselor for every fifty students; some counselors (drawn from both the Derner Institute and Adelphi's Social Work school) would attend to, as the committee put it, "educational matters," while others would deal with "psychosocial support." Furthermore, professors from diverse departments would serve the program as advisors. Thenceforth, General Studies would be the sole conduit for experimental, probationary admissions at Adelphi.[19]

Some fine-tuning and clarification were required before approval. One professor protested "that [the] program was conceived to get dollars, not to help students," an impression aided by its jumpstart origin. Would it be a two-year program or for freshmen only? Would it be open to transfer students? Might General Studies include a summer component? What curriculum would it follow? Who would teach? Who would hire? Would the all-too-common "faculty exploitation and pay differentials" of adjuncts prevail? Among the few unionized regular faculty in the world of private universities, Adelphi professors clearly wondered about their security if part-time professors in the new program were to proportionately replicate the national picture of adjuncts replacing full-timers at a fraction of the cost. Moreover, the impact of General Studies students eventually flowing into the mainstream of the general Adelphi population continued to agitate some faculty members who raised the specter of contagion. Assuming a freshman-sophomore General Studies structure, one professor made it plain: "We should consider the fact that our classes will be affected in two years. A large percentage of students won't ever get to be high caliber—in two years, standards will go down." The aforementioned equation of low test scores with "special needs" exemplified the attitude. Likewise, the withholding of institutional aid profoundly contradicted the avowal of support.[20]

Further discussion of the proposal envisioned General Studies as an interdisciplinary pre-major program (like Boston University's General

Studies), with courses fitting the core of required Humanities and Social Science general distribution credits taken by all students. The initial administrators assigned came out of the fields of History, Sociology of Education, and English; it was anticipated that they might be in a better position than other administrators to obtain the regular faculty's acceptance of program versions of humanities and social science courses. To an extent, their scholarly predilections followed the thinking of 1960s' education reformers, whose progressive, broad-minded philosophies became pivotal to the operation of the program. The University College associate dean at the time, Dominick Cavallo, rejected conservative principles as "the pervasive, irrational anti-communism that dominated American politics, stifled dissent at home, and inspired a nuclear arms race that threatened human survival." He pointed out, "the United States economy has been marked by gross disparities in wealth and large numbers of poor people." A key inspiration was Michael Katz, historian of education, who sought to show that American elites manipulated the school system to produce obedient and compliant adults. Katz and others, like Samuel Bowles and Herbert Gintis, argued that the educational system squelched initiative in favor of "order." Educational failure, wrote Katz, reflected the larger problem: "that young people do not have a worthy society in which to grow up."[21]

Alan Sadovnik, the assistant dean of University College and another liberal-minded scholar, was appointed to lead the program. In response to the aforementioned doubts about General Studies, he maintained that it would add qualified students to the university, not undermine its quality standards. He insisted that the coursework would be rigorous, to ensure that students who succeeded in General Studies would go on to thrive in the mainstream. "The basic idea is to provide these students intense support, academic and counseling, to develop their skills," explained Sadovnik. Of all the dangers, he warned presciently, the most important would be the "stigma problem" on campus. In advance of modern concepts of learning communities, he forecast for General Studies students a "sense of identity, but also a sense of community"—but the question of how to then integrate that community into a larger community of mainstream students still remained unanswered. Meanwhile, the faculty finally adopted the program in a one-year format (which fell under the supervision of an advisory committee of full-time professors drawn from diverse disciplines) and gave it a home within University College.[22]

Despite assurances that General Studies students would still receive counseling and tutoring services after mainstreaming, some faculty members were uneasy about the effect the integration would have on Adelphi's overall quality. Hence, the "rigor defense" to assuage faculty misgivings. "Rigor" itself became open to various interpretations: grading without embellishment was perhaps the best of these. Rigidity and inflexibility occupied the opposite end. However from the inception, different campus constituencies endowed General Studies with both progressive and conservative ingredients. In any case, Sadovnik rebutted the charge that the university would sink. Nevertheless, it was clear that putting a border around General Studies, while being an insulator, could also be a segregator.[23]

BUILDING THE FIRST GENERAL STUDIES CLASS

Debates over General Studies' value and practical implementation were ultimately foreshortened by the urgency of rapidly delivering a program to bolster recruitment. Although the inclination to challenge traditional notions of college-readiness and -worthiness surfaced amidst the program's formation, it was not the main reason General Studies had been established. Adelphi's newspaper placed the matter quite starkly: "The General Studies program was conceived . . . when the administration realized there was another large enrollment drop . . . [The] program is designed to bring in more students and therefore increase revenues."[24]

From the start, selection of General Studies students from the pool of applicants fell to the Office of Admissions, which announced 150 freshmen enrolled in fall semester 1985 (a fifth of the entire freshman class).[25] Associate Dean Dominick Cavallo disagreed with the Admissions Office-controlled selection process from the get-go. Devoid of academic training, Admissions staffers were entirely lacking in professional judgment of college qualifications and incapable of grasping the program's critique of the SATs, according to Cavallo. Choice of students should not be left to Adelphi novices who had never taught, he maintained, but rather, "Admissions [should] refer potential General Studies students to us, with the final decision regarding acceptance made by us." He continued: "The key issue it seems to me, is not who sends the letters but who accepts the students. I am not concerned with territoriality in regard to a bureaucratic process (stuffing envelopes), but with academic control." Empowering those working in the new program to make admissions decisions would exert academic sobriety over the "helter skelter origins of the Program."[26]

That General Studies might become hostage to "a 'flea market' approach" worried Cavallo and others. They believed it vital to chisel out a ramified working method whereby Adelphi would do more than take the students' money and forget about their prospects. To do this correctly demanded keeping the program's unconventional theory of college eligibility foremost, or at least at eye level with Adelphi's need for bodies. The in-house methodology paired well with the sense of purpose: critical, continuous communication would occur between the faculty, counselors, and tutors; teachers would consult one another about assignments and shared students; syllabi would be openly shared among the faculty. General Studies, in other words, would become a self-contained world.[27]

Cavallo believed the program was most significantly "a product of the democratization of both American society and higher education." In a letter to faculty, Cavallo outlined the kernel of a programmatic ethos: "the existence of a rigorous curriculum that mandates a considerable amount of reading and writing" and ongoing support services, for "otherwise we democratize for failure." There would be no remediation in the classroom. Counseling and tutoring would be connected to coursework—the former geared to improving academic performance, the latter focused on specific in-class work. The program's constituents, said Cavallo, would be in a circle.[28]

Exponents of General Studies insisted that the program be evaluated for meeting a clear and simple set of objectives: providing an undiluted education, while extending support services tied to curriculum to strengthen skills. Judge the program on this foundation, Dominick Cavallo urged, "rather than upon an extrinsic ideology of educational testing, measurements, etc., which are irrelevant to the Program's premises and immaterial . . . to the purposes of a truly higher education." General Studies, he wrote, was "not designed to transform high school graduates with profound (and perhaps structural) reading and writing deficiencies into model students." Rather, the "reasonably intelligent 'underachiever'" would remain the program's main target, a student "fully capable of doing college-level work if exposed to a properly designed academic/pedagogical program whose purpose is to simultaneously challenge and motivate."[29]

STAFFING AND FACULTY

Cavallo sensed a danger of "turning the tutorial program into a lab experience for grad students" who would not be able to engage in the "ongoing identification with the University, the Program, the staff, the faculty, the students." He therefore considered professionalization of the counseling and tutoring staff essential. The handful of full-time counselors first assembled for General Studies was inadequate. But years went by before the budget permitted expanding the ranks of the counselors and tutors beyond graduate students, part-time workers, and a few full-timers. And while the program's directors were clearly dissatisfied with the need to hire adjuncts, they understood that appointing lower-paid academics coincided with the program's money-making premise, and revenue would secure the program's survival. And, indeed, the revenue flowed: General Studies took in $875,000 in 1985, while paying out $220,000. In 1986, it made $1.3 million and spent $230,000. "Why was General Studies founded?" asked Cavallo bluntly in 1987: "For economic reasons. It has worked well in these terms; indeed, the University's current budget surplus is revenue generated by General Studies. Without General Studies, the University would have had severe deficits in 1985/1986, 1986/1987."[30]

No sooner was the program ratified then University College assistant dean Alan Sadovnik commenced to interview adjunct faculty candidates. He gave each a cogent summary of the program's plan and aim. To explain the counseling component, he mentioned possible psychological or emotional problems some of the incoming students might have. By fall semester 1985, Sadovnik had put together a faculty of more than thirty instructors—eight of them full-time Adelphi professors working on overload, including the chair of the History department and veterans in English and Sociology. More than a few of the adjuncts were already teaching at different schools or units of Adelphi.

To the satisfaction of Cavallo, the initial General Studies faculty included a handful of instructors who were inspired by his and others' underlying principles, rather than a paycheck (which was unconscionably low). One had been a pioneer of PRIDE, the General Studies forerunner. Another, the historian Robert Devlin, identified with the Left: he wore a belt buckle adorned with a hammer and sickle logo, and led Adelphi-sponsored tours of the Soviet Union. Three were published poets.

To accommodate the anticipated number of General Studies students, the university offered a core of courses roughly corresponding to generally required distribution basics—a total of thirty-five sections, including Critical Reading and Writing, Origins of Western Culture, Society and the Individual, and Communication and Critical Thinking, among others. Society and the Individual comprised introductory sociology; Western Culture matched the standard Western Civilization survey. English composition sections abounded. An Art History course rounded out the picture. In answer to the university's enrollment shortfall, twice-a-week time-slots not normally granted to freshmen courses were made abundantly available for all General Studies sections.

At the outset, the program took on one full-time and one part-time tutor, both with doctorates in English. Eight graduate students performed the rest of the tutoring duties (precisely as Cavallo feared, but could not avoid). The counseling end, though filled out by doctoral students from the university's Derner Institute for Advanced Psychological Studies (who earned six thousand dollars per academic year), benefited by a few permanent hires, in addition to a coordinator. Every General Studies student was assigned to one counselor and one tutor, with meeting intervals of one to two weeks. Tutors and counselors were obliged to keep careful records, which would have bearing on a student's future if she or he were to come up for possible dismissal by ending the first semester below 2.0. For those in this predicament, a grandly titled General Studies Committee on Academic Performance made the final determination in January of dismissal from Adelphi or probation for spring semester. Furthermore, the Committee's year-end session might put students below a 2.0 at year's end on continued probation for the sophomore year (when they were out of the program), obliging them to still see program counselors and tutors. The counseling and tutoring dimensions were intended to ensure that few fell into the category, hence the monthly meetings to assess students in jeopardy. From the start, it was clear that no other Adelphi bloc would be held to such rigorous standards, or evaluated with such scrutiny, as students in General Studies.[31]

NOTES

1. Nancy Rauch Douzinas, "What Every LI'er Should Know," January 2010, *Long Island Index*, https://lii-production.s3.amazonaws.com/lii-data/download/4c890d6d45548d83382191cb07e8562f/download_2010.01.WELISK.pdf. Accessed June 17, 2011.

2. Long Island Index, *At the Breaking Point? Taxation and Governance on Long Island: A Report Prepared for the Rauch Foundation*, 2005, Long Island Index, 3, 4; Amy Stuart Wells et al., *Why Boundaries Matter: A Study of Five Separate and Unequal Long Island School Districts*, 2009, 1, 2, 3; Amy Stuart Wells et al., *Divided We Fall: The Story of Unequal Suburban Schools 60 Years After Brown v. Board of Education*, The Center for Understanding Race and Education, Teachers College, Columbia University, May 2, 2014, 7; Michael Powell, "Bank Accused of Pushing Mortgage Deals on Blacks," *New York Times*, June 7, 2007, A16; Alan Richter, "Black and White on Long Island: Like Oil and Water," *New York Times*, June 16, 2002, LI1; Eric Schmitt, "Analysis of Census Finds Segregation Along With Diversity," *New York Times*, April 4, 2001, A15; Seth Forman, "Racial Composition of Long Island School Districts, 1991–2001: Change and Stagnation," *Opolis*, Vol. 1, No. 2 (2005), 17–31; Peter Eavis, "Study Strongly Links Baltimore Mortgage Denials to Race," *New York Times*, November 17, 2015, B3; Charlie Savage, "Wells Fargo Will Settle Mortgage Bias Charges," *New York Times*, July 12, 2012, B3; John Kucsera and Gary Orfield, *New York State's Extreme School Segregation: Inequality, Inaction, and a Damaged Future*, The Civil Rights Project, March 2014, 16–18, 128.

3. ERASE Initiative of the Long Island Community Foundation, *Racism and the Opportunity Divide on Long Island*, 2002, 11, 12, 22, 26; Peter Whoriskey, "With Executive Pay, Rich Pull Away From America," *Washington Post*, June 20, 2011, http://mobile.washingtonpost.com/c.jsp?item=http%3a%2f%2fwww.washingtonpost.com%2fbusiness%2feconomy%2fwith-executive-pay-rich-pull-away-from-rest-of-america%2f2011%2f06%2f13%2fAGKG9jaH_mobile.mobile&cid=578815&spf=1. Accessed June 21, 2011; Nancy Rauch Douzinas, "What Every LI'er Should Know," January 2010, *Long Island Index*, https://lii-production.s3.amazonaws.com/lii-data/download/4c890d6d45548d83382191cb07e8562f/download_2010.01.WELISK.pdf. Accessed June 17, 2011.

4. The Brookings Institution, Center on Urban and Metropolitan Policy, *The Rise of New Immigrant Gateways*, 2004, 26; Lee Hachaoorian, Hispanic Immigration on Long Island (Nassau and Suffolk County), Center for Urban Research, The Graduate Center, City University of New York (CUNY), 2007, http://www.urbanresearch.org/resources/latinos-on-long-island-nassau-and-suffolk-county. Accessed December 27, 2011; Liz Robins, "Latinos, in Class-Action Case, Accuse Suffolk County Police of Bias and Harassment," *New York Times*, April 30, 2015, A25; Mariano Torras and Curtis Skinner, *The Economic Impact of the Hispanic Population on Long Island*, New York, Horace Hagedorn Foundation, 2004; Jim Rutenberg, "Ethnicity, Class and Suicide Lead Hamptons School to Reach Out," *New York Times*, June 11, 2013, A20; Long Island Index, *Places to Grow: An Analysis of the Potential for Transit-Accessible Housing and Jobs in Long Island's Downtowns and Station Areas*, 2010, 7, 26–28; Long Island Index, *Long Island Index 2007*,

2007, 4, 6; Long Island Index, *Long Island Index 2004*, 2004, 29; "Struggling in the Suburbs," editorial, *New York Times*, July 7, 2012, SR10; James Mabli et al., *Hunger in America 2010: Local Report Prepared for Long Island Harvest and Long Island Cares*, Mathematica Policy Research, January 2010; Sam Roberts, "Suburbs' Share of Poor Has Grown Since 2000," *New York Times*, March 20, 2013, A19.

5. "The Candidates Get a New York Minute: Mr. Trump Reopens the Wounds of a Hate Crime," editorial, *New York Times*, April 9, 2016, A18; Carolyn Kormann, "Report Says Anti-Immigrant Atmosphere in Suffolk Country Fuels Violence," *27East*, September 15, 2009, http://www.27east.com/news/article.cfm/news/234053/Report-says-anti-immigrant-atmosphere-in-Suffolk-County-fuels-violence. Accessed January 27, 2015; Elissa Gootman, "Old Tensions Surface after Firebombing," *New York Times*, July 14, 2003, B3; Mary Reinholz, "A Harder Line in Farmingville," *New York Times*, June 8, 2003, 14LI.

6. Timothy Bolger, Homeless: More People Live on the Streets Amid Arctic Blasts than Stats Show," *Long Island Press*, February 1, 2014, http://www.longislandpress.com/2014/02/01/homeless-more-people-live-on-the-streets-amid-arctic-blasts-than-stats-show/. Accessed January 27, 2015; Laura Schofer, "Your Neighbors Are Hungry: Churches Step Up to Fill the Need in Wantagh and Seaford," *LI Herald*, November 26, 2014, http://www.liherald.com/stories/Your-neighbors-are-hungry,61104?content_source=&category_id=&search_filter=Poverty&event_mode=&event_ts_from=&list_type=&order_by=&order_sort=&content_class=&sub_type=&town_id. Accessed January 27, 2015; Shaye Weaver, "Amid Wealth and Comfort, Homelessness Persists on the East End," *27East*, December 2, 2104, http://www.27east.com/news/article.cfm/East-End/88338/Amid-Wealth-And-Comfort-Homelessness-Persists. Accessed January 27, 2015; Amanda M. Fairbanks, "Chronic Underemployment, High Poverty," *The East Hampton Star*, June 12, 2014, http://easthamptonstar.com/Education/2014612/Chronic-Underemployment-High-Poverty. Accessed January 27, 2015; Betsy Abraham, "Food Pantry Opens in New Cassel," *Westbury Times*, October 3, 2013, http://www.antonnews.com/westburytimes/news/33049-food-pantry-opens-in-new-cassel-.html. Accessed January 27, 2015; Joseph Pinciaro, "Amid Frigid Winters, Homeless Seek More Help from Shelters," *Riverhead News-Review*, February 27, 2014, http://riverheadnewsreview.timesreview.com/2014/02/52107/amid-frigid-winter-homeless-seek-more-help-from-shelters/. Accessed January 27, 2015; Tatiana B., "Independence," by permission of Tatiana B., Adelphi University, 2015.

7. Charles F. Howlett, "The Long Island Civil Rights Movement in the 1960s, Part Three: Militancy and Black Consciousness *Long Island Historical Journal*, Vol. 9, No. 2 (Spring 1997), 168–88.

8. Barry Fruchter to Dr. Dominick Cavallo, "Comparative Study, General Studies Programs: A Progress Report," September 27, 1989, General Studies Collection (GSC), Adelphi University.

9. Adelphi University Office of Research, Assessment, and Planning, *Results of the Cooperative Institutional Research Program (CIRP) Survey Fall 1991 to Fall 1998*, 2; Adelphi University Office of Research, Assessment and Planning, *Results of the Cooperative Institutional Research Program (CIRP) Survey Fall 2000 to Fall 2010*, April 2011, 19, 23.

10. Charles Raebeck, "Our Major Challenge: The Humanization of Education," *Adelphi Quarterly*, Summer 1966, 12.

11. "PRIDE: Providing an Alternative," *The Delphian*, November 21, 1973, 3; Salvatore Primeggia to author, July 5, 2016.

12. "PRIDE: Providing an Alternative," *The Delphian*, November 21, 1973, 3; Linda Dombrowski, "Women With A Cause," *The Delphian*, October 23, 1974, 15; Ana Barbu, "MAD About Satire," *Adelphi University Magazine*, Fall 2011, 54; Malcolm Howard, "Barbara E. Drotman," *The Delphian*, September 6, 1984, 3.

13. *Adelphi University Bulletin 1970-71: Undergraduate Programs of Study*, 1969, 23; *Minutes of the Faculty Senate*, October 29, 1984, GSC.

14. *Minutes of the Faculty Senate*, February 4, 1985, GSC.

15. Alan Sadovnik to author, August 20, 2015; Peter Katopes to author, August 13, 2015.

16. *Minutes of the Faculty Senate,* February 4, 1985, GSC.

17. *Minutes of the Faculty Senate,* February 4, 1985, GSC.

18. *Minutes of the Faculty Senate,* February 18, 1985, GSC.

19. Faculty Senate Admissions Committee, *Recommendations on General Studies Students,* March 15, 1985, GSC.

20. *Minutes of the Faculty Senate,* March 18, 1985, GSC; Frank, 278.

21. Dotterman, Executive Summary: General Studies Program Panel/Northeast Modern Language Association, March 22, 2013; Dominick Cavallo, *A Fiction of the Past: The Sixties in American History,* New York, 2001, 6-7; Michael B. Katz, *Class, Bureaucracy, and Schools: The Illusion of Educational Change in America,* New York, 1975; Samuel Bowles and Herbert Gintis, *Schooling in Capitalist America,* New York, 1976; Katz, "On Crisis in the Classroom," in Katz, ed., *Education in American History,* New York, 1973, 342. See also Alan R. Sadovnik, ed., *Knowledge & Pedagogy: The Sociology of Basil Bernstein,* Norwood, NJ. 1995; Glen Zeitzer, "The Fellowship of Reconciliation on the Eve of the Second World War: A Peace Organization Prepares," *Peace & Change,* Vol. 3, No. 2–3 (October 1975), 46–51; Peter J. Katopes, with Ruth Miller, "The Harlem Renaissance: Arna W. Bontemps, Countee Cullen, James Weldon Johnson, Claude McKay, and Jean Toomer," in M. Thomas Inge et al., eds., *Black American Writers: Bibliographical Essays, I: The Beginnings through the Harlem Renaissance and Langston Hughes,* New York, 1978.

22. Alan Sadovnik to author, August 20, 2015; *Minutes of the Faculty Senate,* March 18, 1985, GSC.

23. Dominick Cavallo to Dean Starkey, *"Mainstreaming" General Studies Students,* February 21, 1986, GSC; Malcolm Howard, "Faculty Approves General Studies Program for Fall," *The Delphian,* March 20, 1985, 1; Lynne B. Lubash, "General Studies Program Explained," *The Delphian,* April 24, 1985, 3; Howard, "Faculty Approves General Studies Program for Fall."

24. Malcolm Howard, "Faculty Approves General Studies Program for Fall," *The Delphian,* March 20, 1985, 1.

25. Brian O'Sullivan, "Freshman Enrollments Continue Climb," *The Delphian,* October 30, 1985, 1; "Enrollment Increase," *The Delphian,* September 19, 1985; John Donohue to David Newton, *General Studies Graduation Rates,* February 26, 1991, GSC.

26. Dom Cavallo to Provost Heeger, October 15, 1985, GSC.

27. Dom Cavallo to Provost Heeger, January 30, 1986, GSC; Dominick Cavallo to General Studies Faculty, Fall 1986, August 5, 1986, GSC.

28. Dominick Cavallo to Faculty Senate Evaluation Committee, *General Studies Program: Evaluation,* October 31, 1986, 2–4, GSC.

29. *Minutes of the Senate Advisory Committee on General Studies,* October 29, 1986, GSC; Senate Faculty Committee on General Studies Evaluation, *Questions,* December 12, 1986, GSC; Dominick Cavallo to Faculty Senate Evaluation Committee, *General Studies Program: Evaluation,* January 12, 1987, 2, GSC; Dominick Cavallo, *The General Studies Program: A Report on the 1985–1986 Academic Year,* July 1, 1986, 1, GSC.

30. Dominick Cavallo, *The General Studies Program: A Report on the 1985–1986 Academic Year,* July 1, 1986, 5, GSC; Dominick Cavallo to Faculty Senate Evaluation Committee, *General Studies Program: Evaluation,* October 31, 1986, 4–5, GSC; Dominick Cavallo to Professor Robert Edelstein, General Studies Budgets, December 19, 1986, GSC; Malcolm Howard, "Students Foot the Bill at Adelphi," *The Delphian,* February 26, 1986, 3; Juri Fiorello, "Admissions Rated," *The Delphian,* September 17, 1986, 3; Frank, 279; Dominick Cavallo to Faculty Senate Evaluation Committee, *General Studies Program: Evaluation,* January 12, 1987, 1, GSC.

31. Dominick Cavallo to Faculty Senate Evaluation Committee, *General Studies Program: Evaluation,* October 31, 1986, Appendix, GSC; Alan Sadovnik to Dom Cavallo, *Tutoring Line,* March 3, 1986, GSC; Deborah Robottom and Barry Fruchter to Dom

Cavallo, *2nd Year Faculty Referral Report*, November 12, 1986, GSC; Sally Baker to Dom Cavallo, *General Studies Committee on Academic Performance, Fall 1985*, February 12, 1986, GSC.

FIVE

The Program Defines Itself

Despite the straightforward pecuniary aim in establishing the program, General Studies enjoyed the coincidence of pedagogically nontraditional founders. They were universally dubious about quantitative definitions of college readiness. "My research in General Studies this year," wrote sociologist Alan Sadovnik in 1986, "as well as a substantial body of literature on freshman performance, refutes the neatness of the prediction model." Skepticism of test-based student profiles combined with doubts about the lecture method of instruction. Tolerance was shown for teaching outside the box by considering more student-centered course formats, with roundtable discussions, debates, and group presentations. Clearly, alternative and progressive educational method, like Adelphi's PRIDE program once embodied, motivated Sadovnik and his collaborators.[1]

General Studies spokespersons put a good deal of thought to furthering the entity as an experiment. However, the tendency to issue top-down edicts, as when determining how students would be evaluated for continuation or eviction, operated from the start as well. It gathered steam under Adelphi's new president, Peter Diamandopoulos, who came to the school at the time the program began in 1985. He promoted a strict hierarchy in academic administration, which filtered into Adelphi's schools and departments in his twelve years in office. In this regard, he openly declared "the industrial model" his lodestar in campus affairs.[2] Among other signs, the approach animated formal pronouncements and proliferation of regulations. Though General Studies implementers were aware of the bureaucratic impulse (to which the president expected verbal, if not applied, obeisance), they were to an extent caught up in it. Hence, the reiterated message that the General Studies students were lucky to be there, their feet held to the fire within "the experimental freshman General Studies Program."[3]

MODUS OPERANDI

The General Studies Program swam in digits. Faculty submitted mid-semester averages and final grades; counselors compiled the totals and aligned them with student high school grades and SAT scores. Exhaustive charts were issued four times a year (mid-semester and end of semester) and churned on for dozens of pages. Short individual assessments by professors attended the data—"Progress is slow but steady"; "Johnny lacks motivation, resulting in little effort"; "Mary's increased efforts have paid dividends this semester. She still needs to focus more, but is clearly on her way to being a successful student"—and tutors added paragraph-length synopses of each student's progress. Early Microsoft Excel enterprises spouted out graphs, occasionally accompanied by hand-drawn ones. Published results included all the aforementioned components, were circulated to other departments, and weighed several pounds.[4]

Retaining students in the new program depended on close monitoring. In 1985, Dominick Cavallo's guidelines spoke dispassionately of the endeavor "to salvage those willing and able to succeed at this institution." For the others (demonstrated by lackluster grades), probation or discharge from the university was a possibility. In the latter instance, a student could return in a year to Adelphi as a mainstreamed student after earning an overall "C" average somewhere else (a community college, for instance). Templates of letters to students soon covered all eventualities: high achievement, poor performance, excessive absences, probation, dismissal, and reversal of dismissal. Early warning communications rose in severity, first conveying caution, then raising the specter of true risk. Notices of severance, stamped with the dean's signature, delivered bad news quickly: "I am extremely sorry to notify you that your academic performance during the ______ Academic Year . . . warrants dismissal from the General Studies Program and Adelphi University." Revised wording appeared in 1991, opening with a voice of doom and heading downhill from there: "Unfortunately I must tell you that your academic performance during the ________ semester was so poor that it warrants your dismissal from the General Studies Program and Adelphi University."[5]

An extraordinarily structured regimen was instituted to assess grades, probations, and dismissals. The program came with an explicit warning against grade inflation; General Studies instructors were reminded of it constantly, in writing and in person. (General Studies GPAs settled around "C+" for the first five years, conforming in fact to students' high school records.)[6] The implication that General Studies faculty grading practices would be monitored contrasted sharply with marking outside the program. Undergraduates in the other departments of Adelphi maintained much higher averages than their peers in General Studies in the 1980s. Whether they were better students is a matter of conjecture. Within the program, differences emerged between the grading practices of adjuncts and full-time departmental professors initially teaching in it. In General Studies courses like Society and the Individual, Western Culture, and Art, the full-time faculty from Sociology, History, and Art awarded the highest grades.[7]

Their jobs more precarious, adjuncts may have felt the pressure to meet the mandated rigor, which the program wore upon its sleeve. They would be less inclined than full-timers to trust their grading acumen to academic freedom. Program administrators began assessing adjuncts in the classroom from the beginning, presenting written conclusions with recommendations for improvement. In-class observations came with the territory. To be sure, there were jaded or ineffective teachers among the adjuncts too. But with administrators constantly peering over their shoulder, even the most effective and enthusiastic might become weary. Paradoxically, an innovative program often operated in a top-down fashion.[8]

After fall semester 1985, the General Studies Committee on Academic Performance (eventually changed to the rather blunter "Dismissal Committee") scheduled five meetings in the dean's office to decide the fate of forty-six students with a below-C (2.0) average. The lengthy sessions eventually acquired the short-hand "dismissal meetings." The committee included the dean, the two assistant deans of University College for Academic Affairs and Administration, the coordinator of Counseling and Student Services, the General Studies tutors (part- and full-time), and each counselor in turn. The counselors, who had spent four days making initial recommendations for probation or dismissal to the University College dean based on their students' records, entered the meeting room one at a time to present recommendations on their designated students. Like witnesses in a trial, instructors (adjuncts too) would be asked to testify on student work. They waited in an outer room until called upon. Indeed, the atmosphere resembled a genuine council of inquiry.[9]

The participants voted to dismiss twelve of the forty-six students under 2.0. Discharged students had the right to schedule an "appeal" to the dean, which again an instructor might attend by special invitation. In this event, a parent might accompany the student. Although all sub-2.0 students were vulnerable to removal from Adelphi, committee decisions attempted to take each case individually, with final recommendations often turning upon whether a student had worked hard, gone to tutoring, and attended counseling.[10]

The program administrators obliged all teachers (except in math) to assign five papers per semester. The first would be a "summary" paper;

the second, a "critical reaction"; the third, a "compare and contrast," and so forth, with each paper more focused in scope and thicker with detail. Rewrites, if necessary, came at the discretion of the instructor. Dean Cavallo hoped that "a coordinated effort like this will reinforce the evaluative/learning outcomes . . . across the curriculum," encouraging "horizontally cohesive" and "vertically orchestrated" coursework, aided by the tutors and bolstered by the counselors outside the classroom. The imposed assignments, like other aspects of program format, appealed to the hierarchical purview of Adelphi's president Diamandopoulos. At the same time, the five papers provided a platform for development of critical thinking skills throughout the program and connected the courses, making General Studies a unified system.[11]

General Studies students were soon doing more classwork than Adelphi's mainstream freshmen. The workload made it impossible for program members on the school's NCAA teams to meet their academic priorities. An attempt to regulate athletic participation was generous, though short-lived: "Students admitted to the General Studies Program may not play on organized teams during their first semester. With the permission of the dean, they may be allowed to participate in such games in the spring semester if they have achieved an average of at least 3.0 during the fall semester." The spring-only option worked against the fall and winter athletes (cross country, basketball, soccer, indoor track) and in favor of the warm weather ones. But the declining grades among baseball playing General Studies students in the spring of 1986 drove the program to impose a complete ban on student participation with the intercollegiate squads, along with a prohibition on pledging sororities and fraternities. Students with athletic scholarships had to wait until their General Studies year ended before they could play.

The rule provoked sharp opposition from the Athletics Department and the Office of Admissions. General Studies already placed limits upon students: they took a lower number of credits than other freshmen, had appointments with tutors and counselors, could not declare majors until the end of the year, and shouldered additional work. How could this strict and rigorous program, set up to enlarge the freshman class, accomplish the goal of attracting students? But the blunt reasoning of Dean Cavallo (an occasional athlete himself) drove the ban: "To allow demonstrably underprepared students to play organized sports is simply unethical." The student had "one job: to read, write, study, think." Circumstances, wrote Cavallo, dictated that "kicking a spherical object around and between the legs of a fellow citizen may be an incandescent way to pass time between soap operas and sit-coms, but when that activity monopolizes fifteen hours per week of 'practice,'" along with travel time "and the mental energy consumed by imagining the sphere," prohibiting it became a no-brainer.[12]

THE STIGMA OF GENERAL STUDIES

For many students in General Studies, the stigma began the moment they opened their acceptance letters. The Office of Admissions informed them tactlessly, "we are pleased to be able to offer you admission to our new General Studies Program . . . designed especially for students whose high school records do not meet Adelphi's admissions standards." A second letter to students from the program itself soon followed, which contained a rather grudging greeting which emphasized the program's goal of "enabling underachieving high school graduates to become proficient university students."[13] Lukewarm letters of admission from Dominick Cavallo and his successor, David Newton, differed only slightly in tone. A late 1980s congratulatory message from Cavallo to new General Studies students put quotation marks around "Accepted" in informing them of admission. And while Cavallo and Newton went on to stress the advantages of the program, the accent placed upon subpar prior grades was not lost on recipients.[14]

Recipients pointed out that the negative undertone of the greeting letters contradicted the program's enlightened view of college eligibility. "I want to know who you think you are calling me an underachieving graduate," replied high school senior Tammy S. Student Jennifer M. declared, "because I did not do extremely well on the SATs doesn't make me an underachiever." Josephine S., the parent of a General Studies student, said the letter "emotionally upset my daughter." "Maybe you should be a little more selective in your choice of words," student Melanie C. insisted. Newton for one was moved by the protests, apologizing to students, and thanking them for having "sensitized me to a problem with our letter: a problem that will be corrected."[15]

While the program tried to fight notions of second-class Adelphi citizenship, it also catered to them to a degree. But when the students were out of the program and into their majors, program spokesmen spoke out against the prejudice they faced on campus. In 1986, the Faculty Senate reported bias by instructors in the majors against the former General Studies students who had advanced to sophomore status. Proud of the program, Dean Cavallo indignantly complained that some Adelphi professors made former General Studies students "feel conspicuous by identifying them as such in a classroom situation." In fact, he protested, the registrar appended a "designation code" to the names of General Studies alumni, after they had left the program and picked their majors, to signify their General Studies origins "for purposes of tracking and potential dismissal." It became an emblem worn by the student long after she or he finished the program. That the regular faculty, in overwhelmingly approving the General Studies Program the year before, had not been of one mind as to what it was, what it would do, or what to do with it, may explain the bias with which some regarded former General Studies students. By no means were the members of the Faculty Senate unanimous about the sum and substance of the SATs, for example. Moreover, the regular Adelphi faculty in the other departments and schools was about to experience attrition far in excess of national norms, which in fact approached the turnover rate of adjuncts. Attributable to an unstable, eventually proven corrupt, school presidential leadership, the fact that so many full-time instructors came and went made it that much harder for the regular faculty to understand General Studies.[16]

Beyond the designation code, program alumni now entering their majors as sophomores bore no distinguishing marks. As one faculty senator observed, they did not behave differently from other students, and were not distinct in their makeup or composition from the rest of the student body. "It was pointed out that statistically speaking the General Studies population is not uniquely different from the general campus student profile." But he wondered if the code designation itself produced distorted attitudes toward former General Studies students. In fact, faculty apprehensions about the potential damage of lower-scoring freshmen upon the whole fabric of Adelphi were still in play. One could not so easily forget the prior implications that behavioral issues went hand in hand with test deficiencies.[17]

Several Adelphi academic departments, however, were demonstrably friendlier to the new students entering the ranks in their second year. Enabled by a series of General Studies workshops on choosing a major, students found a warm welcome by the dean of the College of Arts & Sciences, who threw a reception for the students at the close of the first year of the program's existence. The Communications Department was especially forthcoming in consolidating former program students. Evidently a convinced supporter of the program, the chair declared: "The General Studies Program has helped these students reach their goal by giving these students the opportunity to prove their ability." A bit presciently in view of current emphasis on the first-year experience, he reflected on the value of what they had undergone: "The Freshman year is an important orientation towards your future communication studies and the first step in your college career."[18]

EARLY EVALUATIONS OF GENERAL STUDIES

But after one year, much of the jury was still out on General Studies. On this score, the Faculty Senate asked the program's counselors what kind of problems they encountered. Proponents of General Studies had gone to great lengths to place counseling in context, as part and parcel of the program's pedagogical formula, indissolubly tied to the integration of teaching and tutoring. Cavallo cautioned: "Once curricula issues and goals are sundered from the daily routines of counselors and tutors—in any educational setting—the former becomes therapy and the latter rather less than therapy." And while "therapy is fine," it did not explain the purpose of General Studies. Yet the Faculty Senate was still unclear about the basics of the program approved so quickly the year before: Who were the students? What was their makeup? What was their profile? Besides their low test scores, was anything else the matter with them?[19]

Perhaps catering to the implicit suggestion that the type of counseling required for such students would have to go well beyond helping pressured freshmen adjust to college, become better organized, and grow more confident, the General Studies counselors produced an exhaustive report on the purported psychological profile of the program's students. (The counselors may have expected to encounter distinct disturbances.) The report posited that General Studies students manifested disordered behaviors in an apparently more exacerbated form than other freshmen. General Studies students, it found, exhibited five types of problems—chief among them, immaturity. Some had a combination of emotional, learning, and cognitive problems. Dean Cavallo intervened before the report acquired momentum, warning the counselors to "avoid substitution of terminology for insight and correction," since "a person is more than his/her 'symptoms.'" However, the image of General Studies students as disturbed or otherwise "different" remained.[20]

Retention of General Studies students suffered substantially as a result of the university policy to not grant them financial aid. The students were ineligible for tuition discounts, and most importantly merit scholarships, which Adelphi based upon the SAT scores. For here was another contradiction in the school's establishment of the program: students were to pay full freight, even though low test scores reflected not college acumen, but more often lower economic status. General Studies administrators attempted to confront the issue, which would fester long, as soon as the Faculty Senate approved the program. Financial obstacles contributed to the withdrawal of thirty students between the fall and spring semesters of the program's inaugural year, no doubt sustaining images of stigma and exceptionalism. Of 150 students finishing fall semester 1994, 47 reported either inability to return or difficulty in obtaining loans and grants on the eve of the following spring. Needless to say, however successful overall, the program evolved in fits and starts because the motives that propelled it did not always mesh or begin from the same premise.[21]

Even after minimal "contingent institutional aid" was established for General Studies students, program advocates sought its wider application in vain. Their arguments were nevertheless pointed and vociferous: "Financing is the one major obstacle prospective GS students have to attending Adelphi," Cavallo had contended. Qualifying to study at the university, "many of them, however, simply cannot afford it." Said Cavallo, "To offer a low income student the opportunity to study at this institution, but then require that individual to assume a debt far in excess of anything realistically manageable, in terms of personal projected income or parental income, is cynical and counterproductive." The policy amounted to discrimination with a vengeance, said David Newton, who replaced Cavallo as University College dean in 1990—discrimination against General Studies students in general, and against working-class and minority students in particular, "who may find it increasingly difficult to use General Studies as an avenue of access to higher education." A supporter of civil rights and an administrator of Open Admissions at the City University of New York, Newton understood how race-based employment discrimination lowered parental income, savings, and net worth, and jeopardized minority enrollment. He correctly anticipated that Latino and African-American students would sink into particularly insidious college loan debt they could not repay.[22]

The university authorized an exhaustive student survey of the program after the first General Studies class of 1985–1986. While students in the program could not declare majors, they indicated a preference for business and the liberal arts over nursing, teaching, and social work. Although students diverged from early speculations that they would feel alienated from the rest of Adelphi, nearly a third detected problems of varying degree in how other Adelphi freshmen regarded them. Fifteen percent recorded being "angry" about being in a separate program, and 16 percent were "confused." A huge majority indicated that they had worked harder in General Studies than in high school, and, based on observations of their peers, had many more assignments than non-program freshmen.

The student profile did not vary from the traditional makeup of the freshman class. Thus, minorities constituted 30 percent of the initial General Studies group. Only in the 1990s did students of color begin to make up the majority of the program's entrants. Not unlike the broader Adelphi constituency, most parents of General Studies students had failed to complete college: some 12 percent of mothers and 20 percent of fathers had bachelor's degrees. Nearly three-quarters of the students held jobs while in school: of these, 35 percent worked at least eighteen hours per week.[23]

Two-thirds of the first class attended their counseling sessions twice a month as assigned. But the proportion making required weekly visits to their tutors was much lower. People who worked in the program attributed this to the stigma of tutorship and the erratic nature of tutoring employment, monopolized by graduate students. A post-year review declared that "the 'irregular' nature of these employees" impaired the tutoring experience—"notwithstanding the intelligence and diligence of tutors . . . the tutoring aspect of the Program, in short, must be stabilized." Even among students keeping counseling appointments, only half found the obligation useful, though responses varied according to whether counseling in general or the counselor in particular was the subject of inquiry. Moreover, a majority of the students reported meeting with their counselors less often in the spring than in the fall semester. The university's poll of General Studies students reflected the program's infancy and fluidity, the rapid transformation of an enrollment booster into an academic experience, and the built-in tensions in the latter process. But at the same time, the answers established a baseline against which future student feedback might be assessed. In a number of areas, student reactions have held steady since the program's origins.[24]

Thus, a student entering in 1989 reported wide-ranging explorations of potential majors with his counselor, which he would have been unlikely to experience outside General Studies, but the program nevertheless delayed his major: "I found it a hindrance to what I really wanted to do . . . because I could not take other classes. I enjoyed the [General Studies] classes I was put in, but by the end . . . I figured out what I wanted, but I was stuck in what I was put in." Yet despite the uneven acceptance of certain stipulations, others students came out strongly in favor of the General Studies Program. In 1987, a student ridiculed the notion that it was "a lower-paced academic program: it is not!" Campus-wide ignorance, he felt, perpetrated more injury than misinformation, for "the program is not recognized as one of Adelphi's major contributions." Presaging the fear that the program could just as easily "grow or die," he opined it was "worth saving."[25] Like-minded students made several attempts to form a General Studies Council, under program auspices, to engage in mutual support and contact between program alumni and each incoming class. But the immersive pull of the former students' new majors may have proved too relentless to permit the envisioned interaction and continuity, for their efforts failed.[26]

Whatever students felt about aspects of the program, few accepted the SATs as truly representative of their abilities. One of the university's highest-achieving General Studies alumnae, who had scored a combined 720 verbal-math total on the College Boards, scolded the test in no uncertain terms: "Low SAT scores have led me and others to feel stupid and rejected in a highly competitive and 'factually-based' society." Excelling in college convinced her of the test's "inability to determine human potential." The student found the exam devoid of creativity, and asked, "how can this test judge prospective college students fairly?"[27]

Students outside the program were not totally oblivious to its advantages. A student columnist remarked in 1988 that different General Studies classes were studying the same topic from diverse angles. Such a "coordinate approach" might lead students to "think deeply about a whole range of major issues." The discussion-based pedagogy favored by Alan Sadovnik and other program developers was evidently bearing fruit. Another student recounted that her program courses concentrated "on the expression of the mind and its reaction to what it is being exposed to, not just the meaningless retrieval of trivial facts that have no significance whatsoever on intellectual development." She went on:

> One of the things I have learned as a former General Studies student is that you do not need to recite data and quotes to prove your intellect. If you can find an inner meaning in what you learn, find how it relates to you, you will learn to make connections and therefore it will stay in your memory and contribute to your development. I would never have realized this under "uniform school."[28]

ACADEMIC RESULTS OF THE FIRST PERIOD

From the outset, General Studies organized annual celebrations for students earning at least a 3.0 GPA in their first semester. Nineteen of the first group of 157 received academic achievement awards the first time around. Seven placed on the Dean's List. Given the students' massive workload and the open cautions against grade inflation, University College dean Dominick Cavallo pronounced the award winners' achievement genuine because "we hit them with a cannon." One later General Studies student (who went on to take her master's at Northwestern University) remembered feeling as if she had written fifty-two papers "within one particular month." In fact, protagonists of General Studies often amplified the point that because their students were "in a tough program" their gains were more authentic. Speaking at another ceremony, Cavallo openly contrasted General Studies with academic programs "where narrow vocationalism dominates the pulse and pursestrings." General Studies had principles, Cavallo insisted: "We believe, to put it succinctly, that the higher education we deliver to our freshmen must not be compromised by the whims of the marketplace."[29]

Three years after the first group entered General Studies, the program solicited the reminiscences of its members still at Adelphi. Their impressions were positive—perhaps more so than when they were freshmen. Most credited the program with preparing them well for their remaining college years. A decisive majority called their program instructors more accessible than professors in their majors, and considered the counseling and tutoring helpful. However, only 35 percent of the first General Studies students graduated in four years.[30]

University College associate dean John Donohue observed contextually that leading college assessors deemed four-year graduation "a thing of the past for the vast majority of students." Figures adduced by Adelphi's own Office of Institutional Research in 1990 proved that merely 38 percent of the school's regularly admitted freshmen finished in four years, (logically undercutting assumptions of General Studies' "slower" students). The first generations of General Studies members attended Adelphi at a time when a multitude of national studies showed likewise.

National data showed four-year graduation rates under 40 percent, and five-year totals below 60 percent. A federal review of post-1965 countrywide tendencies reported that "students tend to stretch out their college experience more than they used to, taking fewer courses per semester or leaving college and returning." In short, "the average college student is taking longer to complete a degree." Donohue maintained that the early returns for General Studies were positive, considering that many students had been relatively uninspired in high school and ill-prepared for college, had been held to strict standards, and had experienced a mandatory curriculum faced by no other Adelphi freshmen. In the bigger picture, he wrote in 1991, "the actual and imminent graduation rates of General Studies students constitute an unmitigated triumph."[31]

Nevertheless, the program's usefulness would soon run up against the university's emphasis, under Peter Diamandopoulos, on elitist concepts of college. Backed by an array of funders from the far-right sector of academia, pressures upon other administrators to follow suit became more than some could live with, including Dominick Cavallo, who rather suddenly returned to the History Department in 1990. His resignation as dean of University College occurred at the same time as the departures of four peers from Adelphi. This was hardly a coincidence, reasoned the student newspaper, since "it seems that an inability to work with the administration may have contributed to some of the decisions to leave the university." (He hadn't actually left the university.) Resenting the domineering actions of those above them, the other General Studies advocates took steps to protect it from potential threat.[32]

PROFESSIONALIZATION OF FACULTY AND STAFF

More a professional administrator than a scholar, Cavallo's replacement, David Newton, was no less intrigued with the academic advantages of General Studies, which he bluntly called "socially redeeming." Newton began creating full-time General Studies instructor positions in the early 1990s. The idea stemmed from an innovation of Cavallo's that converted one of the adjunct professors into a full-time tutor, with benefits, on an administrative line paying $21,000. (He also taught on an adjunct basis.) With one stroke, "tutor" officially became "Tutor." Newton would later combine the tutoring and instructional capacities into a slightly more exalted job, called "Academic Tutor," on a single non-tenure track salary, thereby creating the nucleus of a professional teaching staff. Though this position too was deemed administrative, instruction was its only charge. Yet the university gave the line a code number signifying a specific managerial grade, which remained in effect until 2016. In previous service at the City University of New York Newton had envisioned a completely part-time teaching staff "inexpensive, expendable, and flexible enough to meet the changing needs of the city economy." While the full-time slots created by Newton were more expensive to Adelphi than part-time lines, they retained the model of employment flexibility imagined by him at CUNY. Ever-sensitive to racism and division, yet favoring newer forms of contingent faculty, Newton himself exemplified paradox in General Studies.[33]

Newton began to surround the adjuncts still teaching in the program with a full-time core of contingent scholars who both taught and tutored. As Academic Tutors, they worked more than regular faculty—all year, almost every day—insofar as they carried out their tutoring work outside the classroom, taught the same number of classes each semester, and came in during the summer and intercessions (though the program ran no courses in these intervals). They worked by the administrative, not academic, calendar. They earned a living wage and salary increases were pegged to annual administrative increments, trailing the pay upgrades accruing to promotion in professor rank. The program continued to be quite profitable, undergirded by the prevalence of this instructional system. Subject to dismissal without protection and ineligible for tenure or membership in the faculty union, the General Studies instructors nevertheless joined faculty committees, including key committees of the Faculty Senate, which solicited their participation. Still, program supporters wondered whether denying General Studies faculty status fed the image that both its students and instructors were substandard.[34]

The ranks of the program's part-time instructors began to thin. New full-time hires with PhDs joined General Studies through Human Resources administrative rules, with academic search undertones. By 1993, Newton could attribute part of the program's ongoing success to the fact that the "tutors are not 'peer tutors,' but rather highly skilled teachers in their own right, credentialed professionals with excellent writing skills." He presented the format into which tutoring had evolved, aided by the stabilization of the position: "In General Studies, students who come to a tutoring session must do the thinking." They were expected to come equipped with outlines, rough drafts, or at least preliminary thoughts on assignments, to discuss with the tutor, with whom they may also have been taking a class: "The tutor will then carefully guide them through the process of reviewing and revising an argument" and the hoped-for adoption of an "independent critical intellectual stance."[35]

Newton, whose PhD was in Psychology, also spoke on the contribution of full-time counselors. He nailed down their academic purpose: to help students "recognize personal problems that may interfere with academic success" and "prioritize their goals . . . and clarify strategies for success." Fundamentally, counseling sessions "are inappropriate for in-depth psychological treatment"—rather, "the central role of counselors is to create a sense of connection and place for students in relation to the college, to make students feel that, despite the demanding stance in the classroom, General Studies is also a program that values the individual, regardless of academic performance."[36]

To an extent, the sporadic student evaluations of General Studies counselors bore out Newton's exposition. That the counselor "was always on top with my concerns," "was always there to answer questions," or "always took the extra step" typified student reaction when elicited. Occasional complaints, with some historical antecedents, were also voiced: "I felt I was not given enough time in my sessions"; "I feel counseling should be at your leisure, not a mandatory meeting." But like Cavallo before him, Newton believed that General Studies, with its three-cornered structure—coursework, faculty tutoring, and academic counseling—marked an alternative to a watered-down, diffuse, introduction to college life. Inadequate preparation for college rendered the program necessary: "Broadly speaking," said Newton, "these students are victims of educational malpractice on the secondary school level," and "they are by no means unique."[37]

Simulating Cavallo, who pinpointed the "powerful complementarity" [sic] between students and "a staff of faculty-counselors-tutors who consistently express a common philosophy of education and a belief that diligence inside and outside the classroom can foster success," Newton underlined the importance of continuous interaction within General Studies: it was a learning community. While the program always had a preliminary procedure for "mainstreaming" students into their designated majors by the end of the freshman year, it was confined to written communications with department chairs and deans. Under Newton, departmental or professional school faculty were solicited to advise students poised to complete General Studies and ready to enter fields of study. General Studies counselors corresponded with the relevant professors in the spring semester, supplied the names of their new advisees, and informed them of credits already gained. Another battery of letters and forms emerged, and counselors provided program students with a full set of evidentiary documents to bring to their new advisors.[38]

EXPLORING POSSIBILITIES

Still, transitioning into the majors was not easy. The university coded program students as General Studies members until they graduated, but the code also labeled the students "undecided" until they declared a major with a new advisor. Some regular faculty undoubtedly found the prospect of brand new second-year majors, who had taken no courses in the field, off-putting or mysterious. This included professors who were sympathetic to the program. Some felt these students were behind the pace. The more detailed communication with a targeted group of departmental advisors aimed to overcome misinterpretation in the attitudes of

Adelphi faculty members to General Studies students, by developing an accessible sympathetic nucleus. Nevertheless, numerous students, upon leaving the program, indeed opted to wait until well into their sophomore year before declaring a major. In keeping with the program's vision, an Adelphi dean had to remind a doubter in the first year that "an Undecided Major at this point in the students' college career is just as valid" as a chosen major in Business, Education, or Art. General Studies would not force students to pick a path, but rather encourage them to explore all the possibilities out there.[39]

NOTES

1. Dom Cavallo to Provost Heeger, *General Studies: Academic Data, Fall 1985,* March 4, 1986, GSC; Alan Sadovnik to Dom Cavallo, *Experimental Admit Report,* February 25, 1986, GSC.
2. Peter Diamandopoulos to Joseph Ruocco, September 20, 1995, in author's possession, courtesy of Joseph Ruocco.
3. Daniel Rosenberg, "The Twilight of Reason: Neo-Conservatism and Corruption at Adelphi University, 1985–1997," *Left History,* Vol. 8, No. 2 (Spring 2003), 71; "New Administrators Enhance Adelphi Community," *Adelphi Record,* February 8, 1988, 2.
4. Meryl Shapiro to Sally Baker, assistant dean for Administration, *Grade Point Averages for Second Year Probation Students,* January 12, 1987, GSC; Barbara Shulman to Dr. Augusto Hacthoun, dean of Academic Attainment, *General Studies Sophomore Probation Students,* January 25, 1991, GSC.
5. Dominick Cavallo, *General Studies: Academic Dismissal,* October 21, 1985, GSC; Dominick Cavallo to C.A., June 11, 1986, GSC; Dominick Cavallo to ____, January 1989, GSC; David Newton to ____, January 1991, GSC.
6. Peter Katopes to the University College Faculty, *Making the Grades,* June 7, 1994, GSC; Dominick Cavallo, *The General Studies Program: A Report on Student Progress 1985–1990,* August 1990, 2, GSC; Meryl Shapiro to Dean Cavallo, *Final Grades,* February 12, 1988, GSC; *Fall 1994 Final Grades, General Studies Freshman Class,* GSC; Della Hudson-Tomlin to David Newton, *Spring 1996 Final Grades,* May 21, 1996, GSC; Della Hudson-Tomlin to David Newton, *Fall 1995 Final Grade Report,* January 2, 1996, GSC.
7. Howard Robinson, chairman, Faculty/Student Senate, *Study on Grading Practices in the Undergraduate Day Division,* 1970, 3, GSC; Dom Cavallo to Provost Heeger, *General Studies Academic Data,* Fall 1985, March 4, 1986, GSC.
8. John Donohue to Dean Cavallo, *General Studies Course GPA's: Averages by Instructor,* January 25, 1990, GSC.
9. Dominick Cavallo to Paul Doherty, acting athletic director, *General Studies Students/Athletic Participation,* February 2, 1986, GSC; Sally Baker to Dom Cavallo, *General Studies Committee on Academic Performance, Fall 1985,* February 12, 1986, GSC.
10. Sally Baker to Dom Cavallo, *General Studies Committee on Academic Performance, Fall 1985,* February 12, 1986, GSC; Barbara Gross to Dean Newton, *General Studies Committee on Academic Performance,* May 29, 1992, GSC; Barbara Gross to General Studies Staff, *Spring 1992 Dismissals,* May 27, 1992, GSC; *GS Dismissals 1994,* GSC; Della Hudson-Tomlin to Augusto Hacthoun, dean, *General Studies Reversals,* January 20, 1995, GSC.
11. Dominick Cavallo to General Studies Faculty, Fall 1986, August 5, 1986, GSC; Dominick Cavallo to Faculty Senate Evaluation Committee, *General Studies Program: Evaluation,* October 31, 1986, 5, GSC.
12. Dom Cavallo to Provost Heeger, *Sports and the Single Student,* January 21, 1986, GSC; Dominick Cavallo to Paul Doherty, acting athletic director, *General Studies Students/Athletic Participation,* February 2, 1986, GSC.

13. Ellen F. Hartigan, Director of Admissions, "Dear ___," circa 1986, GSC; Dominick Cavallo to Provost Heeger, *Experimental Admits/General Studies*, January 30, 1986, GSC; Dominick Cavallo to Acting Provost Zeitzer, *Experimental Admits and the General Studies Program*, January 27, 1987, GSC; David Newton, "Dear Student," January 1991, GSC.

14. David. Newton, "Dear Student," January 1991, GSC; Dominick Cavallo, "Dear Colleague," May 1990, GSC; Dominick Cavallo, "Dear 'Accepted' Student," circa 1988, GSC.

15. Tammy S., "Dear Mr. Newton," January 15, 1991, GSC; Josephine S., "David Newton, Phd," January 15, 1991, GSC; Melanie C., "Dear Mr. David Newton," January 11, 1991, GSC; David Newton to Melanie C., January 29, 1991, GSC.

16. *Minutes of the Senate Advisory Committee/General Studies Program*, October 29, 1986, GSC; Dominick Cavallo to Dean Starkey, College of Arts and Sciences, *"Mainstreaming" General Studies Students*, February 21, 1986, GSC; "Faculty Departures (retirements and terminations), new hires, and length of service by rank," tables supplied by Adelphi office of the American Association of University Professors to the Adelphi University Middle States Sub-Committee on Faculty and Curriculum, January 1998, courtesy Steve Goldberg, Department of Chemistry.

17. *Minutes of the Senate Advisory Committee/General Studies Program*, October 29, 1986, GSC.

18. "Choosing a Major," flyer, October 20, 1987, GSC; Dominick Cavallo to Dean Starkey, Arts & Sciences, *Arts/Sciences Advisement for General Studies Students*, April 11, 1986, GSC; Len Price to Dom Cavallo, September 17, 1986, GSC; Len Price, *Letter to 2nd Year General Studies Students*, September 23, 1986, GSC.

19. Senate Faculty Committee on General Studies Evaluation, *Questions*, December 12, 1986, GSC; Dominick Cavallo, *The General Studies Program: A Report on the 1985–1986 Academic Year*, July 1, 1986, 12-13, GSC.

20. Deborah Robottom to Dom Cavallo, *Categorization of Problems with General Studies Students*, December 19, 1986, GSC; Dom Cavallo to Deborah Robottom, *Categorization of General Studies Students*, January 12, 1987, GSC.

21. Alan Sadovnik and Sally Baker to Provost Heeger, *Adelphi Grant-in-Aid for General Studies Students*, May 7, 1985, GSC; Dom Cavallo to Provost Heeger, *General Studies*, February 3, 1986, GSC; *Spring Registration*, December 12, 1994, GSC.

22. Dominick Cavallo, *Prospective General Studies Student, Fall 1986*, April 7, 1986, GSC; John Donohue, associate dean, University College, to David Newton, dean, University College, *Financial Assistance for General Studies Students*, October 16, 1992, GSC; David Newton to Provost Webb, *Financial Aid and General Studies*, November 18, 1992; "The Widening Racial Scoring Gap on the SAT College Admissions Test," *The Journal of Blacks in Higher Education*, http://www.jbhe.com/features/49_college_admissions-test.html. Accessed August 9, 2011; "The Widening Racial Scoring Gap on SAT II Subject Tests," *The Journal of Blacks in Higher Education*, December 24, 2009, http://www.jbhe.com/latest/index122409_p.html. Accessed August 8, 2011; "Almost No Blacks at the Top of the ACT Scoring Pyramid," *The Journal of Blacks in Higher Education*, August 30, 2007, http://www.jbhe.com/latest/index083007.html. Accessed August 8, 2011; Martin Conroy, *Faded Dreams: The Politics and Economics of Race in America*, Cambridge, 1994; David A. Love, "Blacks and Latinos Will Suffer When the Student Debt Bubble Bursts," *LA Progressive*, August 28, 2011, http://www.laprogressive.com/education-reform/student-debt-bubble/?utm. Accessed August 30, 2011.

23. *General Studies Program Student Survey*, June 1986, 14, 15, 17, 21–22, 30, 94–95, 107, 122, 133.

24. Dominick Cavallo, *The General Studies Program: A Report on the 1985–1986 Academic Year*, July 1, 1986, 13, GSC; *General Studies Program Student Survey*, June 1986, 108, 110, 113–14, 116–18, 120, GSC; Dominick Cavallo, *The General Studies Program: A Report on the 1985–1986 Academic Year*, July 1, 1986, 14, GSC; Deborah Robottom to Dom Cavallo, *Categorization of Problems with General Studies Students*, December 19, 1986, GSC; Dom Cavallo to Deborah Robottom, *Categorization of General Studies Students*,

January 12, 1987, GSC; Della Hudson-Tomlin to David Newton, *General Studies Counselor Evaluation*, May 4, 1994, GSC.

25. Michael Sealing, Roving Reporter: Interview with Robert Hollweg," *The Delphian*, October 13, 1993, 4; Steve Pincus, Letter to the Editor, "General Studies Worth Saving," *The Delphian*, April 29, 1987.

26. "Academic Excellence Honored at Adelphi," *Adelphi Record*, March 21, 1988, 2; Dina Mirabile, "Plea for Campus Life Continues," *The Delphian*, April 20, 1988, 10; Dina Mirabile, "Candidates to Treasure," *The Delphian*, April 13, 1988, 5.

27. Dina Mirabile, "Gardner Redefines 'Smarts,'" *The Delphian*, October 19, 1988, 11.

28. Brian O'Sullivan, "Core Curriculum: Adelphi Must Experiment," *The Delphian*, May 4, 1988, 11; Dina Mirabile, "Gardner Redefines 'Smarts,'" *The Delphian*, October 19, 1988, 11.

29. Earlena Toole, "Success Begins with GS: Meredith Douglass '03," *General Studies Newsletter*, Spring 2007, 7; Meredith Douglass Morales, http://www.linkedin.com/in/meredithmorales. Accessed June 28, 2014; Mike Cunningham, "General Studies Students Honored," *The Delphian*, March 5, 1996, 3; "Academic Excellence Honored at Adelphi," *Adelphi Record*, March 21, 1988, 2.

30. John Donohue to David Newton, *General Studies Graduation Rates*, February 26, 1991, GSC; John Donohue to Dr. David Newton, *The Magic of Numbers: HEOP, General Studies, Apples, Oranges, and Mirrors*, December 14, 1990, GSC; John Donohue to Dean Cavallo, *Graduation Figures for General Studies Cohorts of 1985, 1986*, July 11, 1990, GSC.

31. John Donohue to David Newton, *General Studies Graduation Rates*, February 26, 1991, GSC; College for All? Is There Too Much Emphasis on Getting a 4-year College Degree? January 1999, http://www2.ed.gov/pubs/CollegeForAll/completion.html. Accessed July 14, 2011.

32. Daniel Rosenberg, "The Twilight of Reason: Neo-Conservatism and Corruption at Adelphi University, 1985–1997," *Left History*, Vol. 8, No. 2 (Spring 2003); Gary Jansen, "Resignations Plague Adelphi," *The Delphian*, February 11, 1990, 1.

33. Newt Davidson (Newton) to Governor Nelson Rockefeller, Confidential Memo, "The BHE-PSC Contract and Long-Range Planning for CUNY," September 12, 1973, courtesy the late David Newton.

34. Adelphi University Budget Office, *Adelphi University Tuition and Fee Income Report for 2011-2012*, November 9, 2012; Interview with Della Hudson-Tomlin, June 24, 2014, Garden City, NY.

35. David Newton, *Philosophy of General Studies*, Dean's Report, 1993, in Della Hudson-Tomlin, General Studies Statistics, October 31, 1994, 5, GSC; Dr. David Newton to Concerned Administrators and Faculty, *Pre-College Programs*, August 26, 1991, GSC; Peter Katopes to David Newton, *Curriculum for 1992 Pre-College Program*, February 3, 1992, GSC; Peter Katopes to David Newton, *Final Report—Summer Academy*, August 31, 1993, GSC; Peter Katopes to David Newton, *Final Report—Summer Academy*, August 31, 1994, GSC; Marianne Horan to Pam McClenagen, *Students Dorming for Summer Academy*, July 18, 1995, GSC.

36. Newton, *Philosophy of General Studies*, 5, GSC.

37. Della Hudson-Tomlin to David Newton, *General Studies Counselor Evaluation*, May 4, 1994, GSC; Newton, *Philosophy of General Studies*, 3, 5, GSC.

38. Dominick Cavallo, *The General Studies Program: A Report on Student Progress, 1985–1990*, August 1990, GSC; Barbara Shulman to Frank Friedman, Biology Department, *Undecided Major Advisement/General Studies Students*, March 27, 1991, GSC; Barbara Shulman to Devin Thornburgh, School of Education, *Undecided Major Advisement/General Studies Students*, March 27, 1991, GSC; Barbara Gross to Shirae Cho, Sociology Department, *Undecided Major Advisement/General Studies Students*, March 23, 1992, GSC; Barbara Gross to Judith Johnston, Anthropology Department, *Undecided Major Advisement/General Studies Students*, March 23, 1992, GSC.

39. Sally Baker to Martha Wissman, *General Studies Current Students, Spring 86*, January 30, 1986, GSC; Della Hudson-Tomlin to Augusto Hacthoun, *General Studies Change of Major*, May 9, 1995, GSC.

SIX

The Struggle for Survival

Through the first half of the 1990s, the developing and deteriorating presidency of Peter Diamandopoulos confounded the customary ebb and flow of recruitment. In an atmosphere of division, exemplified by hostility toward the school's workforce and its unions, along with contempt for Adelphi's student constituency, the freshman recruitment class declined sharply. There were 866 freshmen in 1991, 596 in 1992, and 462 in 1993, with greater losses yet to come. Here was a trend that the economic cycle could not explain. More than a third of Adelphi's fall 1991 incoming class did not return for the spring 1992 semester.[1]

Leading administration officials had praised General Studies during its first half-dozen years, citing high standards, hardworking instructors, and no-nonsense philosophy. They painted the program's instructional staff as quite the role model for the regular faculty. Diamandopoulos and others occasionally expressed admiration for the program's firmness, for apparently it resembled their own toughness: "You either produce or you leave," said his assistant Jeffrey Wallin, in praise of the General Studies ethic. General Studies coordinators dropped the word "rigor" at every opportunity, impressing the program's bona fides into the ears of higher-ups. Yet the people running General Studies never felt the program's place secure at Adelphi, and consequently brainstormed to solidify its position. Could the program (which alone on campus gave concentrated attention to the transition from high school) play a larger role in the university-wide freshman orientations?[2] Would it be possible to reheat the concept of General Studies as a two-year stint? In the face of the university's enrollment problems, Adelphi agreed to two offshoots of General Studies in the early 1990s, calculated to attract, consolidate, and retain students.

THE SUMMER ACADEMY

The Summer Academy, an intensive two-week program run by General Studies (but open to all arriving freshmen) began in 1991. It exemplified the "summer bridge" concept germinating around the nation. Originally conceived by Dominick Cavallo in 1989 as a month-long complement to orientation, the project took the florid tone of contemporary Adelphi to suggest the academy focus on writing, five to six hours a day: "Writing may . . . be the archetype of all non-speech/non-gesture modes of communication," wrote Cavallo, "Indeed putting mind to paper through a tool held by the hand and doing so within a medium that allows all who understand the language to partake of the writer's mind, renders writing the most commonly utilized and accessible of artistic and intellectual expression." The writing focus, submitted Cavallo, would foster "a creative merger between observer and observed that can be shared by observers of the writer's observations." Many such phrases wandered through the aims looking for a home. Yet in anticipation of a time when colleges would be forced to grapple comprehensively with the transition from high school, Cavallo's design included two significant iterations of General Studies premises. It would prioritize the effort to prepare freshmen for university life, as "most high school students are uncertain, and confused about, and perhaps emotionally ill-prepared for, the rigors, routines, and autonomy inherent in higher education . . . [And] if we make them feel at home before Fall, we may be able to elevate their chances for success and our chances of retaining them for more than one-two-three semesters." And secondly, Cavallo restated his doubts about standardized success indicators for the entire Adelphi freshmen class: "Wherever our current and prospective students reside on the SAT/high school average rainbow, they are at best pre-intelligent vis a vis a good university's expectations."[3]

The Summer Academy offered two sections of a credit-bearing course in Communication and Critical Thinking. Writing permeated the classes. At its height in 1991, the academy elicited the participation of thirty-nine students, the majority of whom went into General Studies the following fall. The academy classes, taught by two of the full-time General Studies instructors (academic tutors), were among the first on campus to employ computers in the writing process. A writing lab, special talks on time management, a presentation on plagiarism, a seminar on test-taking skills, along with movies and book discussions, rounded out the academy sessions. But as a recruiting instrument, the Summer Academy recorded diminishing returns. Despite thousands of brochures mailed out and scores of high school guidance counselors contacted, the academy drew twenty students in 1992, thirty in 1993, thirty-five in 1994, and a mere handful in 1995 and 1996, its final year.[4]

GENERAL STUDIES II

The second initiative of the early to mid-1990s took advantage of the fact that the university had first contemplated General Studies as a freshman-sophomore package before implementing it in a single year format. It called for "the reinstitution of General Studies as a two-year program," even though it had never actually operated as such. In support of extending the program, proponents reported that many former program students voluntarily visited their old professors, counselors, and tutors for consultations: continuity already inhered. In the wake of Faculty Senate approval, they added an extra year, but only for students who would have otherwise been dismissed or put on probation. Thus, the Committee on Academic Performance would consider for "General Studies II" students who finished the freshman year between 1.5 and 1.9, dismissing from the university anyone falling below the lower benchmark. Second-year General Studies students would still take several in-house sophomore level courses, fall and spring, but could also more freely work within their majors. The rationale recognized that while General Studies freshman were put to the test of "relentless intellectual rigor" without grade inflation, "a substantial number of these students are not being reached." In view of the university's enrollment shortage, "GS II" (as it was commonly called) recognized that, "with a bit more time, many students dismissed from General Studies could make successful students." Continuing under the aegis of the program, students would attend tutoring and counseling as before. Students whose cumulative GPAs did not surpass 1.79 in their sophomore fall semester or 2.0 when the year was done would be discharged.[5]

The program reserved the power to dismiss from the university, but accepted that students at 1.5 and up would remain. Sub-2.0 probation, formerly granted to those who showed potential enough to continue, became an officially structured second year. Some thirty-two members of the 1992–1993 cohort with freshman averages between 1.61 and 1.99 thus began GS II in fall 1993. The University College dean notified them by letter. A new set of missives thus joined the river of notes regularly emanating from General Studies.[6]

The in-house sophomore level courses designed for the new extension reflected concentrations in the humanities and social sciences, chiefly because these were the areas in which the assigned General Studies instructors were trained. The corresponding disciplinary departments in the College of Arts & Sciences reviewed and approved the courses as upper-level equivalents to their own. "Understanding and Analysis I: Science and Technology" was an anthropology course, with an imposing set of readings and questions. "Through the Prism of Language: Representations of American Culture in the Modern Age" challenged students to consider novels, short stories, and plays. Other weightily titled courses, such as "The Quest for Identity: Race, Ethnicity, Gender" and "The Myth of the Frontier," rounded out the selection. During this period, Adelphi's president and board produced a gust of phrase rarely heard in higher education, incorporated in the names given to many university classes and to different levels of the Core Curriculum. In fact, it is likely that GS II would never have been accepted by the higher administration without the course titles mentioned here.

GS II drew upon the level of Core classes meant for all the university's second and third-year enrollees: "Modes of Knowledge and Versions of Understanding." (The Core's senior classes were grouped together under "Values and Actions.")[7] The majority of General Studies II students moved on into the junior year. Students with freshman grade point averages closer to 1.5 tended not to do well in GS II, and were dismissed.[8] The university's policy of withholding grants-in-aid to General Studies students also applied to GS II.[9]

Although a number of students who continued with General Studies into their sophomore year subsequently entered prominent careers and professions (including academia), keeping students under the discipline of a certain regime for a second year did not always have positive effects, even if their responsibilities to the program were fewer than in freshman year. In less benign manifestations, General Studies sounded or felt like an ordeal, an uphill climb, and therefore negatively impacted certain students. Once again, a wall stood behind the door of academic opportunity, in fact one of the original traits of General Studies. Reiteration of the "rigor" principle, which could have draconian meaning beyond precise grading, might have made the second year as daunting as the first. It was difficult for some to sustain consistency and optimism when the light at the end of the tunnel was further away. But given the rumblings from Adelphi's helmsmen, program leaders hoped to use GS II and the Summer Academy to buttress General Studies.

PETER DIAMANDOPOULOS AND NEO-CONSERVATISM

Leaving aside the internal contradictions of the General Studies Program, it was as hurt by the impulsive character of President Diamandopoulos, the corruption of his trustees, and the strident neo-conservative proclivities of his backers as any other department or branch of Adelphi. Fits of shouting and threats became normal features of everyday business as the president and his supporters sought to make Adelphi the foremost standard-bearer of higher education and the embodiment of western values. The Academic Plan proclaimed Adelphi's mission to "rediscover the lost vision of higher education" and supply "fresh power to the all-but-abandoned idea of education as a preparation, achieved through the discipline of reason, for the quest of truth—about one's self, about one's world."[10]

The university's vaunted celestial destiny was a fantasyland impeding practical decisions, impairing admissions, and prohibiting sober assessment. People working in General Studies, from the University College dean on down, did not know what each year would bring, even in flush times; the same could be said for most sectors of the university. Volatility encouraged Adelphi's schools to contemplate survival by pilfering programs from each other, and the question arose of whether General Studies would stay in University College or be consigned to the School of Education or the School of Business. In any case, the program seemed up for grabs. Under the circumstances, General Studies, which depended on understanding and stable attention to the complexities of its task, was not secure. The Diamandopoulos administration never seemed at peace with it, GS II and the Summer Academy notwithstanding.

In retrospect, the administrators who led General Studies in the first decade served the program by chance: Dominick Cavallo was a historian assuredly influenced by the more "inclusive" approaches of the 1960s; Alan Sadovnik was a scholar with strong antipathy for elitism in education; David Newton was a professional bureaucrat who nevertheless favored liberal New Deal-type programs to address exclusions and extend opportunities. As much as they could stomach, Newton and Cavallo swam with the more authoritative Adelphi currents as needed: in campus labor disputes, for example. Yet they also pursued aims closer to their own leanings.[11]

A review of the first six General Studies graduation cohorts outlined the essential benefit of the program. Some 42 percent of the graduates who first entered through General Studies in 1985 and remained at the university would not have attended Adelphi under traditional SAT considerations; 32 percent of graduates who stayed at Adelphi after beginning in the program in 1986 would also have been rejected. More than half of the graduates from the surviving 1990 group would not have been considered for admission, but for the existence of General Studies. Thus, students deemed by standardized measures devoid of merit—such as the cohort of 1987, which brought an SAT average total of 788—found a place at Adelphi through General Studies. General Studies thus accomplished more than the expansion of Adelphi enrollment, because it helped redefine the criteria of a diligent student.[12]

Such notions were far from the minds and policies of the people running Adelphi between the mid-1980s and mid-1990s. To them, General Studies was a cipher, at best a lever for elevating enrollments, but certainly not their definition of a success story. On the moral and theoretical level, the Diamandopoulos-era administration, trustees, and supporters harked back to the most conservative educational premises. They were unfriendly at best to the emergence of nontraditional areas and methodologies of study, like the ones favored by Cavallo and Sadovnik. At Diamandopoulos' inaugural in 1986, Boston University's John Silber urged a return to "the authority of traditional cultural forms" in academia, while condemning the "drift" under whose force "cherished beliefs about the nature of individuals, groups, and nations were abandoned."[13]

University trustees, guest speakers, and commencement laureates during this period held solid neo-conservative credentials, greatly influencing and shaping Adelphi policy. Conservative foundations and think tanks, like the Olin Foundation and the Hudson Institute, readily stocked Adelphi with administrators, trustees, and guest faculty. Adelphi trustee William Simon, head of several foundations, former Nixon administration member, and funder of numerous Adelphi visiting professors, was a case in point. His 1992 Adelphi lecture on the greatness of Christopher Columbus emphasized the man's "entrepreneurial skills," which introduced "a nation of doers." The result of such initiative was "the greatest individual freedom ever known to man." Rightwing guru William F. Buckley spoke along the same lines at Adelphi a year later: group interests and group thinking had spurred crime, unemployment, and poverty, which only individualism and a "reaffirmation of marriage" could solve. Private initiative and the private sector ought to be looked upon for examples of remedy, for "the individual . . . can accomplish more than a collective." Likeminded Irving Kristol, well-known editor of *The Public Interest*, punctuated his appearance at the school in 1994 with an invocation to the contemporary poor to follow the industrious example of their Eastern and Southern European immigrant forebears, who had indeed worked their way up. Social programs on the other hand made people "dependent, weak, and demoralized." Kristol, like Buckley and Simon, spoke on the occasion of Columbus Day, underscoring the frontal assault of their messages.[14]

The message dovetailed with another favored impulse of the Adelphi milieu, a return to classical concepts of education. Presented by Diamandopoulos as a daring thrust, it more resembled a throwback to convention. Rejecting new pedagogies and global changes (like the emergence of independent African states), it emphasized the long-taught view that the West had produced the most important virtues and practices in modern culture. The most significant contribution of the West to contemporary society, according to the administration's Core Curriculum, was in fact "individualism," *the* driving force of modernity. Espousal of individualism took extreme forms under Diamandopoulos, ranging from philosophical abstraction to concrete practice. A pronounced libertarianism came into vogue, partly embodied in Diamandopoulos' devil-may-care style. But its more serious incarnation appeared in the ethic, espoused from platform to classroom, that individual, not group, effort and self-enrichment form the soul of existence.[15]

Elevating this principle to an active moral code, the university's leaders and trustees attracted the scrutiny of the New York Attorney General and the Board of Regents in the 1990s. Both agencies uncovered numerous transgressions against nonprofit statute and widely observed, fundamentally accepted moral expectations. Affronted by the growing cases against them, Adelphi spokesmen attacked pending investigations as another manifestation of government interference in individual realms, resembling communism.[16] Yet the adduced evidence of plunder and misuse of funds, improper decisions, secrecy, plotting, extravagance, and pampering confirmed the distorted mind-set and mode of conduct, however excused by sophisticated argument and political bent. The revealed evidential sources do not come close to representing what was at play.[17]

In Diamandopoulos, the administrators who served him loyally, the trustees who enriched themselves, and the extreme right-wingers who circled the wagons, Adelphi's true constituents confronted formidable foes. The president and his supporters had little time or patience for serious educational work, backward or otherwise. Genuine effort toward improving Adelphi's programs and schools, and serving its students, could not reasonably advance when a different agenda lit the path. To be sure, neo-conservative ends fortified the energy with which the Adelphi leadership asserted and justified itself. Their forceful espousal of a narrow individualism as alpha and omega of being came from the heart.

GENERAL STUDIES UNDER ATTACK

The corruption and political narrowness in the Diamandopoulos administration buttressed doubts about whether such a regime could successfully carry out legitimate tasks in higher education. Subject of course to pressure from faculty and students, as long as they were recognized, compromise might be reached and solutions hammered out. But temporary easing of tension and meeting of minds always yielded to renewed conflict, the emergence of new obstacles, seemingly bound to arise. Erupting initially from the inner chamber, ostensibly saner minds put the tantrums into rational policy form. Programs like General Studies, which proposed an expanded idea of a learning community, could not possibly have been in safe hands under the circumstances. Nor could the "socially redeeming" nature of General Studies, which gave equal attention to the individual and the collective, be expected to win lasting friendship from such power brokers in these conditions.

A decade's worth of General Studies representatives appeared annually before the provost, trustees, and Diamandopoulos, to respond to suspicions about the program's premises. After apparent accommodation, the administration expressed greater reservations, subjecting the program to further scrutiny, even as more than a thousand students passed through it successfully. The faculty and staff, and eventually the students, of the program might realize that the academic trajectory evolved over the year, that positive outcomes were not commonly immediate. But the spirit of evolution was not on Adelphi's schedule. By standard criteria, the numbers put up by General Studies in its first ten years—an SAT mean of 752, high school GPA of 2.19, and first-year college averages of 2.24—were disappointing to administrators. As it came under mounting pressure, General Studies tried to prove how lower-performing but talented students might succeed in college through an initially structured approach, but the numbers were not music to the ears of administrators.[18]

To buttress the program's purpose, General Studies advocates then adduced five- and ten-year charts to show that more than 1,600 students had enrolled in General Studies from 1985 to 1996, of which a thousand finished their initial year in good standing. Nearly four hundred graduated from the university, others departing to finish their degrees elsewhere. Although the graduation rate measures the percentage of the original incoming class that completes degrees, the University College assistant dean Peter Katopes sharply pointed out that this literal calculation was "somewhat misleading" since it "does not take into account [General Studies] students in good standing who transfer from Adelphi and complete their studies elsewhere." The four-year Adelphi graduation rate of the persisting four hundred was 78 percent; taking a fifth year into account, it reached 94 percent. Program freshmen left the university (dismissed, transferred, discontinued) during the first year at a faster clip than any others, but remaining program alumni graduated at rates at the very least comparable to Adelphi's other continuing former freshmen. Chapters 8 and 9 of the present work confirm Katopes' latter point.[19]

But the mind-set at the top, despite allusions to the program's admirable rigor, was neither sophisticated nor patient. Although a General Studies cohort was likely to finish the spring semester with a higher overall GPA than in the previous fall, the heavy concentrations in the C to B- range discouraged higher administrators from boosting the program with conviction. Indeed, outcomes such as those of the class of 1993–1994, in which 62 percent finished at C or above in the fall and 74 percent did so in the spring, took a sense of transition to grasp.[20]

All the while, the university's enrollment suffered. But some administrators honed in on the greater lag in General Studies graduation rates and the lower retention, still finding the program's acceptance of lower-scoring students hard to swallow. They prompted programmatic rebuttals in the mid-1990s, which revisited one of the original observations about General Studies students: that their high school GPAs foretold academic achievement better than their college entrance scores. Assessing the figures anew, a General Studies report to the administration on 1993–1994 grades adamantly repudiated a link between tests and college success. According to the report, "the overall motivation of a student and . . . the student's ability to take advantage of the services we provide" determined their progress. Challenging the doubters, program advocates stressed that student achievement embraces factors such as motivation and maturity, which cannot be enumerated. Regarding conventional success predictors, the General Studies student "defies this type of quantification."[21]

University College dean David Newton identified the style of work responsible for the encouraging results within General Studies: the "incessant flow of information, insight, assistance, guidance, complaints, problems, solutions."[22] But Adelphi officials became more concerned since program students made up an increasing proportion of the freshman class so essential to university health. While phrases like "underprepared" or "underserved" first typified comments of the president and other spokesmen about General Studies students, wording and thinking turned sour in the early 1990s, even as the program facilitated freshman recruitment. Peter Katopes' frank recollection summarizes the administrative bias: "General Studies didn't square with Diamandopoulos' view of an elite institution." Its constituents "were the low-lives, the underachievers." General Studies entrants were bluntly termed "undistinguished," although their membership in the freshman class was ironically indispensable to enrollment.[23]

UNDERMINING THE PROGRAM

Although notices for General Studies were placed in periodicals throughout the late 1980s, by 1990 the university stopped publicizing the program altogether. Like the refusal to grant institutional aid, the reluctance to advertise expressed the university leadership's reservations. Program faculty and staff suspected that keeping the program out of the public eye communicated embarrassment or a hint of secrecy. Their pleas and suggestions elicited feeble reply, and then silence. Their recommendations for ads in local papers, including non-English language publications, drew no response. A suggested campaign to meet with guidance counselors and students in local high schools never materialized. A proposal by University College assistant dean John Donahue to host a conference on "The Underachiever in Higher Education" found no takers among leading university officials. Donahue sensed that the school's foremost spokesmen interpreted General Studies as "Adelphi watered down for the mediocre," and thus treated it as "Adelphi's step-child program." And yet, General Studies remained remarkably lucrative for the university.[24]

The university administration had tinkered with General Studies, prior to GS II. Enrollments beyond the capacity of the program were at times encouraged, despite lip service to academic integrity and the administration's deep-seated, upper-level allegiance to elitist notions. The head count in fall 1990 was 211. Annual fluctuation presupposed labor flexibility in staffing courses, antithetical to programmatic stability. Numbers flowed and ebbed—152 in 1989, 211 in 1990, 171 in 1991, 149 in 1992—but high officers of the university occasionally readmitted students who were dismissed by the program for academic reasons, to the chagrin of General Studies faculty and counselors. In a debate that likely forecast his eventual resignation as dean, Dominick Cavallo protested that only the program's staff should properly determine its policy: there were "program-specific rules and guidelines," which the institution must acknowledge. To do otherwise "is playing a dangerous game indeed."[25]

While these instances of interference by university administrators were rare at first, they swelled into concerted pressure on the program not to dismiss its failing students, thus to ignore "rigor."[26] Adelphi policy makers managed to twin the elitist notion of higher education with the retention of every warm body. The fall 1990 class evidenced the most problematic example of university recruitment troubles dictating General Studies policy. With more than half of the original 211 students finishing the fall semester below "C," the General Studies Committee on Academic Performance dismissed fifty-four and place seventy-one on probation for spring 1991. Within two days, the president's office, long consumed with Adelphi's academic reputation, ironically charged the program with being "vindictive" and "hasty." General Studies administrator John Donohue defended the "rigorous policy concerning the General Studies dismissals" as indispensable.[27]

The matter was not laid to rest. The Admissions Office demanded that General Studies explain every one of the fifty-four dismissal decisions. Donohue complied by submitting documentation from the program's instructors and counselors. But urged on by the leading school officials, the Admissions Office unilaterally restored fifteen dismissed students, mainstreaming them into the freshman class in spring 1991. Ten actually returned, of whom only one finished the academic year above a 2.0, despite in-progress Admissions reports that all "were doing splendidly." The episode left a bad taste, made worse by further repudiations of program decisions the following summer. Not normally one to bite the hand that fed him, dean David Newton declared himself "astonished and distressed" when a student finishing the academic year with a 1.47 was dismissed by the program but pushed into sophomore year by the Office of Academic Attainment: "Standards do exist in the General Studies Program and neither the faculty nor I, as Dean, have any intention of seeing them vitiated." He wondered who has "the authority to countermand a judgment on the part of the General Studies faculty" and, suggesting that the impetus to undermine program policy came from above, he warned "this feckless approach to admissions and inexplicable assumption of authority endangers the entire University."[28]

After the spring 1991 semester, the General Studies Committee on Academic voted to dismiss another twenty students below 2.0 from Adelphi. An explanation by a program statistician pointed out that the "high number of dismissals in the 1990/91 cohort reflects a relaxation of admissions standards for the program, in which students with VSATs [verbal SATs] lower than 250 were admitted in larger than numbers than [in] previous years." Program staff members charged the Admissions office with bending standards to fill the classrooms. General Studies had always questioned the SATs. But program instructors nevertheless suspected that a score below 250 on the verbal component signified a problem: they credited the standardized exam to this extent. Without giving credence to conventional SAT implications about college learning, General Studies personnel believed that the Admissions Office had diluted the criteria on explicit instruction from above.[29]

According to the 1990–1991 General Studies report of final grades and dismissals, 83 percent of the students with SAT verbals below 300 were dismissed. But other figures give pause, for the highest achieving student in the program in 1991, who went on to graduate with Latin honors in three—not four—years, had attained only 320 on the verbal component of the SATs. The student with the second highest freshman grade point average in 1991 (who later became a lawyer) had a 380. Others who met or exceeded a freshman GPA of 3.0 had generally averaged between the high 300s and the mid-400s on the verbal SAT. Students finishing the first Adelphi year in the middle GPA range showed slightly lower SAT verbal results overall, one (who went on to graduate) as low as 220. Two groups vulnerable to dismissal, ending the year between 1.0 and 1.49, and 1.5 and 1.9, respectively, evidenced virtually identical SAT verbal profiles. In turn, their verbal average was not much below those who earned freshman GPAs between 2.0 and 2.7. However, the students who finished the freshman year below 1.0 clearly recorded lower SAT verbal scores than these two groups.[30]

The following year, the Office of Admissions admitted a General Studies cohort whose SAT verbal averaged 320. On the eve of fall semester 1991, a counselor perused the incoming records and warned: "This appears to be one of the weakest groups we've had in the General Studies Program with close to one third of the students beneath 300 SAT Verbal. This indicates that a large group of students are entering the program with poor written and comprehensive skills." In light of the previous year's conflict with Admissions, stated the counselor, "it is safe to assume that we will not be allowed to dismiss" the students warranting severance from the program.[31]

The semester bore out her expectations. More than half the 171 students attained Adelphi fall GPAs below 2.0. This included three-quarters of program entrants with sub-300 SAT verbal scores. Wrestling with the possibilities, she projected thirty dismissals and twice that number on probation in the spring. There were not enough hours in the week, she feared, to be able to handle the weekly appointments of probationary students and the biweekly rendezvous with the rest. Yet she also predicted a precipitous attrition of the large pool of students who should not have been admitted. And indeed, General Studies dwindled from 171 students in September 1991 to 123 by May 1992. By semester's end however, the remaining students had acquitted themselves, belying some of the dire forecasts. Most of the survivors of the beginning 171 completed their freshman year above 2.0.[32]

Questionable admissions decisions precipitated similar concerns in the year that followed. When fall semester 1992 was over and the Committee on Academic Performance reviewed the returns, forty-eight students had finished under 2.0. In response to higher pressures to retain all of these students, the committee agreed in nearly every case, namely by eschewing past practice and criteria. Bending to stronger winds, General Studies advanced members of the cohort into the second semester holding fall GPAs of .61, .99, .46, and .30. The committee voted to dismiss only a handful. Upon appeal, four dismissals were reversed, benefiting individuals whose closing fall semester averages were .93, .76, and .84. The policy stood in stark contrast with the exacting grading expected in General Studies.[33]

Adelphi's leaders wielded General Studies as a lever, first to elevate total freshman turnout, then suddenly to cut its percentage of the whole. Stuck in the mix were impulsive and contradictory messages about the university's direction and reputation. Flights of fancy, underscored by the approval of the allegedly levelheaded, had become arbitrarily imposed plan. General Studies was clearly a moneymaker, evidenced in the undiscounted tuition of the students and the miniscule pay and colossal workloads of the counselors. Still listed as administrators, the program's full-time instructors taught more classes than the unionized faculty, but earned significantly less. Decision makers may have used General Studies to boost numbers, but were paradoxically sensitive about having too many program students within the university, which apparently undermined the institution's status as a prestigious private school. A large General Studies cohort could be considered both necessary and distasteful.

RACE AND DIVISION

The increasing diversity of General Studies brought in a rich multicultural Adelphi contingent every year. Program students represented a broader range of races, ethnicities, and religions than the rest of the freshman class. There was however an Adelphi program specifically devoted to serving a large number of African-American and Latino students, among others: there were also a few white students. The university had operated the Higher Education Opportunity Program (HEOP) for several years, to help facilitate minority enrollment. HEOP had no connection to General Studies, though the academic profiles were similar. Both programs accepted high school grades lower than the Adelphi admissions standard. HEOP students were eligible for grants-in-aid: General Studies students were not. But with Adelphi's enrollment struggling in the early 90s, high administrators decided to eliminate HEOP, thus saving the university the funds dedicated to financial aid and personnel. Now, potential HEOP beneficiaries were counseled to seek admission through General Studies.[34]

Besieged with minority students' criticism, Peter Diamandopoulos cajoled and patronized, but did not manifest sensitivity. He boasted of his thick skin and was amply defended by his appointees and trustees. "I owe you nothing," he once told African-American students. "I didn't have slaves." Diamandopoulos was no friend of dialogue, particularly with minority students. "My record was brutal with the blacks," he admitted.[35]

The president's message was not lost on dean David Newton, then in charge of General Studies, whose sympathies had been with the Civil Rights Movement, and who now called attention to the discriminatory thrust of these new pronouncements. While General Studies was the most racially diverse undergraduate unit, minority and working class students within it long suffered the denial of institutional aid. General Studies included many lower income students whose SAT scores reflected the inability to afford expensive prep courses.[36]

The elimination of HEOP in 1992 provoked demonstrations. The limitations on aid to General Studies students caused immediate hardship to ten would-be HEOP students (six African-American, two Latino, one white, one Asian-American) joining General Studies in the fall of 1993. They were all that remained of HEOP, but for a few counselors kept on staff. Entering General Studies under the subheading "Opportunity Students," several reported great difficulty in coming up with tuition and fees. A General Studies inquiry indicated that one student could not afford the commute to Adelphi by train, and requested administration support allowing the student to live on campus. A General Studies counselor described another enrollee, with a part-time job, as "very concerned with the cost of attending Adelphi. She has stated that it cost $12.50 per day in transportation plus lunch," leading her to seek "additional employment that would provide an adequate salary to cover the cost of her commute." Anxiety "about her ability to finance her education" also plagued a third student, who would go on to take her doctorate and teach at the college level. Wrote the counselor: "She informed me that she had to go door-to-door in her project to pay the required $500.00 for her to register. We provided her with a book loan because she had no available funds."[37]

Not least among the extensive Adelphi sectors alienated by the Diamandopoulos administration, minority students also commented on the differences between HEOP and General Studies. A former General Studies student suggested that the university leadership considered HEOP an unsightly project for a prestigious school, opting to have its remnants digested by the apparently more acceptable General Studies. In the race to "excellence," Adelphi had its public image to consider. The handful of HEOP students would be left virtually without institutional aid. General Studies, he granted, would maintain the educational, tutoring, and counseling components of HEOP. The student pointed out that removing HEOP marked a disturbing precedent: "Can we expect a trend? Will other programs that attract a huge number of minorities, including the learning disabled program and the General Studies Program, be terminated next?"[38]

One student doubted that General Studies could support student progress in the same way, for "I know first-hand that its academic services are considerably lacking. The current tutorial services can be described as shallow at best. Furthermore, General Studies lacks the family unit and the close relationship between student and faculty that HEOP possessed." Others believed General Studies would provide adequate services, but focused on the indignity of canceling HEOP itself. Another student observed: "Adelphi didn't want the H.E.O.P., so they did away with it."[39]

Responding to criticism, Adelphi promised to provide full tuition and living expenses to the ten prospective HEOP students who found themselves rerouted to General Studies. Diamandopoulos agreed to appoint a Monitoring Committee to make sure the students obtained proper services. In a related move, in 1993 Adelphi appointed Raymond A. Davis associate dean for Minority Student Affairs, who outlined a lengthy series of cultural events, campus-wide educational activities, internships, and career counseling. He recommended that the university keep a database of complaints alleging racial discrimination, each of which should be investigated. As he met with upper-level officials over time, Davis learned that racial bias pulsated in Adelphi's leadership. He admitted "finding it so high in the administrative structure was revealing." Davis resigned after two years.[40]

Raymond A. Davis' proposals were ignored. The administration did not keep a pledge to retain ex-HEOP personnel available to the specific students bound for General Studies in 1993. Instead, Adelphi terminated all remaining former HEOP staff members, despite student outcry. A university spokesman averred that HEOP had separated minority students in an "isolationist" category, which dispersal on a minimal basis into General Studies would now resolve. The decision to get rid of HEOP, according to another former General Studies student, reflected the university's desire to become "great" by eliminating "those who hold them back."[41] Another HEOP supporter wondered: "Does the administration believe that by offering us this cheap HEOP imitation, General Studies based program, that we will be appeased?" A student found it "amazingly hilarious that the administration would actually consider comparing this program [General Studies] to H.E.O.P." For "let us not be deceived into thinking that General Studies is a program of foundation or strength. That is not the case. General Studies is a rather weak program that offers tutoring which is inadequate and not readily available." Students came through General Studies "with no major educational improvements." A third had "witnessed General Studies students who struggle through the program without the initiative or motivation to seek help. It would not be a fabrication to say that such students left the program with no better academic standing than when they started."[42]

On the other hand, a nurse-in-training formerly in General Studies appreciated the "dedicated mentors, counselors, and so forth," while worrying that General Studies itself might be discarded by Adelphi. Indeed, warned another report by an African-American student, "General Studies . . . will probably be no exception to the ax of restructuring." According to a reporter in a student newspaper, "General Studies may not be a success story for everyone but its overall track record can be commended in its own light"—but nothing could truly fill "the gaping hole caused by the phasing out of H.E.O.P." Interestingly, former General Studies students were among those condemning the dissolution of HEOP, while still defending General Studies. They joined student organizations on campus, including the African People's Organization and the National Association for the Advancement of Colored People, in protest. A number wrote for the short-lived *Afrika Unbound*. In addition, a leading General Studies student (who later became a college instructor) pioneered the multiracial group CALIBER (Cause to Achieve Leadership Intelligence Brotherhood Excellence and Respect), to which many General Studies students would contribute over the years. CALIBER sponsored a multicultural event each year known as "The Black and White Affair," which brought not only African-Americans and whites together for a celebration, but also members of Adelphi's Caribbean, Latino, Asian, and Muslim student groups.[43]

But just as it trifled with the idea of moving General Studies to another division of Adelphi—Business, Education, or Arts and Sciences—the Diamandopoulos administration fomented division among students. It promoted vulnerability of departments, programs, and people, pitting them against one another. Hence, the administration made frequent observations to the faculty union that General Studies instructional work schedules should be a model for all: everyday, all year, all day, no tenure. And when it came to minority students, school leaders did their utmost to make allies into rivals.

The university was not immune to the racial animus percolating in the larger environment. Contemporary observations connected the stigma (by no means universal) toward General Studies students with the test-fixation of some academics, but there were other biases. More than one early sage had deemed General Studies students suspect. One recalls the apprehension about General Studies at the very inception: it would bring down the rest of the school; it would depress the conditions of all; behavioral problems of the incoming low scorers would be made manifest; entrants should be kept strictly apart for two years, or one year; they carried psychological baggage no one else did. Additionally, the higher administration's arrogance dodged universal recoil for far too long, because it corresponded with an ivory tower image others on campus held dear.

From the time of HEOP'S demise, one can begin to discern the increasing proportion of minority students in General Studies. Already more heterogeneous than Adelphi's regular freshman classes, General Studies increasingly became a portal for hundreds of Latino, African-American, and Asian-American students into the university. Hence, General Studies turned into a program with many minority students, coexisting with white students, amidst the discolored views of university executors and others, under inhospitable administration in the segregated Long Island landscape. African-American, Latino, Asian-American and other minority students composed nearly half of each incoming class through the 1990s. By 1996, they constituted a majority.[44]

DOWNSIZING THE PROGRAM

Yet even with campus-wide enrollment in crisis, the administration moved to drastically cut the number of students entering Adelphi through the General Studies gateway. The reduction was made in close proximity to the elimination of HEOP. The General Studies Program into which the few HEOP-eligible students would go was thus diminished. Lowering the proportion of General Studies and HEOP students within the freshman class would be used to raise the school's academic profile. If decision makers were at all discomfited by the expansion of minority participation in General Studies (which may similarly have prompted the suspension of HEOP) and through General Studies into the mainstream of Adelphi, slicing the numbers might ease their concerns.

President Diamandopoulos proposed shrinking the 1995–1996 General Studies group to 80 from 163 the year before. On the other hand, he called for expanding Adelphi's Honors College, including additional funds for new hires and the hefty scholarships given to its students. Indeed, said Diamandopoulos, the formula would "allow the university to combine quantity with quality in the population of new students."[45] Within General Studies, the intended downsizing by half came as a shock, evoking dismay among the full-time core of instructors developed by University College dean David Newton. The effect of the announcement on the program's enduring half-dozen adjunct professors was even more palpable: they were terrified.[46]

Diamandopoulos' proposition stirred up consternation among pro-General Studies faculty in Adelphi's various schools and departments, who objected to damaging a successful program. A Political Science professor questioned the appropriation of resources for the Honors wing while General Studies, a proven commodity, was slashed. The Math chair wondered whether Adelphi would shut the door entirely on Adelphi's traditional student base. The Faculty Senate, with especially vehement intervention by Arts & Sciences professors, insisted that admissions decisions should pair "academic integrity and fiscal responsibility."[47]

In the end, only sixty-two students entered the General Studies in the fall of 1995, a hundred fewer than in fall of 1994. The enforced shrinkage coincided with a plummet in freshman registration from 850 to 385 between 1985 and 1995. The decline brought cuts in the teaching staff. Only two adjuncts survived. Two of the full-time instructors were let go. The fall 1996 and 1997 General Studies cohorts enrolled fifty-seven and sixty-one students, respectively.[48]

With Adelphi on the ropes, evidence surfaced that the trustees had disregarded their fiduciary responsibility to the school by improperly determining the president's compensation, perks, and privileges. The New York Board of Regents launched an investigation. As a trustee himself, Diamandopoulos had deployed school funds for personal use, including the purchase of jewelry and art, which the other board members either approved or ignored—a blatant infringement of regulations governing non-profit corporations. The board also violated conflict of interest statutes. In February 1997, the Regents ordered the removal of the trustees, and consequently Diamandopoulos, for having violated non-profit statute.[49]

GENERAL STUDIES REVIVED

The experienced administrator Dolph Norton (who had led the University of Maryland and Case Western Reserve University, among others) took over for the dismissed Diamandopoulos. With a basically new administration, he moved to stabilize and rebuild Adelphi. Like the rest of the university, General Studies would begin to benefit from an atmosphere now fostering serious work. By fall semester 1998, the program was up to 121 students. Despite the new enrollment growth, the university administration kept the General Studies counseling and teaching staff as small as it had been when the program was decimated several years before, on the grounds that the staff to student ratio was still workable with twice as many students. Therefore, a handful of people could teach more classes, counsel more students. The disposal of Diamandopoulos had left his industrial model intact. In protest, then-University College dean Peter Katopes wondered whether there were too many pencil pushers at Adelphi: perhaps the ratio of accountants to students should be adjusted. At stake, he ventured, was "the appropriate relationship of academic authority to fiscal authority." Until the school's treasurer could prove some sort of "superior academic wisdom," he recommended additional hires in General Studies to support the real "business of this institution--which I believe still is educating students."[50]

However, General Studies carried out its work on terrain considerably more stable in contrast with the contention under the former administration, even while facing budgetary challenges and renewed questioning of its role and mission. Despite continued ineligibility for institutional aid, General Studies students recorded improved retention rates in the years following Diamandopoulos' exit. While less than half of those entering in 1998 remained at Adelphi a year later, the percentage who stayed in 2000 was 64 percent. With slight dips, about two-thirds of each class entered the school's mainstream as sophomores over the next ten years.[51]

In cooperation with the new administration, the university revisited the question of where General Studies should be housed, in its original home (University College) or somewhere else. The prospect of relocating General Studies had surfaced under the former leadership, but as a reflection of broad disequilibrium. As a whole, University College had been ostensibly equal to the other schools of Adelphi, with its own dean and administration. As the nontraditional branch mainly serving adults, it had elicited covetous glances from its sister units in former days, as they sought to stem their own loss of students. Through somewhat cumbersome deliberations, the faculty and administration first approved the absorption of University College into the College of Arts & Sciences (which was announced as its only proper home) within two years of the end of the old regime. But University College migrated again in 2001, this time into the School of Business, likewise declared to be its natural habitat. University College departed the space it had inhabited in a long-empty dormitory and settled into the building of the Business School. General Studies was obliged to move too, but the new Business quarters were too small for its offices. Administratively still leagued with University College, the itinerant General Studies found rooms in the building where the College of Arts & Sciences had its offices. Eventually the university split General Studies from University College and put it in the College of Arts & Sciences in 2002, apparently its rightful place all along.[52]

AMENDING THE RULES

Liberated from the most deleterious restraints, the once again growing General Studies Program functioned as intended. Most original procedures and rules stayed in effect. Probation, dismissal, and other crucial issues remained the province of the General Studies Committee on Academic Performance, though the formality of the title had begun to fade. The essential embargo of Greek-organization pledging also held constant. The university itself treated the right to responsibly join a fraternity or sorority as part of overall participation in student groups and associations. But while General Studies students freely joined and assumed leadership in clubs and organizational activity, Greek life initially remained closed to them, which caused resentment among many students. Their parents, however, largely agreed with the program's educational emphasis, an attitude common among parents of General Studies-profile students throughout the country.[53]

But no longer prodded by the hierarchical values of the Diamandopoulos administration, the program considered certain structural modifications. By 2000, General Studies began to loosen its restrictions on joining Adelphi's NCAA teams. Recruited athletes in the program received permission to practice (but not travel or compete) with the squads. Program members became free to participate in the parallel athletic dance and cheerleading teams, whose coach by then was a General Studies alumnus teaching in a public school. But Peter Katopes, the associate dean of Business, who administered General Studies at the time, recalled that "the prohibition was originally imposed to insure that General Studies students, who take a rigorous mandatory curriculum, would not become overburdened by any extracurricular activity which requires extensive practice time or traveling." Katopes stood by the essence of the policy, however flexed. Academics remained the priority, and he reserved "the right to summarily ban" a student from even limited participation "if in my judgment the student's academic performance is suffering as a result."[54]

The Athletics Department and the Office of Admissions had pushed for sports participation for years; General Studies' grudging concession was the first revision of its original tenets. Another dispensation came soon after. Since 1985, General Studies students had been held to a fixed thirteen-credit course load in their opening semester. A spring term increase hinged upon a 3.0 GPA in the fall. But every new cohort included scholarship-eligible dancers, musicians, and artists, who were prohibited by the thirteen-credit ceiling from taking classes in their fields right away. Through the College of Arts & Sciences, the pertinent departments negotiated with the program to permit some leeway in this regard, allowing students to take a credit or two from the outset in addition to their regular course schedule. Katopes agreed, on the condition that no other aspects of General Studies would change: the Arts majors were held to the discipline of the program, including the obligation to maintain a "C" average or risk dismissal. Were a sub-"C" student to be placed on probation after the fall semester, he or she would not be permitted to take a course in the Arts in the spring, scholarship notwithstanding.

As the air continued to clear, the provost established a committee to review the program in 2002. Chaired by an associate provost and equipped with several outside faculty members as well as the dean of the College of Arts & Sciences, the committee functioned for nearly half a year, heard witnesses, examined documents, and debated the program's restrictions and bans. Seeking to explain why more General Studies students left Adelphi after the first year than their mainstream counterparts, the committee report "observed that the attrition rate is not mainly or necessarily tied to what is done in the GS program."[55]

The review committee recommended continuing the program and drawing it more deeply into the College of Arts & Sciences, by way of committee memberships and decision making. It proposed extending grants-in-aid to General Studies students to bolster retention. It noted that General Studies students remaining at Adelphi lagged relatively behind their peers in four-, five-, and six-year graduation rates. As possible remedy, it urged "changes in the financial aid policies. We recommend that GS students receive any needs based aid to which they are entitled including Adelphi grants." More than ten years would elapse before this proposal was adopted. The final document supported eliminating the General Studies coding next to the names of program alumni once they advanced into the majors, in hopes of reducing occasionally insensitive reactions to them by faculty. In all, the admission of qualified college students, despite lower SATs, was welcomed. After detailing the integrated work of students, counselors, tutors, and instructors, the committee concluded "it is ethically and educationally sound to offer students at risk a chance to succeed at the college level."[56]

While the review did not put to rest all qualms about General Studies, its vote of confidence strengthened the program. Other instances of bringing General Studies into line with the university's brighter outlook soon followed. The program began to issue a regular newsletter, with articles written by past and present students. It publicized successful students, interviewed former ones who had moved on into professions, and presented features on counselors and faculty. At the same time, the program's letters to accepted applicants underwent revision, gradually eliminating suggestions that the students were less than bona fide admits. The university's General Studies brochures acquired a more welcoming tone. The developing webpage reiterated the program's suitability for students who "demonstrate potential for success but require more personalized attention to reach their goals." The revisions were incremental nonetheless. Deleting "not" and "but" from all public language was easier imagined than accomplished, for the changes were not for program protagonists alone to approve. Thus a publication outside the program continued to put it more conventionally: the "General Studies program . . . provides an opportunity for a limited number of freshmen who have not qualified for regular admittance to Adelphi."[57]

ENROLLMENT TRENDS

As the university experienced continued recovery after Diamandopoulos, freshman enrollment climbed. More than five hundred first-year students came to Adelphi in 1998, a figure to be doubled within ten years. General Studies entrants made up a fifth of the freshman class of 1998, a sixth in 2000. Adelphi acted to keep General Studies numbers consistent. When all was said and done, Admissions capped the program at ninety in 2001, ultimately raising it to one hundred, roughly 10 to 12 percent of all freshmen. The new association with the College of Arts & Sciences created a powerful advocate for controlling the numbers. The target of one hundred reinforced the stability of the General Studies full-time teaching and counseling staff, and made resort to adjuncts less likely.

While the goal held steady on paper, it nevertheless varied in practice in accordance with Adelphi admissions trends and needs. Rarely did the actual number diverge dramatically from the target. But it was subject to objective, as well as orchestrated, ebb and flow—including old worries about the impact of a lower-scoring entering cohort upon Adelphi's reputation—from which no program of this type is immune. Enrollment managers nationwide have at least one eye on the published ratings of college rank and selectivity, superficiality notwithstanding. This may impact the relative size of certain programs within the whole. With so many factors affecting admissions, the potential that General Studies could expand or contract always existed. Since full-time General Studies instructors were never deemed "regular" faculty, they might be dismissed if the program's compression was in the offing. But in 2016 they solidified their status by earning the designation "lecturer," becoming part of the regular faculty and members of the Adelphi branch of the American Association of University Professors.[58]

NOTES

1. William Romano, "Freshman Class Decrease Rumored Larger Than Figures," *The Delphian*, February 20, 1991, 3; Kathleen Slavin, "'93 Freshman Enrollment Decreases, Total Enrollment Remains Steady," *The Delphian*, October 6, 1993, 1; Letter to the editor, *The Delphian*, September 6, 1995, 7.
2. Romano, "Freshman Class Decrease Rumored Larger Than Figures;" Dom Cavallo, *Summer Orientation for Freshmen*, April 14, 1989.
3. Dom Cavallo, *Summer Orientation for Freshmen*, April 14, 1989, 3, 4, 6, GSC.
4. *Pre-College Program for General Studies Students*, 1991, GSC; *Summer Academy for College-Bound Students*, 1994, GSC; Deborah Ziff, "Pre-college Camps Help Incoming Students Learn How to Learn," *Wisconsin State Journal*, August 13, 2011, http://m.host.madison.com/mobile/article_7007dc26-c52e-11e0-87b2-001cc4c03286.html. Accessed

August 15, 2011; General Studies Program, *Proposal for a College Preparation Program*, February 4, 1991, GSC.

5. John Donohue, *General Studies II: Proposal for the Reinstitution of General Studies as A Two-Year Program for Probationary Students*, September 25, 1992, GSC.

6. John Donohue, *General Studies II: Proposal for the Reinstitution of General Studies as A Two-Year Program for Probationary Students*, September 25, 1992, GSC; David Newton to Dr. Diamandopoulos, May 20, 1993, GSC; David Newton to ______, May 27, 1993, GSC; David Newton to A.V., January 18, 1995, GSC; David Newton to ________, January 6, 1994, GSC.

7. John Vetter, chair, Anthropology to John Donohue, associate dean, May 5, 1993, GSC; Peter Farley, chair, English, to Peter Katopes, director of Academic Affairs, April 15, 1993, GSC; Adelphi University, "Adelphi University Core Curriculum: Values and Actions Senior Seminar Courses," Fall 1994, GSC.

8. Della Hudson-Tomlin to Dr. Augusto Hacthoun, *General Studies Dismissals Spring 1994*, June 14, 1994, GSC; Peter Katopes to Dean Newton, *GS Dismissals, Fall Semester 1994*, January 9, 1995, GSC; *Committee on Academic Performance*, May 22, 1995, GSC.

9. David Newton to Dr. Diamandopoulos, May 20, 1993, GSC.

10. Adelphi University Planning Committee, *Adelphi University Academic Plan 1991-1996*, SpecialCollections, Adelphiana Collection, Swirbul Library, Adelphi University.

11. Interview with David Newton, vice-provost for Faculty Relations, January 5, 1998.

12. Della Hudson-Tomlin to David Newton, *General Studies Statistics*, October 31, 1994, 17, 20, 24, 28, 35, GSC; Meryl Shapiro to Dean Cavallo, *Breakdown of Students Accepted to General Studies*, June 1987, GSC.

13. Adelphi University, *Presidential Inauguration Addresses: The Inauguration of Peter Diamandopoulos as the Seventh President of the University*, April 18, 1986, 18–22, Adelphiana Miscellany, Presidents, Diamandopoulos, P., Inauguration Folder, Swirbul Library, Adelphi University.

14. "William E. Simon Inaugurates New Lecture Series," *The Delphian*, October 14, 1992, 1, 3; Suzy Edwards, "William F. Buckley, Jr. Lectures on American Civilization and Values," *The Delphian*, October 6, 1993, 5; "Irving Kristol Lectures on American Values and the Welfare State," *The Delphian*, October 26, 1994, 3.

15. Memorandum from Elliot Pruzan, Associate Provost to Carl Buxbaum, chair, Faculty Senate Academic Affairs Committee, April 10, 1996, Subject: A New Core Curriculum Proposal, in author's possession; Tibor R. Machan, "What is Morally Right with Insider Trading," http://genius.iscd.edu/~john/p/libuniv_dir/Machan_dir/Machan.InsTrad. Accessed July 7, 2000.

16. Igor Webb, "Letter to the Editor," *The Delphian*, October 4, 1995, 10; Edith Kurzweil, "Letter to the Editor," *The Delphian*, February 7, 1996, 12–13; Minutes of the Board of Trustees, September 2, 1993, Board of Regents of the University of the State of New York, *Hearings in Re: Adelphi*, Exhibit P-217; Minutes of the Board of Trustees, September 28, 1994, *Hearings*, Exhibit 211; Vincent Passaro, "Letter to the Editor," *The Delphian*, October 25, 1995, 9; Bruce Lambert, "Court Order Halts Ouster at Adelphi U.," *New York Times*, February 12, 1997, B1.

17. Bruce Lambert, "Examining Adelphi President's Perks, From a Mercedes to a Million-Dollar Condo," *New York Times*, August 12, 1996, B4; Bruce Lambert, "Adelphi Trustees Ignored Auditor's Advice," *New York Times*, September 1, 1996, 44; Furniture Purchased by Adelphi for Apartment at 422 E. 72nd Street, NYC, *Hearings*, Exhibit P-272; Interview with Chris Toften, August 3, 2011; Lionel Lewis, *When Power Corrupts: Academic Governing Boards in the Shadow of the Adelphi Case*, Piscataway, 2000.

18. Peter Katopes to David Newton, *General Studies Stats*, June 19, 1997, GSC.

19. Peter Katopes to David Newton, *General Studies Stats*, June 19, 1997, GSC; *Adelphi Data Book Fall 2006*, 119.

20. Marianne Krasinski, *Fall 1993 Grades*, Series 1, GSC; *Spring 1994 Grades*, Series 1, GSC.

21. Della Hudson-Tomlin, *May 1996 Graduates*, June 10, 1996, GSC; "Introduction to the Statistical Profile of the 10 Year History of the General Studies Program," in Della Hudson-Tomlin to David Newton and Peter Katopes, *General Studies Statistics*, October 31, 1994, GSC.

22. David Newton, *Philosophy of General Studies*, Dean's Report, 1993, in Della Hudson-Tomlin, *General Studies Statistics*, 1994, 7, GSC.

23. William Romano, "Freshman Class Decrease Rumored Larger Than Figures," *The Delphian*, February 20, 1991, 3; *Provost's Report on Enrollments in University College*, November 14, 1995, 7, GSC; Interview with Peter Katopes, June 20, 2014, New York City; University College: A Report, *Cohort Attrition, 1985–1993*, 1994, GSC.

24. John Donohue to David Newton, *General Studies Marketing*, April 9, 1992, GSC; John Donohue to David Newton, *General Studies Recruitment Initiatives*, September 11, 1992, GSC; John Donohue to David Newton, *General Studies Marketing*, June 25, 1992, GSC.

25. University College: A Report, *Cohort Attrition*, 1985–1994, 1994, GSC; "1995 Graduates: Former General Studies Students Who were Awarded Bachelors or Masters Degrees from Adelphi in May 1995," in *General Studies 1994-95 Final Grades*, GSC; Dominick Cavallo to Augusto Hacthoun, dean of Academic Attainment, *Readmission of E.A.*, October 2, 1989, GSC.

26. Adelphi University, Office of Research, Assessment and Planning, *General Studies Heads and FTEs by Major*, July 9, 2007.

27. *GS Dismissals* January 1991, 2-7, GSC; Barbara Shulman to Dean Newton, *General Studies Committee on Academic Performance*, January 7, 1991, GSC; John Donohue to Dr. David Newton, *General Studies Dismissals*, January 9, 1991, GSC.

28. John Donohue to Dr. John Russel, Dean of Admissions, *Requested List of Selected General Studies Dismissals*, February 1, 1991, GSC; John Donohue to Dr. David Newton, *GS Students Dismissed from Program and Re-Admitted to Adelphi*, June 6, 1991, GSC; Dr. John Russel to Ms. J.P., July 30, 1991, GSC; David Newton to Dr. Augusto Hacthoun, August 8, 1991, GSC.

29. University College: A Report, *Cohort Attrition, 1985–1993*, 1994, GSC; Kenneth Stevenson, Dean of Admissions, to Harvey Weiner, vice-provost for Academic Affairs, *Flexibility Regarding General Studies Admissions* Criteria, February 23, 1996, GSC.

30. Barbara Shulman to Dr. Augusto Hacthoun, *General Studies Dismissals*, June 7, 1991, GSC; Barbara Gross to Dean Newton, *General Studies Class Fall 1991*, September 12, 1991, GSC; *University College: A Report*, "Cohort Attrition," 1994, 22, GSC.

31. Barbara Gross to Dean Newton, *General Studies Class Fall 1991*, September 12, 1991, GSC.

32. Barbara Gross to Dean Newton, *General Studies Class Fall 1991*, September 12, 1991, GSC; Barbara Gross to Dean Newton, *Final Report on General Studies Students for the Fall of 1991*, January 2, 1992, GSC; Barbara Gross to Dean Newton, *Breakdown of Grades for General Studies Students*, May 26, 1992, GSC,

33. Della Hudson-Tomlin to Dean Newton, *General Studies Head Count for Spring 1993*, January 1993, GSC.

34. Peter Diamandopoulos to the University, December 9, 1992, 3, GSC; Della Hudson-Tomlin to Igor Webb, provost, *Adelphi Opportunity Program Update*, September 8, 1993, GSC; Vincent Natale, "Minority Students Stage Sit-In To Voice Discontent at Adelphi," *The Delphian*, November 18, 1992, 1; Vincent Natale, "President Addresses Minority Student Concerns in Forum," *The Delphian*, December 2, 1992, 5; Carrie Gerkey, "First Faculty Meeting of the Semester," *The Delphian*, September 14, 1993, 3; John Donohue to Dr. David Newton, *The Magic of Numbers: HEOP, General Studies, Apples, Oranges, and Mirrors*, December 14, 1990, GSC.

35. Carrie Gerkey, "Administrators Present at Faculty Senate Meeting," *The Delphian*, November 30, 1994, 5; Shabnam Shah, "Students Attend Open Forum in Record Numbers," *The Delphian*, February 14, 1996, 4; Jonathan Giovanni and Shabnam Shah, "President Diamandopoulos Speaks on Education, the Media, Program Cuts, and the

Core Curriculum," *The Delphian*, February 28, 1996, 1; "2 Problem Schools, 2 Problem-Solvers: Diamandopoulos of Adelphi," *Newsday*, June 6, 1986.

36. David Newton to Provost Webb, *Financial Aid and General Studies*, November 18, 1992.

37. Della Hudson-Tomlin to Igor Webb, provost, *Adelphi Opportunity Program Update*, September 8, 1993, GSC; Della Hudson-Tomlin to Monitoring Committee, *Opportunity Program*, December 1, 1993, GSC.

38. Chuck Green, "HEOP: What Really Happened?" *Afrika Unbound*, October 29, 1992, 4, 12.

39. Chuck Green, "HEOP: Where Do We Go From Here?" *Afrika Unbound*, February 1993, 17; Lawrence Brown, A Bounced Check," *Afrika Unbound*, February 1993, 6; Della Hudson-Tomlin to David Newton, *Midterm Grades for Fall 1993: Opportunity Students*, October 27, 1993, GSC; Della Hudson-Tomlin to Academic Attainment, *Students Who May Withdraw on or before December 14, 1993*, December 3, 1993, GSC.

40. "President Updates University on Minority Affairs," *Adelphi Gazette*, October 25-November 14, 1993, 1; Peter Diamandopoulos to the University, *African-American and Latino Student Concerns*, October 9, 1993, courtesy Dean Della Hudson; Raymond A. Davis to Carl J. Rheins, vice president and dean, Student Life and Development, *Proposed Programs for the Office of Minority Student Affairs*, August 31, 1993, courtesy of Dean Della Hudson; "Is Anyone Listening," *Afrika Unbound*, November 1994, 12; Janine Brown, "Time to Fill the Vacant Office," *Afrika Unbound*, October 1995, 4.

41. Kevin Moorer, "An Indecent Proposal," *Afrika Unbound*, April 1993, 4; Sheila Guerine, "The Roving Questioner," *Afrika Unbound*, November 1994, 11.

42. Editorial, "'The Op-poor-tunity' Program," *Afrika Unbound*, October 1994, 10; Editorial, "The General Studies Scam," *Afrika Unbound*, September 1993, 8; Chuck Green, "General Studies Plot?" *Afrika Unbound*, April 1993, 7.

43. Jenner Zetrenng, "Black Capitalism," *Afrika Unbound*, October 1993, 5; Jennifer Remy, "The Roving Question," *Afrika Unbound*, November 1995, 8; Editorial, "'Prestigious' Adelphi," *Afrika Unbound*, October 1994, 11; Marie Alzi, "Just a Phase," *Afrika Unbound*, May 1996, 5; Marie Alzi, "Skepticism in the Phasing Out of H.E.O.P.," *Afrika Unbound*, March 1996, 6; Amy Demner, "Students Discuss Racism," *The Delphian*, April 4, 1990, 1; CALIBER, ad for "Black and White Affair," *The Delphian*, November 16, 1994, 2.

44. Della Hudson-Tomlin, *Final 1993–94 Statistics: Ethnic Breakdown of General Studies*, May 18, 1994, GSC; Della Hudson-Tomlin, *1992–93 Final Statistics: Grades by Ethnic Background*, May 20, 1993, GSC; Della Hudson-Tomlin, *General Studies Headcount—Fall 1996*, September 16, 1996, GSC.

45. Carrie Gerkey, "President Diamandopoulos Discusses Recruitment, Fundraising," *The Delphian*, February 1, 1995, 3.

46. David Newton to Igor Webb, senior vice president, June 1, 1995, GSC.

47. Kathleen Slavin and Carrie Gerkey, "First Faculty Meeting of Spring Semester Ends in Anger," *The Delphian*, March 1, 1995, 5, 4; Jill Kerr, "Faculty Senate Discusses CRAP," *The Delphian*, May 3, 1995, 4.

48. *Provost's Report on Enrollments in University* College, November 14, 1995, 7, GSC; Interview with Della Hudson-Tomlin, June 24, 2014, Garden City, NY; Gayle Insler et al., The Committee to Save Adelphi, Petitioners against Peter Diamandopoulos et al., Respondents, *To the Board of Regents*, 1996, 26; General Studies Deposits and Enrolled, May 28, 1998, GSC; *General Studies Head Count 1996*, Fall 1996, GSC; Debra Marks to David Newton, *Spring 1997 Final Grades*, June 9, 1997, GSC; *General Studies Head Count 1997*, Fall 1997, GSC.

49. Board of Regents of the University of the State of New York, *Report to the Honorable Members of the Board of Regents, re the Committee to Save Adelphi et al., Petitioners, against Peter Diamandopoulos et al., Respondents*, February 5, 1997.

50. *Adelphi University Databook*, Fall 2009, 33, 108; Peter Katopes to Mathew Goldstein, president, *Staffing for GS: 98/99*, July 7, 1998, courtesy of Peter Katopes.

51. *Adelphi University Databook,* Fall 2009, 33, 108; Interview with Peter Katopes, June 26, 2013, New York City.

52. Les Baltimore et al., *Report of the General Studies Review Committee,* May 17, 2002, 4, GSC.

53. Center for Student Involvement, Adelphi University, *Student Life Satisfaction Survey,* January 23, 2013; Dotterman, Executive Summary: General Studies Program Panel/Northeast Modern Language Association, March 22, 2013.

54. Peter Katopes to Robert Hartwell, director of Athletics, *GS and Cheerleading Squad,* March 1, 2000, GSC; Dan Rosenberg to Robert Hartwell, *Women's Lacrosse,* September 5, 2002, GSC.

55. Les Baltimore et al., *Report of the General Studies Review Committee,* May 17, 2002, 2, GSC; *Minutes of the General Studies Review Committee,* April 19, 2002, GSC.

56. Les Baltimore et al., *Report of the General Studies Review Committee,* May 17, 2002, 2-7, GSC.

57. *A Note of Welcome to Accepted Students,* http://academics.adelphi.edu/gns/welcome.php. Accessed August 25, 2011; *About General Studies,* http://academics.adelphi.edu/gns/about.php. Accessed August 25, 2011; *Special Academic Programs,* http://academics.adelphi.edu/specialprograms.php. Accessed August 25, 2011; *Adelphi University Databook,* Fall 2007, ix.

58. *Adelphi University Databook,* Fall 2009, 33; Tom Westermann, "Faculty Senate Update," *The Delphian,* February 21, 2001, 9; Adelphi University, Office of Research, Assessment and Planning, GS: 200 Deposits, *Fall 2016 Admissions Comparisons,* June 2, 2016.

SEVEN

The Grades of General Studies Students

This chapter analyzes the grades of students in the program while they are in it, and after they enter their Adelphi majors, using grade point average as the key measurement. It confirms that high school GPA is a superior predictor than standardized test scores, but nevertheless problematic, precisely because secondary school education is in crisis. It regards college grades as one of the better demonstrations of achievement, but no single instrument can tell the whole story.

GRADE INFLATION IN COLLEGE

College grades generally are quite high in the United States. Burnout and overwork may impact the grading by the increasingly preponderant contingent faculty. Full-timers exhibit some of these burdens. With an eye on competitive school ranking, college administrators may rather turn a blind eye to, if not sing the praises of, grades that beg the truth. For once again, they often channel the inducement to get students through college quicker down to the professors, to amplify school image. Resultant impacts upon public college faculty of tying state funding to student performance may also lead to grade inflation. As Rudy Fichtenbaum, head of the AAUP puts it, "faculty will face a 'subtle pressure' to pass more students." However, a recent study in *Educational Policy and Analysis* casts the "benefit" of connecting state aid to retention and completion outcomes as "often not distinguishable" from states where this policy is not followed. Nevertheless, grades, grad stats, and SAT scores are key ingredients for institutional braggadocio.[1]

A Columbia Teachers College critique of grading recognizes that college grades ballooned at several points in the twentieth century. However, the inflation of grades over the past twenty-five years seems unrelated "to increases in student achievement. . . . Students are increasingly disengaged from their studies . . . and the literacy of graduates has declined." What seems different about college grading since the 1980s is "the now common practice of requiring student-based evaluations of college teachers." Inflation occurs relatively more often at private institutions of higher learning. An adamant mid-1990s *New York Times* editorial illumines the tradition at prestigious Stanford, where "an astonishing 93 percent of all letter grades are 'As' and 'Bs,' a huge increase over twenty years ago." What "an odd way to prepare students for an ever more competitive world," says the paper. Nonetheless, a school's reputation among students rests upon whether it can advance them to doctoral and masters studies: "And that means transcripts loaded with 'As.'" Thus, many students emerge from college with difficulty in problem-solving and serious analysis. Contemporary surveys of new alumni echo the Columbia graduate who questioned his critical thinking skills after graduation: "I think of the things I didn't know, and of the pains and perils to which my ignorance exposed me!"[2]

The average GPAs accrued by students at the University of Michigan soared from 2.57 in 1951 to 3.27 in 2008. Michigan represents a trend leading educators to speculate: "It is likely that at many selective and highly selective schools, undergraduate GPAs are now so saturated at the high end that they have little use as a motivator of students and as an evaluation tool for graduate and professional schools and employers."[3] But they look good on paper and fit appropriately into the numbers-based game of college reputation, thus luring new fish. Post-baccalaureate programs are not immune. Revelations in 2012 of administrative grade-fixing at Baruch College's Zicklin School of Business (City University of New York) substantiates the "suspicion that some graduate schools inflate grades to keep programs with high tuitions full."[4]

HOW STUDENTS HAVE FARED IN GENERAL STUDIES

The gap between highest and lowest-finishing program members was widest through the 1980s and most of the 1990s. Comprehensive and regular measurements of how General Studies students fared in the program and beyond, in light of high school and SAT performance, only began in 2003. But even the piecemeal earlier data shows a trend. Through most of the program's first period, the numbers ending freshman year below 2.0 substantially exceeded those above 3.0. One may take the 1987–1988 class as typical. A full 30 percent of its students completed the first year of college under 2.0, either put on probation or dismissed.

Six percent breathed the thin vapors beyond 3.0, two upon the Dean's List. "C" was the group mean. From a starting class of 167, 41 were dismissed during the year.[5]

The 1989–1990 entrants showed similar results. Among the 123 who completed both semesters, 39 finished below 2.0: 10 were under 1.49. Thirteen made it to 3.0 or higher. Yet a solid majority ended the year in good academic standing, with 2.2 the average. Individual student experiences nonetheless caution against taking the numerical outcome as the bellwether of all that is to come. Hence one former General Studies student who went on to become a teacher reminisced that she resented being placed in the General Studies Program in the fall of 1989, because "she could not jump into her desired field of study." Thus she did not do well at first. Yet she would eventually find in the program "a support system I could use to my full advantage." She identified the regular interactions with counselors and faculty as crucial dimensions in becoming a confident student: "The offices felt safe, and I could get help on anything."[6]

The 1993–1994 cohort slightly amended the grade breakdown. In the first semester, fifty-two students ended below 2.0 and ten prevailed above 3.0, in a class of 136. With the cohort reduced to 118, the ten ended the spring once again in the highest ranks, but thirty-one of their classmates wrapped up the spring under "C." The proportion under 2.0 diminished between fall and spring from 38 to 26 percent. The share over 3.0 however barely rose. But even in less successful instances, concrete experience demonstrates that a student's first-year experience may not be conclusive in the bigger picture. Thus a student—later professor of Health Education at Maryland's Coppin State—who was dismissed after her first year, then readmitted upon appeal, readily comments, "I had a difficult time living away from home and being a college student, and my GPA dropped."[7]

Relative improvement in first-year outcomes was not accompanied by parallel growth in SAT profiles. Thus, the College Board math-verbal average of the 1994–1995 group essentially matched its predecessors, totaling 740. But the incoming high school average was now 2.3, a peak. In no sense did the year's results then arc naturally upward, because 94 of the 169 students (56 percent) composing the starting unit found themselves below 2.0 by the middle of their Adelphi Fall semester. Only one student in the class at this point rose above 3.0 and headed for the Dean's List. But she had been nowhere near the top performers on the SAT. Seventeen of the vanguard SAT group above 740 labored in academic peril as college freshmen beneath 2.0. Yet after the next semester, the class by then reduced to 114 for various reasons (including financial), the proportion in academic distress shrunk dramatically, to a year-ending 22 percent. The concluding freshman GPA rested at 2.3.[8]

In the significantly reduced General Studies class of 1995–1996, 73 percent of the students attained an average of 2.0 or better in the fall term.

The final semester report observed editorially, "two of our students who entered the program with combined SAT scores above 950 received final averages below 1.0. The student with the lowest combined SAT score of 670 received a final average 2.38." Thus was noted one of the recurrent tendencies in the General Studies Program. In any case, the class SAT mean barely scraped 700. The term witnessed ten students surpassing 3.0 as college freshmen, two on the Dean's List. None of them had exceeded 840 on the SATs. Half of the ten had stellar high school averages, while the others had entered Adelphi at 2.3, 2.5, 2.0, 1.6, and 2.7. Sixteen fellow students ended in below "C" territory. The number under 2.0 once again exceeded the ones beyond 3.0, but the gap was narrowing.[9]

The years immediately following 1998 evidenced final freshman year GPA improving from 2.3 to 2.76. In the crucial category of students liable to dismissal after completing the program, the concluding percentages are striking. Thus 21 percent in 2001–2002 ended their first year at Adelphi under a 2.0. Thirteen percent of GS students found themselves in this predicament in 2004–2005, 15 percent in 2005–2006. In the succeeding years, this proportion dropped to between 2 and 7 percent. Likewise, the numbers finishing above 3.0 also increased, averaging 30 to 40 percent of the whole, while earlier in the decade the figure was as low as 13 percent. Finally, sources demonstrate a reduction in those winding up the first year in the 2.0 to 2.49 range and an expansion of the stratum at the 2.5 to 2.9 level.[10]

The sharp decline in academic jeopardy cases is a key change in the program's thirty plus years. Text box 7.1 at the end of this chapter illustrates the tendency of grades earned in the program over the past decade, including developments in evolving high school and SAT averages. It will be clear that while the former have increased, the latter, for all intents and purposes, have remained much the same.

GENERAL STUDIES AND GRADE INFLATION

In the beginning, regular tenured or tenure-track faculty from other departments who taught in General Studies tended to grade higher than the program's adjuncts. But initially expressed fears that General Studies students would otherwise ruin Adelphi standards energized a hard programmatic line against inflationary grading. On their own, program organizers openly agitated against dilution of standards. The program's invocation to grade rigorously eventually struck deeper roots among the least established instructors, more likely to take literally the word from on high. Eventually, David Newton appointed full-time professors designated "administrators" but like adjuncts subject to termination at any point. The tenure-less new instructors (classified at "grade 10" on the managerial scale) came likewise under the sway of unbending grading. While containing a valid premise, this could seem an ultimatum: grade low or else. Though logically and legally no veto operated over grades determined by faculty, the full-time instructors worked contingently, and thus were more susceptible to suggestion from above.

Originally, grading fell under a peculiar harshness, as if "rigor" meant that General Studies was a "boot-camp," bringing to mind the negative characterizations contained in the program's early letters of acceptance. Several instructors would "pride themselves on how rarely they give an 'A' or 'B,' and how frequently they give 'Cs,' 'Ds,' or 'Fs.'" Invocation to sober grading led some faculty to lose perspective with grades, like many of their students.[11] In principle, however, the original proponents of General Studies reminded professors to be impervious to everything but the authentic results of student endeavor, which made sense. One therefore took General Studies grades as the cold truth, the pure fruit: no additives, no enhancers. The university recognized a General Studies student making the Dean's List as the real deal. If any academic department worked hard to remind instructors not to yield to tears or rising grade trends outside, it was General Studies.

Naturally, fluctuation in grading has always been evident in different sections of the same General Studies courses. But in General Studies, grade differentials between same-course sections were narrower, and once again on average lower than in the rest of Adelphi. Taking the early version of the Adelphi Freshman Seminar in General Studies in spring 1994 for example, average marks ranged between 2.0 and 2.7 through seven sections. Eight Writing sections averaged from 2.1 to 2.88, the same number of History sections from 1.6 to 2.6. No section of any course, out of thirty-three total sections, crossed the 3.0 average. This greatly irked the Diamandopoulos administration at the time, as witnessed in the previous chapter. For, while making elitist pretensions, it bitterly resented the program's tight standards and interfered with them.[12]

TRENDS IN GRADES AT ADELPHI UNIVERSITY

All Adelphi undergraduate units manifested rising overall grades between 2000 and 2013. For most of this period, a greater percentage of students inside the program received failing grades than outside. Fewer "As" are earned in General Studies than in any other area of the university. The average grade on campus is a "B+," with big majorities obtaining "As" in some units. At the same time, General Studies in the recent past has led all Adelphi divisions in "B" (58 percent of all grades), "C" (20 percent) and "D" (3.6 percent).[13] Still, more General Studies students met or exceeded a "B" average by the end of freshman year 2008–2009 than at any point in the history of the program: 42 percent. But 84 percent of their Adelphi peers in the freshman mainstream obtain "B" and "A."[14] Even while increasing relatively, "A" grades remain so small a portion of all earned returns as to be stark in contrast: the General Studies "A" has never exceeded 17 percent of marks.[15]

Since the mid-1990s, bachelor's level grades within the various Adelphi schools have risen. General Studies was one of only three undergraduate units where the average grade was lower than 3.0 in 1995. Most professional majors settled in the "B" framework. With a dip or two, grades then rose in degrees in all units, eventually including General Studies. Education majors saw their averages improve from 3.11 in 1995 to 3.33 in 2010. Students in Arts & Sciences fields experienced average increases from 2.91 in 1995 to 3.31 in 2011. Social Work undergrads touched 3.3 territory by 2010. Though facing a more challenging curriculum and stiffer examinations, Nursing majors never dipped below 3.19 and averaged as high as 3.37. Psychology majors also steadily improved, near "B" in the 1990s and realizing Nursing school dimensions by 2011. Business majors rose crisply as well, breaking the overall 3.0 level in 1998, tripping slightly in 2002, topping off at 3.23 in 2009. However, the Business School's grade fermentation has appeared more moderate.[16]

Adelphi grade development is reflected below, according to school. University sources include General Studies with the others, though it is a program comprising only first-year students. While General Studies is a constituent of the College of Arts & Sciences, its GPAs are presented on a separate line. The abbreviation IAPS refers to the Institute of Advanced Psychological Studies, the Derner Institute. NYSUT, noted in figure 7.2, is a nondegree graduate education program.[17]

Adelphi professors outside of General Studies have stated, "'most' of the students they teach lack the basic skills for college-level work." Nevertheless, the high school GPAs of all Adelphi freshmen have exhibited consistent improvement. The proportion bringing 3.7–4.0 secondary school averages into Adelphi has swelled: 36 percent in 2000, 44 percent in 2005, 47 percent in 2010. This matches the anticipations of many entering freshmen: that their college grades will be equally high, albeit surveyed instructors disagree. But posted final grades belie the faculty doubts cited above.[18]

Adelphi faculty themselves have criticized inflationary grade tendencies. In contrast with General Studies, which had once witnessed higher grades administered more by regular than adjunct professors, a 2006 faculty probe proposed that the latter were now more culpable across the board. While adjuncts had all but disappeared from General Studies after the mid-1990s, part-time instructional labor had become prevalent university-wide. Carried out by professors from a range of Adelphi schools and departments, the faculty study noted that the disproportionate use of part-timers was in regrettable conformity with national occurrences in the educational field. However, the report also found that the "grades assigned by all faculty have steadily risen during the period studied,"

Trends in Grade Point Average (GPA)[1]:
Fall 1995 to Fall 2006

	1995	1997	1999	2000	2001	2002	2003	2004	2005	2006
Undergraduate										
Arts & Sciences	2.91	3.06	3.09	3.10	3.16	3.20	3.20	3.21	3.21	3.19
Business	2.85	2.98	2.94	3.06	3.00	3.03	3.11	3.12	3.09	3.17
Education	3.11	3.07	3.09	3.04	3.12	3.09	3.19	3.19	3.29	3.15
IAPS	•••	•••	2.98	3.18	3.14	3.20	3.29	3.18	3.33	3.28
Nursing	3.25	3.18	3.25	3.20	3.36	3.32	3.31	3.35	3.25	3.29
Social Work	3.23	3.04	3.15	3.18	3.30	3.31	3.32	3.36	3.29	3.29
University College	3.22	3.26	3.24	3.29	3.27	3.23	3.26	3.35	3.23	3.23
General Studies	2.23	2.33	2.44	2.46	2.63	2.37	2.33	2.42	2.15	2.48
Total	**3.05**	**3.10**	**3.11**	**3.12**	**3.16**	**3.17**	**3.20**	**3.22**	**3.20**	**3.14**
Graduate										
Arts & Sciences	3.57	3.62	3.67	3.66	3.77	3.74	3.76	3.71	3.72	3.68
Business	3.34	3.35	3.32	3.42	3.53	3.59	3.46	3.56	3.47	3.53
Education	3.49	3.53	3.60	3.62	3.64	3.66	3.68	3.65	3.67	3.67
IAPS	•••	3.61	3.28	3.70	3.47	3.62	3.67	3.70	3.75	3.70
Nursing	3.89	3.77	3.71	3.63	3.68	3.75	3.71	3.80	3.84	3.79
Social Work	3.43	3.47	3.45	3.45	3.50	3.44	3.56	3.55	3.50	3.48
Total	**3.47**	**3.50**	**3.53**	**3.57**	**3.60**	**3.61**	**3.63**	**3.63**	**3.62**	**3.64**

[1] Semester GPA

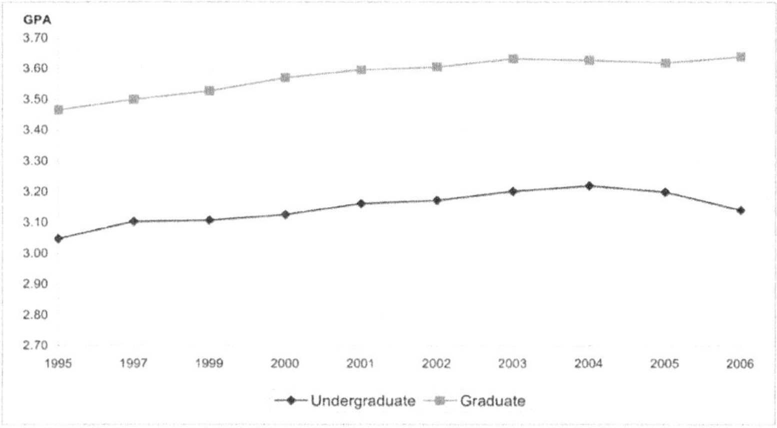

Figure 7.1. Trends in Grade Point Average (GPA): Fall 1995 to Fall 2006. Source: Adelphi University 2006 Data Book, page 150.

emphasizing that "As" "rose each year," with increasing "influence on the overall GPA." A focused examination of grade changes also found that the greatest number were from a lesser grade to "A," with regular faculty making most of the alterations. The faculty report cited General Studies as the lone exception.[19] The Adelphi faculty also traced heightening averages in key departments and professional schools over time, producing a "B" plus across the board. Statistics showed somewhat more modest grades awarded in certain professional subdivisions, but with increases all around. The faculty's survey pointed out, for example, that

Trends in Grade Point Average (GPA)[1]: Fall 2004 to Spring 2014[2]

	Fall 2004	Fall 2005	Fall 2006	Fall 2007	Fall 2008	Fall 2009	Spring 2010	Spring 2011	Spring 2012	Spring 2013	Spring 2014
Undergraduate											
Arts & Sciences	3.21	3.21	3.19	3.23	3.23	3.26	3.31	3.30	3.30	3.32	3.35
Business	3.12	3.09	3.17	3.15	3.10	3.23	3.20	3.12	3.16	3.18	3.24
Education	3.19	3.29	3.15	3.30	3.26	3.27	3.33	3.28	3.32	3.25	3.32
IAPS	3.18	3.33	3.28	3.35	3.32	3.36	3.40	3.36	3.45	3.44	3.50
Nursing	3.35	3.25	3.29	3.37	3.36	3.27	3.34	3.37	3.45	3.44	3.46
Social Work	3.36	3.29	3.29	3.22	3.19	3.31	3.33	3.29	3.36	3.42	3.48
University College	3.35	3.23	3.23	3.33	3.30	3.40	3.34	3.34	3.41	3.36	3.40
General Studies	2.42	2.15	2.48	2.45	2.75	2.77	2.87	2.68	2.81	2.86	2.84
Total	**3.22**	**3.20**	**3.19**	**3.25**	**3.23**	**3.27**	**3.30**	**3.29**	**3.33**	**3.33**	**3.37**
Graduate											
Arts & Sciences	3.71	3.72	3.68	3.66	3.67	3.71	3.76	3.87	3.78	3.81	3.77
Business	3.56	3.47	3.53	3.54	3.53	3.54	3.61	3.56	3.40	3.48	3.52
Education	3.65	3.67	3.67	3.69	3.58	3.75	3.73	3.74	3.76	3.76	3.77
IAPS	3.70	3.75	3.70	3.76	3.47	3.77	3.86	3.86	3.87	3.85	3.86
Nursing	3.80	3.84	3.79	3.70	3.83	3.71	3.69	3.71	3.64	3.72	3.62
Social Work	3.55	3.50	3.48	3.53	3.20	3.49	3.36	3.53	3.63	3.64	3.63
University College	•••	•••	•••	3.55	3.75	3.78	3.25	3.40	3.63	3.68	3.24
Total	**3.63**	**3.62**	**3.64**	**3.64**	**3.65**	**3.66**	**3.73**	**3.67**	**3.68**	**3.69**	**3.77**

[1] Semester GPA (Excluding NYSUT)
[2] Spring data were used because fall data are not available before February.

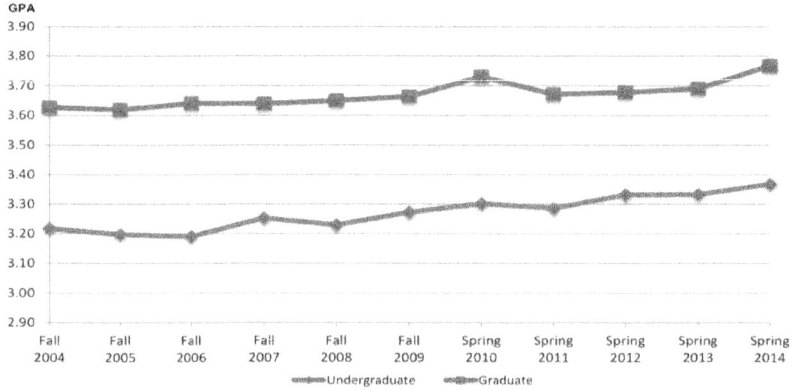

Figure 7.2. Trends in Grade Point Average (GPA): Fall 2004 to Spring 2014. Source: Adelphi University 2014 Data Book, page 168.

the GPA of Finance majors shifted impressively between 2003 and 2005, from 2.7 to 3.0.[20]

GENERAL STUDIES AND THE MAJORS

An examination of the majors is pertinent to a review of the grades of General Studies when they leave the program. Adelphi offers undergraduate concentrations in several noted professional areas: Education, Nursing, Psychology, Business, and Social Work. It has been possible to earn a master's degree in a few of these fields at Adelphi with one additional year of study. But, as has been demonstrated countrywide, the number of college graduates working in the field they studied is shrinking; and this is not to mention the number unemployed.

Many focus in majors deemed concrete. However a good number in General Studies go into the sophomore year "undecided." The push to rapidly enter a career track grates against the recognized benefits of continuing to explore and reflect on choices a bit more, and as well clouds the advantages of a broad education en route to a career. The Commission on the Humanities and Social Sciences of the American Academy of Arts and Sciences warns that material questions "have caused some to question the liberal arts tradition itself, on the grounds that its elements do not all contribute visibly and directly to near-term employment. But this concern misses the ways in which the liberal arts train people to adapt and change over a lifetime." Indeed, "[A]t a time when economic anxiety is driving the public toward a narrow concept of education focused on short-term payoffs, it is imperative that colleges, universities, and their supporters make a clear and convincing case for the value of liberal arts education."[21]

For both General Studies alumni and other Adelphi students, the majors perceptibly leading to occupations in health care, entrepreneurship, education, and mental health careers may seem a better bet. The choices of General Studies students bear out both the predilection for study in these areas and the nationally reported reluctance among freshman to be pressured into premature decisions. With many majors to choose from, 10 percent of the General Studies enrollees in 2008–2009 opted for Nursing after freshman year. A larger proportion went into Education. Business and Psychology barely trailed Nursing in major choice. The four areas accounted for roughly half of all academic concentrations. But "Undecided" made up another quarter of relevant student declarations. Together, Psychology and "Undecided" were far and away the most selected options of General Studies students one year later, totaling 25 percent of the students completing the program. Fewer prospective nurses and business people emerged; a good number of would-be teachers identified themselves, equaling those majoring in Physical Therapy.[22]

Needless to say, the fields of education, counseling, social work, psychology, and health care have also been subjected to privatization, standardization, and erosion of standards. When examining the other majors which attract General Studies students, the expanse is wide: History, Math, Sports Management, English, Environmental Studies, Criminal Justice, Biology, Chemistry, Physical Education, Communications, Speech Pathology, Theatre, Dance, Art, Music. The latter four naturally hinge on portfolios or auditions. Selecting from the humanities or social sciences departments without also affiliating with the School of Education is rare. But every General Studies cohort contains a handful entering these disciplines as such. The smallness of the number and the scattering of choices are characteristic.[23]

Assuming a chosen major, concentration on professional training and a diffusion of interests outward are the two main trends. Nursing, Physical Education, Education, Business Management, and Psychology led the way for the 2002 group: the Class of 2006. A number concentrated on training as teachers, with a partnered major in one of the humanities: History and Philosophy, especially the former. A diversity of areas made up the rest: Biology, Political Science, Sociology, Theatre, and Anthropology. Few opted for Social Work after General Studies. A higher number than usual entered the sophomore ranks as "undeclared" in the following year. Nevertheless, common options gradually stood out for the Class of 2007: Nursing, Business Management, Business Administration, and Psychology, with diverse Arts and Sciences dotting the map. But fewer linked the last mentioned with the School of Education. And not a one keyed in on Social Work.[24]

Adelphi's five-year bachelor's-master's program in Education—STEP—meanwhile grew apace, and this was reflected in the calculations of General Studies students who began college in 2004. Hence, Education attracted a greater number than in the previous years, and the teaching profession took a visible place beside the other hopefully practical paths after General Studies. Among the twinned STEP-Arts and Sciences majors were History, English, and Math. (Here and there went an eventual social worker or psychologist, a journalist, or even a political scientist unattached to teaching.) The rest lined up in Nursing and the Business branches. The Class of 2009 continued the movement toward teacher training (linked to Sociology and History), but Nursing became the dominant track. Business Management still held its own among students who came into General Studies in 2005. And then an assortment of expressed interests: Biology, Communications, Social Work, Psychology.[25]

Cohorts from 2006 to 2008 sent out students according to the patterns. Business, Psychology, Nursing, and something of an awakening of Social Work, characterize the majors. But the percentage of "undecided" students dropped. By 2008, nearly every General Studies student had declared a major following freshman year, perhaps in light of the incipient economic crisis. Tie-ins between Education and History, Sociology, Psychology, and English constituted a persistent current, though a few students opted to steer these disciplines away from teaching careers. New or improved Adelphi offerings beckoned as well, for example in Criminal Justice, Physical Therapy, and Sports Management, also in the "concrete" vein.[26]

From 2009 to 2012, the cohorts made key amendments to the bigger picture, sparked by the strengthening of Psychology and Education and the relative decline of the Business options. The first two, together with Nursing, led other majors. Once again, most program alumni had made up their minds before sophomore year, rather than delaying major choice. Students designating Social Work breathed among each collective, alongside appellants spanning Computer Science, Communications Disorders, Theatre, Biology, Accounting, and Art Education. Ebbs and flows were evidenced: the most popular areas of study often switched places, and "Undecided" constituted the official status of many in the second year. A full third of the 2012–2013 cohort went into sophomorehood without a major. But where Business concentrations used to lead in subject choice, other professional orientations competed for student allegiance, as the economic recession worsened. In 2011–2012 for example, only six General Studies students inclined toward Business areas for the sophomore year. But eight preferred Psychology, and twenty-one went into Nursing. Twice the number went into Biology than those who picked Business fields after the 2012–2013 academic year; the ratio of Nursing to Business majors was also two to one. One is struck by the presence of General Studies students in occupational programs with tough criteria for entering and remaining.[27]

Table 7.1 at the end of the chapter reveals declarations of major by each student at the outset of the first college semester in General Studies. It covers four cohorts. The proliferation of "undecided" students is marked. The earlier in the first semester that students are asked to indicate a major, the greater the number choosing "undecided." Evidence appearing later in this study will include graduation rates of the selected classes. It will demonstrate a good deal of change and clarification of major choices in the years leading to commencement. Once again, most General Studies students do not begin fields of concentration until they are sophomores.

THE RISE IN GPAS AFTER GENERAL STUDIES

What happens to the grades of former General Studies students remaining at Adelphi once they have left the program? Aside from an occasional special study, no agency consistently tracked post–General Studies development until after the provost's investigation into General Studies in 2002. Thereafter the program produced in-depth annual surveys exemplifying the unmistakable trend: as the former program students progressed through the university, their grades went up. The results transcended the earliest, somewhat hazy, reports in 1987 finding "the vast majority of those who left General Studies in good academic standing have maintained that status this Fall." Fragmentary sources survive which highlight the sophomore grades of former program members placed on probation at the end of the program's first year, 1985–1986. Having finished General Studies below 2.0, but not dismissed, most of the twenty-two students overcame probation by the time of their second sophomore semester. They were, for the most part, Business majors. The students not placed on probation by General Studies went on in the fall of sophomore year to do no worse than they had in the program. They compiled a GPA of 2.32; the previous semester, while still in General Studies, the class average had been 2.31.[28]

Since 2000, the percentage of former program students thereafter attaining 3.0 or better as upperclassmen increased as well. The number of dismissed students—whose exodus certainly enhances the net performance level of the cohort—has diminished to about half a dozen a year as the entering high school grades have improved and the program has cohered as a learning community: but the SAT scores have barely budged. Withdrawals and transfers have rested primarily on financial reasons, explaining the departure of many of the strongest former General Studies students.

While 15 percent scored 3.0 or better in the General Studies group of 2002–2003, close to 40 percent of the remaining students had reached that level by senior year. Once again, students still at Adelphi from the entering class reflected all gradations of academic strength and by no means comprised only the most outstanding of the original group. Indeed, the percent of the cohort over 3.0 at Adelphi doubled between the final freshman semester in General Studies (Spring 2003) and the second sophomore term in the majors (Spring 2004).[29]

The weakest students in 2003–2004 were dismissed after the fall semester, in which 16 percent of the entire group averaged 3.0 or beyond. Still only 17 percent of the cohort in spring semester garnered averages in this happy range by term's end. Grades blossomed after General Studies. A striking—by General Studies terms—65 percent of the continuing students produced 3.0 and sweeter by 2007, senior year. About 70 percent of the 2004–2005 cohort still at Adelphi belonged to this category. Here too, evidence shows individual GPAs improving every year.[30]

General Studies witnessed a high number of dismissals after fall 2005, when the collective average was 2.14 and only nine percent wound up in "B" territory or better. The program's 3.0 and higher rate rose to 21 percent in spring 2006. Once done with General Studies and launched upon the majors, the 2005–2006 alumni greatly improved their GPAs, with well over half landing at 3.0 and above as second-year students. More impressive, the degree of 3.0 attainment by persisting students would mount to 67 percent by senior year. Among the former entrants in this formidable group were several whom the program had placed on probation for sub-2.0 performance in the first year. The academic year 2006–2007 marked a General Studies class in which the proportion of supra-"B" students rose to breakthrough levels. When nearly twenty left Adelphi after the fall, some 41 percent of those remaining matched or bettered 3.0 in the spring, bringing the year's net to 36 percent in this range. Most of the class went to sophomore year at Adelphi. Entering the majors proved of immediate benefit: the percentage above 3.0 went up 23 points. By four-year graduation time—spring 2010—75 percent were thus ensconced.[31]

The enrollees of 2007–2008 also ranked high (in General Studies, not Adelphi, context) in above-average program grades. The dismissals were minimal, thus with little effect on the class mean. "B" and beyond students made up no less than a third of the whole, fall and spring. Several of the highest-achieving General Studies freshmen did not continue at Adelphi. But grades rose at a faster clip once the remaining members were done with General Studies and became sophomores: fully half the group earned no less than 3.0 in their majors now. Junior year was better still, with 63 percent doing likewise. The cohort of 2008–2009 had the same experience. Early on, the program removed several students from the university for academic reasons, but grades otherwise ascended in General Studies. Essentially 40 percent of the class never dipped below 3.0 all year. But the proportion went up when the students began their majors the next year, and it nearly doubled between sophomore and senior years. The grades of the continuing majority increased annually. Thus, 71 percent of the persisting General Studies Class of 2012 resided in the 3.0 and up camp by the time of commencement.[32]

The General Studies "B" minimum sector was just as heavy in fall 2009. Only three members of the cohort were ruled ineligible to return for spring 2010 on academic grounds. Students who left the university voluntarily after the fall semester were among the program's best. No consistency prevails among the students who dropped out, transferred, or took leaves over the three years to follow: strong, middling, and weaker ones were among them. As the former cohort students entered their concentration subjects, their averages expanded. By the end of sophomore year, 56 percent of the program's alumni were in 3.0 condition at least. When senior year came, 63 percent of the surviving Class of 2013 were at this level. The following year, General Studies dismissed three students from the fall 2010 cohort, but reinstated one. The other non-returnees occupied the grade range from below 2.0 to well above 3.0. A third of the 2010–2011 collective entered their sophomore year majors with a minimum 3.0 Adelphi index. Though steady expansion of grades typified much of the cohort as it wound its way through the university, the proportion in the thriving category at and beyond 3.0 grew more slowly: 46 percent in sophomore year, 58 percent by junior year.[33]

General Studies was clearly in a new phase by 2011–2012. The group GPA waxed bright. Students who chose not to continue from fall to spring were at all academic levels. In general, their departure was unrelated to "weeding out" the weakest students. The dismissal of a handful carried out the latter mission. Upon enrolling in the concentrated fields of study, student averages scaled new heights, improving smartly over the two sophomore semesters. By the close of the second year, 60 percent lived in the atmospheres beyond "B."

GRADES IN PERSPECTIVES

The record is replete with students whose academic standing substantially improved across the majors after having completed below-average work in General Studies. Cases include students placed on first-year probation by General Studies, of which a number took academic honors at graduation. But the GPA evolution of former General Studies students is not identical, assuming both commitment to the major and the existence of grade inflation in certain fields. Of course, many former program members have seen their fortunes rise in the warm air of different grading practices. Yet attributing the success of the students in general to grade inflation negates their possession of genuine skills and assumes questionable instructional practice across the board, for which there is no evidence. In any case, constituents at the lower end of General Studies passing standards indeed do better when they join the majors, but not as well as their confreres who did better in the program.[34]

Grades are a piece of the puzzle of success, but do not define intelligence. Bright students come in all guises, their grades subject to growth, but as well to stress, financial circumstances, and other situations. Thus, tuition was a major hurdle during most of General Studies' history. As long as their lower SAT scores made them ineligible for scholarships (since they were deemed "at-risk"), hundreds of program members might become discouraged about their prospects, with potential influence on coursework. Assuming that SAT scores connoted success potential performed a genuine disservice to the financial well-being of General Studies students. The university's reversal of this policy in 2016 tacitly recognized that deeper circumstances factored into student progress beyond General Studies, and that the SAT mark was a problematic criterion of academic merit.[35]

The doubts so often expressed about the horizons of students of the General Studies type—"underperforming" in standardized tests or in high school—traditionally stereotype the abilities of all of them, not merely a layer. Ideally, students solidify, organize, and establish themselves as college students through General Studies, hence progressing through their majors. Certainly many become genuinely interested in their fields and the hope of earning a living thereby. No doubt, improving grades involve several facilitating combinations, including what the students bring to the table. In all, their academic outcomes disprove the College Boards with even greater force.[36]

Text box 7.1 shows totals of student performance while in the program. It includes SAT scores and high school averages, and supplies overall freshman outcomes. For certain years, a slight discrepancy may exist between the numbers of students given in text box 7.1 and the figures for the 2003, 2006, and 2010 cohorts in chapters 8 and 9. The disparate sources of decline from fall to spring (financial blocks, transfers, dismissals, or non-returns) are not known at the same time. In some cases the status of non-returnees is not clear until a bit later.[37] Table 7.1, which follows, shows choices of majors of four General Studies cohorts.[38]

Textbox 7.1. General Studies GPA Trends 2002–2014

Keys: HS GPA: High School GPA
VSAT: Verbal SAT
MSAT: Math SAT
WSAT: Writing section of the SAT
AA: Academic Achievement Award in General Studies

2013–2014 Academic Year

The Cumulative GPA at the completion of the **2013–2014** Academic Year, calculated on 72 students

44% received a grade of 3.0 or higher
31% received a grade of 2.50–2.99
18% received a grade of 2.0–2.49
7% received a grade under a 2.0
93% of the students are in Good Academic Standing with a GPA of 2.0 or higher
The average GPA is: 2.79

The GPA Breakdown for Spring 2014, calculated on 72 students

42% received a grade of 3.0 or higher
33% received a grade of 2.50–2.99
17% received a grade of 2.0–2.49
8% received a grade under a 2.0
92% of the students are in Good Academic Standing with a GPA of 2.0 or higher
The average GPA is: 2.8
Four students made Dean's List
One student from Fall 2012 was readmitted for Spring
One student withdrew before finals
Twenty-eight retained an AA
Three of the seven students on Probation for Spring attained over a 2.0 cum for the year

The GPA breakdown for Fall 2013, calculated on 81 students

38% received a grade of 3.0 or higher
29% received a grade of 2.5–2.99
17% received a grade of 2.0–2.49
16% received a grade below a 2.0

84% of the students are in Good Academic Standing
The average GPA is: 2.0
Two students made Dean's List with a GPA of 3.5 or higher
Thirty-one students qualified for an AA
Five students withdrew—three before the semester started, one after midterms, one student went to half time after end of semester

Academic Profile of the Class of 2017
HS GPA 2.91
VSAT 455
MSAT 455
WSAT 453
SAT 1367

2012–2013 Academic Year

The Cumulative GPA at the completion of the **2012–2013** Academic Year, calculated on 85 students

40% received a grade of 3.0 or higher
35% received a grade of 2.50–2.99
21% received a grade of 2.0–2.49
4% received a grade under a 2.0
96% of the students are in Good Academic Standing with a GPA of 2.0 or higher
The average GPA is: 2.86

The GPA Breakdown for Spring 2013, calculated on 85 students

44% received a grade of 3.0 or higher
28% received a grade of 2.50–2.99
21% received a grade of 2.0–2.49
7% received a grade under a 2.0
93% of the students are in Good Academic Standing with a GPA of 2.0 or higher
The average GPA is: 2.85
Nine students made Dean's List
One student withdrew before finals
One student was on Probation

The GPA breakdown for Fall 2012, calculated on 90 students

38% received a grade of 3.0 or higher
36% received a grade of 2.5–2.99
9% received a grade of 2.0–2.49
6% received a grade below a 2.0
94% of the students are in Good Academic Standing

The average GPA is: 2.81
Four students made Dean's List with a GPA of 3.5 or higher
Thirty-six students qualified for an AA
A total of seven students withdrew—five before the semester started, one before midterms

Academic Profile of the Class of 2016

HS GPA 3.05
VSAT 445
MSAT 458
WSAT 458
SAT 1361

2011–2012 Academic Year

The Cumulative GPA at the completion of the **2011–2012** Academic Year, calculated on 88 students

33% received a grade of 3.0 or higher
43% received a grade of 2.50–2.99
19% received a grade of 2.0–2.49
5% received a grade under a 2.0
95% of the students are in Good Academic Standing with a GPA of 2.0 or higher
The average GPA is: 2.78
Twenty-three students maintained AA status, eight retained monetary award

The GPA breakdown for Spring 2012, calculated on 88 students

38% received a grade of 3.0 or higher
36% received a grade of 2.50–2.99
18% received a grade of 2.0–2.49
8% received a grade under a 2.0
92% of the students are in Good Academic Standing with a GPA of 2.0 or higher
The average GPA is: 2.78
Seven students made Dean's List with a GPA of 3.5 or higher
Six students were dismissed in the fall
Five students did not return for financial reasons, two were on Probation, one was a monetary AA winner

The GPA Breakdown for the Fall 2011 Academic Year, calculated on 99 students

32% received a grade of 3.0 or higher
36% received a grade of 2.5–2.99
20% received a grade of 2.0–2.49

12% received a grade below a 2.0
88% of the students are in Good Academic Standing
The average GPA is: 2.62
Eight students made Dean's List with a GPA of 3.5 or higher
Thirty-two students qualified for an AA status, with thirteen receiving a monetary award
A total of six students withdrew—one after midterms on a Medical

Academic Profile of the Class of 2015
HS GPA 2.8
VSAT 446
MSAT 462
WSAT 395
SAT 1303

2010–2011 Academic Year

The Cumulative GPA at the completion of the **2010–2011** Academic Year calculated on 103 students

33% received a grade of 3.0 or higher
40% received a grade of 2.50–2.99
21% received a grade of 2.0–2.49
7% received a grade under a 2.0
93% of the students are in Good Academic Standing with a GPA of 2.0 or higher
The average GPA is: 2.76
Thirty-one students maintained the AA
Three additional students qualified for the AA

The GPA breakdown for Spring 2011, calculated on 103 students

30% received a grade of 3.0 or higher
36% received a grade of 2.50–2.99
22% received a grade of 2.0–2.49
22% received a grade under a 2.0
88% of the students are in Good Academic Standing with a GPA of 2.0 or higher
The average GPA is: 2.66
Thirty-one students maintained the AA
Five students made Dean's List with a GPA of 3.5 or higher
Five students did not return for financial reasons
One student did not return due to Medical w/d in the fall

The GPA breakdown for Fall 2010, calculated on 112 students with 1 student getting Medical Incomplete

40% received a grade of 3.0 or higher
35% received a grade of 2.5–2.99
17% received a grade of 2.0–2.49
8% received a grade below a 2.0
92% of the students are in Good Academic Standing
The average GPA is: 2.74
Three students made Dean's List with a GPA of 3.5 or higher
Forty-five students qualified for an AA
A total of seven students withdrew—two after midterms
Three students were dismissed—one was reinstated
Five students were placed on probation but one of them withdrew from the university

Academic Profile of the Class of 2014
HS GPA 2.88
VSAT 449
MSAT 455
WSAT 456
SAT 1360

2009–2010 Academic Year

The Cumulative GPA at the completion of the **2009–2010** Academic Year

38% received a grade of 3.0 or higher
40% received a grade of 2.50–2.99
20% received a grade of 2.0–2.49
2% received a grade under a 2.0
98% of the students are in Good Academic Standing with a GPA of 2.0 or higher
The average GPA is: 2.84
Thirty students maintained the AA
Five additional students qualified for the AA

The GPA breakdown for Spring 2010, calculated on 86 students

44% received a grade of 3.0 or higher
33% received a grade of 2.50–2.99
16% received a grade of 2.0–2.49
7% received a grade under a 2.0
93% of the students are in Good Academic Standing with a GPA of 2.0 or higher
The average GPA is: 2.86
Thirty students maintained the AA
Fourteen students made Dean's List
Three students dismissed

Seven students did not return for financial reasons
Four students transferred

The GPA breakdown for Fall 2009, calculated on 100 students

35% received a grade of 3.0 or higher
39% received a grade of 2.5–2.99
19% received a grade of 2.0–2.49
7% received a grade below a 2.0
93% of the students are in Good Academic Standing
The average GPA is: 2.77
Seven students made Dean's List with a GPA of 3.5 or higher
Thirty-five students received an AA
A total of ten students withdrew—five before the semester began, five after the semester began
Three students were dismissed
Four students were put on probation

Academic Profile of the Class of 2013
HS GPA 3.4
VSAT 448
MSAT 448
WSAT 450
SAT 1342

2008–2009 Academic Year

The Cumulative GPA at the completion of the **2008–2009** Academic Year

42% received a grade of 3.0 or higher
27% received a grade of 2.50–2.99
25% received a grade of 2.0–2.49
6% received a grade under a 2.0
94% of the students are in Good Academic Standing with a GPA of 2.0 or higher
The average GPA is: 2.82
Thirty-two students maintained the AA (additional course increased GPA)

The GPA breakdown for Spring 2009, calculated on 84 students

43% received a grade of 3.0 or higher
24% received a grade of 2.50–2.99
17% received a grade of 2.0–2.49
7% received a grade under a 2.0
92% of the students are in Good Academic Standing with a GPA of 2.0 or higher

The average GPA is: 2.81
Thirty-one students maintained the AA
Eleven students made Dean's List (additional course increased GPA)
One student withdrew from the university after the semester began
One student on Probation did not return
Five students did not return for financial reasons
Two students transferred
Two students re-admitted from 2007–2008 year

The GPA breakdown for Fall 2008, calculated on 94 students

40% received a grade of 3.0 or higher
27% received a grade of 2.5–2.99
20% received a grade of 2.0–2.49
13% received a grade below a 2.0
87% of the students are in Good Academic Standing
The average GPA is: 2.75
Nine students made Dean's List with a GPA of 3.5 or higher
Thirty-eight students received an AA
A total of five students withdrew—two before the semester began, three after the semester began
Three students were dismissed
Nine students were put on probation

Academic Profile of the Class of 2012
HS GPA 2.9
VSAT 448
MSAT 435
SAT 883

2007–2008 Academic Year

The Cumulative GPA at the completion of the **2007–2008** Academic Year

34% received a grade of 3.0 or higher
34% received a grade of 2.50–2.99
27% received a grade of 2.0–2.49
5% received a grade under a 2.0
95% of the students are in Good Academic Standing with a GPA of 2.0 or higher
The average GPA is: 2.74
Twenty-seven students maintained the AA

The GPA breakdown for Spring 2008, calculated on 80 students

35% received a grade of 3.0 or higher
31% received a grade of 2.50–2.99
20% received a grade of 2.0–2.49
14% received a grade under a 2.0
86% of the students are in Good Academic Standing with a GPA of 2.0 or higher
The average GPA is: 2.7
Twenty-seven students maintained the AA
Four students withdrew from the university after the semester began (three Medical)
Four students made Dean's List

The GPA breakdown for Fall 2007, calculated on 102 students

31% received a grade of 3.0 or higher
25% received a grade of 2.5–2.99
23% received a grade of 2.0–2.49
21% received a grade below a 2.0
79% of the students are in Good Academic Standing
The average GPA is 2.46
Seven students made Dean's List with a GPA of 3.5 or higher
Thirty-two students will receive an AA
A total of eight students withdrew—three before the semester began, five after the semester began.
Two students were dismissed by the university for disciplinary reasons

Academic Profile of the Class of 2011
HS GPA 2.90
VSAT 448
MSAT 435
SAT 883

2006–2007 Academic Year

The Cumulative GPA at the completion of the **2006–2007** Academic Year

36% received a grade of 3.0 or higher
24% received a grade of 2.50–2.99
36% received a grade of 2.49–2.0
4% received a grade below 2.0
96% of the students are in Good Academic Standing with a GPA of 2.0 or higher
The average GPA is: 2.75
Twenty-three students maintained the AA
Six students will qualify for an award

The GPA Breakdown for Spring 2007, calculated on 81 students

41% received a grade of 3.0 or higher
26% received a grade of 2.40–2.99
31% received a grade of 2.49–2.0
2% received a grade below a 2.0
98% of the students are in Good Academic Standing with a grade of 2.0 or higher
The average GPA is: 2.81
Eleven students made the Dean's List with a 3.5 or higher
Two students withdrew before the end of the semester

The GPA Breakdown for Fall 2006, calculated on 103 students

27% received a grade of 3.0 or higher
26% received a grade of 2.5–2.99
24% received a grade of 2.0–2.49
23% received a grade below a 2.0
77% of the students are in Good Academic Standing
The average GPA is: 2.44
Twenty-seven students were awarded AA
Five students made Dean's List with a 3.5 or higher
Eight students are on probation
Seventeen students were dismissed—three decisions were reversed
Six students did not return after Fall 2006
A total of seven students withdrew—three before the semester began, four after the semester began

Academic Profile of the Class of 2010
HS GPA 2.4
VSAT 430
MSAT 440
SAT 870

2005–2006 Academic Year

The Cumulative GPA at completion of the **2005–2006** Academic Year

13% received a grade of 3.0 or higher
40% received a grade of 2.50–2.99
32% received a grade of 2.49–2.0
15% received a grade below 2.0
85% of the students are in Good Academic Standing with a GPA of 2.0 or higher
The average GPA is: 2.51
Eight out of nine students maintained their AAs

Two students achieved AA status

The GPA Breakdown for Spring 2006, calculated on 80 students

21% received a grade of 3.0 or higher
39% received a grade of 2.50–2.99
26% received a grade of 2.49–2.0
14% received a grade below a 2.0
86% of the students were in Good Academic Standing with a GPA of 2.0 or higher
The average GPA is: 2.59
Three students made the Dean's List with a GPA of 3.5 or higher

The GPA is Breakdown for Fall 2005, calculated on 102 students

9% received a grade of 3.0 or higher
28% received a grade of 2.5–2.99
29% received a grade of 2.0–2.49
36% received a grade below a 2.0
64% of the students are in Good Academic Standing with a GPA of 2.0 or higher
The average GPA is 2.14
Two students made Dean's List with a 3.5 or higher
Nine students received AAs
A total of two students withdrew before the end of the semester—two are pending Medical
Twenty-two students were dismissed
Four students were reinstated
Three students did not return to Adelphi

Academic Profile of the Class of 2009
HS GPA 2.5
VSAT 450
MSAT 440
SAT 890

2004–2005 Academic Year

The Cumulative GPA at completion of the **2004–2005** Academic Year

29% received a grade of 3.0 or higher
24% received a grade of 2.50–2.99
34% received a grade of 2.49–2.0
13% received a grade below 2.0
87% of the students are in Good Academic Standing with a GPA of 2.0 or higher
The average GPA is: 2.57

The GPA Breakdown for Spring 2005, calculated on 76 students

24% received a grade of 3.0 or higher
29% received a grade of 2.5–2.99
33% received a grade of 2.0–2.49
14% received a grade below 2.0
86% of the students are in Good Academic Standing with a GPA of 2.0 or higher
The average GPA is: 2.57
Four students made Dean's List with a GPA of 3.5 or higher
Twenty-two students received the AA
Fourteen students on Probation

The GPA Breakdown for Fall 2004, calculated on 90 students

23% received a grade of 3.0 or higher
24% received a grade of 2.5–2.99
26% received a grade of 2.0–2.49
27% received a grade below 2.0
73% of the students are in Good Academic Standing
The average GPA is: 2.38
One student made Dean's List with a GPA over 3.5 or higher
A total of eight students withdrew (six personal reasons, two Medical)
Ninety-eight students starting Fall 2004
Eight students withdrew before end of the semester
Eight students were dismissed
Three students transferred
1 student withdrew for financial reasons
Two students did not return

Academic Profile of the Class of 2008
HS GPA 2.5
VSAT 462
MSAT 455
SAT 917

2003–2004 Academic Year

The Cumulative GPA at completion of the **2003–2004** School Year

17% received a grade of 3.0 or higher
32% received a grade of 2.5–2.99
39% received a grade of 2.0–2.49
12% received a grade below 2.0
88% of the students are in Good Academic Standing with a GPA of 2.0 or higher
The average GPA is: 2.52

The GPA Breakdown for Spring 2004, calculated on 72 students

29% received a grade of 3.0 or higher
38% received a grade of 2.0–2.49
19% received a grade of 2.5–2.99
14% received a grade below a 2.0
86% of the students are in Good Academic Standing with a GPA of 2.0 or higher
The average GPA is: 2.55
Five students made Dean's List with a GPA of 3.5 or higher

The GPA Breakdown for Fall 2003, calculated on 89 students

17% received a grade of 3.0 or higher
23% received a grade of 2.5–2.99
35% received a grade of 2.0–2.49
25% received a grade below a 2.0
75% of the students are in Good Academic Standing
The average GPA is: 2.34
Four students made the Dean's List with a GPA of 3.5 or higher
Ninety-four students starting this semester
Five students withdrew before end of semester
Nine students were dismissed
Four students transferred
One student left for financial reasons
Seventy-five students beginning Spring 2004 semester—one readmitted
Four students withdrew before end of semester
Sixty-eight students completing program: 72% of the 94 students enrolled for 2003–2004
Five students retained on probation for 04/09

Academic Profile of the Class of 2007
HS GPA 2.62
VSAT 458
MSAT 444
SAT 902

2002–2003 Academic Year

The Cumulative GPA at the completion of the **2002–2003** Academic Year

16% received a grade of 3.0 or higher
38% received a grade of 2.5–2.99
37% received a grade of 2.0–2.49
9% received a grade below a 2.0

91% of the students are in Good Academic Standing with a GPA of 2.0 or higher
The average GPA is: 2.60

The GPA Breakdown for Spring 2003, calculated on 68 students

26% received a grade of 3.0 or higher
34% received a grade of 2.5–2.99
28% received a grade of 2.0–2.49
12% received a grade below a 2.0
88% of the students are in Good Academic Standing with a GPA of 2.0 or higher
The average GPA is: 2.64
Nine students made Dean's List with a GPA of 3.5 or higher

The GPA Breakdown for Fall 2002, calculated on 81 students:

16% received a grade of 3.0 or higher
31% received a grade of 2.5–2.99
32% received a grade of 2.0–2.49
21% received a grade below a 2.0
78% of the students are in Good Academic Standing with a 2.0 or higher
The average GPA is: 2.38
Two students made Dean's List with a GPA of 3.5 or higher

Academic Profile of the Class of 2006
HS GPA 2.37
VSAT 458
MSAT 436
SAT 894

Source: *2013–2014 Final Grades*, May 19, 2014, GSC.

Table 7.1. General Studies Majors, Selected Years, Declared in Fall semester Freshman year

Class of '12	*Class of '13*	*Class of '16*	*Class of '17*
Und	Bmg	Nur	Psy
Theater	Com	Und	Che
Eng/STEP	His/CrimJ	Comm	Und
Nur	Und	Und	PolSci
Bus	Und	Und	Bio
Mus	Bio	Und	Mgmt
Und	Bmg	Comm	Art
Com/Jou	Eng/STEP	Und	ExPhys
Und	Dance	Mktg	Nur
Spe	SpePath	CrimJ	Psy
PhysTher	Psy	Health	Und
Und	His	Und	SpMgmt
Psy	Swk	Bio	Und
Und	SpMgmt	ComDis	Und
Und	Psy	Und	Mth/STEP
Acc	Bio	Bio	Eng/STEP
Bus	Psy	Bio	Bio
Bus	Und	CrimJ	Nur
Und	Und	ComDis	Und
CrimJ	Und	Und	SpMgmt
CIS	Und	ExSci	Nur
Bio	Psy	Bus	Nur
Und	Und	Art	Und
Mus	Psy	Nur	Nur
Nur	Und	Mth	Und
Acc	EnvStu	Psy	Und
Nur	Und	Acc	Und
Acc	EnvStu/STEP	Und	Und
CrimJ	PT/Bio	ExSci	Und
Und	Mth/STEP	CompSci	Mgmt
Nur	Nur	Und	Comm
Bus	Com	Und	CrJ
Und	PT/Bio	PolSc	Bio
PhysEd	Und	Int'l St/Bus	Und

Class of '12	***Class of '13***	***Class of '16***	***Class of '17***
CrimJ	PT/Ed	Bio	Psy
Psy	Art	Und	Nur
Eng/STEP	Dance	Und	Und
Mth/STEP	PT/Bio	Und	Und
Und	Mth/STEP	Chem	Und
Und	Nur	Und	Und
Com/Jou	Psy	Nur	Und
Com	Und	Nur	Und
Bus	PT/Bio	Bio	Und
Und	Psy	Und	Und
Psy	HealthEd	Comm	Nur
Theater	Com	ExSci	Und
Art	SpePath	Nur	Und
Nur	PT/Bio	Und	Nur
Und	Eng	Und	Und
Bus	Art	Und	Und
Psy/STEP	Art	Physics	Eng/STEP
Und	Psy	Comm	Und
Bus	Nur	Bio	MusEd
Bus	Und	Und	Und
Eng/STEP	Und	Und	Und
Und	EnvStu	Und	Che
Psy	Psy	Und	Und
Und	Psy	Und	CompSci
Und	Und	Bus	Und
Bus	Bio	Bio	Und
Psy/STEP	Psy	Und	Und
Nur	Und	Bio	PE
Nur	Bio	Und	Nur
Psy/Eled	PE	Und	Com
Nur	Psy	Und	Und
Bus	Und	Und	Bio
Und	Und	Und	Bio
Und	SptMgmt	Und	Und
SWK	Eng	Und	Comm
Spe	Art	Nur	Und

Class of '12	***Class of '13***	***Class of '16***	***Class of '17***
Und	Swk	Psy	Bio
SWK	Bio	Und	Bio
Eng	Eng/STEP	Nur	Und
Und/SpEd	Eng/STEP	Nur	Und
Und	Psy	Und	
Und	Und	Nur	
Psy	Bio	Bio	
PhysEd	Mus	Nur	
His	The	Und	
SptMgt	Art	Swk	
Und	STEP/Early/Mth	ComDis	
Und	Psy	Und	
Und	Psy	Und	
Eng/STEP	PE	Und	
EnvSt	Psy	Psy	
Nur	Und	Und	
Und	Psy		
His/STEP			
Und			
Nur			
Und			
Nur			
Und			
Und			

Source: *GS Majors 08-09*, GSC; *GS Majors 09-10*, GSC; *General Studies Majors Spring 2010*, GSC; *GS Majors 12-13*, GSC; *GS Majors 13-14*, GSC. Note: Designed by Daniel Rosenberg. I Acc (Accounting), Bio (Biology), BMG (Business Management), Bus (Business), Che or Chem (Chemistry), Com or Comm (Communications), ComDis (Communication Disorders), ComJou (Communications/Journalism), CompSci (Computer Science), CrimJ or CrJ (Criminal Justice), Early (Early Childhood Education), Ed (Education), Eng (English), EnvStu (Environmental Studies), ExPhys (Exercise Physiology), ExSci (Exercise Science), His (History), Int'l St (International Studies), Mgmt (Management), Mktg (Marketing), Mth (Math), Mus (Music), Nur (Nursing), PE or Phys Ed (Physical Education), PolSci (Political Science), Psy (Psychology), PT or PhysTher (Physical Therapy), SpePath or Spe (Speech Pathology), SpMgmt (Sports Management), STEP or Step (Scholar Teacher Education Program), Swk (Social Work), The (Theater), Und (Undecided)

NOTES

1. Rudy Fichtenbaum, quoted in Hechinger Report, *Community College Spotlight*, http://communitycollegespotlight.org/tags/performance-funding/. Accessed January 9, 2015; Nicholas W. Hillman et al., "Evaluating the Impacts of 'New' Performance Funding in Higher Education," *Educational Evaluation and Policy Analysis*, Vol. 20, No. 10, 14.

2. Stuart Rojstaczer and Christopher Healey, "Grading in American Colleges and Universities," *Teachers College Record*, March 4, 2010, http://www.tcrecord.org ID Number 15928. Accessed March 4, 2010; "Making the Grades," editorial, *New York Times*, June 5, 1994, A16; Upton Sinclair, *The Goose-Step: A Study of American Education*, New York, 1936 (1922), 17.

3. Mark Perry, "High GPAs Have Little Use As Student Motivator Or Evaluation Tool For Grad Schools And Employers," *Daily Markets*, July 15, 2011, http://www.dailymarkets.com/economy/2011/07/15/high-gpas-have-little-use-as-student-motivator-or-evaluation-tool-for-grad-schools-and-employers/. Accessed August 1, 2011; Stuart Rojstaczer and Christopher Healy, "Where A Is Ordinary: The Evolution of American College and University Grading, 1940–2009," *Teachers College Record*, Vol. 114, No. 7 (2012). http://www.tcrecord.org/Content.asp?ContentId=16473. Accessed August 1, 2011.

4. Ross Buettner, "Guilty Plea in Grade-Fixing at Baruch," *New York Times*, December 20, 2012, A30.

5. Meryl Shapiro to Dean Cavallo, *General Studies Student's* [sic] *Fall 1987 GPAs*, January 1988, GSC; Meryl Shapiro to Dean Cavallo, *Breakdown of Grades for General Studies Students*, May 19, 1988, GSC; Meryl Shapiro to Dean Cavallo, *General Studies Committee on Academic Performance*, May 20, 1988, GSC; University College: A Report, *Cohort Attrition, 1985–1994*, 1994, GSC.

6. Joanna LoRe, "Alumni Spotlight: Gloria Hernandez," *General Studies Newsletter*, Spring 2005, 3; Jordan Griffith, "Gloria Hernandez-Croce '94: Teaching and Reaching Young Minds," *General Studies Newsletter*, Spring 2014, 6; Barbara Shulman to Dean Cavallo, *Breakdown of Grades for General Studies Students*, June 4, 1990, GSC.

7. General Studies I, *Fall 1993 and Spring 1994 Grades*, Series I, 1994, GSC; Della Hudson-Tomlin to Dr. David Newton, *Final 1993–94 Statistics*, May 18, 1994, GSC; Jeffrey Blaine, "Alumni Highlight: Dr. Hamidah Sharif-Harris '98," *General Studies Newsletter*, Spring 2010, 10.

8. Jim Wilshire to Della Hudson-Tomlin, *Average Scores for General Studies I Class of 1994–95*, September 1, 1994, GSC; Della Hudson-Tomlin, *Midterm Grades Fall 1994 General Studies*, circa November 1994, GSC; *General Studies 1994–95 Final Grades, GSC.*

9. Della Hudson-Tomlin to David Newton, Dean, *1995–1996 General Studies Freshman Class*, September 13, 1995, GSC; Della Hudson-Tomlin to David Newton, *General Studies Fall 1995 Final Grade Report*, January 2, 1996, GSC.

10. *Adelphi University Databook*, Fall 2009, 166; *2006–2007 Final Grades*, GSC; *2010–2011 Final Grades*, May 18, 2011, GSC.

11. Peter J. Markie, *Professor's Duties: Ethical Considerations in College Teaching*, Lanham, MD, 1994, 55, 190.

12. *Spring 1994 Final Grades*, GSC.

13. *Adelphi University Databook*, Fall 2009, 165, 167; *Adelphi University Databook*, Fall 2010, 163–64; *Adelphi University Databook*, Fall 2013, 173–74.

14. Deirdre Donat, *2008-2009 Final Grades*, May 27, 2009, GSC; *Adelphi University Databook*, Fall 2009, 165; *Adelphi University Databook*, Fall 2010, 163; *Adelphi University Databook*, Fall 2011, 163; James B. Mullin, *Report of the Task Force on Grades*, May 26, 2006, GSC.

15. *Adelphi University Databook*, Fall 2006, 149; *Adelphi University Databook*, Fall 2007, 155; *Adelphi University Databook*, Fall 2008, 159; *Adelphi University Databook*, Fall 2009, 165; *Adelphi University Databook*, Fall 2010, 163; *Adelphi University Databook*, Fall 2011, 163; *Adelphi University Databook*, Fall 2012, 167.

16. *Adelphi University Databook,* Fall 2008, 160; *Adelphi University Databook,* Fall 2011, 164.

17. *Adelphi University Databook,* Fall 2006, 150; *Adelphi University Databook,* Fall 2014, 168.

18. Office of Research, Assessment and Planning, Adelphi University, "Selected Findings from the HERI Faculty Survey," *ORAP Research Bulletin,* January 2006; Office of Research, Assessment and Planning, Adelphi University, *Results of the Cooperative Institutional Research Program (CIRP) Survey Fall 2000 to Fall 2010,* April 2011, 23.

19. James P. Mullin et al., *Report of the Task Force on Grades,* May 26, 2006, 5–14, GSC.

20. James P. Mullin et al., *Report of the Task Force on Grades,* "Mean GPA by Academic Unit," May 26, 2006, GSC.

21. American Academy of Arts and Sciences, Commission on the Humanities and Social Sciences, *The Heart of the Matter,* Cambridge, MA, 2013, 32.

22. College Board, *Adelphi University,* https://bigfuture.collegeboard.org/college-university-search/adelphi-university. Accessed July 5, 2013; Deirdre Donat, *GS Majors 08–09,* GSC; Deirdre Donat, *GS Majors 09–10,* GSC; Deirdre Donat, *General Studies Majors Spring 2010,* GSC.

23. Deirdre Donat, *GS Majors 08–09,* GSC; Deirdre Donat, *GS Majors 09–10,* GSC; Deirdre Donat, *General Studies Majors Spring 2010,* GSC.

24. Deirdre Donat, *Class of 2006 Tracking,* May 2008, GSC; Deirdre Donat, *Class of 2007 Tracking,* May 2010, GSC.

25. Deirdre Donat, *Class of 2008 Tracking,* May 2009, GSC; Deirdre Donat, *Class of 2009 Tracking,* May 2010, GSC.

26. Deirdre Donat, *Class of 2010 Tracking,* May 2010, GSC; Deirdre Donat, *Class of 2011 Tracking,* May 2011, GSC; Deirdre Donat, *Class of 2012 Tracking,* May 2012, GSC.

27. Deirdre Donat, *Class of 2013 Tracking,* May 2013, GSC; Deirdre Donat, *Class of 2014 Tracking,* May 2013, GSC: Deirdre Donat, *Class of 2015 Tracking,* May 2013, GSC; Deirdre Donat, *2012–2013 Final Grades,* May 17, 2013, GSC.

28. Meryl Shapiro to Sally Baker, *Grade Point Averages for Second Year Probation Students,* January 12, 1987, GSC; Meryl Shapiro to Diane Beltrani, *General Studies Students,* May 29, 1987, GSC; Meryl Shapiro to Dean Cavallo, *Second Year General Studies Students,* January 29, 1987, GSC.

29. Deirdre Donat, *Class of 2006 Tracking,* May 2008, GSC.

30. Deirdre Donat, *Class of 2007 Tracking,* May 2008, GSC; Deirdre Donat, *Class of 2008 Tracking,* May 2009, GSC.

31. Deirdre Donat, *Class of 2009 Tracking,* May 2010, GSC; Deirdre Donat, *Class of 2010 Tracking,* May 2010, GSC.

32. Deirdre Donat, *Class of 2011 Tracking,* May 2011, GSC; Deirdre Donat, *Class of 2012 Tracking,* May 2012, GSC.

33. Deirdre Donat, *Class of 2013 Tracking,* May 2013, GSC; Deirdre Donat, *Class of 2014 Tracking,* May 2013, GSC.

34. James P. Mullin et al., *Report of the Task Force on Grades,* "Mean GPA by Academic Unit," May 26, 2006, GSC; Deirdre Donat, *Class of 2006 Tracking,* May 2008, GSC; Deirdre Donat, *Class of 2007 Tracking,* May 2010, GSC; Deirdre Donat, *Class of 2008 Tracking,* May 2009, GSC; Deirdre Donat, *Class of 2009 Tracking,* May 2010, GSC; Deirdre Donat, *Class of 2010 Tracking,* May 2010, GSC; Deirdre Donat, *Class of 2011 Tracking,* May 2011, GSC; Deirdre Donat, *Class of 2012 Tracking,* May 2012, GSC; Deirdre Donat, *Class of 2013 Tracking,* May 2013, GSC; Deirdre Donat, *Class of 2014 Tracking,* May 2013, GSC: Deirdre Donat, *Class of 2015 Tracking,* May 2013, GSC.

35. Robert A. Scott, *Adelphi University Master Plan 2004,* Appendix: Identify Programs of Distinction and Areas of Opportunity.

36. Les Baltimore et al., *Report of the General Studies Review Committee,* May 17, 2002, 2-7, GSC.

37. Deirdre Donat, *2013–2014 Final Grades,* May 19, 2014, GSC.

38. Deirdre Donat, *GS Majors 08–09*, GSC; Deirdre Donat, *GS Majors 09–10*, GSC; Deirdre Donat, *General Studies Majors Spring 2010*, GSC; Deirdre Donat, *GS Majors 12–13*, GSC; Deirdre Donat, *GS Majors 13–14*, GSC.

EIGHT

College Graduation and High School Average

The experiential distance between a person's days as a high school senior and commencement day in college is immense, though a relationship remains. Academically it is likely that the student will bear a certain resemblance to what she or he was four or six years ago. But while prior educational paths form part of every college grad's makeup, they logically exert less force over time. Assuming significant growth between high school and college graduation, the SAT, taken on one terrifying day as a secondary school senior, will offer even less barometric utility than four years' worth of high school.

FACTORS INFLUENCING GRADUATION AND RETENTION

Graduation is an achievement under any circumstances, no matter how long it takes. Key factors have contributed to increasingly strong General Studies retention rates over the history of the program. These include the eventual granting of some institutional assistance to incoming students in the early 2000s, the full-time consolidation and professionalization of faculty and counselors, and the genuine elements included in the improved academic profiles of General Studies entrants. Prior to these changes, graduation and retention rates of students who passed through the program were low. For example, some 69 percent of the students arriving in 1990 advanced to spring semester and 46 percent of the original group stayed on as sophomores. The further a student goes beyond the freshman year, the less her or his fate has to do with General Studies. Yet gradual retention improvements in all regards characterize General Studies, even when the university denied grants-in-aid. Hence the preservation of student numbers from fall to spring inched upward through the 1990s and first decade of the twenty-first century: roughly 80 percent by 2000, 87 percent by 2011. Similarly, persistence into sophomore-hood ticked upward: 63 percent in 2000, 78 percent in 2011. A third of the entering 2000 cohort graduated in four years, with close to half finishing in another two. Both levels have held steady.[1]

The larger the General Studies cohort, the lower the rates of retention and graduation. The changing national contours of retention and graduation rates aside, only 17 percent of the 204 students in General Studies in 1990 had finished their studies by 1994, equaling a historic low; the six-year rate was 24 percent. Then again, only 37 percent of 1990 mainstream freshmen graduated Adelphi in 1994. Of the large General Studies group (167) in 1994, 19 percent went to commencement in 1998. But ironically, one third of the students in the slashed entering classes of 1995 and 1997 (sixty-two and sixty-one students) completed their degrees in the traditional span. Recovering from the basic decline of the Diamandopoulos years, the university set an annual target of 100 program students after the 1990s, while keeping the number of full-time faculty (still "administrators") stable. The program thus enjoyed a fifteen-year period of protection from the accordion tendencies of enrollment managers.[2]

Retention and graduation records remain inseparable from internal General Studies academic policies, covering dismissals, probations, prohibition from athletics and discouragement of Greek-letter pledging, all of which may facilitate attrition. They are connected as well to larger societal tensions affecting higher education, as well as shifting sands of high school integrity, funding, debt, exam fixation, debates over standards and the influx of managing strategies that have more to do with the marketplace than the classroom. As shall be demonstrated in a later chapter, General Studies includes a higher proportion of Adelphi freshmen whose lives are affected by discrimination. At nearly every pertinent chart spot, General Studies retention and graduation levels trail the rest of the freshman class at Adelphi. A 10 to 20 point differential prevailed in this regard until roughly 2008. While 17 percent of the 1990 GS entrants graduated in four years, 34 percent of the rest of that freshman class did so. As a bit more than two-thirds of that General Studies class stuck it out for second semester, 80 percent of the other freshmen returned. The glad tidings of freshman-to-sophomore stability in General Studies by the year 2000 accompanied even better news among their fellow first-year finishers. However, recent years disclose a narrowing of the gap in both relevant continuities.[3]

LOCAL AND NATIONAL FEATURES

Referring to freshmen as the "Class of" a time to come four years later no longer makes sense. Interruption and elongation of the higher education experience clearly belong to a national picture, struck by evolving economic conditions, government and education policies, employment patterns, wealth distribution, discrimination, and social perceptions influencing the decisions of students and families. Students who have had to work and take longer to graduate are hardly less qualified in their professions than their peers who finished sooner. Moreover, the encounters of General Studies students who continued into majors become less attributable to what they went through in the first year. Freshman year may well determine if a student becomes engaged at first. It sets the tone, not the outcome.

While General Studies' initial cohorts were still making their way through Adelphi in the late 1980s, one U.S. survey estimated that only 31 percent of private university freshmen would be done in four years. The first program groups were sizable: 159 in 1985, 124 in 1986, and 163 in 1987. All told, 240 of the three-year total of 446 were upperclassmen in their majors at Adelphi by fall 1988. Of the 1985 group, ninety-eight became sophomores at Adelphi. From the inaugural class, the program had dismissed twenty-eight. Others withdrew during the year or transferred afterward. Graduation records of the latter were unavailable. Of the continuing former program students, sixty-six of the ninety-eight who started the second year went on to become juniors. In any case, thirty-seven of the ninety-eight graduated in June 1989, four years after beginning Adelphi. Another seventeen received diplomas by January 1990. More than a third of the original 1985 class, and over 50 percent of those who survived to become Adelphi sophomores, had graduated within four and half years.[4] But General Studies admits in 1986 did not move on at the same pace. Seventy-one of the arriving 124 became Adelphi sophomores, of whom twenty-eight were able to graduate in four years, a rate of 20 percent. By the end of 1990 another seven students completed their degrees. The four-and-a-half year graduation rate, so to speak, of the second GS cohort was 28 percent.[5]

Responding to dismay about this pace to commencement, the program's backers pointed out that over a four-year period "the national graduation rate for freshmen with a General Studies profile is approximately 6 percent." The perseverance of the first two General Studies cohorts, even with a 25 percent to 28 percent dismissal rate in the 1990s, was not far behind that of regular freshmen. The high school records of the first two cohorts were indeed weaker than those compiled by mainstream peers. Moreover, as shown above, some sectors of the university attached a stigma to General Studies, and treated program alumni ungraciously. Negative assumptions (first raised at the inception of General Studies) may affect morale, retention, and graduation. Program advocates observed that the notion (held by many outside the program, but some inside as well) that the members carried some type of "handicap" and were congenitally poor students littered the landscape. Similar was a counselor's estimate to Dominick Cavallo that General Studies students' "maturation and learning problems," along with "emotional problems," were more acute than in the freshman class as such. In addition to such pejorative views amidst genuine academic difficulties, students struggled, as Cavallo put it, with "the challenge, academic discomfort, pain and rigor provided by a mandatory liberal arts curriculum." Cavallo thus drew a connection between the program's touted grading precision and perceived student demoralization.[6]

Based on more traditional assumptions about college careers, the tempo at which former General Studies students earned degrees generated understandable concern against the backdrop of American grad trajectories. Slower graduation rates especially characterized the sophomore-to-senior arc of General Studies alumni with low high school averages but higher SATs. The 1987 group, for instance, brought in a collective verbal-math SAT average of 770, but included students whose totals had exceeded 1000. Fewer than half their number made it from fall to spring in good academic standing, equaling the fall to spring returns of students admitted with scores below 600. Admits gaining between 600 and 1000 on the entrance test did better at Adelphi.[7]

The college completion records of retained students who came through General Studies over the first ten years of the program's operation suggest that higher SAT scores presaged lower college GPAs as well as a longer road to graduation. Half of 1985's sub-800 test takers remaining at Adelphi after the program went on to graduate, but less than a third of those who had surpassed 900. Once again, half of those who entered General Studies in 1987 after scoring between 600 and 700 on the SAT—and who stayed at Adelphi—graduated. The 1989 entering class sustains the point. Data shows five-year totals for the retained students as follows: 13 percent of those with combined math and verbal marks above 900 had graduated by May 1994; 26 percent of those scoring between 800 and 900; 30 percent of those scoring between 700 and 800; and 25 percent of those scoring between 600 and 700.[8]

Many earlier General Studies graduates would not have been accepted under shifting Adelphi SAT and GPA admissions criteria in the 1990s. One from the group of 1991 who graduated from Adelphi *cum laude* in a four-year span would have been ineligible for admission under late 1990s dictates. Similarly, three of seven late 1980s students achieving master's degrees from the university in 1995 would have fallen short of eligibility requirements had they applied that year. The same holds for five of the six master's winners in 1996, along with dozens who then acquired bachelor's degrees.[9]

A malaise simultaneously thickened over Adelphi in the early 1990s, casting the university into crisis with disastrous impact on enrollment. University leaders toyed with making the school the embodiment of "excellence" by abolishing General Studies. Dean David Newton argued instead that the program provided unprecedented opportunity for previously talented but excluded students to obtain degrees. The facts showed, he declared quite plainly, "that SAT scores and high school GPAs for purposes of admitting students to our General Studies Program are meaningless criteria." Counselor Della Hudson seconded the point: student initiative and willingness to work with faculty and counselors counted for more. The arguments underlined the evolving view in higher education that "students need more emphasis on developing their intellectual capabilities and less time spent memorizing tests such as the ACT and the SAT." Preferable, said Hudson, was the approach that encouraged "work on fewer, but more comprehensive and involved projects" and portfolios that "provide a far better idea of students' capabilities than traditional tests and grades."[10]

TRENDS IN COMPLETION RATES

After 2000, mainstream Adelphi freshmen continued to advance to commencement at a faster pace, but the program's four-year graduation rates also improved over time, rising to at least 30 percent in the mid to latter years of this century's first decade, but again trailing other finishers by double digits. At the same time, half of General Studies alumni achieved their degrees within six years, a substantial increase. The figure for their freshman counterparts stood between 60 and 70 percent.[11] But the retention and graduation rates among Adelphi's schools and disciplines vary, within essentially improving persistence levels of all their freshmen. Nursing, Education, Arts & Sciences, Social Work, and Business students take differing intervals to complete bachelor's work. As seen above, grade distribution from "A" to "F" is not uniform in the different fields of study.[12]

Thus, Adelphi's School of Nursing has witnessed a longer road to commencement than the School of Education. Certainly, the Nursing School represents the widest distribution of generational groups in Adelphi. Age, demographics, gender, work requirements, and family situations obviously influence the speed of degree completion. Similarly, discrepancies between graduation rates of students of color and white students are in abundant evidence. Here, one must take caution before making concepts like "behind" or "ahead" of the pace into iron clad evaluations. Broader impacts, such as race, class, or gender discrimination in society, complicating the road to college are not confined to history. Projecting the completion of college as if a level playing field exists can only diminish accuracy. A recent ACT study on "college readiness" is superficial when it alleges that lower career aspirations among African-American college applicants explain higher education difficulties, while raising no questions about the reality and pressure of systemic bias. Moreover, all indicators point to the ever-stronger intervention of material factors (such as age, gender, and work requirements) in the prolongation of college careers, thus making simple deployment of "pace" beyond shorthand terminology rather superficial. It would be better indeed not to view any path as more advanced than another.[13]

THE HIGH SCHOOL GPA

Among graduation forecasting tools like high school records and SAT scores, the former hold greater reliability. Educators have come to consider high school GPA a better predictor, with all its question marks, because it still more closely matches college outcomes. Even so, the secondary school GPA may have more than one meaning. High school students function in widely divergent conditions, according to school budgets, state of equipment and infrastructure, local economies, and politics. No doubt, these phenomena affect the quality of high school education. Additionally, two scholars have noted: "For some students, GPA may reflect academic ability, while for others it might reflect ability to show up for class, and for others it might represent their tendency to get along with their peers." They add that high school "teachers differ in the elements used to assign a grade, and in the relative importance of those elements." Of course, college professors also differ in computing grades.[14]

Relative to their incoming high school average, final Adelphi GPAs of former General Studies students between 2007 through 2014 are shown below. Overall the higher the high school performance, the better the college result. The exceptions are unmistakable, but the graph nevertheless shows that General Studies recruits with the best high school indices do finish college with the highest GPAs. In most cases, the final college averages of those completing Adelphi are consistent with their points on the high school continuum.[15]

Tracking data for several cohorts can now be used to correlate their Adelphi four- and six-year graduation rates with both high school averages and SAT exams (total scores, and verbal and math scores taken separately. High school grades as college graduation prognostics are examined in this chapter, entrance exams in the next. A word of caution before presenting and dissecting more statistics: numbers do not do justice to the debates over the results of the college experience. Rating students by exams or graduation time, like superficial rankings of higher educational institutions by newspapers and magazines, reduces higher

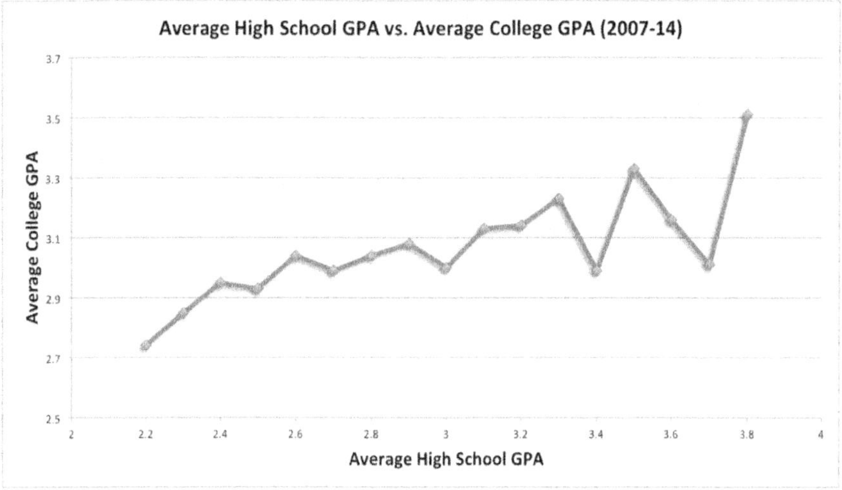

Figure 8.1. Average High School GPA vs. Average College GPA (2007–2014). Note: Figure designed by Gabriel Rosenberg. Statistics were used with permission from Deirdre Donat and were compiled by Gabriel Rosenberg.

education to a competition. Unless all factors affecting college persistence and graduation are acknowledged, only shallow conclusions will be drawn.

The entering cohorts of 2003, 2006, and 2009 have been selected from an epoch of graduation rate data dating back to 2002. The evidence from the three cohorts corresponds to the results for the entire period in which it was collected: nothing within the period contradicts the findings for the chosen groups. The logic of the intervals and the availability in all cases of both four- and six-year graduation results helped determine the years selected.

Each arriving cohort will inevitably become smaller on academic grounds by the time of the second freshman semester for reasons intrinsic to General Studies. The prerogative of General Studies to dismiss students below 2.0 after only one semester has been unique at Adelphi. The program is marked by the apparently inherent contradictions of admitting qualified students on broader grounds, while reserving the right to dismiss them after one semester. The historical lack of equivalent institutional and merit aid for General Studies students, long viewed pejoratively as not worth the risk of financial assistance, also quickly diminished the size of every cohort. It is useful to assess General Studies outcomes by taking these factors into account. The narratives accompanying the three tables therefore make clear two sets of results: the graduation rate of the original cohort and that of the returning sophomores. The tables feature documentation of the latter. It is suggested here that conditions specific to General Studies be considered.

THE CLASS OF 2007

The ninety program students who came to Adelphi in fall 2003 had a collective SAT mark of 902 and a high school average of 2.62. Attrition went into effect almost immediately, with several withdrawals before the fall was over: eighty-six finished the semester. Dismissals and transfers brought the spring 2004 starting numbers to seventy-two. Subtracting the handful dismissed after the spring and the greater number who did not return for financial or other reasons, sixty-one members of the Class of 2007 returned as sophomores at Adelphi. In smaller increments, former General Studies students left, took leaves, or transferred over the next three years, for reasons having little to do with what they did as freshmen. By spring 2007, thirty-seven were left at Adelphi. All told, twenty-eight graduated that year. Five more followed in their wake in 2008, with another on their heels in 2009. The four-year graduation rate, based on a starting figure of ninety, was 31 percent. The six-year graduation rate stood at 38 percent of the beginning cohort.[16]

As mentioned above, the fall-off between fall and spring of freshman year in General Studies, while not nearly as sharp as originally, always remains greater than for the mainstream freshmen. When transfers and students beset with financial difficulties are also taken into account, reducing the cohort once again, the number of former members commencing sophomore-hood at Adelphi is used as a second point of reference for four- and six-year graduation rates of program alumni. This purview brings the four-year graduation level of the returnees to 46 percent, and the six-year proportion to 56 percent. Further investigation shows variation between different components of the cohort.[17]

Of the students coming into General Studies in fall 2003, twenty-one brought overall high school mean scores of 3.0 or better. None surpassed 1000 on the SAT. Fourteen of them stayed at Adelphi for sophomore year, with seven advancing to commencement in May 2007. An eighth member of this stratum, a Biology major, graduated three years later. Hence, the four-year rate of graduation of this subgroup was 33 percent of their original number. But half of those who stayed at Adelphi after freshman year graduated "on time." Their combined high school average had been 3.2. Their cumulative grade point average when they accepted Adelphi diplomas was 3.38. Their majors, supplemented by their classmate who gained her degree later, show a rather narrow concentration: Psychology, Biology, and the Social Sciences.[18]

Out of the beginning ninety, another thirty-six students came in fall 2003 with high school benchmarks between 2.5 and 2.99. Three broke the

1000 mark on the combined verbal and math SAT. A year later, twenty-three moved on to become sophomores at Adelphi (several had discontinued for financial reasons, including two with Dean's List qualifications of 3.49 and 3.55). Eleven graduated in 2007, followed by two others by 2009. Therefore, only 31 percent of the incoming segment made it to commencement in the traditional span, and 36 percent in the now more widely accepted six-year interval. However, 48 percent of students who stayed for the second year obtained diplomas "on time," and well over half within six years. Fields of study focused within the Arts and Sciences, most tied to teacher training: Art, History, Sociology, and especially Communications. Business majors were also prominent within the 2.5–2.99 high school GPA segment completing college work. But only one of the proposed Nursing majors made it to graduation (the others left the university by junior year) while all the Business majors did.[19]

Twenty-eight of the entering ninety carried high school levels between 2.0 and 2.49 in to General Studies, with eighteen continuing into the second year (dismissals and financial difficulties explain the attrition). Here also could be found the greatest concentration of combined verbal-math exam marks beyond 1000. (The previously discussed subgroups scored lower on the SAT, albeit doing better in high school). Eleven walked "on time," signaling a graduation rate of 39 percent of the original arrivals with 2.0 to 2.49 high school averages, but nearly two-thirds of the surviving sophomores. Two more went to commencement by 2009. Like the preceding segment, more than fifty percent of the students who made it through freshman year were able to end their Adelphi studies in the four-year frame. All told, the first eleven had a composite 2.0 in high school, toward the bottom of the stratum, while exiting the university with a grade point average of nearly 3.0. By way of initial retention, eventual continuity, and subsequent completion, their final record is notable. The Communications and Psychology departments furnished several graduates, but a good number of those earning Adelphi degrees majored in associated Business fields.[20]

To be sure, two cohort members with high school averages below 2.0 also graduated in 2007, one with Latin honors in Political Science. This student was a rare composite, having done well on the SAT, beautifully at Adelphi, but poorly in high school. The Class of 2007 was one of the last of the General Studies groups to include students from sub-"C" high school terrain.[21]

Table 8.1, which organizes the Class of 2007 by high school GPA, gives a picture of the pace and trends, including majors, averages obtained in General Studies and beyond, and Latin honors bestowed. SAT totals, and for math and verbal parts, are also provided. The table delineates all semesters following the first year for fall and spring. After fall 2003 (the first freshman semester), all other grade indications reflect each student's performance in the indicated semester, followed by the cumulative GPA.

One sees for example that the third student on the list entered Adelphi with a high school GPA of 3.6, earned a 3.38 in fall 2003, ended the freshman year at 3.37, recorded a 3.57 in the spring term of senior year, and graduated in May 2007 *cum laude* in History. Students who withdrew (the majority of whom left before the fall semester) are not counted in the tabulations, but are indicated at the bottom in the order in which they left the university.[22] Abbreviations are as follows:

> **Majors**: Acc (Accounting), BBA or BMG (Management), Bio (Biology), Bfn (Finance), Bus (Business), Chem (Chemistry), Cis (Computer and Management Information Systems), Comm (Communications), CSD (Communication Disorders), ComJou (Communications/Journalism), CompSci (Computer Science), CrimJ (Criminal Justice), Early (Early Childhood Education), Ed (Education), Eng (English), EnvStu (Environmental Studies), ExPhys (Exercise Physiology), ExSci (Exercise Science), Health Ed (Health Education), His (History), Int'l St (International Studies), Mgmt (Management), Mktg (Marketing), Mth (Math), Mus (Music), Nur (Nursing), PE, (Physical Education), PolSci (Political Science), Psy (Psychology), PT (Physical Therapy), Soc (Sociology), Spa (Spanish), SpePath or Spe (Speech Pathology), SpMgmt (Sports Management), STEP or Step (Scholar Teacher Education Program), Swk (Social Work), The (Theater), Und (Undecided). **Other**: Dis: Dismissed, DNR: Did Not Return, W/D: Withdrew, $: Financial issues, Tran: Transferred, Abroad: Studied abroad, VSAT: Verbal SAT, MSAT: Math SAT, Tot. SAT: Total SAT, HS GPA: High school grade point average, GS-avg: General Studies average, F: Fall semester (F03 = Fall 2003), S: Spring semester (S04 = Spring 2004), cr: Credits

Class of 2007 Adelphi Graduation by Rate by High School GPA

Number of Students	**90**	**72**		**61**	**54**	**45**	**42**	**39**	**38**	
% of Original class		84%		70%	64%	52%	49%	45%	40%	
% Returning sophomores				100%	89%	74%	69%	64%	62%	
% 3.0 or higher semester	16%	17%		37%	40%	58%	55%	46%	65%	
% semester GPA Increase				75%	63%	69%	74%	79%	76%	
Number Graduate*									32	2
% Graduate*									52%	3%
*** Returning**										

HS GPA	**VSAT**	**MSAT**	**Total SAT**	**Major**	**F03**	**S04**	**GS-avg**	**F04**	**S05**	**F05**	**S06**	**F06**	**S07**	**5 Year S08**	**6 Year S09**
3.70	400	480	880	PolSci	2.93	3.0	2.96	DNR							
3.70	350	510	860	Nur	2.98	tran									
3.60	470	460	930	His	3.38	3.37	3.37	3.47/3.4	3.56/3.48	3.06/3.4	3.65/3.48	3.5/3.44	3.57/3.46 **Laude**		
3.60	400	400	800	Bio	2.84	2.7	2.73	2.2/2.57	2.3/2.5	1.49/2.28	2.74/2.35	.51/2.05	1.3/1.96		7 yrs **Grad** 5/10
3.50	480	370	850	Psy	2.92	2.25	2.58	2.9/2.67	3.24/2.79	3.88/3.06	3.8/3.22	3.48/3.26	3.06/3.23 **Grad**		
3.40	420	420	840	Und	2.21	2.13	2.17	2.35/2.22	1.35/2.1	2.5/2.29	1.0/2.21	3.0/2.24	4.0/2.33	60 cr	60 cr
3.30	430	430	860	Und	2.31	tran									
3.30	400	430	830	Music	3.18	w/d									
3.30	440	390	830	Comm	3.61	3.51	3.56	3.6/3.57	3.88/3.65	3.46/3.61	3.86/3.66	3.83/3.68	3.81/3.7 **Magna**		
3.30	510	380	890	Psy	2.56	3.34	2.95	2.4/2.75	2.56/2.69	3.37/2.82	3.14/2.89	3.94/3.06	2.73/3.02 **Grad**		
3.30	430	470	900	Psy	3.61	3.93	3.76	3.64/3.71	3.94/3.79	4.0/3.84	4.0/3.86	3.54/3.62	4.0/3.89 **Summa**		
3.20	480	400	880	Und	1.54	2.25	1.89	2.88/2.16	3.02/2.39	DNR					

HS GPA	VSAT	MSAT	Total SAT	Major	F03	S04	GS-avg	F04	S05	F05	S06	F06	S07	5 Year S08	6 Year S09
3.20	420	370	790	Bio	2.77	3.0	2.88	2.69/2.81	3.31/2.94	2.86/2.92	3.0/2.94	3.04/3.01	2.36/2.94 **Grad**		
3.20	400	440	840	Bio	0.72	dis									
3.17	360	430	790	Bfn	2.55	3.0	2.77	2.75/2.76	DNR						
3.12	400	460	860	Und	2.18	1.53	1.86	2.43/2.0	2.85/2.28	DNR					
3.10	410	450	860	Bio	2.62	1.51	2.06	2.36/2.16	2.0/2.13	.97/1.99	2.08/1.84	1.04/1.79			
3.10	430	410	840	Spa	2.14	2.36	2.25	2.94/2.5	1.62/2.26	0.0/1.86	DNR $				
3.10	380	400	780	Bfn	2.86	3.16	3.01	3.43/3.17	3.76/3.27	3.54/3.31	3.42/3.33	3.94/3.42	3.57/3.45 **Laude**		
3.00	410	420	830	Dance	1.86	tran									
3.00	410	400	810	Und	2.35	2.44	2.4	DNR							
2.90	380	420	800	Comm	2.45	2.44	2.44	3.42/2.75	3.34/2.97	3.68/3.12	3.21/3.14	3.55/3.2	3.14/3.19 **Grad**		
2.90	460	430	890	Psy	2.45	1.76	2.1	DNR							
2.90	400	470	870	Soc	2.01	2.21	2.11	2.02/2.23	2.88/2.39	2.6/2.45	2.86/2.52	3.14/2.61	3.14/2.68 **Grad**		
2.90	430	470	900	Mgt	2.70	2.67	2.68	3.3/2.75	3.6/2.93	DNR					
2.90	410	480	890	PE	2.78	w/d									
2.90	400	400	800	His	2.77	3.06	2.91	3.07/2.92	3.06/2.97	3.28/3.08	3.54/3.15	3.54/3.21	3.66/3.26 **Grad**		
2.90	400	420	820	Und	1.61	2.09	1.85	1.87/1.85	DNR						
2.90	510	460	970	Nur	3.38	3.06	3.49	DNR							
2.80	430	480	910	PE	2.38	tran									
2.80	440	440	880	Und	2.23	2.87	2.55	1.66/2.42	1.0/2.16	DNR					
2.80	440	450	890	Nur	2.07	2.67	2.37	2.65/2.48	2.77/2.55	2.43/2.53	DNR $				
2.80	380	420	800	Nur	2.16	2.67	2.41	3.39/2.74	2.73/2.74	3.18/2.84	2.94/2.85	2.85/2.85	2.65/2.83 **Grad**		
2.80	380	500	880	Mth	1.79	dis									
2.80	450	430	880	Mgt	2.02	2.6	2.31	2.5/2.57	2.67/2.59	3.05/2.75	2.23/2.69	2.5/2.67	3.0/2.7 **Grad**		

HS GPA	VSAT	MSAT	Total SAT	Major	F03	S04	GS-avg	F04	S05	F05	S06	F06	S07	5 Year S08	6 Year S09
2.70	430	480	910	Nur	2.82	2.93	2.87	4.0/3.18	2.56/3.0	2.53/2.88	2.7/2.87	1.3/2.73	DNR$		
2.70	520	400	920	PE	2.14	2.16	2.15	2.12/2.13	1.85/2.07	2.8/2.18	1.9/2.15	2.32/2.18	2.32/2.19	**Grad**	
2.70	410	420	830	Und	1.18	dis									
2.64	560	330	890	Comm	3.63	3.46	3.55	DNR							
2.60	410	420	830	Und	2.63	2.53	2.58	1.44/2.20	.7/1.83	DNR					
2.60	470	400	870	Comm	2.61	2.72	2.66	DNR							
2.60	520	460	980	Soc	3.00	2.48	2.72	2.82/2.76	2.88/2.84	3.17/2.9	3.75/3.03	3.67/3.12	2.95/3.4 **Grad**		
2.60	430	330	760	Mgt	2.18	2.37	2.28	2.67/2.4	2.06/2.32	2.56/2.37	3.07/2.47	3.16/2.59	2.56/2.59	115 cr	115 cr
2.60	460	420	880	Comm	2.32	2.46	2.39	2.92/2.56	2.77/2.61	3.0/2.7	2.38/2.64	2.87/2.71	2.55/2.68 **Grad**		
2.60	410	460	870	CIS	2.45	2.6	2.52	2.65/2.55	2.6/2.63	tran					
2.50	490	420	910	Csd	3.00	2.86	2.93	3.7/3.18	3.5/3.26	3.22/3.28	3.18/3.26	3.28/3.29	3.58/3.32 **Laude**		
2.50	410	440	850	Soc	1.95	w/d									
2.50	460	430	890	Dance	1.38	dis									
2.50	410	520	930	Comm	1.68	dis									
2.50	410	410	820	Comm	1.82	tran									
2.50	440	440	880	Und	2.00	2.16	2.08	3.46/2.54	2.88/2.64	2.24/2.55	1.39/2.41	4.0/2.88	DNR$		
2.50	510	520	1030	Eng	2.39	2.28	2.33	2.61/2.43	1.0/2.24	.65/1.98	DNR				
2.50	520	610	1130	Mgt	2.47	3.37	2.93	3.6/3.18	3.54/3.27	3.45/3.31	3.63/3.37	3.46/3.39	3.68/3.42 **Laude**		
2.50	460	440	900	Und	1.95	2.23	2.09	1.65/2.01	2.4/2.32	2.5/2.34	2.2/2.31	3.12/2.37	1.97/2.32	**Grad**	
2.50	590	500	1090	Eng	0.53	dis									
2.50	440	310	750	His	3.38	3.21	3.36	3.5/3.4	3.3/3.41	3.22/3.37	3.31/3.36	3.25/3.36	3.76/3.4 **Laude**		
2.50	450	500	950	Art	1.63	3.21	2.54	3.04/2.7	3.17/2.82	2.72/2.8	abroad	1.8/2.63	3.17/2.7 **Grad**		
2.40	400	410	810	Acting	2.15	2.46	2.30	2.4/2.33	3.0/2.49	3.38/2.73	3.2/2.82	3.55/2.96	3.83/3.09 **Grad**		

HS GPA	VSAT	MSAT	Total SAT	Major	F03	S04	GS-avg	F04	S05	F05	S06	F06	S07	5 Year S08	6 Year S09
2.40	460	460	920	Und	2.31	1.0	1.68	DNR							
2.40	410	530	940	Nur	0.46	dis									
2.40	440	450	890	Mgt	2.28	2.74	2.51	1.91/2.34	2.91/2.5	2.6/2.52	2.83/2.61	2.99/2.68	2.98/2.73 **Grad**		
2.40	490	400	890	Nur	2.58	w/d									
2.40	510	510	1020	Psy	3.08	3.46	3.27	3.06/3.15	3.92/3.30	3.73/3.4	3.6/3.42	3.6/3.48	3.68/3.34 **Laude**		
2.40	410	430	840	Nur	2.77	2.48	2.62	3.12/2.88	3.01/2.91	2.07/2.77	2.17/2.71	DNR			
2.40	480	440	920	Bio	2.22	2.88	2.55	tran$							
2.40	500	460	960	Mgt	2.53	1.93	2.23	2.33/2.25	DNR $						
2.40	540	410	950	His	2.63	2.7	2.66	2.82/2.81	DNR						
2.30	430	490	920	Comm	3.35	3.48	3.41	3.77/3.54	3.54/3.54	3.8/3.59	3.78/3.63	2.32/2.18	3.75/3.68 **Magna**		
2.30	460	420	880	PE	1.79	1.28	1.53	dis							
2.30	360	430	790	His	2.45	2.48	2.46	2.66/2.53	2.45/2.51	2.86/2.68	3.25/2.76	3.06/2.84	2.98/2.73 **Grad**		
2.30	480	420	900	Psy	2.42	2.39	2.7	2.77/2.53	2.69/2.57	3.09/2.65	3.51/2.83	3.55/3.07	3.66/3.11 **Grad**		
2.30	500	590	1090	Mgt	2.12	1.83	1.97	2.5/2.27	2.5/2.32	1.5/2.24	2.76/2.3	2.53/2.39	1.54/2.25 **Grad**		
2.30	420	400	820	Psy	2.18	0	1.02	dis							
2.30	580	550	1130	Comm	2.00	2.02	2.01	2.6/2.21	1.0/2.15	2.76/2.24	2.86/2.37	3.49/2.49	2.8/2.62 **Grad**		
2.20	500	550	1050	Und	3.38	1.21	2.39	WD							
2.20	400	490	890	Comm	1.95	2.37	2.16	2.56/2.26	3.32/2.62	3.26/2.76	3.02/2.81	3.94/2.99	2.77/2.94 **Grad**		
2.20	480	390	870	Und	2.00	21.6	2.08	2.7/2.24	DNR						
2.20	570	420	990	Comm	0.46	dis									
2.14	480	460	940	Mgt	3.45	3.53	3.49	2.92/3.13	2.4/3.09	2.84/3.05	3.37/3.1	3.12/3.1	3.0/3.09 **Grad**		

HS GPA	VSAT	MSAT	Total SAT	Major	F03	S04	GS-avg	F04	S05	F05	S06	F06	S07	5 Year S08	6 Year S09
2.10	530	440	970	Und	2.02	2.07	2.04	0.0/1.52	0/ 1.18	DNR					
2.00	470	380	850	Comm	2.00	1.67	1.83	2.9/2.11	DNR						
2.00	500	630	1130	His	3.18	3.09	3.0	3.3/3.12	w/d 3/21						
2.00	470	490	960	Psy	0.92	dis									
2.00	500	480	980	PE	1.93	2.97	2.0	2.65/2.55	3.0/2.44	3.5/2.64	3.02/2.71	2.93/2.82	3.37/2.98 **Grad**		
2.00	480	490	970	Mgt	2.77	2.60	2.68	3.0/2.76	2.35/2.64	2.37/2.58	2.74/2.6	2.66/2.61	2.06/2.55 **Grad**		
1.90	620	530	1150	Psy	2.84	3.06	2.95	3.57/3.15	3.38/3.19	3.28/3.2	2.15/3.04	DNR			
1.90	410	410	820	Nur	1.70	2.32	2.01	DNR							
1.80	600	510	1110	PolSci	3.68	3.6	3.64	3.06/3.42	3.2/3.36	3.22/3.33	3.68/3.39	3.34/3.38	3.41/3.39 **Laude**		
1.70	430	480	910	Mgt	1.18	2.44	1.81	3.1/2.22	2.0/2.17	2.0/2.14	2.44/2.17	3.4/2.38	3.23/2.52 **Grad**		
1.70	520	430	950	Und	1.70	3.07	2.38	2.5/2.42	2.66/2.55	DNR					
3.0	350	440	890			w/d									
2.9	370	460	830			w/d									
2.5	520	390	910			w/d									
3.2	360	500	860			w/d									
3.5	410	460	870			w/d									

Note: Table created by Daniel Rosenberg. Statistics used with permission from Deirdre Donat.

THE CLASS OF 2010

The students beginning courses in General Studies in the fall of 2006 numbered 103. Their overall secondary school standing was 2.4, alongside an SAT verbal-math combination of 870. After departures due to financial issues, transfers and dismissals, eighty-three returned for spring 2007. In 2007, sixty-nine inaugurated the sophomore year. The four-year graduation rate was 34 percent, but also more than half the former sophomores. The next two years found fifteen more students completing their Adelphi degrees, constituting a 49 percent six-year completion rate of the whole, or practically three-quarters of the sophomore carryovers.[23]

A robust thirty-nine of the initial freshmen carried high school GPAs at or above 3.0, of which twenty-seven became second-year students at Adelphi. Eighteen graduated in 2010, some 46 percent of the original subgroup, or 66 percent of the sophomores. A second push toward Adelphi degrees supplemented the first, with another six accomplishing the goal within two more years. In the context of the subgroup's starting numbers, the six-year graduation rate was well over 60 percent. From the perspective of the sophomore carryovers, it was almost 90 percent. The starting thirty-nine had an SAT average (852) lower than the cohort's. But the ones who graduated Adelphi had scored even lower on the SATs, roughly 847. However, the high school GPA of the entrants and graduates alike was 3.2. And the concluding college average of the latter was also 3.2. The diploma winners under review demonstrated a propensity for Business (specifically Management) and Psychology. This was replicated throughout the entire graduating group of the Class of 2010, no matter the incoming high school average. To be sure, Social Work, Nursing, Math, and Biology (give or take a tie-in with teacher training) could be found among the roster, but manifested in rather isolated totals. Half of this highest high school GPA (lowest SAT) subgroup received Latin honors at Adelphi commencement.[24]

The number of General Studies freshmen in the 2.5 to 2.99 level of high school achievement was forty-one in fall 2006. After a year, twenty-six entered the Adelphi sophomore class. Thirteen finished college work on time, producing a graduation rate of 32 percent of the starting subgroup, or half of the sophomores. Another six obtained Adelphi degrees over the next two years. Altogether, the graduates comprised 46 percent of the original enrollees and 73 percent of the sophomore survivors. None of the originals had over a thousand on the SATs, but the 2.5–2.9 subgroup nevertheless scored higher on the exam than the GPA category above it, and also beat the cohort standard. The graduates held a slightly higher high school GPA than that of the original forty-one. However, the graduates exited Adelphi with a 3.0. Among them were more Psychology majors (three with Latin honors) and a matching number with Business Management degrees. The supremacy of these fields of study over others, previously seen, remained. History, Communications, and Accounting also put in an appearance.[25]

Twenty-three students arrived at Adelphi in fall 2006 with high school records between 2.0 and 2.49. Their SAT mean was nearly seventy points higher than the cohort average, and well over the students with better secondary school GPAs. In any case, fifteen entered sophomore year. Five graduated in 2010 (22 percent of the original members, a third of the sophomores) and another five within six years (43 and 66 percent, respectively). Of the five supra-1000 SAT scorers in this grouping, all would complete degrees, but only one in the quadrennial frame. Pertinently, the ten graduates had taken a high school average of 2.28 into Adelphi's General Studies Program. The top SAT achievers produced an Adelphi GPA of 2.7, about the same as the concluding averages of the other diploma recipients in their subgroup. Business Management majors made up a healthy proportion of degree earners.[26]

Like the preceding table, 8.2 indicates the graduation rates and associated specifics of the cohort, showing the academic progress of continuing students, while presenting some of the reasons for departures.[27] Students who withdrew (the majority left before the fall semester) are not counted in the tabulations, but are indicated at the bottom in the order in which they left the university. The numbers of students given in Table 8.2 and the figures for the 2006 cohort in Table 7.1 may not add up exactly. The causes of decline from fall to spring (financial blocks, transfers, dismissals, or non-returns) are not identified simultaneously, affecting the data to a small degree. Abbreviations are as follows:

> **Majors**: Acc (Accounting), BBA or BMG (Management), Bio (Biology), Bfn (Finance), Bus (Business), Chem (Chemistry), Cis (Computer and Management Information Systems), Comm (Communications), CSD (Communication Disorders), ComJou (Communications/Journalism), CompSci (Computer Science), CrimJ (Criminal Justice), Early (Early Childhood Education), Ed (Education), Eng (English), EnvStu (Environmental Studies), ExPhys (Exercise Physiology), ExSci (Exercise Science), Health Ed (Health Education), His (History), Int'l St (International Studies), Mgmt (Management), Mktg (Marketing), Mth (Math), Mus (Music), Nur (Nursing), PE (Physical Education), PolSci (Political Science), Psy (Psychology), PT (Physical Therapy), Soc (Sociology), Spa (Spanish), SpePath or Spe (Speech Pathology), SpMgmt (Sports Management), STEP or Step (Scholar Teacher Education Program), Swk (Social Work), The (Theater), Und (Undecided). **Other**: Dis: Dismissed, DNR: Did Not Return, W/D: Withdrew, $: Financial issues, Tran: Transferred, VSAT: Verbal SAT, MSAT: Math SAT, Tot. SAT: Total SAT, HS GPA: High school grade point average, GS-avg: General Studies average, F: Fall semester (F06 = Fall 2006), S: Spring semester (S07 = Spring 2007), cr: Credits

Class of 2010 Adelphi Graduation by Rate by High School GPA

	F06	S07	F07	S08	F08	S09	F09	S10	5 Year S11	6 Year S12	7 Year
Number of students	**103**	**83**	**69**	**66**	**61**	**60**	**55**	**54**			
% of Original class		81%	66%	64%	59%	58%	53%	52%			
% Returning sophomores			100%	96%	88%	87%	80%	78%			
% with 3.0 or higher semester		40%	57%	56%	57%	60%	85%	76%			
% semester GPA increase			70%	70%	69%	75%	85%	78%			
Number graduate*							2	36	13	2	2
% Graduate*							3%	52%	19%	3%	3%
*** Returning**											

HS GPA	**VSAT**	**MSAT**	**Total SAT**	**Major**	**F06**	**S07**	**GS-avg**	**F07**	**S08**	**F08**	**S09**	**F09**	**S10**	**5 Year S11**	**6 Year S12**	**7 Year**
3.9	370	430	800	Mgt	3.52	3.84	3.68	3.66/3.67	3.46/3.61	3.94/3.68	3.73/3.69	3.63/3.68	3.71/3.68 **Magna**			
3.7	360	540	900	Bio	2.18	2.31	2.24	1.86/2.11	2.12/2.11	1.59/2.02	1.54/1.95	2.24/1.99	1.9/1.98	**Grad**		
3.5	410	460	860		2.45	DNR										
3.5	390	520	910	Mth	3.05	3.37	3.21	3.86/3.44	3.53/3.41	3.36/3.38	3.62/3.42	3.6/3.44	3.54/3.45 **Laude**			
3.5	410	410	820	Psy	3.32	3.54	3.43	3.81/3.6	3.74/3.63	3.86/3.68	3.93/3.71	3.94/3.75	3.94/3.77 **Magna**			
3.4	420	400	820	His	2.84	3.54	3.19	3.85/3.39	3.32/3.38	3.54/3.41	3.6/3.45	3.68/3.49	3.6/3.5 **Laude**			
3.4	410	430	840	Mgt	3.31	3.70	3.50	3.74/3.59	3.28/3.5	3.66/3.53	3.36/3.51	3.08/3.44	3.9/3.51 **Laude**			
3.4	470	420	890	Psy	2.93	3.55	3.24	3.46/3.31	3.34/3.32	3.5/3.35	3.57/3.38	3.86/3.45	3.93/3.51 **Laude**			
3.4	380	390	770	Swk	2.61	3.09	2.85	3.2/2.98	3.0/2.98	3.48/3.09	3.52/3.15	3.67/3.21	3.10/3.2 **Grad**			
3.4	370	480	850	Swk	3.05	3.47	3.26	2.66/3.06	3.21/3.1	3.18/3.12	3.4/3.16	3.07/3.15	3.25/3.16	**Grad**		
3.4	380	530	910		1.00	Dis										
3.3	360	460	820		0.00	Dis										
3.3	420	430	850	Nur	2.55	2.61	2.58	2.9/2.68	3.52/2.91	3.69/3.07	3.55/3.15	wd	2.57/3.06	**Grad**		
3.3	380	470	850		3.02	3.39	3.21	DNR								

HS GPA	VSAT	MSAT	Total SAT	Major	F06	S07	GS-avg	F07	S08	F08	S09	F09	S10	5 Year S11	6 Year S12	7 Year
3.3	440	400	840	Mgt	3.55	3.68	3.62	3.61/3.61	4.0/3.71	4.0/3.78	3.82/3.78	4.0/3.82	3.85/3.82 **Magna**			
3.3	430	450	880		3.07	3.25	3.16	tsf								
3.2	390	550	940	Mgt	3.23	3.48	3.36	3.75/3.52	3.06/3.39	3.4/3.39	3.7/3.45	3.54/3.48	3.66/3.50 **Magna**			
3.2	480	410	890		2.68	3.38	3.03	DNR $								
3.2	450	410	860	Mgt	3.38	3.77	3.57	3.79/3.65	3.6/3.64	3.6/3.63	4.0/3.69	3.75/3.7	3.88/3.73 **Magna**			
3.2	410	340	750	Mgt	3.00	3.32	3.16	3.77/3.4	3.32/3.38	3.51/3.42	3.85/3.48	4.0/3.55	3.8/3.58 **Magna**			
3.2	360	500	860		2.68	DNR										
3.2	380	400	780	Nur	3.39	3.16	3.28	3.18/3.24	3.64/3.31	2.92/3.23	1.48/3.04	2.3/2.99	3.0/2.99	**Grad**		
3.1	380	470	850	Mgt	3.54	3.39	3.47	3.88/3.59	DNR							
3.1	400	490	890	Mth	3.23	3.23	3.23	3.83/3.43	3.78/3.52	2.73/3.30	3.86/3.4	3.29/3.38	3.17/3.35 **Laude**			
3.1	430	430	860	Nur	2.40	2.54	2.47	3.52/2.87	3.55/3.03	3.37/3.11	1.93/2.91	DNR				
3.1	410	490	900	Psy	2.02	2.45	2.23	2.46/2.31	2.67/2.39	DNR						
3.1	450	450	900		1.38	0.00	0.69									
3.1	410	430	840		3.38	2.68	3.03	DNR								
3.1	440	450	890		2.02	0.31	1.17	Dis								
3.0	410	420	830	PE	2.91	2.47	2.69	2.36/2.6	2.34/2.53	2.9/2.62	2.1/2.56	3.57/2.68	3.57/2.8 **Grad**			
3.0	510	380	890	Comm	2.18	2.02	2.10	1.15/1.8	2.67/2.01	2.77/2.15	2.83/2.27	2.9/2.34	1.53/2.26	**Grad**		
3.0	370	460	830	Eng	3.09	2.42	2.75	1.61/2.35	1.94/2.25	2.94/2.34	3.55/2.55	3.68/2.74	3.74/2.88	**Grad**		
3.0	380	410	790	Psy	2.77	3.07	2.92	3.27/3.03	2.54/2.9	3.14/2.95	3.32/3.01	3.86/3.15	**3.61/3.22 Grad**			
3.0	450	360	810	Mgt	2.15	2.46	2.30	3.12/2.6	2.34/2.53	2.06/2.43	2.93/2.51	3.07/2.58	2.79/2.6 **Grad**			
3.0	350	440	890	Nur	3.09	DNR$										
3.0	420	400	820	Psy	3.32	3.09	3.21	3.54/3.32	3.74/3.46	3.82/3.52	3.86/3.59	3.83/3.62	3.94/3.64 **Magna**			
3.0	450	440	890	Psy	3.16	3.47	3.32	2.87/3.15	3.7/3.29	3.51/3.33	3.43/3.35	4.0/3.43	3.94/3.5 **Laude**			

HS GPA	VSAT	MSAT	Total SAT	Major	F06	S07	GS-avg	F07	S08	F08	S09	F09	S10	5 Year S11	6 Year S12	7 Year
3.0	400	510	910	Bio	2.93	3.84	3.38	3.26/3.33	2.52/3.11	3.3/3.16	3.15/3.17	3.68/3.29 **Grad**				
3.0	420	470	890	Mgt	2.79	3.38	3.08	2.82/2.93	2.8/2.9	3.13/2.94	2.5/2.87	3.4/2.93	3.75/3.02 **Grad**			
2.9	420	410	830		2.28	2.47	2.38	DNR								
2.9	450	420	870	Soc	2.09	2.02	2.06	2.68//2.28	3.2/2.53	2.88/2.6	2.75/2.62	3.46/2.74	3.13/2.79	**Grad**		
2.9	430	450	880	Comm	2.55	2.52	2.53	2.66/2.58	3.14/2.73	3.14/2.86	3.61/3.01	3.34/3.05	3.06/3.05 **Grad**			
2.9	430	460	890	Psy	3.39	3.84	3.62	3.74/3.66	3.94/3.74	3.94/3.78	3.94/3.81	4.0/3.83	3.88/3.84 **Magna**			
2.9	370	460	830		2.84	DNR										
2.9	460	410	870	Psy	2.91	3.16	3.03	3.53/3.2	3.28/3.22	3.8/3.49	3.42/3.36	3.73/3.42	3.6/3.44 **Laude**			
2.9	450	440	890	Comm	2.70	2.32	2.51	2.32/2.8	3.62/2.91	3.02/2.93	3.34/3.02	3.4/3.09	3.32/3.12	**Grad**		
2.8	480	370	850		0.53	Dis										
2.8	480	370	850	Psy	3.31	3.70	3.50	3.31/3.43	2.42/3.2	3.5/3.26	2.8/3.17	3.68/3.26	2.41/3.18 **Grad**			
2.8	430	420	850	Psy	1.78	2.38	2.08	2.25/2.13	3.08/2.4	3.3/2.67	2.88/2.71	3.75/2.87	3.66/2.97 **Grad**			
2.7	410	440	850		2.24	DNR										
2.7	500	380	880	Swk	2.84	3.07	2.95	3.43/3.13	3.13/3.12	2.2/2.94	3.17/2.97	3.47/3.04	3.56/3.09	**Grad**		
2.7	410	430	840	Mgt	2.00	2.77	2.38	2.58/2.46	2.35/2.43	1.84/2.31	2.22/2.3	2.77/2.42	2.53/2.5 **Grad**			
2.7	450	390	840		1.22	Dis										
2.7	380	500	880	Mgt	2.37	2.22	2.29	2.92/2.51	2.49/2.5	2.33/2.46	2.75/2.5	3.16/2.62	2.5/2.6			
2.7	420	420	840		1.39	Dis										
2.68	450	420	870	PE	2.61	2.52	2.56	3.4/2.86	3.86/3.13	3.27/3.15	3.52/3.18	3.94/3.3	4.0/3.37	**Laude**		
2.66	420	420	840	His	2.14	2.46	2.30	2.86/2.5	1.88/2.33	2.25/2.32	2.69/2.38	DNR				
2.6	410	440	850	His	2.53	2.68	2.60	3.2/2.82	3.43/2.99	3.0/2.99	2.65/2.91	DNR	3.07/2.95		**Grad**	
2.6	410	420	830	Psy	2.48	2.38	2.43	3.0/2.62	3.03/2.7	2.82/2.73	2.92/2.76	1.45/2.53	3.5/2.7	**Grad**		
2.6	490	400	890	Psy	3.02	2.82	2.92	3.67/2.88	3.26/2.96	3.7/3.11	3.75/3.19	3.92/3.27	3.77/3.3 **Laude**			

HS GPA	VSAT	MSAT	Total SAT	Major	F06	S07	GS-avg	F07	S08	F08	S09	F09	S10	5 Year S11	6 Year S12	7 Year
2.6	440	410	850	Mgt	2.30	2.63	2.47	2.78/2.69	2.09/2.54	2.6/2.64	3.0/2.68	3.32/2.75	3.82/2.86 **Grad**			
2.6	350	480	830	Mgt	1.79	2.30	2.05	3.31/2.54	3.11/2.71	2.68/2.7	3.11/2.78	3.38/2.87	3.24/2.92 **Grad**			
2.6	370	540	910		2.22	0.00	1.11	Dis								
2.55	420	410	830	Dance	3.61	3.70	3.65	3.29/3.45	3.47/3.46	DNR						
2.5	510	370	880		2.52	2.61	2.56	DNR								
2.5	520	390	910		2.84	DNR										
2.5	430	460	890	Acc	2.61	2.92	2.76	3.26/2.94	2.8/2.9	3.43/3.02	2.32/2.89	3.16/2.94	2.6/2.9 **Grad**			
2.5	470	480	950	Acc	3.02	3.16	3.09	3.34/3.17	3.25/3.19	2.85/314	2.86/3.09	3.88/3.2 **Grad**				
2.5	460	410	870		0.39	Dis										
2.5	440	430	870		2.63	2.02	2.33	DNR								
2.5	430	470	900	Mgt	2.22	2.61	2.41	2.3/2.37	2.63/2.43	2.73/2.53	2.22/2.49	2.94/2.59	2.18/2.53 **Grad**			
2.5	420	510	930	CrimJ	2.39	2.40	2.40	2.8/2.55	2.79/2.61	2.2/2.53	3.46/2.68	DNR				
2.5	430	410	840		1.86	2.09	1.98	1.56/1.87	DNR							
2.5	390	480	870		2.30	2.45	2.37	2.83/2.52	0/2.09	0/1.67	DNR					
2.5	410	480	890		1.53	2.07	1.80	DNR								
2.5	420	410	830	His	2.75	3.00	2.87	3.0/2.91	2.57/2.83	3.36/2.97	3.24/3.02	3.14/3.04	3.0/3.05 **Grad**			
2.5	410	390	800		1.52	Dis										
2.5	480	430	910		1.53	Dis										
2.5	440	420	860		1.01	Dis										
2.5	440	420	860	Acting	2.91	2.63	2.77	3.2/2.93	3.15/2.97	2.87/2.99	2.65/2.92	3.14/2.96	2.71/2.93 **Grad**			
2.47	430	450	880		0.78	Dis										
2.4	420	480	900		1.15											
2.4	370	440	810	PolSci	2.47	2.09	2.28	2.8/2.47	2.52/2.48	2.98/2.58	3.48/2.74	3.07/2.78	3.17/2.82 **Grad**			
2.4	490	480	970		3.23	2.58	2.90	DNR								

HS GPA	VSAT	MSAT	Total SAT	Major	F06	S07	GS-avg	F07	S08	F08	S09	F09	S10	5 Year S11	6 Year S12	7 Year
2.4	390	410	800		2.31	2.54	2.42	2.62/2.49	2.46/2.48	DNR						
2.4	490	460	950		1.85	2.47	2.16	3.07/2.44	3.1/2.6	DNR						
2.4	460	380	840		1.09											
2.4	440	510	960	PE	2.63	2.84	2.73	3.49/3.02	3.39/3.11	3.08/3.1	3.46/3.16	3.6/3.2	3.32/3.24 **Grad**			
2.4	470	550	1020	CrimJ	2.32	2.05	2.19	1.64/1.98	2.45/2.08	1.43/1.99	2.46/2.06	2.65/2.19	3.17/2.29		**Grad**	
2.35	540	550	1090	Mgt	2.92	2.78	2.85	2.65/2.78	2.52/2.7	2.22/2.62	2.6/2.61	2.57/2.61	2.0/2.57	**Grad**		
2.3	410	510	920		3.54	3.31	3.42	tsf								
2.3	480	390	870	Mgt	2.82	2.77	2.79	3.02/2.87	3.2/2.96	2.74/2.91	3.58/3.03	3.79/3.15	3.8/3.22 **Grad**			
2.3	440	420	860	Mgt	2.07	2.70	2.38	3.22/2.69	2.78/2.71	3.37/2.86	2.45/2.78	2.9/2.8	3.54/2.89 **Grad**			
2.3	450	400	850		1.24											
2.27	580	600	1180	Art	3.30	3.48	3.39	.85/3.1	1.85/2.94	3.33/2.85	3.02/2.88	3.85/2.95	3.85/3.02		**Grad**	
2.2	480	530	1010	PE	1.91	3.07	2.49	3.32/2.76	3.2/2.86	2.95/2.88	2.77/2.86	2.75/2.86	2.96/2.89	**Grad**		
2.2	420	400	820	Nur	2.52	2.28	2.40	2.83/2.56	2.31/2.51	3.14/2.62	3.39/2.75	1.59/2.57	DNR			
2.1	440	480	920	Swk	1.91	2.55	2.23	3.3/2.59	2.95/2.68	3.17/2.77	2.66/2.76	2.17/2.67	2.32/2.63		**Grad**	
2.1	420	420	840		2.15	1.95	2.05	2.2/2.08	.59/1.64	DNR						
2.1	520	540	1060	Mgt	2.22	2.02	2.12	2.8/2.36	2.86/2.5	2.92/2.59	3.94/2.84	2.88/2.84	3.5/2.91 **Grad**			
2.0	400	520	920		1.63	2.43	2.03	1.46/1.88	DNR$							
2.0	490	410	900		3.22	2.77	2.99	DNR								
					1.85	DNR										
3.0	350	440	790	w/d												
2.9	370	460	830	w/d												
2.5	520	390	910	w/d												
3.2	360	500	860	w/d												
3.5	410	460	870	w/d												
2.7	410	440	850	w/d												

Note: Table created by Daniel Rosenberg. Statistics used with permission from Deirdre Donat.

THE CLASS OF 2013

The entering class in 2009 consisted of a hundred students. It was a particularly strong group in secondary school average, boasting a 3.4 overall, to go with a total SAT verbal-math score of 896. The incoming class GPA strongly overshadowed the high school record (2.9) of the previous cohort. The second year witnessed the return of seventy-four of the originals, nearly 75 percent. Only twenty-seven finished degrees in 2013. The sophomore quadrennial graduation rate was therefore 36 percent. Nineteen followed directly in 2014, fashioning a five-year graduation rate of 46 percent of the starting group, or 62 percent of the sophomores. As two others earned diplomas in 2015, the six-year completion rate became 48 percent of the originals and 65 percent of the second-year returnees.[28]

Well over a third of the students (thirty-six) held a high school GPA of 3.0 and above, a number of them well above. Nevertheless, their combined math-verbal mean score on the SAT lagged behind the general class average of 896 by more than thirty points. In the history of General Studies, high school GPA and SAT scores rarely, if ever interweave, but exhibit nearly magnetic repulsion. Fall 2010 saw twenty-seven sophomores return, with fifteen graduating in 2013 (42 percent of the original subgroup). A half dozen took degrees by 2015, bringing the rate to as 58 percent of the constituent core, or 78 percent of those who came back for the second year.[29]

The subgroup boasted a clutch of Latin honors, as well as other 3.0 and higher final Adelphi averages upon completion. It is safe to say that "B+" typified the subgroup at the time it finished college work. This might be expected among students who had done strong work in grades 9 through 12. But they were also the bearers of the lowest SAT mean of the Class of 2013. One notes the *magna* laureate with 860 on the College Boards and the Social Work alumnus (also *magna*) with 880. The graduates showed a certain bent toward Psychology. Otherwise, their fields of concentration spread out to Education-tied areas of Social Science and Humanities, Nursing, Communications, Social Work, Business Management, and Art.[30]

A much larger subdivision of the cohort filled out the high school average range between 2.5 and 2.99. Of the forty-eight students occupying this space, thirty-five came back for sophomore year. The source indicates that students who withdrew, or were dismissed for academic reasons, were generally well beyond the SAT average of the cohort. One finds here several who broke 1,000 on the SAT. In fact, nobody in the 3.0 and over high school GPA classification came close to that score.[31]

Of the sophomore returnees, twenty-two earned diplomas in 2013. This constituted 46 percent of the original subgroup, or 63 percent of the sophomores. Within the next two years, five others graduated as well. They made the six-year graduation rate 58 percent of the whole, thus 80 percent of the post-program students. Two scientifically oriented (Nursing and Environmental Studies) students had struggled on the math component of the SAT, one scoring 380, the other 420: but they excelled at the college level. The graduates' college GPA upon completion came to roughly 3.3, no different than the segment averaging over 3.0 in high school. Peaks included particular success in the arts departments, Psychology, English, Business Management, and Nursing. The bent toward Psychology manifested itself again. The same was true in Education-rooted fields. Latin honors are discernible in the grouping's mid and upper strata, while the lower range included near-*laude* graduates. Other alumni of interest also appear, for example, the two Psych *laude* designees (one a 2.7 in high school, the other 2.6) who achieved 790 and 800 respectively on the SAT.[32]

The portion of the 2009 cohort drawing high school averages between 2.0 and 2.49 was rather small, but it deserves recognition for escalating the collective SAT mean. Sixteen students entered General Studies with this profile in fall 2009, bearing an overall secondary index of 2.3 and an SAT math-verbal average of 970, towering over the subgroup with the best high school record. "DNR" ("did not return") surfaces at several points in this subgroup: indications are that money issues led a few students to leave, one in the second year and another in senior year. (The ones who left the university midway were at different points on the academic spectrum: one departed Adelphi with a 2.0, another with a 2.8, a third with a 3.0, and a fourth with a 2.1.) Twelve students came back in the second year, of whom five graduated in 2013 and another the following year. The graduation rate was 31 percent of the first sixteen, or 42 percent of the second-year enrollees, over four years. The six-year rate was 38 percent and 50 percent, respectively. The grads averaged just under 3.0 at Adelphi, a significant rise in GPA from high school, yet the lowest college GPA of any segment of the Class of 2013. The majors make for an interesting spread, including several in Physical Education or Physical Therapy, and a faint iteration of the Psychology/Humanities/Teaching refrain struck up by the cohort.[33]

Table 8.3 below conveys the academic trajectory of all members of the cohort, listed according to entering GPA from high school, and including final Adelphi graduating averages.[34] Students who withdrew (who left mainly before the fall semester) are not counted in the tabulations, but are indicated at the bottom in the order in which they left the university. Abbreviations are as follows:

> **Majors**: Acc (Accounting), BBA or BMG (Management), Bio (Biology), Bfn (Finance), Bus (Business), Chem (Chemistry), Cis (Computer and Management Information Systems), Comm (Communications), CSD (Communication Disorders), ComJou (Communications/Journalism), CompSci (Computer Science), CrimJ (Criminal Justice), Early (Early Childhood Education), Ed (Education), Eng (English), EnvStu (Envi-

ronmental Studies), ExPhys (Exercise Physiology), ExSci (Exercise Science), Health Ed (Health Education), His (History), Int'l St (International Studies), Mgmt (Management), Mktg (Marketing), Mth (Math), Mus (Music), Nur (Nursing), PE (Physical Education), PolSci (Political Science), Psy (Psychology), PT (Physical Therapy), Soc (Sociology), Spa (Spanish), SpePath or Spe (Speech Pathology), SpMgmt (Sports Management), STEP or Step (Scholar Teacher Education Program), Swk (Social Work), The (Theater), Und (Undecided). **Other**: Dis: Dismissed, DNR: Did Not Return, W/D: Withdrew, $: Financial issues, Tran: Transferred, Abroad: Studied abroad, VSAT: Verbal SAT, MSAT: Math SAT, Tot. SAT: Total SAT, HS GPA: High school grade point average, GS-avg: General Studies average, F: Fall semester (F09 = Fall 2009), S: Spring semester (S10 = Spring 2010), cr: Credits

Class of 2013 Adelphi Graduation by Rate by High School GPA

Number of students	**100**	**86**	**74**	**67**	**61**	**59**	**58**	**56**		
% of Original class		86%	74%	67%	61%	59%	58%	56%		
% Returning sophomores			100%	91%	82%	80%	78%	76%		
% w 3.0 or higher semester*	33%	44%	53%	60%	59%	53%	62%	73%		
% with gpa increase in semester*		54%	61%	66%	57%	58%	67%	80%		
Number Graduate*								41	11	2
% Graduate*								55%	15%	3%
*** Returning**										

HS GPA	**VSAT**	**MSAT**	**Tot SAT**	**Major**	**F09**	**S10**	**GS-avg**	**F10**	**S11**	**F11**	**S12**	**F12**	**S13**	**5 Year S14**	**6 year S15**
3.8	380	540	920	Bio	3.48	3.77	3.63	3.75/3.69	3.73/3.7	2.95/3.56	3.83/3.61	3.6/3.61	3.76/3.62 **Magna**		
3.7	420	490	910	Und	3.58	3.68	3.63	DNR							
3.7	440	470	910	Psy	3.93	3.93	3.93	3.62/3.82	3.72/3.79	3.91/3.83	4.0/3.84	4.0/3.87	3.87 **Magna**		
3.7	440	440	880	Psy	3.30	3.16	3.23	2.78/3.05	2.45/2.92	3.07/2.94	2.0/2.84	2.16/2.72	3.6/2.82 106 cr	**Grad**	
3.7	460	360	820	Art	2.91	2.84	2.87	3.4/3.15	3.42/3.21	3.86/3.32	3.34/3.33	3.08/3.29	4.0/3.36 **Laude**		
3.6	490	380	870	Und	3.84	3.93	3.88	DNR							
3.6	410	400	810	Eng	2.35	2.52	2.43	3.5/2.8	2.78/2.8	3.7/3.0	3.7/3.13	3.64/3.22	3.75/3.29 **Grad**		
3.5	430	430	860	EnvStu	2.70	2.91	2.80	3.43/2.96	3.66/3.12	3.35/3.14	2.9/3.1	2.9/3.08	3.39/3.12 82 cr	**Grad**	
3.5	460	390	850	Psy	3.07	3.15	3.11	3.94/3.41	2.86/326	3.6/3.34	3.58/3.38	3.82/3.45	3.94/3.51 **Laude**		
3.5	380	450	830		2.54	DNR$									

HS GPA	VSAT	MSAT	Tot SAT	Major	F09	S10	GS-avg	F10	S11	F11	S12	F12	S13	5 Year S14	6 Year S15
3.5	410	410	820	Mth	3.16	3.23	3.20	3.0/3.13	1.5/2.69	3.22/2.68	3.35/2.9	2.64/2.87	2.94/2.88 104 cr	**Grad**	
3.4	460	450	910	HealthEd	2.82	2.85	2.83	2.71/2.79	2.92/2.82	2.94/2.9	2.56/2.79	3.79/2.91	3.34/2.97 **Grad**		
3.4	430	430	860	CSD	3.42	3.65	3.53	3.45/3.5	3.12/3.4	3.75/3.48	3.94/3.55	4.0/3.61	3.84/3.65 **Magna**		
3.4	440	400	840	His	2.91	2.77	2.84	2.8/2.82	2.25/2.69	1.08/2.33	2.75/2.4	2.76/2.46	2.71/2.49 107 cr	DNR	
3.4	410	420	830		3.93	DNR$									
3.3	420	490	910	Nur	2.77	2.95	2.86	2.58/2.75	3.4/2.96	2.3/2.8	2.3/2.76	2.55/2.73	2.91/2.75 105 cr	**Grad**	
3.3	390	500	890	Mus	2.40	2.68	2.54	1.2/2.37	DNR cred						
3.3	420	450	870		3.39	DNR									
3.3	460	380	840	Eng	3.00	2.47	2.73	DNR							
3.2	440	440	880	Eng	2.86	2.61	2.73	3.57/3.0	DNR						
3.2	410	460	870	Art	2.91	3.14	3.02	3.2/3.08	3.54/3.24	3.72/3.34	3.68/3.42	3.86/3.48	4.0/3.53 **Laude**		
3.2	390	460	850		2.91	DNR$									
3.2	430	420	850	Psy	2.70	2.15	2.42	3.1/2.59	2.08/2.44	DNR					
3.2	390	420	810	Psy	2.24	3.12	2.68	2.29/2.54	2.74/2.59	2.29/2.53	2.76/2.56	1.91/2.46	2.63/2.56 103 cr	**Grad**	
3.2	370	430	800	Com	2.84	3.14	2.99	3.82/3.25	3.92/3.41	3.67/3.46	3.74/3.51	3.65/3.55	3.42/3.53 **Laude**		
3.1	430	460	890	Psy	2.42	2.52	2.47	2.39/2.44	3.66/2.8	3.2/2.89	2.66/2.84	2.56/2.79	2.33/2.73 **Grad**		
3.1	400	480	880	SpMgt	1.46	2.00	1.73	2.25/1.89	2.35/2.0	3.0/2.19	2.17/2.199	2.92/2.29	3.03/2.39 100 cr	**Grad**	
3.1	420	460	880	und	2.61	1.77	2.19	2.1/2.6	DNR$						
3.1	440	440	880	Swk	3.28	3.84	3.56	3.51/3.58	3.76/3.63	3.94/3.69	3.56/3.67	3.92/3.7	3.66/3.69 **Magna**		

HS GPA	VSAT	MSAT	Tot SAT	Major	F09	S10	GS-avg	F10	S11	F11	S12	F12	S13	5 Year S14	6 Year S15
3.0	500	390	890	Soc	2.24	3.16	2.70	2.81/2.73	3.07/2.82	3.28/2.92	3.66/3.06	3.56/3.14	2.81/3.07 **Grad**		
3.0	510	380	890	Mgt	3.58	3.68	3.63	3.85/3.72	3.46/3.65	3.62/3.64	abroad 3.64	3.37/3.86	3.85/3.59 **Laude**		
3.0	450	430	880	Mgt	2.61	1.84	2.22	1.38/1.98	2.42/2.09	2.8/2.26	2.46/2.29	3.23/2.43	2.32/2.42 90 cr	DNR	
3.0	410	460	870	PE	3.07	2.91	2.99	3.0/2.99	3.13/3.03	3.4/3.11	2.56/3.01	2.97/2.99	3.01/3.0 **Grad**		
3.0	430	430	860	Und	3.07	3.32	3.20	DNR							
3.0	440	420	860	und	2.23	0.23	1.23	Dis							
3.0	390	460	850	Swk	3.16	2.91	3.03	2.65/2.91	2.18/2.7	2.76/2.71	2.67/2.71	2.85/2.72	2.12/2.63 **Grad**		
2.9	470	450	920	PE	3.07	3.23	3.15	3.28/3.19	3.26/3.21	3.75/3.33	3.83/3.42	3.35/3.41	3.3/3.4 **Laude**		
2.9	450	440	890	Art	2.68	2.79	2.73	3.14/2.88	3.17/2.94	3.42/3.05	3.82/3.19	3.66/3.26	3.34/3.27 **Grad**		
2.9	470	380	850	Nur	2.98	3.07	3.03	3.02/3.02	3.24/3.07	2.93/2.9	3.22/3.1	2.64/3.02	2.85/2.99 107 cr	**Grad**	
2.9	330	380	710	Psy	3.07	3.54	3.30	3.26/3.28	DNR						
2.85	460	370	830	Und	2.77	3.21	2.99	DNR							
2.8	460	550	1010	Mgt	3.91	3.61	3.76	3.46/3.67	3.86/3.76	3.4/3.7	3.2/3.61	3.21/3.58	3.6/3.58 **Laude**		
2.8	450	460	910	Psy	2.75	2.68	2.71	2.98/2.8	DNR						
2.8	470	440	910	Nur	2.91	3.07	2.99	3.38/3.14	3.19/3.15	2.68/3.05	2.66/2.99	2.42/2.92	3.28/2.97 **Grad**		
2.8	420	470	890	Und	3.28	3.45	3.37	DNR							
2.8	420	460	880		2.16	DNR									
2.8	360	490	850	PE	2.75	2.84	2.79	3.16/2.93	3.35/3.03	3.52/3.13	3.01/3.11	2.76/3.06	3.18/3.04 **Grad**		
2.8	410	400	810	PE	2.75	1.82	2.28	2.97/2.51	3.5/2.8	3.75/3.04	2.62/2.96	2.51/2.91	3.02/2.9 **Grad**		

HS GPA	VSAT	MSAT	Tot SAT	Major	F09	S10	GS-avg	F10	S11	F11	S12	F12	S13	5 Year S14	6 Year S15
2.75	450	420	870	Psy	3.28	3.61	3.45	2.38/3.09	3.08/3.08	2.32/2.92	3.37/3.04	3.05/3.04	3.66/3.15 **Grad**		
2.73	390	440	830	Psy	2.79	3.09	2.94	2.7/2.85	2.54/2.76	2.73/2.76	abroad 2.76	3.28/2.85	2.75/2.83 **Grad**		
2.7	430	530	960		1.56	Dis									
2.7	430	470	900	ExSci	3.00	3.02	3.01	2.84/2.95	1.97/2.71	DNR					
2.7	440	460	900		2.09	DNR									
2.7	430	450	880	Mth	2.68	3.40	3.04	DNR							
2.7	430	440	870	Dance	3.16	3.52	3.34	3.38/3.38	3.76/3.48	3.84/3.56	3.91/3.65	3.87/3.67	3.96/3.71 **Magna**		
2.7	430	400	830		2.38	DNR									
2.7	430	380	810	Psy	3.00	2.68	2.84	2.56/2.73	3.46/2.92	2.76/2.89	3.37/2.98	3.71/3.09	3.51/3.15 **Grad**		
2.7	440	350	790	Psy	2.84	2.45	2.64	3.25/2.83	3.46/3.01	3.25/3.05	3.6/3.2	3.64/3.28	3.88/3.37 **Laude**		
2.7	390	310	700	Swk	2.24	2.84	2.54	2.95/2.69	2.5/2.65	3.17/2.74	3.1/2.78	3.56/2.85	3.8/2.99 **Grad**		
2.68	460	380	840	und	2.98	3.18	3.08	DNR							
2.67	420	440	860	Psy	3.00	2.98	2.99	2.58/2.83	3.28/2.95	2.82/2.92	2.77/2.89	3.88/3.03	3.52/3.09 **Grad**		
2.6	480	530	1010		1.35	Dis									
2.6	440	540	980		2.72	DNR$									
2.6	500	470	970	Eng	3.16	3.68	3.42	3.25/3.36	3.48/3.39	3.38/3.29	3.2/3.35	3.48/3.37	3.34/3.37 **Laude**		
2.6	520	440	960	The	3.00	3.09	3.05	3.34/3.17	3.21/3.19	Abroad	3.57/3.26	3.87/3.37	3.85/3.44 **Laude**		
2.6	470	470	940	SpMgt	2.15	1.86	2.00	2.94/2.34	2.32/2.34	3.0/2.48	2.86/2.55	2.66/2.61	2.71/2.61 **Grad**		
2.6	470	460	930	Psy	2.77	2.63	2.70	2.5/2.62	3.48/2.84	3.2/2.92	3.45/3.01	3.35/3.07	3.66/3.17 **Grad**		
2.6	490	420	910	Bio	2.70	2.25	2.48	0/1.95	0/1.43	DNR					

HS GPA	VSAT	MSAT	Tot SAT	Major	F09	S10	GS-avg	F10	S11	F11	S12	F12	S13	5 Year S14	6 Year S15
2.6	420	460	880	Und	2.77	2.45	2.61	1.76/2.32	1.23/2.05	2.3/2.08	3.52/2.3	DNR			
2.6	420	460	880	Bio	2.23	2.75	2.49	DNR							
2.6	500	380	880	Psy	3.54	2.89	3.22	2.68/3.03	2.34/2.85	2.94/2.87	3.0/2.89	3.7/2.97	3.5/3.06 110 cr	**Grad**	
2.6	450	420	870	EnvSci	2.93	3.00	2.97	3.16/3.03	3.04/3.01	3.46/3.16	abroad	3.41/3.20	4.0/3.23 107	137 cr	**Grad**
2.6	420	450	870	Nur	3.09	3.07	3.08	3.18/3.11	3.42/3.19	3.49/3.25	2.67/3.14	3.06/3.13	3.28/3.15 100 cr	**Grad**	
2.6	410	420	830	Psy	2.86	3.23	3.05	3.16/3.08	3.11/3.09	3.55/3.18	2.67/3.1	3.38/3.15	3.52/3.2 **Grad**		
2.6	400	400	800	Psy	3.16	3.77	3.47	2.86/3.36	3.75/3.45	3.55/3.47	3.68/3.51	3.82/3.58	3.74/3.58 **Laude**		
2.6	380	390	770		2.14	DNR$									
2.5	510	510	1020	Psy	1.95	2.16	2.06	2.85/2.3	2.67/2.39	DNR					
2.5	540	460	1000	Nur	2.68	2.45	2.56	DNR							
2.5	460	500	960	Eng	3.32	3.25	3.29	2.6/3.13	1.16/2.6	2.75	DNR$				
2.5	430	470	900	ExSci	3.09	3.16	3.13	2.76/3.08	3.26/3.07	2.94/3.04	2.54/2.85	2.34/2.77	1.74/2.63 **Grad**		
2.5	470	420	890	Nur	2.84	2.22	2.53	3.32/2.79	3.95/3.06	3.28/3.13	3.65/3.2	2.91/3.15	3.13/3.15 105 cr	120 cr	**Grad**
2.5	430	430	860	Art	2.91	2.68	2.79	3.2/2.86	3.6/3.08	3.52/3.17	3.44/3.21	3.63/3.26	3.5/3.28 **Grad**		
2.5	440	410	850	Psy	2.58	2.70	2.64	2.75/2.67	1.63/2.37	2.67/2.57	2.8/2.68	inc/2.67	3.35/2.91 **Grad**		
2.5	440	400	840	Dance	1.98	2.77	2.38	2.92/2.55	1.89/2.39	1.97/2.32	DNR				
2.4	510	620	1130	PE	3.16	3.55	3.36	3.56/3.46	2.23/3.18	2.83/3.11	2.72/3.06	3.23/3.07	3.61/3.17 **Grad**		
2.4	520	500	1020	Mgt	1.93	2.23	2.08	1.76/2.0	1.42/1.85	DNR					
2.4	450	530	980	Mgt	3.07	3.00	3.03	3.4/3.22	DNR						
2.4	450	500	950	Psy	2.18	2.55	2.37	3.0/2.61	3.23/2.75	3.14/2.89	3.76/2.98	3.53/3.07	3.41/3.11 **Grad**		

HS GPA	VSAT	MSAT	Tot SAT	Major	F09	S10	GS-avg	F10	S11	F11	S12	F12	S13	5 Year S14	6 Year S15
2.4	520	410	930	His	3.16	2.70	2.93	3.42/3.08	DNR						
2.4	430	480	910		2.09	DNR$									
2.4	450	460	910	Eng	2.84	2.40	2.62	2.46/2.58	2.73/2.65	no ret	3.26/2.78	3.22/2.85	3.18/2.93 102 cr	**Grad**	
2.4	470	440	910	ExSci	2.22	2.93	2.57	3.05/2.75	3.73/3.02	3.7/3.14	3.18/3.13	3.7/3.22	3.5/3.22 **Grad**		
2.4	470	400	870	PE	2.93	2.84	2.88	2.77/2.84	2.92/2.86	3.0/2.88	2.93/2.89	2.82/2.88	DNR $		
2.3	580	420	1000		0.00	Dis									
2.3	520	460	980	und	2.68	2.12	2.40	2.67/2.48	1.2/2.13	1.0/2.01	DNR				
2.3	490	480	970		3.07	DNR									
2.3	450	470	920	PE	2.75	2.63	2.69	3.16/2.87	2.91/2.87	2.2/2.74	2.2/2.66	2.03/2.55	2.57/2.55 **Grad**		
2.22	490	470	960	Mgt	2.40	2.38	2.39	2.66/2.48	3.23/2.69	2.9/2.73	2.93/2.76	3.48/2.74	3.16/2.92 **Grad**		
2.21	470	520	990	Com	2.38	1.90	2.14	2.9/2.37	3.17/2.57	1.5/2.39	2.42/2.42	1.78/2.31	2.16/2.31 98cr	124 cr	
2.0	550	550	1100	und	2.45	2.12	2.28	DNR							
2.7	520	400	920	w/d											
3.2	480	260	740	w/d											
2.55	550	410	960	w/d											
2.5	540	460	1000	w/d											
3.2	360	490	850	w/d											
2.7	470	430	900	w/d											
2.1	510	540	1050	w/d											
2.5	520	540	1060	w/d											
3.2	400	410	810	w/d											
2.7	460	470	930	w/d											

Note: Table created by Daniel Rosenberg. Statistics used with permission from Deirdre Donat.

NOTES

1. *Adelphi University Databook*, Fall 2006, 83; *Adelphi University Databook*, Fall 2012, 106.

2. *Adelphi University Databook*, Fall 2000, "Retention and Graduation Rates of First-Time, Full-time Freshmen: General Studies: Fall 1990 to Fall 2003," 1; *Adelphi University Databook* Fall 2003, "Retention and Graduation Rates of First-Time, Regularly Admitted Students: Fall 1990 to Fall 2003," 1.

3. National Student Clearinghouse, *National College Progression Rates*, Herndon, Virginia, 2013, 10–11; *Adelphi University Databook*, Fall 2007, 119; *Adelphi University Databook*, 2012, 129.

4. John Donohue to David Newton, *General Studies Graduation Rates*, February 26, 1991, GSC; John Donohue to Dean Cavallo, *85/09 GS Update*, January 9, 1990, GSC; John Donohue to Dean Cavallo, *Graduation Figures for General Studies Cohorts of 1985, 1986*, July 11, 1990, GSC; Dominick Cavallo, *The General Studies Program: A Report on Student Progress, 1985-1990*, August 1990, GSC; John Donohue to Dr. David Newton, *The Magic of Numbers: HEOP, General Studies, Apples, Oranges, and Mirrors*, December 14, 1990, GSC.

5. John Donohue to Dean Cavallo, *Graduation Figures for General Studies Cohorts of 1985, 1986*, July 11, 1990, GSC; John Donohue to Dean Cavallo, *Graduation Figures for General Studies Cohorts of 1985, 1986*, July 11, 1990, GSC; Dom Cavallo to Dr. Newton, *"Mainstreamed" General Studies Students*, October 7, 1988, GSC; Meryl Shapiro to Dean Cavallo, *Sophomore General Studies Students*, January 1988, GSC; Dominick Cavallo, *The General Studies Program: A Report on Student Progress, 1985-1990*, August 1990, GSC.

6. John Donohue to Dean Cavallo, *Graduation Figures for General Studies Cohorts of 1985, 1986*, July 11, 1990, GSC; Deborah Robottom to Dom Cavallo, *Categorization of Problems with General Studies Students*, December 19, 1986, GSC; Dominick Cavallo, *The General Studies Program: A Report on Student Progress, 1985-1990*, August 1990, GSC.

7. Meryl Shapiro to Dean Cavallo, *Final Grades*, February 12, 1988, GSC.

8. Della Hudson-Tomlin, *General Studies Statistics*, October 31, 1994, 16, 19, 24, 31, GSC.

9. Della Hudson-Tomlin to David Newton, Dean, *General Studies 1995 Graduates*, June 1, 1995, GSC; Della Hudson-Tomlin to Dr. Diamandopoulos et al., *May 1996 Graduates*, June 10, 1996, GSC.

10. David Newton, dean of University College, to Igor Webb, senior vice president, June 1, 1995, GSC; Della Hudson-Tomlin to Dr. Diamandopoulos et al., *May 1996 Graduates*, June 10, 1996, GSC; Clifford H. Edwards, "Grade Inflation: The Effects on Educational Quality and Personal Well-Being," *Education*, Vol. 120, No. 3 (Spring 2000), 544.

11. *Adelphi University Databook*, Fall 2006, "Retention and Graduation Rates of First-Time, Full-time Freshmen: General Studies: Fall 1990 to Fall 2006," 98; *Adelphi University Databook*, Fall 2006, "Retention and Graduation Rates of First-Time, Full-Time Freshmen, Regularly Admitted Students: Fall 1990 to Fall 2006, 120; *Adelphi University Databook*, Fall 2006, "Retention and Graduation Rates of First-Time, Full-time Freshmen: Honors College Entrants: Fall 1995 to Fall 2006, 85; *Adelphi University Databook*, Fall 2012, "Retention and Graduation Rates of First-Time, Full-Time Freshmen, Honors College Entrants: Fall 2002 to Fall 2012, 93; *Adelphi University Databook*, Fall 2012, "Retention and Graduation Rates of First-Time, Full-time Freshmen: General Studies: Fall 2002 to Fall 2012, 106; *Adelphi University Databook*, Fall 2012, "Retention and Graduation Rates of First-Time, Full-Time Freshmen, Regularly Admitted Students: Fall 2002 to Fall 2012, 130.

12. *Adelphi University Databook*, Fall 2006, Retention and Graduation Rates of First-Time, Full-Time Freshmen: College of Arts & Sciences: Fall 1990 to Fall 2006, 121; *Adelphi University Databook*, Fall 2006, Retention and Graduation Rates of First-Time, Full-Time Freshmen: School of Business: Fall 1990 to Fall 2006, 129; *Adelphi University Databook*, Fall 2006, Retention and Graduation Rates of First-Time, Full-Time Fresh-

men: School of Education: Fall 1990 to Fall 2006,123; *Adelphi University Databook,* Fall 2006, Retention and Graduation Rates of First-Time, Full-Time Freshmen: School of Nursing: Fall 1990 to Fall 2006, 125; *Adelphi University Databook,* Fall 2006, Retention and Graduation Rates of First-Time, Full-Time Freshmen: School of Social Work: Fall 1990 to Fall 2006, 126; *Adelphi University Databook,* 2006, "Grade Distribution Within Undergraduate and Graduate Courses: Fall 2006 Percentages," 149; *Adelphi University Databook,* 2012, "Grade Distribution Within Undergraduate and Graduate Courses: Spring 2012 Percentages, 167.

13. *Adelphi University Databook,* Fall 2012, Retention and Graduation Rates of First-Time, Full-Time Freshmen: School of Education: Fall 2002 to Fall 2012, 137; *Adelphi University Databook,* Fall 2012, Retention and Graduation Rates of First-Time, Full-Time Freshmen: School of Nursing: Fall 2002 to Fall 2012, 139; *Adelphi University Databook,* Fall 2012, "Undergraduate Enrollment by Age Category: Fall 2012," 67; *Adelphi University Databook,* 2012, "Retention and Graduation Rates of First-Time, Full-Time Freshmen: Women, Fall 2002 to Fall 2012, 131; *Adelphi University Databook,* 2012, "Retention and Graduation Rates of First-Time, Full-Time Freshmen: Men, Fall 2002 to Fall 2012, 132; *Adelphi University Databook,* "Graduation Rates of First-Time, Full-Time Freshmen By Race/Ethnicity: Fall Cohorts 2000 to 2008, 133; National Student Clearinghouse, *National College Progression Rates,* Herndon, Virginia, 2013, 12–14, 28–31; ACT, *The Condition of College Readiness 2013,* Iowa City, 2013, 5, 9.

14. Ross Markle and Steve Robbins, "A Holistic View of Course Placement Decisions: Avoiding the HS GPA Trap," *Educational Testing Service,* March 2013, 2.

15. Compiled by Gabriel Rosenberg, March 2016, from Deirdre Donat, *Class of 2007 by HS GPA, Class of 2008 by HS GPA, Class of 2009 by HS GPA, Class of 2010 by HS GPA, Class of 2011 by HS GPA, Class of 2012 by HS GPA, Class of 2013 by HS GPA, Class of 2014 by HS GPA,* February 26, 2016, GSC.

16. Deirdre Donat, *Track Class of 2007,* 2010, GSC; Deirdre Donat, *Class of 2007 by HS GPA,* August 2013, GSC.

17. Deirdre Donat, *2012–13 Final Grades,* May 17, 2013, GSC; Deirdre Donat, Class of 2007 by HS GPA, August 2013, GSC.

18. Deirdre Donat, *Class of 2007 by HS GPA,* August 2013, GSC.

19. Deirdre Donat, *Class of 2007 by HS GPA,* August 2013, GSC.

20. Deirdre Donat, *Class of 2007 by HS GPA,* August 2013, GSC.

21. Deirdre Donat, *Class of 2007 by HS GPA,* February 2016, GSC.

22. Deirdre Donat, *Class of 2007 by HS GPA,* February 2016, GSC.

23. Deirdre Donat, *2012-13 Final Grades,* May 17, 2013, GSC; Deirdre Donat, *Class of 2010 by HS GPA,* August 2013, GSC.

24. Deirdre Donat, *Class of 2010 by HS GPA,* August 2013, GSC.

25. Deirdre Donat, *Class of 2010 by HS GPA,* August 2013, GSC.

26. Deirdre Donat, *Class of 2010 by HS GPA,* August 2013, GSC.

27. Deirdre Donat, *Class of 2010 by HS GPA,* February 2016, GSC.

28. Deirdre Donat, *2013-2014 Final Grades,* May 19, 2014, GSC; Deirdre Donat, *Class of 2013 by HS GPA,* July 2015, GSC.

29. Deirdre Donat, *Class of 2013 by HS GPA,* July 2015, GSC.

30. Deirdre Donat, *Class of 2013 by HS GPA,* July 2015, GSC.

31. Deirdre Donat, *Class of 2013 by HS GPA,* July 2015, GSC.

32. Deirdre Donat, *Class of 2013 by HS GPA,* July 2015, GSC.

33. Deirdre Donat, *Class of 2013 by HS GPA,* July 2015, GSC.

34. Deirdre Donat, *Class of 2013 by HS GPA,* February 2016, GSC.

NINE

The SATs and General Studies

Like the previous chapter, this one assumes that finishing college is a major accomplishment, regardless of timing. Contemporary figures show that roughly two-thirds of students graduate in six years. Data collectors have not entirely eschewed the tracking of four-year completion rates. In 2013, the College Board supplied these statistics for several of Adelphi's local competitors: Molloy College (37 percent), St. John's (the same), C. W. Post (27 percent), and the Old Westbury (20 percent) and Farmingdale (17 percent) branches of the State University.[1]

But on the whole, longer graduation rates have characterized the sophomore-to-senior arc of General Studies alumni with higher SATs but lower high school averages. Overall, they have not done as well in the General Studies Program or Learning Community as the lower SAT-scoring program members. The 1987 group, for instance, brought in a combined verbal-math SAT average of 770, but included students whose totals had exceeded 1000. Fewer than half the latter made it from fall to spring in good academic standing, equaling the fall to spring returns of students admitted with scores below 600.[2]

Half of 1985's sub-800 test takers remaining at Adelphi after the program went on to graduate, but less than a third of those who had surpassed 900. Once again, half of those who entered General Studies in 1987 after scoring between 600 and 700 on the SAT—and who stayed at Adelphi—graduated. The 1989 entering class substantiates the point. While information is lacking on six-year completions, data shows a five-year graduation rate for the retained students as follows: 13 percent of those scoring above 900 had graduated by May 1994; 26 percent of those scoring between 800 and 900; 30 percent of those scoring between 700 and 800; and 25 percent of those scoring between 600 and 700. Reference has been made in chapter 6 to the Diamandopoulos administration's decision to admit students scoring in the vicinity of 300 on the SAT verbal in 1990. A good number of them graduated in four years.[3]

This chapter, which analyzes graduation rates of General Studies students in light of their SAT scores, focuses on the most recent period of the program. A large collection of evidence facilitates comparison of SAT scores with Adelphi grades upon graduation. Figure 9.1 shows that the very highest Adelphi finishers were polar opposites on the SAT spectrum. In between the SAT extremes, poorer test takers essentially match or exceed the cumulative Adelphi averages of their higher-scoring classmates.[4]

The data allow for further critique of the exam instrument and its customary presumptions. The outcomes of the classes of 2007, 2010, and 2013, depicted below, again represent the bigger picture. Concentration upon the three example cohorts owes much to the greater availability of tracking data after 2000, and a more attentive approach to compilation. Roughly, the lower the SAT score, the higher the final Adelphi GPA upon graduation and the speedier time to completion. The exception occurs only at the very highest SAT marks, a handful of cases. Even when solid Adelphi GPAs are earned, higher SAT scorers move toward graduation at a slower pace.

The tables for the three graduating classes to be discussed flow from the same premise as their counterparts in the previous chapter. For programmatic reasons intrinsic to its functioning, the size of the General Stud-

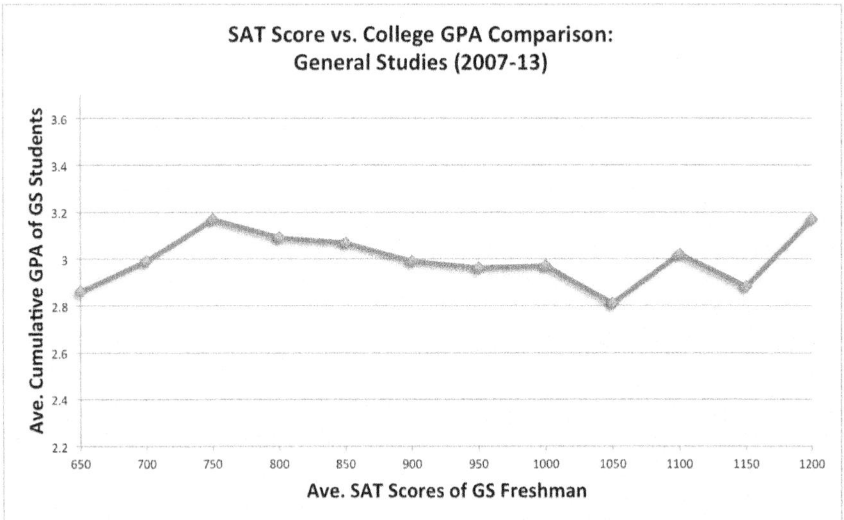

Figure 9.1. SAT Score vs. College GPA Comparison: General Studies (2007–2013). Note: Figure designed by Gabriel Rosenberg. Statistics were used with permission from Deirdre Donat and were compiled by Gabriel Rosenberg.

ies cohort is expected to decline between first and second semesters, and between first and second years. While placing students below 2.0 after one semester on probation remains an option, the program's faculty and counselors may choose to dismiss. Therefore, unique conditions impact retention from first to second semester. Additionally, the decades-long denial of scholarships to General Studies students on the basis of their SAT scores, no matter how well they did in high school, contributed to transfers out of Adelphi.

In this sense, the SAT's underestimation of potential in students who scored low because they could not afford expensive prep classes or who did not attend well-funded funded high schools (or ones with fully staffed college counseling) negatively affected admitted program students. This is not to mention the dim value of a one-shot, one-size-fits-all exam taken under duress. It is worth recalling the *New York Times'* insight that standardized tests tell us more about "parental education and income" than college acumen. For this reason, the National Association for College Admission Counseling has for years advised higher education institutions to "eliminate test scores as a measure of institutional quality."[5]

As before, the analysis here will draw the distinction between the completion rates of the original registrants and those of the second-year returnees. In a program of the General Studies type, sophomore to senior conversion holds special value. The tables follow the outcomes of General Studies students who became sophomores and continued at Adelphi.

THE CLASS OF 2007

Verbal and math SAT totals of the ninety students beginning General Studies in fall 2003, already briefly mentioned in the discussion of secondary school GPA (2.62), crystallized at 902. Ten held topmost rank above 1000. Eight of the ten supra-1000 students began the sophomore year in fall 2004. The record shows that three exited Adelphi as upperclassmen before the quadrennial commencement. The five remaining secured diplomas in 2007. With such a small segment, the graduation rate was 50 percent of the original subgroup in four years: 63 percent of the sophomores. Adelphi awarded Latin honors to three (whose high school averages incidentally were 2.5, 2.4, and 1.8). Business Administration was the choice major of two of the five finishers.[6]

While twenty-seven began in 2003 with SAT marks ranging from 900 to 990, nineteen took sophomore classes in fall 2004. Thirteen were registered at Adelphi by customary senior year measurement. Eleven appeared at 2007 commencement, 41 percent of the first entrants, but more than half of the ex-sophomores. Two more accomplished their goal by the six-year point. This brought the graduation rate to 48 percent of all arriving at Adelphi with SAT scores from 900 to 990, and 68 percent of the second-year enrollees. All the category's students on the rolls as of 2007 became college graduates by 2009. Four of the 900–990 finishers received Latin honors, including one *summa,* and one *magna.* The last two boasted high school GPAs of 3.3 and 2.3, respectively. Common majors spanned Business areas to Nursing to Psychology, with a smaller presence in Education-tied concentrations like History and Sociology.[7]

The group of forty-seven freshmen carrying 800–890 entrance exam marks into General Studies suffered attrition after the first year. Only twenty-seven signed up for sophomore classes at Adelphi. Afterwards, Adelphi recorded significant losses among these students. Table 9.1 shows transfers, students leaving for financial reasons, and others departing for unexplained cause. Ten nevertheless successfully graduated in 2007, making a four-year rate, relative to retained sophomores, of 37 percent: but the grads amounted to 21 percent of the first 47. Another graduated after seven years. Thus, 40 percent of the sophomores advanced to degrees. The graduation rate was lower than the ones recorded by the SAT takers above them. Communications and Psychology headed up the fields of concentration. A student with an 830 SAT won a *magna cum laude* designation.[8]

Freshman to sophomore retention among the six students who joined General Studies in 2003 with sub-800 SATs was 100 percent. Four graduated in 2007, two with honors. The four ended baccalaureate work with final Adelphi averages between 2.7 and 3.45. Of interest within the group were the two who took Education degrees with a History specialization.[9]

The cohort's average math score was 444. Of the most outstanding math test takers (above 500), three earned Adelphi GPAs worthy of *laude,* but others finished at 2.25, 2.62, and 2.7. Business majors dominated the finishers. An examination of students dismissed for academic reasons from the Class of 2007 finds an SAT math composite nearly thirty points higher than the group mean. The number of program students with math marks between 400 and 444 dwindled, primarily due to financial causes and transfers. Eight (whose university GPAs triumphed over the high school averages by a score of 3.1 to 2.5) passed through commencement in four years. However, two students graduated *laude* at the 2007 ceremonies. The finishers displayed a range of concentrations: Psychology, History (tied to Education), Communication and Speech Disorders, Nursing, Business, and Theatre, among them. The quadrennial graduates achieved better final college GPAs than the averages they brought from high school: 3.1 as opposed to 2.6.[10]

The nine GS freshmen with sub-400 math marks reappeared as eight Adelphi sophomores. Six registered in spring 2007, five going to commencement. While one encounters the small numbers with caution, the concluding Adelphi GPA of the graduated lowest-scoring SAT takers was 3.3, matching the average with which they finished high school. Adelphi bestowed Latin honors on two students in this category. Fields of specialization followed several directions: Psychology, Communications, and History (pinned to Education). An entrant in Biology, where the math SAT reputedly augurs much, maintained a 3.0 to the end of her Adelphi degree, despite a 370 on the SAT math.[11]

Evaluating the significance of SAT math scores to future doings of General Studies students depends on how much one enjoys asterisks. This or that achievement level indicates a direction of interest, a fact that advertises something before panning out or trailing off. But the evidence suggests that the exam and its all-crucial math component convey little that is definitive with respect to final college outcomes, retention, and graduation of former General Studies students. After the program's specific first-year academic conditions are considered, the ongoing erosion of a portion of the General Studies base at Adelphi after the first year has less to do with how matriculates came in, while increasingly mirroring the American scene: elongation of college careers, transferring out, taking leaves of absence, attending part-time, working more hours and so forth. The bearing of the latter upon rates of progress in and through higher education is more decisive than test-based reasons.

A verbal mark of 458 characterized the General Studies collective at the start of freshman year 2003. More than a quarter of the cohort had scored no less than 500 (two scaling the heights of 600), ten of whom also equaled or topped 500 on the math counterpart. Yet results like 540 on the verbal, 410 in the math; 530 in the verbal, 440 on the math; or 510 and 460, give pause. Attrition clearly haunted the 500 plus verbal achievers. One departed the university after junior year, carrying a 3.0 in Psychology. In four years, seven reached commencement. The 3.16 final Adelphi GPAs levels represented by the seven graduates in 2007 (three of whom earned Latin honors) contrasted with the 2.4 held by these same students in secondary school. The graduates majored in disparate areas, but showed a predilection for the Social Sciences and Business. No one entered the Natural Sciences.[12]

To be sure, there were also students possessing SAT verbal scores higher than the class average of 458 but lower than 500. Eleven turned into sophomores, with seven graduating in four years—"the normal" length of time. Two achieved Latin honors. Several demonstrated a genuine leap from high school to college final grades. But they had higher high school GPAs than the students in the 500 and up camp. When they went to commencement, the four-year grads held a final Adelphi mean of 3.06, fairly close to the level of the highest SAT verbal students. Majors leaned in no particular direction, but the Humanities, Social Sciences, and Business all had their say.[13]

A larger 2003 cluster was composed of starters with verbal totals between 400 and the class average of 458. Eleven graduated in four years, just over a quarter of the originals: in sophomore perspective, nearly 40 percent. Two more attended commencement after five-year Adelphi careers. A Bio major took seven years, but walked out with her diploma in 2010. The four-year grads carried a high school GPA of 2.6, but finalized college with a hearty 3.2 (buttressed by five students in the upper gradient of Latin honors). Needless to say, their academic achievement at the university overshadowed the performance of the upper verbal classifications. Humanities, Psychology, and Social Sciences majors, including linkage to Education, involved several students.[14]

Seven sub-400 verbal registrants belonged to the original 2003 class. Four were on hand to graduate, three in the traditional four-year span. They split major disciplines, as one went into History (with its many term papers and lengthy final thesis), the others in Communications and Fine Arts. The miniscule contingent owned a high school mean superior to all of the groups discussed above. The four-year grads completed Adelphi with a GPA of 3.12, on par with the majority of students who scored higher on the SAT verbal than they did.[15]

Similar to the math scores, it is difficult to know where to place SAT verbal results on the list of criteria worth analyzing. That all students must learn and extend verbal skills is indisputable, regardless of chosen or hoped-for occupation. But they comprise an essential group of competencies better gauged by examining how students use words over time and in stages and projects, not in standardized exams.

Table 9.1 below presents the Class of 2007 graduation rate according to total SAT scores (with math and verbal scores indicated, along with majors and high school index), in descending order. Data includes year of completion or departure, major, and possible Latin honors, along with in-progress and final college GPA. Students who withdrew (the majority left before the fall semester) are not counted in the tabulations, but are indicated at the bottom in the order in which they left the university.[16] Abbreviations are as follows:

Majors: Acc (Accounting), BBA (Business Administration), Bio (Biology), Bfn (Finance), Bus (Business), BMG (Management), Chem (Chemistry), Cis (Computer and Management Information Systems), Comm (Communications), CSD (Communication Disorders), ComJou (Communications/Journalism), CompSci (Computer Science), CrimJ (Criminal Justice), Early (Early Childhood Education), Ed (Education), Eng (English), EnvStu (Environmental Studies), ExPhys (Exercise Physiology), ExSci (Exercise Science), His (History), Int'l St (International Studies), Mgmt (Management), Mktg (Marketing), Mth (Math), Mus (Music), Nur (Nursing), PE (Physical Education), PolSci (Political Science), Psy (Psychology), PT (Physical Therapy), Soc (Sociology), Spa (Spanish), SpePath or Spe (Speech Pathology), SpMgmt (Sports Management), STEP or Step (Scholar Teacher Education Program), Swk (Social Work), The (Theater), Und (Undecided). **Other**: Dis: Dismissed, DNR: Did Not Return, W/D: Withdrew, $: Financial issues, Tran: Transferred, Abroad: Studied abroad, VSAT: Verbal SAT, MSAT: Math SAT, Tot. SAT: Total SAT, HS GPA: High school grade point average, GS-avg: General Studies average, F: Fall semester (F03 = Fall 2003), S: Spring semester (S04 = Spring 2004), cr: Credits

Class of 2007 Graduation by Total SAT

Number of Students				**90**	**72**		**61**	**54**	**45**	**42**	**39**	**38**			
% of Original class					84%		70%	64%	52%	49%	45%	40%			
% Returning sophomores							100%	89%	74%	69%	64%	62%			
% 3.0 or higher semester				16%	17%		37%	40%	58%	55%	46%	65%			
% semester GPA Increase							75%	63%	69%	74%	79%	76%			
Number Graduate*												32	2		
% Graduate*												52%	3%		
*** Returning**															
														5 Year	**6 Year**
HS GPA	**VSAT**	**MSAT**	**Total SAT**	**Major**	**F03**	**S04**	**GS-avg**	**F04**	**S05**	**F05**	**S06**	**F06**	**S07**	**S08**	**S09**
1.90	620	530	1150	Psy	2.84	3.06	2.95	3.57/3.15	3.38/3.19	3.28/3.2	2.15/3.04	DNR			
2.00	500	630	1130	His	3.18	3.09	3.0	3.3/3.12	wd 3/21						
2.50	520	610	1130	Mgt	2.47	3.37	2.93	3.6/3.18	3.54/3.27	3.45/3.31	3.63/3.37	3.46/3.39	3.68/3.42 **Laude**		
2.30	580	550	1130	Comm	2.00	2.02	2.01	2.6/2.21	1.0/2.15	2.76/2.24	2.86/2.37	3.49/2.49	2.8/2.62 **Grad**		
1.80	600	510	1110	PolSci	3.68	3.6	3.64	3.06/3.42	3.2/3.36	3.22/3.33	3.68/3.39	3.34/3.38	3.41/3.39 **Laude**		
2.30	500	590	1090	Mgt	2.12	1.83	1.97	2.5/2.27	2.5/2.32	1.5/2.24	2.76/2.3	2.53/2.39	1.54/2.25 **Grad**		
2.50	590	500	1090	Eng	0.53	dis									
2.20	500	550	1050	Und	3.38	1.21	2.39	w/d							
2.50	510	520	1030	Eng	2.39	2.28	2.33	2.61/2.43	1.0/2.24	.65/1.98	DNR				
2.40	510	510	1020	Psy	3.08	3.46	3.27	3.06/3.15	3.92/3.30	3.73/3.4	3.6/3.42	3.6/3.48	3.68/3.34 **Laude**		
2.20	570	420	990	Comm	0.46	dis									
2.00	500	480	980	PE	1.93	2.97	2.0	2.65/2.55	3.0/2.44	3.5/2.64	3.02/2.71	2.93/2.82	3.37/2.98 **Grad**		

HS GPA	VSAT	MSAT	Total SAT	Major	F03	S04	GS-avg	F04	S05	F05	S06	F06	S07	5 Year S08	6 Year S09
2.60	520	460	980	Soc	3.00	2.48	2.72	2.82/2.76	2.88/2.84	3.17/2.9	3.75/3.03	3.67/3.12	2.95/3.4 **Grad**		
2.00	480	490	970	Mgt	2.77	2.60	2.68	3.0/2.76	2.35/2.64	2.37/2.58	2.74/2.6	2.66/2.61	2.06/2.55 **Grad**		
2.90	510	460	970	Nur	3.38	3.06	3.49	DNR							
2.10	530	440	970	Und	2.02	2.07	2.04	0.0/1.52	0/ 1.18	DNR					
2.00	470	490	960	Psy	0.92	dis									
2.40	500	460	960	Mgt	2.53	1.93	2.23	2.33/2.25	DNR $						
2.50	450	500	950	Art	1.63	3.21	2.54	3.04/2.7	3.17/2.82	2.72/2.8	abroad	1.8/2.63	3.17/2.7 **Grad**		
1.70	520	430	950	Und	1.70	3.07	2.38	2.5/2.42	2.66/2.55	DNR					
2.40	540	410	950	His	2.63	2.7	2.66	2.82/2.81	DNR						
2.40	410	530	940	Nur	0.46	dis									
2.14	480	460	940	Mgt	3.45	3.53	3.49	2.92/3.13	2.4/3.09	2.84/3.05	3.37/3.1	3.12/3.1	3.0/3.09 **Grad**		
2.50	410	520	930	Comm	1.68	dis									
3.60	470	460	930	His	3.38	3.37	3.37	3.47/3.4	3.56/3.48	3.06/3.4	3.65/3.48	3.5/3.44	3.57/3.46 **Laude**		
2.30	430	490	920	Comm	3.35	3.48	3.41	3.77/3.54	3.54/3.54	3.8/3.59	3.78/3.63	2.32/2.18	3.75/3.68 **Magna**		
2.40	460	460	920	Und	2.31	1.0	1.68	DNR							
2.40	480	440	920	Bio	2.22	2.88	2.55	tran$							
2.70	520	400	920	PE	2.14	2.16	2.15	2.12/2.13	1.85/2.07	2.8/2.18	1.9/2.15	2.32/2.18	2.32/2.19	**Grad**	
2.80	430	480	910	PE	2.38	tran									
1.70	430	480	910	Mgt	1.18	2.44	1.81	3.1/2.22	2.0/2.17	2.0/2.14	2.44/2.17	3.4/2.38	3.23/2.52 **Grad**		
2.70	430	480	910	Nur	2.82	2.93	2.87	4.0/3.18	2.56/3.0	2.53/2.88	2.7/2.87	1.3/2.73	DNR$		
2.50	490	420	910	Csd	3.00	2.86	2.93	3.7/3.18	3.5/3.26	3.22/3.28	3.18/3.26	3.28/3.29	3.58/3.32 **Laude**		
2.90	430	470	900	Mgt	2.70	2.67	2.68	3.3/2.75	3.6/2.93	DNR					

HS GPA	VSAT	MSAT	Total SAT	Major	F03	S04	GS-avg	F04	S05	F05	S06	F06	S07	5 Year S08	6 Year S09
3.30	430	470	900	Psy	3.61	3.93	3.76	3.64/3.71	3.94/3.79	4.0/3.84	4.0/3.86	3.54/3.62	4.0/3.89 **Summa**		
2.50	460	440	900	Und	1.95	2.23	2.09	1.65/2.01	2.4/2.32	2.5/2.34	2.2/2.31	3.12/2.37	1.97/2.32	**Grad**	
2.30	480	420	900	Psy	2.42	2.39	2.7	2.77/2.53	2.69/2.57	3.09/2.65	3.51/2.83	3.55/3.07	3.66/3.11 **Grad**		
2.20	400	490	890	Comm	1.95	2.37	2.16	2.56/2.26	3.32/2.62	3.26/2.76	3.02/2.81	3.94/2.99	2.77/2.94 **Grad**		
2.90	410	480	890	PE	2.78	w/d									
2.40	440	450	890	Mgt	2.28	2.74	2.51	1.91/2.34	2.91/2.5	2.6/2.52	2.83/2.61	2.99/2.68	2.98/2.73 **Grad**		
2.80	440	450	890	Nur	2.07	2.67	2.37	2.65/2.48	2.77/2.55	2.43/2.53	DNR $				
2.50	460	430	890	Dance	1.38	dis									
2.90	460	430	890	Psy	2.45	1.76	2.1	DNR							
2.40	490	400	890	Nur	2.58	w/d									
3.30	510	380	890	Psy	2.56	3.34	2.95	2.4/2.75	2.56/2.69	3.37/2.82	3.14/2.89	3.94/3.06	2.73/3.02 **Grad**		
2.64	560	330	890	Comm	3.63	3.46	3.55	DNR							
2.80	380	500	880	Mth	1.79	dis									
3.70	400	480	880	PolSci	2.93	3.0	2.96	DNR							
2.80	440	440	880	Und	2.23	2.87	2.55	1.66/2.42	1.0/2.16	DNR					
2.50	440	440	880	Und	2.00	2.16	2.08	3.46/2.54	2.88/2.64	2.24/2.55	1.39/2.41	4.0/2.88	DNR$		
2.80	450	430	880	Mgt	2.02	2.6	2.31	2.5/2.57	2.67/2.59	3.05/2.75	2.23/2.69	2.5/2.67	3.0/2.7 **Grad**		
2.30	460	420	880	PE	1.79	1.28	1.53	dis							
2.60	460	420	880	Comm	2.32	2.46	2.39	2.92/2.56	2.77/2.61	3.0/2.7	2.38/2.64	2.87/2.71	2.55/2.68 **Grad**		
3.20	480	400	880	Und	1.54	2.25	1.89	2.88/2.16	3.02/2.39	DNR					
2.90	400	470	870	Soc	2.01	2.21	2.11	2.02/2.23	2.88/2.39	2.6/2.45	2.86/2.52	3.14/2.61	3.14/2.68 **Grad**		
2.60	410	460	870	CIS	2.45	2.6	2.52	2.65/2.55	2.6/2.63	tran					

HS GPA	VSAT	MSAT	Total SAT	Major	F03	S04	GS-avg	F04	S05	F05	S06	F06	S07	5 Year S08	6 Year S09
2.60	470	400	870	Comm	2.61	2.72	2.66	DNR							
2.20	480	390	870	Und	2.00	21.6	2.08	2.7/2.24	DNR						
3.70	350	510	860	Nur	2.98	tran									
3.12	400	460	860	Und	2.18	1.53	1.86	2.43/2.0	2.85/2.28	DNR					
3.10	410	450	860	Bio	2.62	1.51	2.06	2.36/2.16	2.0/2.13	.97/1.99	2.08/1.84	1.04/1.79			
3.30	430	430	860	Und	2.31	tran									
2.50	410	440	850	Soc	1.95	w/d									
2.00	470	380	850	Comm	2.00	1.67	1.83	2.9/2.11	DNR						
3.50	480	370	850	Psy	2.92	2.25	2.58	2.9/2.67	3.24/2.79	3.88/3.06	3.8/3.22	3.48/3.26	3.06/3.23 **Grad**		
3.20	400	440	840	Bio	0.72	dis									
2.40	410	430	840	Nur	2.77	2.48	2.62	3.12/2.88	3.01/2.91	2.07/2.77	2.17/2.71	DNR			
3.40	420	420	840	Und	2.21	2.13	2.17	2.35/2.22	1.35/2.1	2.5/2.29	1.0/2.21	3.0/2.24	4.0/2.33	60 cr	60 cr
3.10	430	410	840	Spa	2.14	2.36	2.25	2.94/2.5	1.62/2.26	0.0/1.86	DNR $				
3.30	400	430	830	Music	3.18	w/d									
3.00	410	420	830	Dance	1.86	tran									
2.60	410	420	830	Und	2.63	2.53	2.58	1.44/2.20	.7/1.83	DNR					
2.70	410	420	830	Und	1.18	dis									
3.30	440	390	830	Comm	3.61	3.51	3.56	3.6/3.57	3.88/3.65	3.46/3.61	3.86/3.66	3.83/3.68	3.81/3.7 **Magna**		
2.90	400	420	820	Und	1.61	2.09	1.85	1.87/1.85	DNR						
2.50	410	410	820	Comm	1.82	tran									
1.90	410	410	820	Nur	1.70	2.32	2.01	DNR							
2.30	420	400	820	Psy	2.18	0	1.02	dis							
2.40	400	410	810	Acting	2.15	2.46	2.30	2.4/2.33	3.0/2.49	3.38/2.73	3.2/2.82	3.55/2.96	3.83/3.09 **Grad**		
3.00	410	400	810	Und	2.35	2.44	2.4	DNR							
2.90	380	420	800	Comm	2.45	2.44	2.44	3.42/2.75	3.34/2.97	3.68/3.12	3.21/3.14	3.55/3.2	3.14/3.19 **Grad**		

HS GPA	VSAT	MSAT	Total SAT	Major	F03	S04	GS-avg	F04	S05	F05	S06	F06	S07	5 Year S08	6 Year S09
2.80	380	420	800	Nur	2.16	2.67	2.41	3.39/2.74	2.73/2.74	3.18/2.84	2.94/2.85	2.85/2.85	2.65/2.83 **Grad**		
2.90	400	400	800	His	2.77	3.06	2.91	3.07/2.92	3.06/2.97	3.28/3.08	3.54/3.15	3.54/3.21	3.66/3.26 **Grad**		
3.60	400	400	800	Bio	2.84	2.7	2.73	2.2/2.57	2.3/2.5	1.49/2.28	2.74/2.35	.51/2.05	1.3/1.96		7 yrs **Grad** 5/10
2.30	360	430	790	His	2.45	2.48	2.46	2.66/2.53	2.45/2.51	2.86/2.68	3.25/2.76	3.06/2.84	**2.98/2.73 Grad**		
3.17	360	430	790	Bfn	2.55	3.0	2.77	2.75/2.76	DNR						
3.20	420	370	790	Bio	2.77	3.0	2.88	2.69/2.81	3.31/2.94	2.86/2.92	3.0/2.94	3.04/3.01	**2.36/2.94 Grad**		
3.10	380	400	780	Bfn	2.86	3.16	3.01	3.43/3.17	3.76/3.27	3.54/3.31	3.42/3.33	3.94/3.42	3.57/3.45 **Laude**		
2.60	430	330	760	Mgt	2.18	2.37	2.28	2.67/2.4	2.06/2.32	2.56/2.37	3.07/2.47	3.16/2.59	2.56/2.59	115 cr	115 cr
2.50	440	310	750	His	3.38	3.21	3.36	3.5/3.4	3.3/3.41	3.22/3.37	3.31/3.36	3.25/3.36	**3.76/3.4 Laude**		
3.0	350	440	890			w/d									
2.9	370	460	830			w/d									
2.5	520	390	910			w/d									
3.2	360	500	860			w/d									
3.5	410	460	870			w/d									

Note: Table created by Daniel Rosenberg. Statistics used with permission from Deirdre Donat.

THE CLASS OF 2010

The Class of 2010 brought an SAT math-verbal average of 870 when arriving at Adelphi in 2006. (One member of the class of 103 did not take the SAT). Among the students staying at Adelphi after General Studies, the ubiquity of Business Management majors at all levels of SAT prowess is remarkable. Nearly as noteworthy is the dispersal of Social Work majors throughout the SAT range: this particularly holds for the six-year graduates. Two Business Management majors emerge among the five achievers of 1000 or better on the combined verbal and math. The five averaged 2.3 in high school. All came back for the second year and completed their undergraduate studies by the six-year mark. Their collective Adelphi GPA upon graduation was 2.7.[17]

Twelve out of twenty-one from the original 900–990 SAT-scoring category returned for sophomore year. Five (24 percent of the original subgroup and 42 percent of the sophomores) acquired degrees in four years, two with Latin honors. Business Management, Biology, Math, Physical Education, and Accounting comprised their concentrations. Another two followed over the next two years. The six-year graduation rate was 33 percent of the starting segment, or 58 percent of the sophomores. The concluding Adelphi GPA of all the graduates was nearly 3.0, about the same as their high school index.[18]

Between 800 and 890 on the SAT were grouped seventy-two students in the Class of 2010. Of the forty-eight enrolled in sophomore year, thirty-one graduated in 2010, another seven by 2012. The four-year graduate rate was thus 43 percent of the original subgroup, or 65 percent of the second-year students. But the six-year rate was 53 percent of the freshman entrants, or 79 percent of the sophomores. While many won Latin honors, the final college GPAs in this category constitute a nearly unbroken tableau of 3.0 and above. Business Management and Psychology majors were prominent. Social Work was also well represented. Students at the lower end of this SAT stratum could be found among the four-year graduates.[19]

All four students who joined General Studies in 2006 with a sub-800 score on the SAT came back for sophomore year. Three walked in commencement in 2010, one *magna cum laude*: the latter had the lowest SAT score in the entire cohort (a phenomenon witnessed more than once in General Studies). Tellingly, these students had a high school GPA of 3.2, the same average they earned in college. The academic achievement of a small grouping, which the "testocracy" (to use law professor Lani Guinier's term) would construe as having "bombed" the SATs is noteworthy.[20]

An SAT math level of 440 characterized the fall 2006 cohort. The students dismissed by the program for academic reasons came in somewhat below this figure, at 425. But those leaving Adelphi for financial reasons after

General Studies had bettered the group's math norm. One cohort member reached 600 on the math section, going on to graduate in six years with an Adelphi average of 3.0 (a jump from a 2.3 high school GPA). Most students scoring a minimum of 500 made it into the second year, and most were done by 2012. Math, Biology, and particularly Business Management, stick out among the chosen majors. In this instance, the math SAT apparently previewed certain fields of (but not necessarily strengths within) study, since the final college GPAs were uneven.[21]

Students attaining between 400 and 490 on the math section made up the great majority of the 2006 cohort. A third earned diplomas in 2010, a full half by 2012. A sizable number of below average math scorers received Latin honors, including students in such fields as Business Management and Psychology, which were the leading choice of this category.[22] Finally, the cohort contained thirteen students whose math scores were under 400. Seven came back for the second year, most finishing degrees in time to graduate with their class. The six-year completion rate of the former sophomores was 100 percent, respectively. The grouping's high school and final Adelphi GPAs were the highest in the Class of 2010. Business Management retained strength at this level, while Social Work emerged in two instances. The lowest math scorer of all, at 340, graduated *magna cum laude* in Business Management.[23]

The fall 2006 collective averaged 430 on the verbal SAT. After subtracting dismissed students (whose scores were in line with the group), students leaving after the first year because of financial hardship (whose verbal marks averaged less than 430), and transfer students, several categories of persisting students remain. The record shows seven students entering the freshman year with scores at or over 500. The number reduced to five in the second year. Only one finished in 2010, but the other four earned degrees by 2012. Rough approximation existed between the grads' high school (2.5) and final college (2.8) averages.[24]

The huge preponderance of students between 400 and 490 on the verbal dimension nearly mirrored the number in the same range on the math section. More than half the originals graduated Adelphi within six years, about 80 percent of the returning sophomores. The cohort's predisposition to Psychology and Business Management is exhibited here, as well as its small History contingent. The SAT verbal scores do not broadly preview any inclination toward reading- and writing-heavy majors (like History and Psychology) from the 400–490 bracket. The History major graduating Adelphi *laude* had a 420 on the verbal exam. The same holds for the Psychology major finishing *magna cum laude*. One of the Business Management laureates scored higher on the verbal than on the math. The Accounting alumnus held virtually equivalent scores on the two SAT sections, and graduated a year early. The Criminal Justice graduate, with plenty of writing assigned, had achieved a math score nearly 100 points better than the verbal one.[25]

The 2006 cohort members under 400 on the verbal SAT were more numerous than their peers above 500. In fact, twice as many entrants fell below 400 on the verbal than on the math. Almost a third (seven) of the originals graduated in the quadrennial span: the number rose to eleven in 2012. Hence, 50 percent of the beginning subgroup were done in six years. The graduates brought a 3.2 high school record to Adelphi, basically matched by their bachelors' degrees at 3.1. Of course, the grouping contained a host of individual trajectories to shape the trend. The student who successfully earned a degree in English had a 370 verbal mark, having done much better on the math. Matching the latter's verbal score was the graduate in Political Science, where research papers are par for the course. One must take note as well of the continuing prevalence of Business students.[26]

Inasmuch as the evidence protests against using the SAT to understand four-year graduation rates, the exam's relevance to longer completion rates is an absurdity. Table 9.2 also makes clear that the winners of Latin honors (of which there were many) came from every point of SAT rank, except the very top. Yet all the honorees graduated in four years. One discovers among the five and six-year grads all the supra-1000 College Board scorers (including Physical Education, Business, and Criminal Justice majors), who were almost universally poorer high school students. However, the degree earners after 2010 also included lower-graded SAT students with better high school GPAs than the highest test takers. Those who required more than four years to graduate had test marks equivalent to the cohort average.

Whether verbal and math exam components were close or far apart, the five- and six-year finishers were within range of their earlier fellow graduates: in one case, a student with 510 on the verbal and 380 on the math finished in five years with a "C+" average; in a second instance, a student with 360 on the verbal and 540 on the math finished in five years with a "C" average. One must also mention the cohort member with a 580 on the verbal and 600 on the math, who graduated Adelphi with 3.0 in six years.[27] Yet the longer one takes to finish college, the more irrelevant even the better handles (like high school GPA) become. For the now lengthier college experience conjoins with work, family, and finances. The prolonging influences have little to do with high school average, and even less to do with the problematic SAT. They are instead tied to the bigger questions in capitalist society.

The following table shows the rate of graduation in four- through six-year spans, the incoming SAT totals in descending order (bundled with majors, verbal and math scores, high school averages, and majors). Students who withdrew (the majority left before the fall semester) are not counted in the tabulations, but are indicated at the bottom in the order in which they left the university. The numbers of students given in Table 9.2 and the figures for the 2006 cohort in Table 7.1 may differ slightly. There is sometimes a delay in ascertaining the various reasons for the decline from fall to spring, which may account for the discrepancy.[28] Abbreviations are as follows:

> **Majors**: Acc (Accounting), BBA or BMG (Management), Bio (Biology), Bfn (Finance), Bus (Business), Chem (Chemistry), Cis (Computer and Management Information Systems), Comm (Communications), CSD (Communication Disorders), ComJou (Communications/Journalism), CompSci (Computer Science), CrimJ (Criminal Justice), Early (Early Childhood Education), Ed (Education), Eng (English), EnvStu (Environmental Studies), ExPhys (Exercise Physiology), ExSci (Exercise Science), His (History), Int'l St (International Studies), Mgmt (Management), Mktg (Marketing), Mth (Math), Mus (Music), Nur (Nursing), PE (Physical Education), PolSci (Political Science), Psy (Psychology), PT (Physical Therapy), Soc (Sociology), Spa (Spanish), SpePath or Spe (Speech Pathology), SpMgmt (Sports Management), STEP or Step (Scholar Teacher Education Program), Swk (Social Work), The (Theater), Und (Undecided). **Other**: Dis: Dismissed, DNR: Did Not Return, W/D: Withdrew, $: Financial issues, Tran: Transferred, VSAT: Verbal SAT, MSAT: Math SAT, Tot. SAT: Total SAT, HS GPA: High school grade point average, GS-avg: General Studies average, F: Fall semester (F06 = Fall 2006), S: Spring semester (S07 = Spring 2007), cr: Credits

Class of 2010 Graduation by Total SAT

Number entering				**103**	**83**		**69**	**66**	**61**	**60**	**55**	**54**				
% Original of class					81%		66%	64%	59%	58%	53%	52%				
% Returning sophomores							100%	96%	88%	87%	80%	78%				
% with 3.0 or higher semester					40%		57%	56%	57%	60%	85%	76%				
% semester GPA increase							70%	70%	69%	75%	85%	78%				
Number graduate*											2	36	13	2	2	
% Graduate*											3%	52%	19%	3%	3%	
*** Returning**																
														5 Year	**6 Year**	**7 Year**
HS GPA	**VSAT**	**MSAT**	**Total SAT**	**Major**	**F06**	**S07**	**GS-avg**	**F07**	**S08**	**F08**	**S09**	**F09**	**S10**	**S11**	**S12**	
2.27	580	600	1180	Art	3.30	3.48	3.39	.85/3.1	1.85/2.94	3.33/2.85	3.02/2.88	3.85/2.95	3.85/3.02		**Grad**	
2.35	540	550	1090	Mgt	2.92	2.78	2.85	2.65/2.78	2.52/2.7	2.22/2.62	2.6/2.61	2.57/2.61	2.0/2.57	**Grad**		
2.1	520	540	1060	Mgt	2.22	2.02	2.12	2.8/2.36	2.86/2.5	2.92/2.59	3.94/2.84	2.88/2.84	3.5/2.91	**Grad**		
2.4	470	550	1020	CrimJ	2.32	2.05	2.19	1.64/1.98	2.45/2.08	1.43/1.99	2.46/2.06	2.65/2.19	3.17/2.29			**Grad**
2.2	480	530	1010	PE	1.91	3.07	2.49	3.32/2.76	3.2/2.86	2.95/2.88	2.77/2.86	2.75/2.86	2.96/2.89	**Grad**		
2.4	490	480	970		3.23	2.58	2.90	DNR								
2.4	440	510	960	PE	2.63	2.84	2.73	3.49/3.02	3.39/3.11	3.08/3.1	3.46/3.16	3.6/3.2	3.32/3.24 **Grad**			
2.5	470	480	950	Acc	3.02	3.16	3.09	3.34/3.17	3.25/3.19	2.85/314	2.86/3.09	3.88/3.2		**Grad**		
2.4	490	460	950		1.85	2.47	2.16	3.07/2.44	3.1/2.6	DNR						
3.2	390	550	940	Mgt	3.23	3.48	3.36	3.75/3.52	3.06/3.39	3.4/3.39	3.7/3.45	3.54/3.48	3.66/3.50 **Magna**			
2.5	420	510	930	CrimJ	2.39	2.40	2.40	2.8/2.55	2.79/2.61	2.2/2.53	3.46/2.68	DNR				
2.0	400	520	920		1.63	2.43	2.03	1.46/1.88	DNR$							
2.3	410	510	920		3.54	3.31	3.42	tsf								
2.1	440	480	920	Swk	1.91	2.55	2.23	3.3/2.59	2.95/2.68	3.17/2.77	2.66/2.76	2.17/2.67	2.32/2.63			
2.6	370	540	910		2.22	0.00	1.11	Dis								
3.4	380	530	910		1.00	Dis										
3.5	390	520	910	Mth	3.05	3.37	3.21	3.86/3.44	3.53/3.41	3.36/3.38	3.62/3.42	3.6/3.44	3.54/3.45 **Laude**			

HS GPA	VSAT	MSAT	Total SAT	Major	F06	S07	GS-avg	F07	S08	F08	S09	F09	S10	5 Year S11	6 Year S12	7 Year
3.0	400	510	910	Bio	2.93	3.84	3.38	3.26/3.33	2.52/3.11	3.3/3.16	3.15/3.17	3.68/3.29 **Grad**				
2.5	480	430	910		1.53	Dis										
2.5	520	390	910		2.84	DNR										
3.7	360	540	900	Bio	2.18	2.31	2.24	1.86/2.11	2.12/2.11	1.59/2.02	1.54/1.95	2.24/1.99	1.9/1.98			
3.1	410	490	900	Psy	2.02	2.45	2.23	2.46/2.31	2.67/2.39	DNR						
2.4	420	480	900		1.15										**Grad**	
2.5	430	470	900	Mgt	2.22	2.61	2.41	2.3/2.37	2.63/2.43	2.73/2.53	2.22/2.49	2.94/2.59	2.18/2.53 **Grad**			
3.1	450	450	900		1.38	0.00	0.69									
2.0	490	410	900		3.22	2.77	2.99	DNR								
3.1	400	490	890	Mth	3.23	3.23	3.23	3.83/3.43	3.78/3.52	2.73/3.30	3.86/3.4	3.29/3.38	3.17/3.35 **Laude**			
2.5	410	480	890		1.53	2.07	1.80	DNR								
3.0	420	470	890	Mgt	2.79	3.38	3.08	2.82/2.93	2.8/2.9	3.13/2.94	2.5/2.87	3.4/2.93	3.75/3.02 **Grad**			
2.9	430	460	890	Psy	3.39	3.84	3.62	3.74/3.66	3.94/3.74	3.94/3.78	3.94/3.81	4.0/3.83	3.88/3.84 **Magna**			
2.5	430	460	890	Acc	2.61	2.92	2.76	3.26/2.94	2.8/2.9	3.43/3.02	2.32/2.89	3.16/2.94	2.6/2.9 **Grad**			
3.1	440	450	890		2.02	0.31	1.17	Dis								
3.0	450	440	890	Psy	3.16	3.47	3.32	2.87/3.15	3.7/3.29	3.51/3.33	3.43/3.35	4.0/3.43	3.94/3.5 **Laude**			
2.9	450	440	890	Comm	2.70	2.32	2.51	2.32/2.8	3.62/2.91	3.02/2.93	3.34/3.02	3.4/3.09				
													3.32/3.12			
3.0	350	440	890	Nur	3.09	DNR$										
3.4	470	420	890	Psy	2.93	3.55	3.24	3.46/3.31	3.34/3.32	3.5/3.35	3.57/3.38	3.86/3.45	3.93/3.51 **Laude**			
3.2	480	410	890		2.68	3.38	3.03	DNR $						**Grad**		

HS GPA	VSAT	MSAT	Total SAT	Major	F06	S07	GS-avg	F07	S08	F08	S09	F09	S10	5 Year S11	6 Year S12	7 Year
2.6	490	400	890	Psy	3.02	2.82	2.92	3.67/2.88	3.26/2.96	3.7/3.11	3.75/3.19	3.92/3.27	3.77/3.3 **Laude**			
3.0	510	380	890	Comm	2.18	2.02	2.10	1.15/1.8	2.67/2.01	2.77/2.15	2.83/2.27	2.9/2.34	1.53/2.26			
2.7	380	500	880	Mgt	2.37	2.22	2.29	2.92/2.51	2.49/2.5	2.33/2.46	2.75/2.5	3.16/2.62	2.5/2.6			
3.3	430	450	880		3.07	3.25	3.16	tsf								
2.9	430	450	880	Comm	2.55	2.52	2.53	2.66/2.58	3.14/2.73	3.14/2.86	3.61/3.01	3.34/3.05	3.06/3.05 **Grad**			
2.47	430	450	880		0.78	Dis										
2.7	500	380	880	Swk	2.84	3.07	2.95	3.43/3.13	3.13/3.12	2.2/2.94	3.17/2.97	3.47/3.04	3.56/3.09			
2.5	510	370	880		2.52	2.61	2.56	DNR								**Grad**
2.5	390	480	870		2.30	2.45	2.37	2.83/2.52	0/2.09	0/1.67	DNR					
2.5	440	430	870		2.63	2.02	2.33	DNR						**Grad**		
2.9	450	420	870	Soc	2.09	2.02	2.06	2.68//2.28	3.2/2.53	2.88/2.6	2.75/2.62	3.46/2.74	3.13/2.79			
2.68	450	420	870	PE	2.61	2.52	2.56	3.4/2.86	3.86/3.13	3.27/3.15	3.52/3.18	3.94/3.3	4.0/3.37			
2.9	460	410	870	Psy	2.91	3.16	3.03	3.53/3.2	3.28/3.22	3.8/3.49	3.42/3.36	3.73/3.42	3.6/3.44 **Laude**			
2.5	460	410	870		0.39	Dis										
2.3	480	390	870	Mgt	2.82	2.77	2.79	3.02/2.87	3.2/2.96	2.74/2.91	3.58/3.03	3.79/3.15	3.8/3.22 **Grad**			
3.2	360	500	860		2.68	DNR										
3.5	410	460	860		2.45	DNR								**Grad**		
3.1	430	430	860	Nur	2.40	2.54	2.47	3.52/2.87	3.55/3.03	3.37/3.11	1.93/2.91	DNR				
2.5	440	420	860		1.01	Dis										
2.5	440	420	860	Acting	2.91	2.63	2.77	3.2/2.93	3.15/2.97	2.87/2.99	2.65/2.92	3.14/2.96	2.71/2.93 **Grad**			
2.3	440	420	860	Mgt	2.07	2.70	2.38	3.22/2.69	2.78/2.71	3.37/2.86	2.45/2.78	2.9/2.8	3.54/2.89 **Grad**			

HS GPA	VSAT	MSAT	Total SAT	Major	F06	S07	GS-avg	F07	S08	F08	S09	F09	S10	5 Year S11	6 Year S12	7 Year
3.2	450	410	860	Mgt	3.38	3.77	3.57	3.79/3.65	3.6/3.64	3.6/3.63	4.0/3.69	3.75/3.7	3.88/3.73 **Magna**			
3.4	370	480	850	Swk	3.05	3.47	3.26	2.66/3.06	3.21/3.1	3.18/3.12	3.4/3.16	3.07/3.15	3.25/3.16	**Grad**		
3.3	380	470	850		3.02	3.39	3.21	DNR						**Laude**		
3.1	380	470	850	Mgt	3.54	3.39	3.47	3.88/3.59	DNR							
2.6	410	440	850	His	2.53	2.68	2.60	3.2/2.82	3.43/2.99	3.0/2.99	2.65/2.91	DNR	3.07/2.95			
2.7	410	440	850		2.24	DNR										
3.3	420	430	850	Nur	2.55	2.61	2.58	2.9/2.68	3.52/2.91	3.69/3.07	3.55/3.15	wd	2.57/3.06			
2.8	430	420	850	Psy	1.78	2.38	2.08	2.25/2.13	3.08/2.4	3.3/2.67	2.88/2.71	3.75/2.87	3.66/2.97 **Grad**			
2.6	440	410	850	Mgt	2.30	2.63	2.47	2.78/2.69	2.09/2.54	2.6/2.64	3.0/2.68	3.32/2.75	3.82/2.86 **Grad**			
2.3	450	400	850		1.24											
2.8	480	370	850		0.53	Dis										
2.8	480	370	850	Psy	3.31	3.70	3.50	3.31/3.43	2.42/3.2	3.5/3.26	2.8/3.17	3.68/3.26	2.41/3.18 **Grad**			
3.4	410	430	840	Mgt	3.31	3.70	3.50	3.74/3.59	3.28/3.5	3.66/3.53	3.36/3.51	3.08/3.44	3.9/3.51 **Laude**			
3.1	410	430	840		3.38	2.68	3.03	DNR								
2.7	410	430	840	Mgt	2.00	2.77	2.38	2.58/2.46	2.35/2.43	1.84/2.31	2.22/2.3	2.77/2.42	2.53/2.5 **Grad**			
2.7	420	420	840		1.39	Dis										
2.66	420	420	840	His	2.14	2.46	2.30	2.86/2.5	1.88/2.33	2.25/2.32	2.69/2.38	DNR				
2.1	420	420	840		2.15	1.95	2.05	2.2/2.08	.59/1.64	DNR						
2.5	430	410	840		1.86	2.09	1.98	1.56/1.87	DNR							
3.3	440	400	840	Mgt	3.55	3.68	3.62	3.61/3.61	4.0/3.71	4.0/3.78	3.82/3.78	4.0/3.82	3.85/3.82 **Magna**			

HS GPA	VSAT	MSAT	Total SAT	Major	F06	S07	GS-avg	F07	S08	F08	S09	F09	S10	5 Year S11	6 Year S12	7 Year
2.7	450	390	840		1.22	Dis										
2.4	460	380	840		1.09											
2.6	350	480	830	Mgt	1.79	2.30	2.05	3.31/2.54	3.11/2.71	2.68/2.7	3.11/2.78	3.38/2.87	3.24/2.92 **Grad**			
3.0	370	460	830	Eng	3.09	2.42	2.75	1.61/2.35	1.94/2.25	2.94/2.34	3.55/2.55	3.68/2.74	3.74/2.88			
2.9	370	460	830		2.84	DNR										
3.0	410	420	830	PE	2.91	2.47	2.69	2.36/2.6	2.34/2.53	2.9/2.62	2.1/2.56	3.57/2.68	3.57/2.8 **Grad**			
2.6	410	420	830	Psy	2.48	2.38	2.43	3.0/2.62	3.03/2.7	2.82/2.73	2.92/2.76	1.45/2.53	3.5/2.7			
2.9	420	410	830		2.28	2.47	2.38	DNR								
2.55	420	410	830	Dance	3.61	3.70	3.65	3.29/3.45	3.47/3.46	DNR						
2.5	420	410	830	His	2.75	3.00	2.87	3.0/2.91	2.57/2.83	3.36/2.97	3.24/3.02	3.14/3.04	3.0/3.05 **Grad**			
3.3	360	460	820		0.00	Dis										
3.5	410	410	820	Psy	3.32	3.54	3.43	3.81/3.6	3.74/3.63	3.86/3.68	3.93/3.71	3.94/3.75	3.94/3.77 **Magna**			
3.4	420	400	820	His	2.84	3.54	3.19	3.85/3.39	3.32/3.38	3.54/3.41	3.6/3.45	3.68/3.49	3.6/3.5 **Laude**			
3.0	420	400	820	Psy	3.32	3.09	3.21	3.54/3.32	3.74/3.46	3.82/3.52	3.86/3.59	3.83/3.62	3.94/3.64 **Magna**			
2.2	420	400	820	Nur	2.52	2.28	2.40	2.83/2.56	2.31/2.51	3.14/2.62	3.39/2.75	1.59/2.57	DNR			
2.4	370	440	810	PolSci	2.47	2.09	2.28	2.8/2.47	2.52/2.48	2.98/2.58	3.48/2.74	3.07/2.78	3.17/2.82 **Grad**			
3.0	450	360	810	Mgt	2.15	2.46	2.30	3.12/2.6	2.34/2.53	2.06/2.43	2.93/2.51	3.07/2.58	2.79/2.6 **Grad**			
3.9	370	430	800	Mgt	3.52	3.84	3.68	3.66/3.67	3.46/3.61	3.94/3.68	3.73/3.69	3.63/3.68	3.71/3.68 **Magna**			
2.4	390	410	800		2.31	2.54	2.42	2.62/2.49	2.46/2.48	DNR				**Grad**		
2.5	410	390	800		1.52	Dis										

HS GPA	VSAT	MSAT	Total SAT	Major	F06	S07	GS-avg	F07	S08	F08	S09	F09	S10	5 Year S11	6 Year S12	7 Year
3.0	380	410	790	Psy	2.77	3.07	2.92	3.27/3.03	2.54/2.9	3.14/2.95	3.32/3.01	3.86/3.15	3.61/3.22 **Grad**			
3.2	380	400	780	Nur	3.39	3.16	3.28	3.18/3.24	3.64/3.31	2.92/3.23	1.48/3.04	2.3/2.99	3.0/2.99			
3.4	380	390	770	Swk	2.61	3.09	2.85	3.2/2.98	3.0/2.98	3.48/3.09	3.52/3.15	3.67/3.21	3.10/3.2 **Grad**			
3.2	410	340	750	Mgt	3.00	3.32	3.16	3.77/3.4	3.32/3.38	3.51/3.42	3.85/3.48	4.0/3.55	3.8/3.58 **Magna**			
					1.85	DNR										
2.7	520	400	920	w/d												
3.2	480	260	740	w/d												
2.55	550	410	960	w/d												
2.5	540	460	1000	w/d												
3.2	360	490	850	w/d												
2.7	470	430	900	w/d												
2.1	510	540	1050	w/d												
2.5	520	540	1060	w/d												
3.2	400	410	810	w/d												
2.7	460	470	930	w/d												

Note: Table created by Daniel Rosenberg. Statistics used with permission from Deirdre Donat.

THE CLASS OF 2013

The class of 2013 (100-strong) took the stage in the fall 2009 semester with an average SAT score of 896, divided into even 448 math and verbal indices. As indicated above, the cohort bore the strong high school GPA of 3.4. Only eight students met or exceeded 1000: two were dismissed from Adelphi. Four returned as sophomores. Two graduated in 2013 with final college grades of 3.17 and 3.58 (*cum laude*). The four-year graduation rate was 25 percent of the original number, 50 percent of the second-year survivors. The two students who did not graduate Adelphi both left the university after sophomore year. One had majored in Business Management, the other Psychology. The first built a 1.9 GPA, the second a 2.4, through two years.[29]

A larger subgroup inhabited the SAT range from 900 to 990. Of thirty-one constituents, twenty-five came back to Adelphi as sophomores, 80 percent. One of the non-returnees earned a freshman GPA of 3.63 in the program. Fourteen students gained degrees in 2013, making a graduation rate of 45 percent of the original grouping, or 56 percent of the second-year enrollees. Joined by another three by 2015, the coterie as a whole boasted a six-year graduation rate of 55 percent overall, in other words 68 percent of the sophomores. Five received Latin honors, headed by students whose secondary school mean was 3.8 and 3.7 respectively, but who totaled 920 and 910 on the College Boards. The degree earners emphasized Psychology, Nursing, Biology, and Physical Therapy, with several students tying in with teacher training. Students in English, and once again Psychology, pursued the pedagogical route.[30]

The category attaining 800–890 SAT totals returned forty-two of its fifty-seven members for sophomore year. Their four-year completion rate nearly matched that of their fellow students in the group above: twenty-four, or 42 percent, walked in 2013 ceremonies. They comprised well over half the sophomores. Within the next two years, seven more would earn diplomas, rendering a six-year rate of 54 percent (74 percent of sophomores), not too different from the subgroup above them. The Class of 2013 leaned heavily toward the Psychology major. Art, Nursing, Social Work, and Business attracted students here and there. Latin awards highlighted several diplomas.[31]

Four students joined the General Studies ranks in 2009 with sub-800 SAT scores. Their secondary school GPA reached 2.7, slightly higher than their confreres in the 1000 and up camp (2.4), who were more numerous. Three became sophomores. Though one left school during the second year (carrying a 3.3 in Psychology), the other two graduated. One was *cum laude* in 2013, having majored in Psychology, tied to Education. In her wake followed a Social Work major completing the bachelor's with a 3.0.[32]

On the math SAT, the fourteen scorers above 500 fell well below the 3.4 high school average of the whole collective. But the attrition that struck at leaders in total SAT did not affect the math vanguard to the same degree. Many came back in the second year. Four of the sophomores took degrees in a four-year period. Adelphi awarded Latin honors to two of the four program alumni. Fields of study for the modestly sized contingent included Biology, Physical Education, Psych with an Education twist, and Business Management. The graduates' collective final Adelphi GPA excelled over their high school mean, 3.4 to 2.6.[33]

Many more entering GS students in 2009 dwelled in the math SAT environs between 400 and 490. They included a good number above 3.0 in high school. Thirty graduated by 2013. Ten others received diplomas within the six-year framework. Altogether, 57 percent of the first arrivals completed college work over a six-year period. The majors distributed along the lines of the entire cohort, headed by Psychology, Nursing, Business, and English. Education concentrations were in evidence as well. Latin honors abounded. But for those in Nursing, there were few others in this segment to test the alleged predisposition of low math scorers to flounder in the sciences. However, one student majoring in math deserves notice, insofar as this student attained a 410 on the math SAT, but stayed close to an Adelphi index of 3.0 until graduating.[34]

The 2009 cohort fielded a modest grouping of 15 with SAT math marks beneath 400, albeit holding an average high school GPA of 3.0. Two-thirds turned into sophomores. (Low math scorers who left Adelphi thereafter had been in good academic standing for the most part: attention is drawn to such GPAs as 3.89 and 3.30 at the time of departure.) Six went on to finish their studies at Adelphi in 2013, while three others followed suit in the longer span. The alumni completed Adelphi at a collective 3.2. Standout majors feature the ubiquitous Psychology, with and without a link to pedagogical training. The Nursing student with an SAT math score of 380 who graduated Adelphi with an essential 3.0 is worthy of note.[35]

The Class of 2013 averaged the same SAT mark in the math and verbal sections (448). As witnessed for previous classes (and the ones that followed), a near equivalence between math and verbal scores appears throughout the documentary record, sufficient to wonder whether the test outcomes signify equal strengths, parallel weaknesses, or very little. Those with verbal scores meeting or exceeding 500 held a high school GPA of 2.5: they numbered thirteen. The program dismissed the highest verbal achiever from Adelphi on academic grounds after one term. But a substantial majority registered for second-year classes. Six went on to finish at the university, all but one in four years. All told, their diplomas represented an Adelphi GPA of 3.3, a healthy leap from high school. Several of the graduates majored in areas involving writing, for example

Humanities and Social Science areas leading to teaching, and also Psychology.[36]

Most of the Class of 2013 occupied SAT verbal ground between 400 and 490. Losses reduced the subgroup of seventy-three by nearly a third before the second year. Just over half the originals earned Adelphi degrees by 2016. Among the four-year graduates, 50 percent won Latin honors. As much as this entourage played a central role in the cohort's overall 448 verbal SAT index, it was just as influential in shaping its whopping 3.4 high school GPA. The graduates' final Adelphi average was close. Major choices were disparate, but as always included Psychology, with interesting inroads into Art, Dance, and Sports Management.[37]

Twelve freshmen joined General Studies in fall 2009 having scored below 400 on the verbal SAT, yet carrying a 3.1 high school average. Nine registered as sophomores in 2010. Six obtained diplomas in 2013, "on time." Another student soon followed. The alumni bore a college GPA of 3.0 upon completion of degrees, consistent with their high school index. Social Work and Psychology keynoted the areas of study. At the bottom of the verbal scorers, one finds Latin honors at commencement.[38]

Table 9.3 traces the Adelphi completion rate, final college GPA, and majors in descending order by total SAT scores of the Class of 2013. Students who withdrew (the majority left before the fall semester) are not counted in the tabulations, but are indicated at the bottom in the order in which they left the university.[39] Abbreviations are as follows:

> **Majors**: Acc (Accounting), BBA or BMG (Management), Bio (Biology), Bfn (Finance), Bus (Business), Chem (Chemistry), Cis (Computer and Management Information Systems), Comm (Communications), CSD (Communication Disorders), ComJou (Communications/Journalism), CompSci (Computer Science), CrimJ (Criminal Justice), Early (Early Childhood Education), Ed (Education), Eng (English), EnvStu (Environmental Studies), ExPhys (Exercise Physiology), ExSci (Exercise Science), His (History), Int'l St (International Studies), Mgmt (Management), Mktg (Marketing), Mth (Math), Mus (Music), Nur (Nursing), PE (Physical Education), PolSci (Political Science), Psy (Psychology), PT (Physical Therapy), Soc (Sociology), Spa (Spanish), SpePath or Spe (Speech Pathology), SpMgmt (Sports Management), STEP or Step (Scholar Teacher Education Program), Swk (Social Work), The (Theater), Und (Undecided). **Other**: Dis: Dismissed, DNR: Did Not Return, W/D: Withdrew, $: Financial issues, Tran: Transferred, Abroad: Studied abroad, VSAT: Verbal SAT, MSAT: Math SAT, Tot. SAT: Total SAT, HS GPA: High school grade point average, GS-avg: General Studies average, F: Fall semester (F09 = Fall 2009), S: Spring semester (F10 = Spring 2010), cr: Credits

Class of 2013 Graduation by Total SAT

Number of Students	**100**	**86**	**74**	**67**	**61**	**59**	**58**	**56**		
% of Original class		86%	74%	67%	61%	59%	58%	56%		
% Returning sophomores			100%	91%	82%	80%	78%	76%		
% w 3.0 or higher semester*	33%	44%	53%	60%	59%	53%	62%	73%		
% with gpa increase in semester*		54%	61%	66%	57%	58%	67%	80%		
Number Graduate*								41	11	2
% Graduate*								55%	15%	3%

*** Returning sophomores**

HS GPA	VSAT	MSAT	Tot SAT	Major	F09	S 10	GS-avg	F 10	S 11	F11	S12	F12	S13	5 Year S14	6 year S15
2.4	510	620	1130	PE	3.16	3.55	3.36	3.56/3.46	2.23/3.18	2.83/3.11	2.72/3.06	3.23/3.07	3.61/3.17 **Grad**		
2.0	550	550	1100	und	2.45	2.12	2.28	DNR							
2.5	510	510	1020	Psy	1.95	2.16	2.06	2.85/2.3	2.67/2.39	DNR					
2.4	520	500	1020	Mgt	1.93	2.23	2.08	1.76/2.0	1.42/1.85	DNR					
2.6	480	530	1010		1.35	Dis									
2.8	460	550	1010	Mgt	3.91	3.61	3.76	3.46/3.67	3.86/3.76	3.4/3.7	3.2/3.61	3.21/3.58	3.6/3.58 **Laude**		
2.3	580	420	1000		0.00	Dis									
2.5	540	460	1000	Nur	2.68	2.45	2.56	DNR							
2.21	470	520	990	Com	2.38	1.90	2.14	2.9/2.37	3.17/2.57	1.5/2.39	2.42/2.42	1.78/2.31	2.16/2.31 98cr	124 cr	
2.3	520	460	980	und	2.68	2.12	2.40	2.67/2.48	1.2/2.13	1.0/2.01	DNR				
2.6	440	540	980		2.72	DNR$									
2.4	450	530	980	Mgt	3.07	3.00	3.03	3.4/3.22	DNR						
2.6	500	380	980	Psy	3.54	2.89	3.22	2.68/3.03	2.34/2.85	2.94/2.87	3.0/2.89	3.7/2.97	3.5/3.06 110 cr	**Grad**	

HS GPA	VSAT	MSAT	Tot SAT	Major	F09	S 10	GS-avg	F 10	S 11	F11	S12	F12	S13	5 Year S14	6 year S15
2.6	500	470	970	Eng	3.16	3.68	3.42	3.25/3.36	3.48/3.39	3.38/3.29	3.2/3.35	3.48/3.37	3.34/3.37 **Laude**		
2.3	490	480	970		3.07	DNR									
2.6	520	440	960	The	3.00	3.09	3.05	3.34/3.17	3.21/3.19	Abroad	3.57/3.26	3.87/3.37	3.85/3.44 **Laude**		
2.5	460	500	960	Eng	3.32	3.25	3.29	2.6/3.13	1.16/2.6	2.75	DNR$				
2.22	490	470	960	Mgt	2.40	2.38	2.39	2.66/2.48	3.23/2.69	2.9/2.73	2.93/2.76	3.48/2.74	3.16/2.92 **Grad**		
2.7	430	530	960		1.56	Dis									
2.4	450	500	950	Psy	2.18	2.55	2.37	3.0/2.61	3.23/2.75	3.14/2.89	3.76/2.98	3.53/3.07	3.41/3.11 **Grad**		
2.6	470	470	940	SpMgt	2.15	1.86	2.00	2.94/2.34	2.32/2.34	3.0/2.48	2.86/2.55	2.66/2.61	2.71/2.61 **Grad**		
2.6	470	460	930	Psy	2.77	2.63	2.70	2.5/2.62	3.48/2.84	3.2/2.92	3.45/3.01	3.35/3.07	3.66/3.17 **Grad**		
2.4	520	410	930	His	3.16	2.70	2.93	3.42/3.08	DNR						
2.9	470	450	920	PE	3.07	3.23	3.15	3.28/3.19	3.26/3.21	3.75/3.33	3.83/3.42	3.35/3.41	3.3/3.4 **Laude**		
3.8	380	540	920	Bio	3.48	3.77	3.63	3.75/3.69	3.73/3.7	2.95/3.56	3.83/3.61	3.6/3.61	3.76/3.62 **Magna**		
2.3	450	470	920	PE	2.75	2.63	2.69	3.16/2.87	2.91/2.87	2.2/2.74	2.2/2.66	2.03/2.55	2.57/2.55 **Grad**		
2.4	450	460	910	Eng	2.84	2.40	2.62	2.46/2.58	2.73/2.65	no ret	3.26/2.78	3.22/2.85	3.18/2.93 102 cr	**Grad**	
2.6	490	420	910	Bio	2.70	2.25	2.48	0/1.95	0/1.43	DNR					
2.4	430	480	910		2.09	DNR$									
2.8	470	440	910	Nur	2.91	3.07	2.99	3.38/3.14	3.19/3.15	2.68/3.05	2.66/2.99	2.42/2.92	3.28/2.97 **Grad**		
2.4	470	440	910	ExSci	2.22	2.93	2.57	3.05/2.75	3.73/3.02	3.7/3.14	3.18/3.13	3.7/3.22	3.5/3.22 **Grad**		

HS GPA	VSAT	MSAT	Tot SAT	Major	F09	S 10	GS-avg	F 10	S 11	F11	S12	F12	S13	5 Year S14	6 year S15
3.4	460	450	910	HealthEd	2.82	2.85	2.83	2.71/2.79	2.92/2.82	2.94/2.9	2.56/2.79	3.79/2.91	3.34/2.97 **Grad**		
3.3	420	490	910	Nur	2.77	2.95	2.86	2.58/2.75	3.4/2.96	2.3/2.8	2.3/2.76	2.55/2.73	2.91/2.75 105 cr	**Grad**	
3.7	420	490	910	Und	3.58	3.68	3.63	DNR							
3.7	440	470	910	Psy	3.93	3.93	3.93	3.62/3.82	3.72/3.79	3.91/3.83	4.0/3.84	4.0/3.87	3.87 **Magna**		
2.8	450	460	910	Psy	2.75	2.68	2.71	2.98/2.8	DNR						
2.5	430	470	900	ExSci	3.09	3.16	3.13	2.76/3.08	3.26/3.07	2.94/3.04	2.54/2.85	2.34/2.77	1.74/2.63 **Grad**		
2.7	430	470	900	ExSci	3.00	3.02	3.01	2.84/2.95	1.97/2.71	DNR					
2.7	440	460	900		2.09	DNR									
3.0	500	390	890	Soc	2.24	3.16	2.70	2.81/2.73	3.07/2.82	3.28/2.92	3.66/3.06	3.56/3.14	2.81/3.07 **Grad**		
3.0	510	380	890	Mgt	3.58	3.68	3.63	3.85/3.72	3.46/3.65	3.62/3.64	abroad 3.64	3.37/3.86	3.85/3.59 **Laude**		
3.1	430	460	890	Psy	2.42	2.52	2.47	2.39/2.44	3.66/2.8	3.2/2.89	2.66/2.84	2.56/2.79	2.33/2.73 **Grad**		
2.9	450	440	890	Art	2.68	2.79	2.73	3.14/2.88	3.17/2.94	3.42/3.05	3.82/3.19	3.66/3.26	3.34/3.27 **Grad**		
2.5	470	420	890	Nur	2.84	2.22	2.53	3.32/2.79	3.95/3.06	3.28/3.13	3.65/3.2	2.91/3.15	3.13/31.5 105 cr	120 cr	**Grad**
3.3	390	500	890	Mus	2.40	2.68	2.54	1.2/2.37	DNR cred						
2.8	420	470	890	Und	3.28	3.45	3.37	DNR							
2.6	420	460	880	Und	2.77	2.45	2.61	1.76/2.32	1.23/2.05	2.3/2.08	3.52/2.3	DNR			
3.0	450	430	880	Mgt	2.61	1.84	2.22	1.38/1.98	2.42/2.09	2.8/2.26	2.46/2.29	3.23/2.43	2.32/2.42 90 cr	DNR	
3.1	420	460	880	und	2.61	1.77	2.19	2.1/2.6	DNR$						
3.1	440	440	880	Swk	3.28	3.84	3.56	3.51/3.58	3.76/3.63	3.94/3.69	3.56/3.67	3.92/3.7	3.66/3.69 **Magna**		

HS GPA	VSAT	MSAT	Tot SAT	Major	F09	S 10	GS-avg	F 10	S 11	F11	S12	F12	S13	5 Year S14	6 year S15
3.7	440	440	880	Psy	3.30	3.16	3.23	2.78/3.05	2.45/2.92	3.07/2.94	2.0/2.84	2.16/2.72	3.6/2.82 106 cr	**Grad**	
2.8	420	460	880		2.16	DNR									
2.7	430	450	880	Mth	2.68	3.40	3.04	DNR							
3.2	440	440	880	Eng	2.86	2.61	2.73	3.57/3.0	DNR						
3.1	400	480	880	SpMgt	1.46	2.00	1.73	2.25/1.89	2.35/2.0	3.0/2.19	2.17/2.199	2.92/2.29	3.03/2.39 100 cr	**Grad**	
2.6	420	460	880	Bio	2.23	2.75	2.49	DNR							
2.75	450	420	870	Psy	3.28	3.61	3.45	2.38/3.09	3.08/3.08	2.32/2.92	3.37/3.04	3.05/3.04	3.66/3.15 **Grad**		
2.6	420	450	870	Nur	3.09	3.07	3.08	3.18/3.11	3.42/3.19	3.49/3.25	2.67/3.14	3.06/3.13	3.28/3.15 100 cr	**Grad**	
3.6	490	380	870	Und	3.84	3.93	3.88	DNR							
2.7	430	440	870	Dance	3.16	3.52	3.34	3.38/3.38	3.76/3.48	3.84/3.56	3.91/3.65	3.87/3.67	3.96/3.71 **Magna**		
3.2	410	460	870	Art	2.91	3.14	3.02	3.2/3.08	3.54/3.24	3.72/3.34	3.68/3.42	3.86/3.48	4.0/3.53 **Laude**		
2.4	470	400	870	PE	2.93	2.84	2.88	2.77/2.84	2.92/2.86	3.0/2.88	2.93/2.89	2.82/2.88	DNR $		
3.0	410	460	870	PE	3.07	2.91	2.99	3.0/2.99	3.13/3.03	3.4/3.11	2.56/3.01	2.97/2.99	3.01/3.0 **Grad**		
3.3	420	450	870		3.39	DNR									
2.6	450	420	870	EnvSci	2.93	3.00	2.97	3.16/3.03	3.04/3.01	3.46/3.16	abroad	3.41/3.20	4.0/3.23 107	137 cr	**Grad**
3.4	430	430	860	CSD	3.42	3.65	3.53	3.45/3.5	3.12/3.4	3.75/3.48	3.94/3.55	4.0/3.61	3.84/3.65 **Magna**		
2.5	430	430	860	Art	2.91	2.68	2.79	3.2/2.86	3.6/3.08	3.52/3.17	3.44/3.21	3.63/3.26	3.5/3.28 **Grad**		
3.5	430	430	860	EnvStu	2.70	2.91	2.80	3.43/2.96	3.66/3.12	3.35/3.14	2.9/3.1	2.9/3.08	3.39/3.12 82 cr	**Grad**	
2.67	420	440	860	Psy	3.00	2.98	2.99	2.58/2.83	3.28/2.95	2.82/2.92	2.77/2.89	3.88/3.03	3.52/3.09 **Grad**		

HS GPA	VSAT	MSAT	Tot SAT	Major	F09	S 10	GS-avg	F 10	S 11	F11	S12	F12	S13	5 Year S14	6 year S15
3.0	430	430	860	Und	3.07	3.32	3.20	DNR							
3.0	440	420	860	und	2.23	0.23	1.23	Dis							
3.5	460	390	850	Psy	3.07	3.15	3.11	3.94/3.41	2.86/326	3.6/3.34	3.58/3.38	3.82/3.45	3.94/3.51 **Laude**		
2.9	470	380	850	Nur	2.98	3.07	3.03	3.02/3.02	3.24/3.07	2.93/2.9	3.22/3.1	2.64/3.02	2.85/2.99 107 cr	**Grad**	
2.5	440	410	850	Psy	2.58	2.70	2.64	2.75/2.67	1.63/2.37	2.67/2.57	2.8/2.68	inc/2.67	3.35/2.9 1 **Grad**		
2.8	360	490	850	PE	2.75	2.84	2.79	3.16/2.93	3.35/3.03	3.52/3.13	3.01/3.11	2.76/3.06	3.18/3.04 **Grad**		
3.0	390	460	850	Swk	3.16	2.91	3.03	2.65/2.91	2.18/2.7	2.76/2.71	2.67/2.71	2.85/2.72	2.12/2.63 **Grad**		
3.2	390	460	850		2.91	DNR$									
3.2	430	420	850	Psy	2.70	2.15	2.42	3.1/2.59	2.08/2.44	DNR					
2.68	460	380	840	und	2.98	3.18	3.08	DNR							
3.3	460	380	840	Eng	3.00	2.47	2.73	DNR							
3.4	440	400	840	His	2.91	2.77	2.84	2.8/2.82	2.25/2.69	1.08/2.33	2.75/2.4	2.76/2.46	2.71/2.49 107 cr	DNR	
2.5	440	400	840	Dance	1.98	2.77	2.38	2.92/2.55	1.89/2.39	1.97/2.32	DNR				
2.7	430	400	830		2.38	DNR									
2.73	390	440	830	Psy	2.79	3.09	2.94	2.7/2.85	2.54/2.76	2.73/2.76	abroad 2.76	3.28/2.85	2.75/2.83 **Grad**		
3.4	410	420	830		3.93	DNR$									
2.6	410	420	830	Psy	2.86	3.23	3.05	3.16/3.08	3.11/3.09	3.55/3.18	2.67/3.1	3.38/3.15	3.52/3.2 **Grad**		
2.85	460	370	830	Und	2.77	3.21	2.99	DNR							
3.5	380	450	830		2.54	DNR$									
3.7	460	360	820	Art	2.91	2.84	2.87	3.4/3.15	3.42/3.21	3.86/3.32	3.34/3.33	3.08/3.29	4.0/3.36 **Laude**		
3.5	410	410	820	Mth	3.16	3.23	3.20	3.0/3.13	1.5/2.69	3.22/2.68	3.35/2.9	2.64/2.87	2.94/2.88 104 cr	**Grad**	

HS GPA	VSAT	MSAT	Tot SAT	Major	F09	S 10	GS-avg	F 10	S 11	F11	S12	F12	S13	5 Year S14	6 year S15
3.2	390	420	810	Psy	2.24	3.12	2.68	2.29/2.54	2.74/2.59	2.29/2.53	2.76/2.56	1.91/2.46	2.63/2.56 103 cr	**Grad**	
3.6	410	400	810	Eng	2.35	2.52	2.43	3.5/2.8	2.78/2.8	3.7/3.0	3.7/3.13	3.64/3.22	3.75/3.29 **Grad**		
2.7	430	380	810	Psy	3.00	2.68	2.84	2.56/2.73	3.46/2.92	2.76/2.89	3.37/2.98	3.71/3.09	3.51/3.15 **Grad**		
2.8	410	400	810	PE	2.75	1.82	2.28	2.97/2.51	3.5/2.8	3.75/3.04	2.62/2.96	2.51/2.91	3.02/2.9 **Grad**		
2.6	400	400	800	Psy	3.16	3.77	3.47	2.86/3.36	3.75/3.45	3.55/3.47	3.68/3.51	3.82/3.58	3.74/3.58 **Laude**		
3.2	370	430	800	Com	2.84	3.14	2.99	3.82/3.25	3.92/3.41	3.67/3.46	3.74/3.51	3.65/3.55	3.42/3.53 **Laude**		
2.7	440	350	790	Psy	2.84	2.45	2.64	3.25/2.83	3.46/3.01	3.25/3.05	3.6/3.2	3.64/3.28	3.88/3.37 **Laude**		
2.6	380	390	770		2.14	DNR$									
2.9	330	380	710	Psy	3.07	3.54	3.30	3.26/3.28	DNR						
2.7	390	310	700	Swk	2.24	2.84	2.54	2.95/2.69	2.5/2.65	3.17/2.74	3.1/2.78	3.56/2.85	3.8/2.99 **Grad**		
2.5	520	540	1060	w/d											
2.1	510	540	1050	w/d											
2.5	540	460	1000	w/d											
2.55	550	410	960	w/d											
2.7	460	470	930	w/d											
2.7	520	400	920	w/d											
2.7	470	430	900	w/d											
3.2	360	490	850	w/d											
3.2	400	410	810	w/d											
3.2	480	260	740	w/d											

Note: Table created by Daniel Rosenberg. Statistics used with permission from Deirdre Donat.

NOTES

1. National Center for Educational Statistics, *Institutional Retention and Graduation Rates for Undergraduate Students*, May 2015, http://nces.ed.gov/programs/coe/indicator_cva.asp . Accessed March 18, 2016; College Board, *Four-Year Graduation Rates for Four-Year Colleges*, 2013, 18.
2. Meryl Shapiro to Dean Cavallo, *Final Grades*, February 12, 1988, GSC.
3. Della Hudson-Tomlin, *General Studies Statistics*, October 31, 1994, 16, 19, 24, 31, GSC; Barbara Shulman to Dr. Augusto Hacthoun, *General Studies Dismissals*, June 7, 1991, GSC; Barbara Gross to Dean Newton, *General Studies Class Fall 1991*, September 12, 1991, GSC; *University College: A Report*, "Cohort Attrition," 1994, 22, GSC.
4. Compiled by Gabriel Rosenberg, March 2016, from Deirdre Donat, *Class of 2007 by Total SAT, Class of 2008 by Total SAT, Class of 2009 by Total SAT, Class of 2010 by Total SAT, Class of 2011 by Total SAT, Class of 2012 by Total SAT, Class of 2013 by Total SAT*, GSC.
5. Nicholas Lemann, "Tinkering with the Test," *New York Times*, September 19, 1999, A19; National Association for College Admission Counseling, *Report of the Commission on the Use of Standardized Tests in Undergraduate Admissions*, 2008, 9, 11, 20, 40.
6. Deirdre Donat, *Class of 2007 by Total SAT*, September 2014, GSC.
7. Deirdre Donat, *Class of 2007 by Total SAT*, September 2014, GSC.
8. Deirdre Donat, *Class of 2007 by Total SAT*, September 2014, GSC.
9. Deirdre Donat, *Class of 2007 by Total SAT*, September 2014, GSC.
10. Deirdre Donat, *Class of 2007 by MSAT*, September 2014, GSC.
11. Deirdre Donat, *Class of 2007 by MSAT*, September 2014, GSC.
12. Deirdre Donat, *2013–2014 Final Grades*, May 19, 2014, GSC; Deirdre Donat, *Class of 2007 by VSAT*, September 2014, GSC.
13. Deirdre Donat, *Class of 2007 by VSAT*, September 2014, GSC.
14. Deirdre Donat, *Class of 2007 by VSAT*, September 2014, GSC.
15. Deirdre Donat, *Class of 2007 by VSAT*, September 2014, GSC.
16. Deirdre Donat, *Class of 2007 Graduation by Total SAT*, February 2016.
17. Deirdre Donat, *Class of 2010 Graduation by Total SAT*, August 2013, GSC; Deirdre Donat, *Class of 2010 Graduation by Total SAT*, July 2015, GSC.
18. Deirdre Donat, *Class of 2010 Graduation by Total SAT*, July 2015, GSC.
19. Deirdre Donat, *Class of 2010 Graduation by Total SAT*, August 2013, GSC; Deirdre Donat, *Class of 2010 Graduation by Total SAT*, July 2015, GSC.
20. Deirdre Donat, *Class of 2010 Graduation by Total SAT*, August 2013, GSC.
21. Deirdre Donat, *Class of 2010 by MSAT*, August 2013, GSC; Deirdre Donat, *Class of 2010 by MSAT*, February 2015, GSC.
22. Deirdre Donat, *Class of 2010 by MSAT*, August 2013, GSC; Deirdre Donat, *Class of 2010 by MSAT*, February 2015, GSC.
23. Deirdre Donat, *Class of 2010 Graduation by MSAT*, August 2013, GSC; Deirdre Donat, *Class of 2010 by MSAT*, February 2015, GSC; Deirdre Donat, *Class of 2010 Graduation by MSAT*, February 2016, GSC.
24. Deirdre Donat, *Class of 2010 Graduation by VSAT*, August 2013, GSC; Deirdre Donat, *Class of 2010 Graduation by VSAT*, February 2015, GSC.
25. Deirdre Donat, *Class of 2010 Graduation by VSAT*, February 2015, GSC.
26. Deirdre Donat, *Class of 2010 Graduation by VSAT*, February 2015, GSC; Deirdre Donat, *Class of 2010 Graduation by VSAT*, February 2016, GSC.
27. Deirdre Donat, *Class of 2010 Graduation by Total SAT*, August 2013, GSC; Deirdre Donat, *Class of 2010 Graduation by VSAT*, August 2013, GSC; Deirdre Donat, *Class of 2010 Graduation by MSAT*, August 2013, GSC.
28. Deirdre Donat, *Class of 2010 Graduation by Total SAT*, February 2016, GSC.
29. Deirdre Donat, *2013–2014 Final Grades*, May 19, 2014, GSC; Deirdre Donat, *Class of 2013 Graduation by Total SAT*, February 2015, GSC.
30. Deirdre Donat, *Class of 2013 Graduation by Total SAT*, February 2015, GSC.
31. Deirdre Donat, *Class of 2013 Graduation by Total SAT*, February 2016, GSC.

32. Deirdre Donat, *Class of 2013 Graduation by Total SAT,* February 2015, GSC; Deirdre Donat, *Class of 2013 Graduation by Total SAT,* February 2016, GSC.
33. Deirdre Donat, *Class of 2013 Graduation by MSAT,* February 2015, GSC; Deirdre Donat, *Class of 2013 Graduation by MSAT,* February 2016, GSC.
34. Deirdre Donat, *Class of 2013 Graduation by MSAT,* February 2015, GSC; Deirdre Donat, *Class of 2013 Graduation by MSAT,* February 2016, GSC.
35. Deirdre Donat, *Class of 2013 Graduation by MSAT,* February 2015, GSC; Deirdre Donat, *Class of 2013 Graduation by MSAT,* February 2016, GSC.
36. Deirdre Donat, *Class of 2013 Graduation by VSAT,* February 2015, GSC; Deirdre Donat, *Class of 2013 Graduation by VSAT,* February 2016, GSC.
37. Deirdre Donat, *Class of 2013 Graduation by VSAT,* February 2015, GSC; Deirdre Donat, *Class of 2013 Graduation by VSAT,* February 2016, GSC.
38. Deirdre Donat, *Class of 2013 Graduation by VSAT,* February 2015, GSC; Deirdre Donat, *Class of 2013 Graduation by VSAT,* February 2016, GSC.
39. Deirdre Donat, *Class of 2013 Graduation by Total SAT,* February 2016.

TEN

Demographics and General Studies

In the years after the dismissal of Diamandopoulos in 1996, freshman enrollment generally improved. From a low of 385 in 1995, the figures rebounded to 556 in 1998, 637 in 2000, 770 in 2005, and 1005 in 2009. There followed a period of stagnation or decline of freshman recruitment at Adelphi.[1] Although officially targeted in the past decade and a half at 100 students, General Studies students constituted 25 to 40 percent of the freshman class in the early 1990s.[2] But when the school's first-year attendance bottomed in 1995, General Studies students made up 16 percent of all freshmen, and this by design, since administrators intentionally slashed the program's numbers. The General Studies component of Adelphi's freshman group has since hovered closer to 10 to 12 percent, no matter the total freshman enrollment. However, a private college in an intense competitive market, notwithstanding contracts with metrics-driven recruitment experts, is susceptible to enrollment volatility.[3]

THE COMPOSITION OF THE STUDENT BODY IN LOCAL CONTEXT

General Studies exerts positive influence on the breadth of enrollment. While the documentation adduced by Adelphi's Office of Research, Assessment and Planning has never completely coincided with the program's own figures, the findings differ little and equally establish key post-Diamandopoulos developments. These embrace the continuation of demographic and geographic spread and gender ratios. Among the most significant processes has been the growing strength in program constituency of African-American, Latino, and Asian-American students. Whites were 65 to 75 percent of all Adelphi freshmen in the decade after Diamandopoulos' release, and counted for roughly 65 percent of the entire student body, including graduate students. Some of Adelphi's branches were more disproportionate in the ratio of white to minority students, in spite of changes in regional demographics. Yet, the university's diversity was deeper than at a number of neighboring Long Island institutions.[4] Recent data bear out both Adelphi's more diverse composition than competitive institutions in close proximity and Adelphi's continuing white majority. Today, white students make up 60 percent of the school's first-year enrollment. White participation within the whole remains consistent within the university's undergraduate population. Improving diversity coexists with and is affected by the bigger picture.[5]

A particular history of excluding minority residents informs Adelphi's home village of Garden City, documented in chapter 4. District and federal courts have found "race-based animus" responsible for the village's absence of affordable housing. Local hearings made this clear "in light of the racial makeup of Garden City and the likely number of members of racial minorities that residents believed would have lived in affordable housing." Housing activists place Garden City housing discrimination on a par with widely contested practices in Westchester County (New York), Marin County (California), and Dallas. Yet important population alterations, especially the growth of local Latino communities in Long Island, have somewhat diversified student bodies in regional high schools, notwithstanding segregated domiciles. This has its limits nevertheless, first by dint of residence. In this connection, more white Adelphi entrants live in virtually all-white communities than attend similarly composed schools.[6]

Still, Adelphi's home county of Nassau presents enough material to fill an encyclopedia of housing and educational segregation. A Columbia Teachers College survey notes, "the boundary lines for the fifty-six school districts . . . intersect with these residential boundaries in rather inconsistent and unpredictable ways, only adding to the degree of fragmentation." Some not particularly large Nassau villages, for instance, are divided into as many as nine districts. In Nassau County, racial and ethnic bifurcation often occurred on either side of the Long Island Railroad tracks (as in West Hempstead), expressing the divided imagery of Duke Ellington's aptly titled "Across the Tracks Blues." A 2006 study by the National Fair Housing Alliance reported a Long Island realtor pattern of steering African-American homebuyers to "communities and school districts with higher African American and Latino populations," including when the prospective purchasers could afford "a wider range of homes from which to choose."[7]

To be sure, the districting of schools represents local government structures. Hence the Nassau-Suffolk area comprises more than a thousand distinct government units: towns, villages, townships, and others.

The Long Island ERASE Racism Initiative contends: "The extreme fragmentation of Long Island government is a tremendous barrier to opportunities for low-income people of color. The more fragmented a region's local governance, the more segregated the region by race and class." The research of Amy Stuart Wells demonstrates how segregation has contributed to education inequalities on Long Island, shaping the notion of what constitutes a "good school." The "bad reputations" of certain districts, Wells indicates, are "more strongly correlated with the race/ethnicity and poverty rates of the students than with an objective measure of school or district quality *per se*." For indeed, the "data on public school reputations clearly underscores the harm of racial/ethnic segregation across the disparate villages and hamlets of Long Island."[8] A recent study by the Civil Rights Project confirms that Nassau and Suffolk schools are among "the most fragmented in the nation." It suggests that "white students are overexposed to other white students, and this proportion has widened instead of narrowed over the last twenty years," despite demographic changes in the region. Similarly, "the typical black student, followed by the typical Latino, remains underexposed to white students," according to the Project.[9]

UNIQUE ELEMENTS IN GENERAL STUDIES

In the freshman context, General Studies has witnessed a greater distribution of race and ethnicity than the university proper. Despite rough identity between university and General Studies sets of data showing the program's configuration, the internally researched materials are more detailed. Moreover, in-house annual tracking of current-year students traditionally draws parallels with previous cohorts in the relevant categories, while providing sources for regular analysis. Figures demonstrate that minority students made up 47 percent of the cohort during 1993–1994, two points below the level of 1992–1993. A fall 1992 compilation also surveyed in-progress grade trends among different ethnic/racial groups in General Studies (which has not been attempted since). With all cohort members clustering near 2.0 in a challenging first semester, Asian students averaged 1.89, African-Americans 1.95, whites 1.97, and Latinos 2.01.[10]

Most cohorts after 1995 witnessed a closer approximation of minority and white student representation. African-American, Latino, Asian-American, and other students of color have more than once formed the greater part of the General Studies groups since the mid-1990s. General Studies has reflected local demographic changes to a greater extent than other programs of traditionally aged undergraduates and freshmen at Adelphi. Aggregating a more extensive range of students, General Studies diverges that much more from Long Island's prevalent high school segregation.[11]

While the entire cohort has comprised an eighth to a tenth of the freshman class in the recent past, it has accounted for a fifth to a quarter of first-year minority students at Adelphi generally. The documentary record reveals some variation. For example, Latino, African-American, and Asian students in General Studies represented a third of all freshmen of color in 1998. In 2000, 29 percent of all minority freshmen at Adelphi were in General Studies, 15 percent were in the program in 2005, 23 percent in 2010, and 17 percent in 2013. When viewed from the vantage point of minority students entering Adelphi as a whole in each new freshman class, it is evident that the university's ethnic-racial breadth would be diminished without the program.[12]

The program's annual reports present comparative calculations dating to 2003. Thus, the minority to white ratio in General Studies in 2003 was 51 to 49, in 2004 53 to 47, in 2005 45 to 55, in 2006 52 to 48, in 2007 48 to 52. Minority students composed 55 percent of the GS entering cohort of 2010, the same a year later, and a somewhat smaller majority in fall 2012. By 2015, Hispanic, African-American, and Asian students made up 54 percent of the General Studies cohort. University-wide figures confirm that African-American and Latino participation rates are generally higher in General Studies than among the university's undergraduate majors, with the exception of the Schools of Social Work and Nursing (which also draw older students). Naturally, General Studies is solely a freshman platform, in contrast with the other undergraduate rungs. However, within the student body, including the graduate programs, the proportion of Latino student involvement in General Studies exceeds that in nearly all other programs. This mirrors the deepening local Latino employment and residential demographic as well as the "Hispanic enrollment spike" at the college level throughout the country.[13]

Between a fifth and a sixth of all Latinos beginning Adelphi have entered through the gate of General Studies over the past fifteen years. Exceptions include 2011, when Latino students in GS comprised only 4 percent of all Latino freshmen, 2005 when they constituted 6 percent, and 1998 when they were 34 percent. The overall prominence of Latino matriculates within Adelphi's General Studies Learning Community appears to channel the increasing participation scale of Latino students in U.S. college life. The latter has featured a higher degree of college enrollment immediately after high school than among whites. Albeit, fewer Latino students attend college full-time.[14]

General Studies has regularly counted for a quarter to a third of Adelphi's African-American freshmen. The tendency has held for well over a decade, during the same time that the program has represented only ten to twelve percent of all first-year students. Nearly half of all Adelphi black freshmen in 1998 were in General Studies, 35 percent were in the program in 2005, and 25 percent in 2013. However, there have been fewer proportional anomalies in the school's African-American representative base in General Studies than are evident among Latinos in the program. The sources consistently show that General Studies has been a vital entry point for African-Americans into Adelphi. The percentage of black students in the program has regularly been 5 to 10 percentage points above their proportion in the freshman class at large.[15]

Minority and immigrant presence in the program touches on related factors, including language and religion. General Studies records a consistently high percentage of Asian Americans, and students from the Caribbean, Central America, and South America. The program also leads Adelphi schools and departments or has been traditionally among the leaders in proportion of foreign-born entrants and students in whose homes a language other than English is spoken. General Studies leads the campus in students whose religion is Hinduism. At a school whose predominant religious affiliation is Catholic, General Studies shares the condition in the main sense, but diverges from it in a greater affirmation of Protestantism and Eastern faiths. Where ten percent of Adelphi students are Jewish, virtually none are in General Studies. Among non-Catholic Christian General Studies students, a higher ratio than in other programs regularly cite adherence to nondenominational Protestant churches. Nationally, the latter are among the few organized Christian units whose followers have increased since 2000, but the actual participation rate of college-age students is low across most doctrinal entities. However Hindu students have a higher degree of observance than their peers in other American faiths. Of course, the conscious devotion of freshmen to religious belief is a different matter for investigation, outside the scope of the present study.[16]

The greater representation of Latinos, Asian Americans, African-Americans, and the foreign born in General Studies is by no means a given, however consistent the pattern. But General Studies has approached the issue of college eligibility by reducing the negative potency of college entrance exams, whose skewing of the college potential of minority applicants (treated in chapter 2) has been noted by scholars for decades. National findings, according to *Insight Into Diversity*, demonstrate that colleges adopting SAT-optional or similar admissions formats show striking improvement in freshman diversity. Keeping in mind the greater location of minority families in the vicinity of poverty levels—and Adelphi's shift toward providing scholarships to program members—General Studies also expands the university's class base.[17]

A multicultural context, particularly in a learning community setting, can provide opportunity for interaction, facilitating improved comprehension of the circumstances of others. Absence of an appropriate milieu deprives students of this potential. A national report indicates that if the freshman experience is approached with "well-crafted opportunities for reflection and learning," cross-cultural encounters may help bridge the "large divide" between diverse groups. Adelphi students themselves report the benefits of cross-cultural classroom experiences.[18]

Among undergraduate sectors, the participation of female students in General Studies aligns with their considerable representation generally throughout Adelphi. Women have long outnumbered men at Adelphi, accounting for a good two-thirds of all students. In fact female students prevail in Adelphi-like proportions in many schools of similar type and size. A number of factors spur the trend, including the perceived need by working women eighteen to twenty-four to go or return to school to improve employment and benefit chances amidst ongoing job discrimination. Nearly half a million have dropped out of the labor force since 2009.[19]

Forming 90 percent of the membership in certain Adelphi graduate schools—Nursing, Social Work—women also provide the great majority in all other areas but Business. Serving only first-year students, General Studies presents a sizeable female majority as well. Figures compiled by Adelphi's research office show that seventy-one of ninety-four program entrants were female in fall 2003, or 76 percent. All other entering General Studies classes since 2000 (when females made up 69 percent of the students) demonstrate comparable results, with some variation. According to the same data, there were 29 men out of a class of 110 in 2006, 26 in a cohort of 110 in 2009, 31 among 120 in 2010, 25 out of 82 in 2013. Inasmuch as the proportions of male and female students remain in keeping with overall Adelphi scales, there may be nothing particularly significant about the program in this regard, besides opening the door to Adelphi to greater numbers of qualified women, as well as men.[20]

Because the students in General Studies are held in general pre-major suspension for freshman year, they are not yet fully connected to occupational choices of other men and women entering college (though the proliferation of "undecided" first-year students in American colleges is calling early career callings into doubt). General Studies is not an area of study at Adelphi, but rather a community of temporary duration. Yet university data covering gender distribution places General Studies along with the multi-year bachelor's categories. The university publishes this first-year program's ratios alongside those embracing students at other stages of college life, who have declared themselves in training for an occupation. Adelphi's greatest female presence is witnessed in the career majors long considered as accessible to women, though often characterized by discriminatory pay and promotion scales: Nursing, Social Work, Psychology, and Education, for instance. Adelphi statistics prove little difference in the proportion of first-year females entering such majors and in the percentage of female undergraduates adhering to them beyond the freshman year. Considering the large number of General

Studies students choosing to concentrate in Nursing after freshman year, the program alumni do eventually join larger Adelphi patterns.[21]

URBAN REPRESENTATION IN GENERAL STUDIES

The program has often attracted a New York City representation out of proportion to the freshman class proper or the Adelphi student body as a whole. Nassau and Suffolk counties, the two divisions of Long Island, have undergone change yet remain predominantly white. Aforementioned notes on Adelphi's developing multiracial enrollment, in the context of abiding local white majorities, segregated high schools, and significant increases in Latino population, pointed out the prevalence of racially segmented home residence among the students. To be sure, both housing and school segregation also significantly mar New York City, despite its cosmopolitan vibe and complexity. Evidence demonstrates that multiracial, multinational communities are not quite so "mixed" in New York City either. It reveals "the persistence of residential segregation in one of the world's most diverse cities," reports the *New York Times*.[22]

And while New York City exhibits more multiracial, multiethnic communities (quite a bit different from Long Island), its schools remain nonetheless unequal. Employing census and Department of Education data, analysts Clara Hemphill and Nicole Mader found a consistent discrepancy between high minority student enrollments in schools on the one hand, and the more diverse population of the respective school districts of those very schools on the other. As they put it, "there are dozens of high-poverty elementary schools that serve mostly black and Latino children that are located in far more racially and economically mixed neighborhoods." Indeed, "the city's racially and economically segregated schools" prevail "in integrated neighborhoods," featuring "enrollments of more than 90 percent black and Latino students in neighborhoods that are racially mixed." Again, Hemphill and Mader demonstrate that schools in "mixed" neighborhoods nearly always have a higher minority representation than the neighborhood themselves. Meanwhile, the nearly universal black and Latino majorities in ghetto schools hold steady.[23]

At the same time, the five boroughs possess a greater range of people than the two Long Island counties, and one may also attribute the improved diversity in General Studies to a larger draw from city high schools, public and parochial. Over half of all Adelphi freshmen hail from Nassau and Suffolk, while 30 percent are city residents. But evidence points to a different occurrence in the General Studies Learning Community (with some exceptions), namely at times a native Long Island membership of less than 50 percent, with city origins as high as 60 percent, as in 2011. An occasional stronger city presence in the General Studies cohort is traceable to at least the late 1990s, when 38 percent of the class hailed from the boroughs, chiefly Manhattan, Queens, and the Bronx. Few programs have reflected a higher New York City presence than General Studies.[24]

INCOMES OF ADELPHI AND GENERAL STUDIES FAMILIES

Adelphi's freshman and overall student bodies, constituted from suburban and urban milieus, tend to belie persisting associations of wealth and private Long Island academe (census statistics still show the region among the nation's wealthiest). The gloss of wealth has not rubbed off on most Adelphi students, no matter where they come from. Many students from New York City, intermittently prevalent in General Studies, would likely experience particular challenges. For "half of New York City residents say they are struggling economically, making ends meet just barely, if at all," according to the *New York Times*. Adelphi students' parental income mirrors the spread at similar private schools, with a slightly higher proportion totaling $100,000 or more. Nevertheless, identification of income trends of Adelphi enrollees rarely details specific programs within the whole. However, figures from the formative period of General Studies show that Adelphi freshmen in general represented families with fewer financial resources than their peers at other private universities. Through the 1990s, 17 percent of Adelphi first-year students "reported a parental income of less than $20,000" (when federal guidelines calculated poverty for a family of four between $13,000 and $17,000) compared to 6 percent nationally at similar schools.[25]

Even with the decline in area manufacturing, Long Island retains a large working-class population of all races, alongside important demographic changes in the labor force. The mid-1990s picture of the Adelphi freshman class drawn largely from "from working class, blue-collar backgrounds" retains its essence in new forms now encompassing growing Latino, African-American, and Asian sectors.[26] All told, nearly 30 percent of Adelphi families, including those represented in the General Studies Program, took home less than $30,000, which represented the U.S. median, in 1991. Nationwide, African-American and Latino household income trailed the median by $12,000 and $8,000 respectively. The Census Bureau drew the poverty line at $13,400 for a family of four in 1991. Adelphi customarily exceeded the lower family income percentages of other private universities. Interestingly, in 2012 Adelphi could still report ten percent of its constituent families earning less than $20,000 (below poverty levels), and 25 percent below $40,000 annually, higher than national levels for private colleges. Moreover, the university's constituent families continued to earn generally less than peers at comparable institutions. Relevantly, fathers and mothers of Adelphi students throughout the 1990s and into the twenty-first century were less likely than those of students of other private schools to have graduated from college, or own their own businesses. However, mothers of Adelphians exceeded national averages in nursing occupations, a reflection of the region's growing health care industry and a contributing factor in the proliferation of nursing majors at Adelphi. The remainder of the 1990s witnessed a relative decline in the very lowest income brackets at the school, but no less a bunching of 30 percent within hailing distance of the poverty line.[27]

Working families remain the base of the university. Adelphi families have featured working and middle class adults, employed or otherwise. However, the university was able to declare in 2010, "the parental income of Adelphi freshmen has increased." Yet a 2012 follow-up report still indicated that families of other private college freshmen earned more than their Adelphi counterparts, which a 2014 study reiterated. Adelphi freshmen were more likely to work full-time than those at comparable schools. Adelphi family earnings were concentrated in the middle ranges, with a quarter of students from units below $30,000 in 2014, and an additional 20 percent hailing from sub-$60,000 households. These are not families brimming with prosperity.[28]

Census returns have found that costs of living—including college prices—had effectively nullified most salary increases. Reduction of real earnings, despite apparent increasing income, was especially marked in cities. National findings of the effects of earnings decline and rising poverty levels upon college students from urban backgrounds and minority communities are compelling. At the same time, suburban poverty growth, including the rise of concentrated areas of poverty, has taken on striking proportions. Both New York City and its Long Island suburbs have manifested the national surge in two-income households, alongside other evolving family types. Nevertheless, taking property affordability as a measurement, the city and the Island both show a tightening market, even sharper in Nassau County: as one real estate think tank put it, "two middle-class incomes don't add up to a home."[29]

However, the ramifications for families of specific groups of Adelphi students, especially freshmen, have escaped documentation but for a handful of figures. The university charted income by academic unit at several points, usually through student surveys. Considering the inconsistent number of Adelphi and General Studies students responding and the unlikelihood that most freshmen would know their family earnings precisely, reported General Studies family income markedly trailed the intake of other students' families between 2000 and 2010. In 2001, program students estimated household revenue at $38,000. Relevantly, minority students comprised 55 percent of this cohort, hailing from a demographic all-too-well documented as lagging in national wage and savings levels. The average family income claimed by Adelphi students in general was $59,000: here too, one may question what sophomores, juniors, and seniors may have understood about family finances.[30]

But in 2003, reported household income by General Studies students surprisingly zoomed to $67,000, in fact surpassing the family earnings of other Adelphi students (only 22 percent answered the survey). Yet Latino, Asian, and African-American students, undoubtedly experiencing the lower family employment and pay scales attested to by every data measurement, again constituted the majority of the General Studies student community. That General Studies family income (as estimated by student respondents), surpassed broader Adelphi figures appears dubious, considering the persistent lag of minority compensation behind that of whites every year, and inevitable depressing effect of salary discrimination upon the average earnings of program families. Later figures would seem to make the 2003 numbers anomalous. For by 2008, Adelphi students on the whole calculated family income at $76,000, while those in General Studies reported an average $52,000. Overall, student-estimated household income dwindled to $62,000 in 2011, General Studies in particular shrinking to $34,000. The vacillation in General Studies students' estimates has its limits, however, for they nearly always estimated a lower household income than other Adelphians.[31]

College financial advisors rightly warn observers against putting too much stock in student survey answers about the economic situation of their families. Their hesitation in employing student replies extends to all undergraduates, not just freshmen. Analysts have been forced to alter survey questions to obtain more reliable information about income, since students actually skip this question more than any other. But other figures indicate the relative difficulty that General Studies freshmen may have in affording college. Though reports show a consistent lag in overall Adelphi family incomes in comparison with peer institutions, General Studies students have little or no representation among the school's wealthiest families. A university report shows that the presence of General Studies families within the three highest income categories trails those of all other academic units. Family incomes above $150,000, which reach close to ten percent in Adelphi's undergraduate schools of Psychology and Business, do not exist in General Studies. Household compensation between $100,000 and $150,000 is less evident in General Studies than any other Adelphi division. Adelphians on the whole face challenging financial circumstances. But aside from the numerous undergraduate working adults in the School of Social Work, General Studies students report more difficulty meeting tuition costs than any other segment on campus.[32]

On the basis of FAFSA (Free Application for Federal Student Aid) filings, Adelphi classified 57 percent of General Studies students who filed as "high need" for financial assistance in 2003, 55 percent in 2013. Adding General Studies applicants in "medium need," one finds 71 percent altogether in the top two hardship levels in 2003, and 64 percent in 2013. "Need" goes beyond earned compensation. It is measured by number in household, number in college, assets and family income levels.

While Adelphi does not customarily publish the needs of applicants by school or department, it includes broad income breakdowns in annual *Databooks*. Relevantly, household earnings surpassing $100,000 are remarkably common among the student filers: 23 percent in 2006, 30 percent in 2008, 35 percent in 2009, 36 percent in 2010, 31 percent in 2011, 36 percent in 2012, and 38 percent in 2014. But understanding that family income increasingly reflects more than one earner in a household may put a total intake of $100,000 in perspective. It seems to require a combination of individual earners to put a child through college.[33]

In an analysis of home ownership in the New York City area, NYU's Furman Institute found that a total household income below $114,000 was insufficient for most New Yorkers to purchase a home, either in Nassau County or the city itself. Only in Suffolk County (further from the employment centers of the city) would low, moderate, and middle income families have a relatively easier time buying a home.[34]

Roughly half of all Adelphi students who request financial assistance come from households taking in less than $60,000 annually. One would be hard-pressed to afford a college education with this income. Again, Adelphi student-family incomes remain lower than at peer institutions. According to the school's FAFSA applications, lower end compensation is as stubborn a fact as airborne income, and presses downward upon the mean. At the lower end for the years shown above, 31 percent of Adelphi FAFSA applicants reported total family income below $30,000 in 2006, 25 percent in 2008, 22 percent in 2009, 24 percent in 2010, 36 percent in 2011, 26 percent in 2012, and 25 percent in 2014. The federal poverty line for a family of four stayed between $21,000 and $22,000 from 2006 to 2010. The government raised the poverty level to nearly $24,000 by 2014. Adelphi figures indeed show a significant portion of FAFSA applicants hovering around federal poverty indices. Approximately ten percent of the university's FAFSA filings indicate household earnings below $12,000, barely surviving.[35]

However, the General Studies FAFSA data may provide only a partial picture, because in the two indicated years of 2003 and 2013, only half the accepted General Studies students submitted financial aid forms. Lest one conclude that failure to apply for aid signifies financial comfort, students with the lowest household incomes are among the least likely to submit FAFSA forms. If more applied, the percentage recorded as being in "high need" could be greater. Upper income applicants, as seen in Adelphi's data, make up the largest percentage of the school's FAFSA filers. This does not mean that they are the majority of Adelphi students, since once again the university is on record demonstrating that its average constituent income is less than at competing institutions. Then why do better-off students send in for aid? Tuition, fees, and room and board, in today's higher education system can imperil a family's savings, even one that makes $100,000. Student debt will eventually tighten around the neck of loan beneficiaries, including students from higher-earning households. The prospect of $60,000 a year in college costs is enough to make anyone freeze. Nevertheless, studies assert that higher rates of financial aid applications can be a sign of better high school counseling, or attendance at high schools with greater funding for student advising generally. When, as is so often the case, budgets for such services are frozen, cut, or inadequate, college counseling at the high school level is impeded and FAFSA information is in short supply. Chapter 3 demonstrated the inadequacy of college counseling in many public high schools, particularly in minority communities. When Long Island's towns have created separate and unequal school systems, a clear difference emerges in funding, advising, and preparation of students for college. New York City's racial dichotomies are equally evident.[36]

Sadly, comparable figures on "need" do not exist for the general Adelphi student body in the years given. Still, both historical and current data demonstrate that African-American and Latino earners are subject to pay inequity greater than the rest of the population, and both student populations are well-represented in the General Studies Learning Community. This fact may contribute to classifying a high proportion of General Studies students who do file FAFSA applications as truly needing financial aid.

NOTES

1. *Adelphi University Databook*, Fall 2009, 33; Office of Research, Assessment and Planning, "Fall 2015 Admissions Comparisons," May 31, 2015.
2. William Romano, "Freshman Class Decrease Rumored Larger Than Figures," *The Delphian*, February 20, 1991, 3; *Provost's Report on Enrollments in University College*, November 14, 1995, 7, GSC; University College: A Report, *Cohort Attrition, 1985–1993*, 1994, GSC.
3. *Adelphi University Databook*, Fall 2009, 33; *Adelphi University Databook*, Fall 2010, 27; *Adelphi University Databook*, Fall 2011, 27; *2006–2007 Final Grades*, May 21, 2007, GSC; *2009–2010 Final Grades*, May 24, 2010, GSC; *2010–2011 Final Grades*, May 18, 2011, GSC; Adelphi University Office of Research, Planning, and Assessment, *Fall 2016 Admission Reports*, June 2, 2016.
4. *Adelphi University Databook*, Fall 2009, 36, 87, 94; Adelphi University Adelphi University Office of Research, Assessment, and Planning, *Results of the Cooperative Institutional Research Program (CIRP) Survey Fall 1991 to Fall 1998*, 1.
5. *Adelphi University Databook*, Fall 2013, 27, 199; *Adelphi University Databook*, Fall 2015, 37.
6. United States Court of Appeals for the Second Circuit, Docket Nos. 14-1634-cv (L), 14-1729-cv (XAP), *Mhany Management, Inc. et al. v. County of Nassau, County of Nassau Planning Commission, County of Nassau Office of Real Estate & Development, Incorporated Village of Garden City, Garden City Board of Trustees*, March 23, 2016, 4–6, 31, 57–58; Lisa W. Foderaro, "Strides, If Not Solution, Seen in Housing Suit," *New York Times*, April 25, 2016, A1; Adelphi University Office of Research, Assessment, and Planning, *Diversity at Adelphi University: Results From Surveys of Students and Faculty*, September 2013, 1, 2.

7. Amy Stuart Wells et al., *Divided We Fall: The Story of Unequal Suburban Schools 60 Years After Brown v. Board of Education,* The Center for Understanding Race and Education, Teachers College, Columbia University, May 2, 2014, 7–9, 32; National Fair Housing Alliance, *Housing Segregation Background Report: Long Island, New York,* Washington, DC, 2006, 6.

8. ERASE Initiative of the Long Island Community Foundation, *Racism and the Opportunity Divide on Long Island,* 2002, 8; Amy Stuart Wells et al., *Why Boundaries Matter: A Study of Five Separate and Unequal Long Island School Districts* (Abridged), Long Island Index, 2009, 6.

9. John Kucsera and Gary Orfield, *New York State's Extreme School Segregation: Inequality, Inaction, and a Damaged Future,* The Civil Rights Project, March 2014, 128; *New York State's Extreme School Segregation: Inequality, Inaction, and a Damaged Future,* Long Island (Suffolk and Nassau Counties), NY Metro Summary, The Civil Rights Project, March 2014, 5, 8.

10. Della Hudson-Tomlin to David Newton, *Final 1993–94 Statistics,* May 18, 1994; Della Hudson-Tomlin, *1992–93 Final Statistics,* May 20, 1993; Della Hudson-Tomlin to John Donohue, *Mid-Term Grade Report,* November 6, 1992, GSC.

11. *General Studies Freshman Class 1995 Profile,* GSC.

12. Adelphi University Office of Research and Planning, *General Studies Students: Recent Trends,* September 2003, "Profile of Students in General Studies Program: Fall 1990 to Fall 2003"; *2006–2007 Final Grades,* GSC; *2010–2011 Final Grades,* May 18, 2011, GSC; *Adelphi University Databook,* Fall 2013, 27, 111, 139.

13. *General Studies Year-End Report,* May 25, 2004, GSC; *2006–2007 Final Grades,* GSC; *Adelphi University Databook,* Fall 2009, 27, 67; *Adelphi University Databook,* Fall 2010, 9, 27, 67, 103; *Adelphi University Databook,* Fall 2011, 27; *Adelphi University Databook,* Fall 2015, 105; *General Studies Year-End Report,* May 17, 2013, GSC; Pew Hispanic Center, *Hispanic College Enrollment Spikes, Narrowing Gaps with Other Groups* August 25, 2011, 5.

14. Adelphi University Office of Research, Assessment, and Planning, *General Studies Students: Recent Trends,* September 2003, "Profile of Students in General Studies Program: Fall 1990 to Fall 2003"; *2006–2007 Final Grades,* GSC; *2010–2011 Final Grades,* May 18, 2011, GSC; *2011–2012 Final Grades,* May 22, 2012, GSC; Deirdre Donat, "Class of 2016 Demographics," Message to the author, September 5, 2012, E-mail; Pew Hispanic Center, *Hispanic High School Graduates Pass Whites in Rate of College Enrollment,* Washington, DC, May 9, 2013; Sarah Hurley and Ann Cole, *College Counseling for Latino and Underrepresented Students,* National Association for College Admission Counseling, 2015.

15. Office of Research and Planning, *General Studies Students: Recent Trends,* September 2003, "Profile of Students in General Studies Program: Fall 1990 to Fall 2003"; *2003–2004 Final Grades,* GSC; *2006–2007 Final Grades,* GSC; *2010–2011 Final Grades,* May 18, 2011, GSC; *Adelphi University Databook,* Fall 2013, 27; *Adelphi University Databook,* Fall 2015, 37, 105.

16. Adelphi University Office of Research, Assessment, and Planning, *Results of the Undergraduate and Graduate Student Experience Surveys, Fall 2003,* 17; Adelphi University Office of Research, Assessment, and Planning, *Results of the 2007–08 Student Experience Surveys,* 12; Adelphi University Office of Research, Assessment, and Planning, *Results of the Undergraduate and Graduate Student Experience Surveys, Spring 2011,* 14; Adelphi University Office of Research, Assessment, and Planning, *Results of the Undergraduate and Graduate Student Experience Surveys, Spring 2014,* 16; Pew Research Center, May 12, 2015, *America's Changing Religious Landscape,* 3, 9, 14, 26, 39.

17. Alexandera Vollman, "Schools See Spike in Diverse Enrollment with Test-Optional Admissions, *Insight Into Diversity,* http://www.insightintodiversity.com/schools-see-spike-in-diverse-enrollment-with-test-optional-admissions/. Accessed September 21, 2015; National Student Clearinghouse, *National College Progression Rates,* Herndon, Virginia, 2013, 4.

18. Jesse D. Rude, Gregory C. Wolniak, and Ernest Pascarella, *Racial Attitude Change during the College Years,* April 12, 2012, 19, cited by permission; Martha J. LaBare, ed.,

First-Year Engagement: Sound Foundations for College, Citizenship, and Democracy, National Resource Center for the First-Year Experience and Students in Transition, 2008, 14; Adelphi University Office of Research, Assessment, and Planning, *Diversity at Adelphi University: Results From Surveys of Students and Faculty,* September 2013, 3–5.

19. "WIA Report Survey: First-Year Enrollments of Women at the Nation's Leading Research Universities," Women In Academia Report, November 22, 2011, http://www.wiareport.com/2011/11/wiareport-survey-first-year-enrollments-of-women-at-the-nations-leading-research-universities/. Accessed November 30, 2011; Catherine Rampell, "Instead of Work, Younger Women Head to School," *New York Times,* December 29, 2011, A1.

20. *Adelphi University Databook,* Fall 2009, 35, 86; *Adelphi University Databook,* Fall 2013, 84, 111; *Adelphi University Databook,* Fall 2015, 105, 203; General Studies Year-End Report, May 25, 2004, GSC; *Adelphi University Databook,* Fall 2009, 35; *Adelphi University Databook,* Fall 2008, 27; *2006–2007 Final Grades,* May 21, 2007, GSC; *2009–2010 Final Grades,* May 24, 2010, GSC; *2010–2011 Final Grades,* May 18, 2011, GSC; *2013–2014 Final Grades,* May 14, 2014, GSC.

21. *Adelphi University Databook,* Fall 2015, 24, 55, 93.

22. Mireya Navarro, "Segregation Issue Complicates de Blasio's Housing Push," *New York Times,* April 15, 2016, A1.

23. Clara Hemphill and Nicole Mader, *Segregated Schools in Integrated Neighborhoods: The City's Schools Are Even More Divided Than Our Housing,* New School Center for New York City Affairs, 2015, http://www.centernyc.org/segregatedschools. Accessed December 16, 2015.

24. Adelphi University Office of Research, Assessment, and Planning, *Diversity at Adelphi University: Results From Surveys of Students and Faculty,* September 2013, 2; Service Employees International Union, Local 32 BJ, Service Employees International Union, *Falling Further Apart: Decaying Schools in New York City's Poorest Neighborhoods,* 2013; *General Studies 1997–1998 Statistical Report: Summary Breakdown of High Schools of Deposited/Registered Students By Location,* GSC; Dee Donat, GS Incoming NYC HS 2011, March 3, 2011, GSC; *Adelphi University Databook,* Fall 2010, 1, 6, 9, 26, 69; *Adelphi University Databook,* Fall 2009, 6, 9; *Adelphi University Databook,* Fall 2011, 6, 9; *2013-2014 Final Grades,* May 14, 2014, GSC; *Adelphi University Databook,* Fall 2015, 2–9, 28.

25. U.S. Census Bureau, *The Geographical Concentration of High-Income Households: 2007–2011,* February 2013, 5, 7; Alexander Burns and Giovanni Russonello, "Poll of New Yorkers Finds Broad Economic Anxiety," *New York Times,* November 19, 2015, A28; *Adelphi University Databook,* Fall 2013, 201; Adelphi University Office of Research, Assessment, and Planning, *Results of the Cooperative Institutional Research Program (CIRP) Survey Fall 1991 to Fall 1998,* 2, 3; Social Security Administration, *Annual Statistical Supplement to the Social Security Bulletin,* April 2015, Table 3.E8: Poverty Guidelines for Families of Specified Size, 1965–2014 (in dollars), 3.19–3.20.

26. Adelphi University Office of Research, Assessment, and Planning, *Results of the Cooperative Institutional Research Program (CIRP) Survey Fall 1991 to Fall 1998,* 2.

27. Adelphi University Office of Research, Assessment, and Planning, *Results of the Cooperative Institutional Research Program (CIRP) Survey Fall 1991 to Fall 1998,* 9; U.S. Department of Commerce, Bureau of the Census, *Money Income of Households, Families, and Persons in the United States: 1992,* xii; *Adelphi University Databook,* Fall 2013, 201; U.S. Census Bureau, *Poverty 2000 and 2012: American Community Survey Briefs,* September 2013; U.S. Department of Commerce, Bureau of the Census, *Poverty in the United States, 1991,* A-8; Adelphi University Office of Research, Assessment, and Planning, *Results of the Cooperative Institutional Research Program (CIRP) Survey Fall 1991 to Fall 1998,* 10, 11; Adelphi University Office of Research, Assessment, and Planning, *Results of the Cooperative Institutional Research Program (CIRP) Survey Fall 2000 to Fall 2010,* 19–20; Adelphi University Office of Research, Assessment, and Planning, *Results of the Cooperative Institutional Research Program (CIRP) Survey Fall 2004 to Fall 2014,* 4, 6; Adelphi University Office of Research, Assessment, and Planning, *Results of the Cooperative Institutional Research Program (CIRP) Survey Fall 2002 to Fall 2012,* 6; Adelphi University Office of

Research, Assessment, and Planning, "CIRP Survey of Freshmen: Trends," *ORAP Research Bulletin*, March 2009, 1.

28. Adelphi University Office of Research, Assessment, and Planning, *Results of the Cooperative Institutional Research Program (CIRP) Survey Fall 2000 to Fall 2010*, 7; Adelphi University Office of Research, Assessment, and Planning, *Results of the Cooperative Institutional Research Program (CIRP) Survey Fall 2002 to Fall 2012*, 6; Adelphi University Office of Research, Assessment, and Planning, *Results of the Cooperative Institutional Research Program (CIRP) Survey Fall 2004 to Fall 2014*, 4, 6; *Adelphi University Databook*, Fall 2015, 192.

29. College Board, *Trends in College Pricing*, 2007; U.S. Department of Commerce, United States Census Bureau, *Income, Poverty, and Health Insurance Coverage in the United States: 2010*, September 2011, 5–7, 10; National Student Clearinghouse, *National College Progression Rates*, Herndon, Virginia, 2013; Elizabeth Kneebone, *The Growth and Spread of Concentrated Poverty*, Brookings Institution, July 31, 2014, http://www.brookings.edu/research/interactives/2014/concentrated-poverty#/M10420. Accessed August 4, 2014; Pew Research Center, May 29, 2013, *Breadwinner Moms*, 11; Redfin Research Center, "Two Middle-Class Incomes Do Not Add Up to a Home," April 3, 2014, https://www.redfin.com/research/reports/special-reports/2014/middle-class-income-housing-affordability.html#.VXG2dOBsPyc. Accessed June 5, 2015.

30. Adelphi University Office of Research, Assessment, and Planning, *Student Experience Survey: Undergraduate Students*, July 2001, 8; Ana M. Aizcorbe et al., "Recent Changes in U.S. Family Finances: Evidence from the 1998 and 2001 Survey of Consumer Finances," *Federal Reserve Bulletin*, January 2003, 4–5, 7, 12–13, 18; Devah Pager and Bruce Western, *Discrimination in Low-Wage Markets: Evidence from an Experimental Audit Study in New York City*, 2005, submission to the Population Association of American Annual Meetings 2005; *Adelphi University Databook*, Fall 2009, 107.

31. Adelphi University Office of Research, Assessment, and Planning, *Results of the Undergraduate and Graduate Student Experience Surveys, Fall 2003*, 35; Adelphi University Office of Research, Assessment, and Planning, *Results of the 2007–08 Student Experience Surveys*, 22; Adelphi University Office of Research, Assessment, and Planning, *Results of the Undergraduate and Graduate Student Experience Surveys, Spring 2011*, 33; Martin Conroy, *Faded Dreams: The Politics and Economics of Race in America*, New York, 1994, 109–26.

32. Nava Lerer, executive director, Office of Research, Assessment and Planning, to author, June 5, 2015; Adelphi University Office of Research, Assessment and Planning, *Results of the Undergraduate and Graduate Student Experience Surveys, Spring 2014*, 19, 35.

33. Sheryl Mihopulos, assistant vice-president, Student Financial Services and Financial Aid Compliance, Adelphi University, to author, June 4, 2015; Sheryl Mihopulos, assistant vice-president, Student Financial Services and Financial Aid Compliance, Adelphi University, to author, June 8, 2015; *Adelphi University Databook*, Fall 2006, 164; *Adelphi University Databook*, Fall 2008, 174; *Adelphi University Databook*, Fall 20 *Adelphi University Databook*, Fall 2013, 2009, 180; *Adelphi University Databook*, Fall 2010, 178; *Adelphi University Databook*, Fall 2012, 182; *Adelphi University Databook*, Fall 2014, 182.

34. NYU Furman Center, *CITI Report on Home Ownership & Opportunity in New York*, August 5, 2016, 3, 4, 6, 20, 21.

35. *Adelphi University Databook*, Fall 2006, 164; *Adelphi University Databook*, Fall 2008, 174; *Adelphi University Databook*, Fall 2009 *Adelphi University Databook*, Fall 2013, 109, 180; *Adelphi University Databook*, Fall 2010, 178; *Adelphi University Databook*, Fall 2012, 182; *Adelphi University Databook*, Fall 2014, 182; Social Security Administration, *Annual Statistical Supplement to the Social Security Bulletin*, April 2015, Table 3.E8: Poverty Guidelines for Families of Specified Size, 1965–2014 (in dollars), 3.19–3.20.

36. J. Cody Davidson, "Increasing FAFSA Completion Rates: Research, Policies, and Practices," *Journal of Student Financial Aid*, Vol. 43 (2013), Issue 1, Article 4, 39.

Conclusion

Can General Studies Endure?

GENERAL STUDIES AND FRESHMEN IN CONTEXT

Adelphi's General Studies Learning Community is one of hundreds of serious initiatives tackling the problems of first-year students. In the climate of higher education today, their continuation depends upon consistent advocacy. Compounded by the challenges facing youth, working and middle class families, and minorities, the matters facing students in their late teens oblige colleges to take notice and action. General Studies operates in league with national findings that freshmen are a special constituency, to which colleges must be more than nominally attentive and for which certain structures must be in place.

Adelphi's experience is one example of the many steps institutions may take to confront the issues of today's freshmen. Robert A. Scott, Adelphi president from 2000–2015, acknowledges that these university initiatives will vary according to the character of an institution and the high school systems from which it draws. Inasmuch as elite colleges find themselves under pressure to broaden their demographic source, Scott speculates that these schools too will need to adapt measures facilitating the move from high school to college.[1]

In any case, the enervating anxieties and worries afflicting all freshmen necessitate action. Increasingly, scholars and researchers (not to mention students and their families) favor the integration of mentoring and counseling in the transition from high school, whether through freshman-wide initiatives or smaller, targeted programs. A program sets out an arranged and systematized process, which may be easier to implement on a limited basis and framework. However, it must also guard against overorchestrating the lives of students, displacing or weakening the innovative spirit.

Adelphi's General Studies establishes a cohort within a matrix of courses and forms of academic support. (As shown in chapter 3, many other institutions are striving toward the same purpose through various methods.) General Studies is also part of the national trend to divest SAT scores of their influence. General Studies frames academic potential through applicants' critical thinking abilities, outside pursuits, community involvements, and secondary school performance. The program has been a gateway to professional training for students considered less deserving of college admission according to archaic models.[2]

Departing from the test mode of student worth was once unconventional. Realizing that college readiness transcends exams, institutions are gradually discarding test-based assumptions of aptitude. They are reaping the lessons of countless studies, including the 2016 survey by Columbia University Teachers College, which shows that standardized testing detracts from genuine instruction.[3] When a school takes other evidence of student qualifications into account, it might then assess student progress during the college freshman year differently as well, including through portfolios, journals, online discussions, longer-term projects, presentations, papers, and group work. Even if a program establishes a fairly controlled environment in working with first-year students, it can also encourage a range of learning and teaching approaches allowing for interaction and individual expression.

Data on General Studies student graduation rates show the SAT to be a feeble tool for outcomes, or as Robert A. Scott puts it, "a lower-level indicator."[4] The record shows a greater correlation between high school performance and college success, which comprise larger time frames of growth. The SAT blurs the intricacy of capability. When an institution commits to a coherent program for freshmen, as cohort or total class, it must take into account the impacts of standardized testing, the current unbalanced economy, and the budget-slashed public education system from which the students are emerging. These elements exert deleterious effects upon student focus, confidence, and equilibrium. To admit freshmen responsibly means to be aware of the influences upon them, and thus to take practical steps to assist and retain them. As it turns out, General Studies' constituents graduate at a healthy clip, with exemplary averages and Latin honors.

Great resourcefulness and effort spur an impressive range of campaigns around the country, fortifying the freshman seminars, pre-college "bridges," creative orientations, test-optional applications, and "exploratory" programs that place less emphasis on early major choice. Educators are more intelligently recasting the meaning of "undecided." Some are integrating "gap years" for accepted students, understanding that many work or take leaves of absence. Learning communities produce useful encounters within cohorts. Increasing availability of counseling (at several schools, for example, counseling is available 24 hours a day) creates a comfortable and caring learning environment for students. Some schools are even embedding counselors in residence halls.[5]

The efforts are laudable, but depend upon the purse strings of their institutions. Funding cuts have placed highly successful college programs in grave jeopardy.[6] In practice, pedagogical priority is not a given. The market mentality in higher education haunts freshman programs. Consequently, their academic value hardly assures their continuation.

People who have worked with students at the sites of instruction, who have engaged with the changing conditions and mindsets of college-age youth, remain the true generators of these worthy endeavors. Guided by experience, they are attempting to meet genuine needs.

DEMOCRATIZING ADMISSIONS

Adelphi University first designed its freshman program in 1985 to reach an untapped group of paying students. The new recruitment was a no-brainer. While obtaining full tuition from each student, the program would operate on a shoestring staff budget, a lucrative arrangement indeed. As shown in chapter 4, Adelphi equipped the program with a contingent teaching/tutoring staff, a band of graduate students from the university's psychoanalytic wing to counsel students, and a handful of lower-level administrators, who were already working at the university but would be redeployed.

But selecting from the body of applicants whose SAT scores, and to some extent high school averages, fell below admissions criteria meant that the rather simple remedy to enrollment shortfall would require a more than ordinary rationale. Pinpointing these students led to an open airing of arguments about who was qualified to attend Adelphi. In rooting an enrollment booster among traditionally rejected applicants, Adelphi forced questions upon itself—for no sooner was this constituency proposed for admission then the discussion unfolded about its purported hazards, which might endanger the university's standards of schoolwork and conduct. In fact, more than one debate participant ventured that lower test scores shared ground with behavioral risk, and expressed fear about turning General Studies students loose among the mainstream. In turn, the debate, especially among the faculty, opened the door to critical re-examination of admission standards.

Nevertheless, it was the very plainest of platforms, rather than the hunt for new answers, which launched the General Studies Program. Adelphi administrators and faculty swiftly sketched parameters and safeguards. The program would accept applicants at the appropriate lower SAT and high school markings. The designated committees fleshed out an admissions profile and ultimately established a one-year term for the program. In approving General Studies, the faculty mandated that tutoring and counseling would be required of all entrants. Given today's recognition of these services, this was a rather innovative concept.

After the program was approved, it remained for the administrators assigned to General Studies to expand the rudimentary outline. Chapters 4, 5, and 6 introduced several of them: Dominick Cavallo, Peter Katopes, Alan Sadovnik, John Donahue, and David Newton; except for Newton, all were under forty at the time, with freshly minted doctorates in the

Humanities and Social Sciences. They shared a consensus view—that traditional college acceptance criteria on the foundation of the College Board were outworn; unique problems in the adjustment of first-year students compelled forms of collaboration with students outside the classroom; and thus, admissions should be "democratized." In clearly revising the notion of college qualifications, they asserted the potential of all accepted students. By this philosophy, the program thereby took a very different shape than the one first proposed.

As long as General Studies thrived, the latent divergence between the pecuniary root and the democratic impulse were in abeyance. Students entered in droves. The program's earliest conductors chafed at its paltry budget, and were able to hire a few more full-time counselors, persuading the higher administration that funding the support would benefit the students. After observing the work in General Studies for several years, University College dean David Newton concluded that adjunct teaching weakened the interlocking components of tutoring, counseling, and instruction. Newton came to believe that General Studies represented something new, which deserved the stability of full-time instructors with job benefits (and thus a greater university investment). However, they were to be listed as administrators, not part of the regular faculty.

In the toxic air of elitism (nourished publicly in the president's cavorts with the best-known spokesmen of neo-conservatism), president Peter Diamandopoulos moved to do away with General Studies in the mid-1990s. Despite the fact that General Studies had long fulfilled both financial and academic mandates, the query resurfaced: who should be allowed to attend Adelphi? The school's foremost leaders had in fact come to see General Studies as an unsightly receptacle for bottom-feeders, not a gateway for students with potential. The university cut General Studies severely, while at the same time eliminating another program that provided financial aid and academic services to a low-income, mostly minority, student base. Meanwhile, powerful personal and political factors entered the picture, leading Adelphi's enrollment and fortunes to plummet, while scandals involving the president and the board became public. Investigating serious conflicts of interest within Adelphi's board and violation of nonprofit procedures, the New York State Board of Regents got rid of the trustees in 1997 and ushered in a new era. Malfeasance, alongside the neo-conservative agenda of the board and president, had thus made Adelphi rather exceptional.

General Studies resumed its place into the twenty-first century, with a stable cadre of counselors and instructors and overall backing for its mission at the highest levels. As the high school records of General Studies entrants rose to meet higher admissions standards, the program saw improvements in graduation rates as well as retention rates from first to second year. General Studies students performed well in the majors, from sophomore year through commencement, producing final grade point averages on par with the university's best. They disproved the SAT's intellectual suppositions year after year, while continuing to advance Adelphi's case for creative work with freshman.

IMPACT OF NEW TRENDS UPON GENERAL STUDIES

Like so many other schools during the first decade and a half of the new century, Adelphi made substantial technological, procedural, promotional, and organizational adaptations, from breathtaking architecture to electronic instructional delivery services. Classrooms shimmered with high-tech modifications—newly installed hardware folding out of walls and disappearing as quickly as it emerged. Adelphi refounded its library on contemporary principles, with new spaces and marvelous multipurpose design. Matching national practice, the university assembled relevant offices under the umbrella of the Office of Enrollment Management and Student Success and increased the number of adjunct professors.[7]

Private institutions with tuition-driven endowments were particularly impacted by such technological and administrative advancements at the beginning of the twenty-first century. Short of mergers and bankruptcies, many colleges consolidated programs, accelerated the trend toward part-time instructors, and raised tuitions. College presidential recruits often leaned to the business world, some aspirants with limited educational experience, and with them stronger battalions of similarly oriented trustees emerged. The latter drew upon their trades, establishing reputations for getting things done, outsourcing presidential searches to companies and consultants.[8] They welcomed technological innovation, which would revolutionize higher education and pedagogy, with the extra boon of reducing operational costs. The electronic apparatus metamorphosed repeatedly, irresistible and at times useful to pedagogy. Schools transformed through apps, social media, and expertly conceived websites. They turned classrooms inside out. Colleges developed virtual dimensions; students and professors needed never to meet. It was a great progression ostensibly in keeping with evolution itself, flipping traditional instruction or ultimately making it superfluous.

Across the country, institutions held learning goals, outcomes, and student and faculty performance up to the fire of graduation rates—the nuts and bolts. Judging faculty success and student learning by these and other numerical indicators made traditional collaborative practice between instructors and administrations less equal. College managers, however, continued to tout the indispensable model of essential contributions from regular faculty to the collaborative project, since cooperation is officially obligatory. Rising student debt shaped the picture of enrollment, along with the prolongation of the time it took to graduate. The six-year span, long the tacit measurement of graduation rates, became the norm. Yet a full third of college students across the country were unable to meet this goal as well.

Among the many preoccupations of enrollment management among similarly situated institutions, none were more important than addressing the freshman admissions yield—the proportion of accepted students who enrolled. Over the past decade, the freshman yield eroded among hundreds of small and medium private schools. Interventions by upper managers into the academic foundation tend to occur when yields sink, even when institutions spend a great deal on other things. In the dilemmas facing collegiate decision makers, the leaner and meaner strategy seems the best option—just as it is when corporate helms in other realms make those same tough decisions. In this light, what might benefit students is weighed against potential savings from elimination of programs, services, and departments, not to mention reduction of personnel.

After years of averaging 25 to 33 percent yields, General Studies enrollment of accepted students dropped after 2010, reaching 18 percent in 2010, 16 percent in 2013, and 14 percent in 2015. While Adelphi freshman yields overall were over 40 percent in the 1980s, with General Studies a few points behind, the figure dropped to 20 percent in 2009[9] and lower still in 2015—particularly severe in light of enrollment competition with regional schools and comparable institutions.[10] Notwithstanding General Studies' long record of successful work with students, the circumstances prompted renewed skepticism about the program. Why did its yield lag behind? Were accepted applicants turned off by the name "General Studies Program"? Despite support service integration into freshman programs nationwide, some at Adelphi sought to abolish the program's counseling and tutoring, deeming them unnecessary encumbrances. Specific mechanisms that had been implemented to aid freshmen were given little value.[11]

Despite little evidence, some believed that student morale was poor. More than one enrollment manager speculated that General Studies students were unhappy being separated from other freshmen, and suggested that the program loosen its rules preventing students from joining sororities and fraternities and playing intercollegiate sports. Stymied by the resistance they encountered, several assiduously but unsuccessfully recommended that the program be disbanded in its thirtieth year.[12]

A new Adelphi leadership repudiated the proposal to dissolve General Studies. Whether to run such a program inevitably brings into the picture what matters most to an institution. Decisions often rest heavily on estimates of academic program cost and resource allocation, which naturally comprise the bigger contexts of instructional expenses, technological development, and institutional marketing.[13] However, public universities, beset by budget reductions, and private colleges, struggling for market share amid declining yields, increasingly reflect a type of decision making in which educational needs and services do not retain centrality (and are in fact dispensable). Originally set up for the public good (to benefit agriculture, mining, and engineering, and to enroll the budding scholars of urban America), state and city institutions have witnessed dramatic rollbacks in government outlays, part and parcel of the withdrawal of government aid to education and other vital spheres of public benefit. They have used rising tuitions and cheap instructional resources to fill the vacuum of drastic defunding, while companies have moved into the breach to supply mechanisms previously run internally.

Despite rising tuition at public colleges, private schools remain generally more expensive.[14] At the same time, private schools of Adelphi's type and size draw a huge population of working and middle class students who opt to bypass or are not accepted at cheaper public institutions. Private schools exert a pull upon local loyalties and beliefs over generations for myriad reasons. Private colleges often have their own relationship to the immediate community. It may be the place where one's friends go, the more familiar pipeline from high school. Querying prospective Adelphi students on their other school choices elicits a list of private colleges close to and much like Adelphi. Yet private colleges are costly. That Adelphi family incomes trail those at comparable institutions—and that General Studies incomes may be lower still—suggests the stakes involved in building affordable freshman-centered programs.[15]

THE CORPORATE UNIVERSITY

The influence of big business on higher education is not necessarily new; more than a century ago, United States representative Henry George, Jr. asked, "Who are the men of means we nowadays find among our university regents and trustees, and who from without contribute so handsomely toward endowment funds? They are Princes of Privilege." But for the land grant schools, college was traditionally a training ground for scions and executors of wealthy power brokers.[16]

Representatives of large manufacturing and financial firms occupied considerable place at institutions of higher learning in the late nineteenth and early twentieth century. As trustees, they were especially sensitive to extramural statements by faculty in opposition to child labor or in support of union rights and fair labor standards. Upton Sinclair's *The Goose-step: A Study of American Education* (1923) contended, "you could not tell a chart of the Columbia trustees from a chart of the New York Central Railroad, or the Remington Arms Company." Corporate weight held constant on the boards of Radcliffe, the private University of Denver (the Colorado Fuel and Iron Company), the University of Pittsburgh (U.S. Steel), the University of Montana, and the University of Minnesota. All told, Sinclair presented information on 143 institutions (each with a minimum of 500 students) and 2500 trustees. "We have allowed the education of our youth," Sinclair quoted a contemporary scholar, "to fall into the absolute control of a group of men who represent not only a minority of the total population but have, at the same time, enormous economic and business stakes in what kind of an education it shall be."[17]

While tens of millions of working class, middle class, and minority students have entered institutions of higher learning, corporate impacts are more widely diffused within schools, and not only at the level of trustees. According to former Adelphi president Robert A. Scott, "greater emphasis on market forces than on institutional mission can distort the purpose of higher education." For it evokes National Public Radio's Heather King's succinct "Our cultural god is money." It shapes what happens in the classroom, and between student and instructor. Enrollment managers and college leaders who see academic challenges through a marketplace lens are all the rage. The "corporate mindset," writes Scott, tends to disrupt the "mission-market balance."[18]

In Benjamin Ginsberg's words, administrators "having the capacity to spout last year's management buzz words during meetings, retreats, and planning exercises" fit the bill. Moreover, "lack of academic credentials or actual experience in the realms of teaching and research is no disqualification for a career as a professional manager." The case of the public institution in the Midwest that with limited faculty input selected a president from the business world with virtually no track record in college administration cannot be considered unusual.[19]

Nearly fifty years ago, the British labor historian E. P. Thompson already observed that university heads "had become so intimately enmeshed with the upper reaches of consumer capitalist society that they are actively twisting the purposes and procedures" of academia. He bore witness to the emergence of "a new kind of vice-chancellor," who "might see himself not so much as an academic organizer and arbitrator as the managing director of a business enterprise." Consequently, higher education would be brought into "symbiotic relationship with the aims and ethos of industrial capitalism," wrote Thompson.[20]

Hence, business methods, business language, business practices, and businesspeople pervade college structures, and are imposed upon the community of learners and teachers. Their prevalence is different, and greater, than it was a hundred years ago. A trustee interviewed for a major study on college boards by Public Agenda declared, "I come out of business environments where one acts with speed, with clarity, with purpose, with precision. I find that in the university environment, because of union relationships or political relationships, change is very difficult to effect. From a board point of view, it is frustrating." College treasurers have been known to speak along the same lines. Particularly exasperating must be the tradition of faculty participation in college decisions. It is reasonable to assume that trustees from the technology, banking, insurance, and investment sectors of the U.S. economy would contest guaranteeing employees a role in policy making. Likewise, they treat as normal the same skewed, uneven compensation structures in higher education that prevail in their own industries. In remunerative terms, higher college executives often mirror American societal inequality. Case in point: the Northern Ohio university president who recently presided over the layoffs of 200 employees (including the entire staff of the Arts Center) and the imposition of extra student fees, while the school spent $1 million to remodel his house, $100,000 to create a new "brand," and $50,000 to subsidize distribution of t-shirts at a Cleveland Cavaliers game.[21]

That salaries cascade to higher education administration is evident across campuses nationwide. This accompanies the steep rise (documented by the Campaign for the Future of Higher Education) "in the numbers of administrative positions, increases in those salaries, and increases in the percentage of college budgets going to these functions." Howard Bunsis, a financial analyst at Eastern Michigan University and a researcher at the American Association of University Professors (AAUP), states, "you see it on every campus: an increase in administration and a decrease in full-time faculty, and an increase in the use of part-time faculty." The term "Administration" extends to the army of staffers (usually uninvolved with faculty), reporting to the ballooning directorate. Benjamin Ginsberg characterizes them as the "arms, legs, eyes, ears, and mouthpieces" of modern college administration.[22]

According to *The New York Times*, "Despite pressure on institutions of higher learning to hold down costs, the compensation of private college presidents continues to climb." In national perspective, observes Tamar Lewin, "The pay for university presidents has risen sharply over the last decade—as has the gap between their pay and that of the average professor." Naturally, managerial benefits vary, with some executives earning increases that lag behind the rate of inflation. Yet a survey of a prominent Boston school's outlays suggests the costs of administration greatly surpassed the expenses of instruction between 2003 and 2011. The school spent twice as much in the final year of this time frame on academic administrators than in the first year, but only 27 percent more on instruction. In fact, instructional cost increases trailed all other expense categories. Noting "administrative overload" at one school, the *Times* comments that it, "like many colleges, spends more on non-faculty salaries than it does on pay for the teachers."[23]

Recent findings indicate that part-time instructors at a major New York-area institution outnumber full-time 724 to 542, but sub-vice-presidents (associate and assistant) proliferate, of whom the lowest-paid outearns the highest-compensated instructor. A respected school outside Los Angeles witnessed a decline in faculty allocations between 2010 and 2013, but a spike in administrative costs. Of the latter, the AAUP's Howard Bunsis asks: "Why is the percentage of total expenses to instruction going down? Why is the percentage of total expenses to institutional support (upper-level administration) going up?" To be sure, "institutional support" comprises planning, renovations, expansion of the physical plant, human resources, and public relations. But the school's stated mission (which emphasizes the value of instructors in enabling "students from diverse backgrounds to excel in a complex global society") is clearly not met when the allocation of funds goes to maintaining the structure of the institution rather than its academic integrity.[24]

Higher college managers often attribute curtailment of programs and layoffs of employees to school-wide financial shortfalls, which must be acted upon rapidly for the greater good. Benjamin Ginsberg writes, "One favorite administrative tactic is the claim that some fiscal or other emergency requires them to act with lightning speed—and without consulting the faculty—to save the university."[25] Frequently, board members may decree a dollar amount for each department to cut, accomplished through a multitude of pinpointed solutions: here, the liquidation of a line; there, reducing a full-timer to part-time (saving the institution health costs); elsewhere, deleting a secretary from the payroll. Every saved penny can help.

Sometimes the small blade is insufficient and a machete is necessary. To be sure, trustees have been known to advocate more draconian steps—perhaps urging the complete abolition of a science department, or relegating it to an online entity. There is a certain mentality in college boards, writes Robert A. Scott: "The goals of a business are for profits now, even when it means casting off products or services whose popularity has waned but whose potential for reinvigoration is known." Too frequently, "the market and short-term thinking" impel trustee decisions. Scott refers to the consequent aspersion cast upon disciplines now viewed as nearly worthless (like English), for purportedly lacking concrete purpose.[26] Belt-tightening follows a downward arc. It can dissolve departments, sever programs, loosen job security, and extract more for health coverage from full-timers (faculty, clerical workers, maintenance personnel, lower administrators) not yet replaced by part-timers. Indeed, "the devaluation of men is in direct proportion to the increasing value of the world of things."[27]

Despite the efforts of educators to foster "exploratory" experiences for students, corporate purviews favor quicker decisions regarding majors and careers. The more targeted the skill set, the easier for employers to fill well-defined niches. Despite evidence of the advantages to students of sorting things through before declaring a major, too many college administrations and boards prefer to hurry students through this process, oblivious to the inevitable twists and turns in academic exploration. An ACT-United Negro College Fund survey of 2014 first-year college students showed that the top two majors listed were "Undecided" and "No Major Indicated." (Nursing was a distant third.) It is equally common for a large block of applicants attending college open houses to register as "Undecided."[28] But even in light of this evidence, schools continue to pressure eighteen- and nineteen-year-old students to pick a career path almost as soon as they enter college.

As shown above, many companies place a low value on college graduates with degrees in humanities and liberal arts. Here, as well, the business model does a disservice to educational needs. In 1947, as a young student at Morehouse College, Martin Luther King, Jr. emphasized the humanistic root of education now too often swept into mere lip service: "The complete education gives one not only power of concentration, but worthy objectives upon which to concentrate." The purpose of education, argued King, "is to teach one to think intensively and to think critically. But education which stops with efficiency may prove the greatest menace to society."[29]

THE BATTLE OVER PRIORITIES

The increasing administrative tendency to make decisions with academic impact for nonacademic reasons cries out for a counterforce of input from students, educators, and related professionals into college decision-making. Unchallenged, the corporate model distorts the mission. On an uneven playing field, the corporate mind-set cannot be entrusted with higher education. Trustees or administrators beholden to it cannot by themselves understand special approaches to freshmen, whether in cohorts or clusters, with services in tow. The unfortunate result, as Robert A. Scott puts it, is that "market trumps mission." In fact, he adds, "in many cases campus missions seem to have been recast in terms of a capitalist rather than a democratic society."[30]

It is hard to knit genuine educational centrality into the sewage of the "brand," tied so strongly to superficiality and show. Needless to say, the marketing enterprises that devise mottos do not consist of students or faculty. It is easier to epitomize a school's purported spirit in a slogan than in the actual value of its pedagogy. It is educators, and those for whom the learning experience is paramount, who pursue the practical requisites of a sound educational program. Continuous pressure must be applied to administrations to implement, fund, staff, and stand by dedicated programs for freshmen, with as much aid to students as possible. And this pressure is best when organized. It is relevant to note that the most steadfast group responsible for the investigation and removal of Peter Diamandopoulos in the 1990s was the faculty. When faculty-administration cooperation broke down, it was their union that led the fight to restore it.[31]

The ingredients of higher education are undergoing colonization, under the benign supervision of far too many presidents, trustees, and other leaders. Academic capitalism presents inhospitable terrain for colleges to do what they are supposed to. Higher education would ultimately benefit from a different system entirely. The march toward corporate-shaped colleges may not be inexorable, though it appears so. Advocacy from faculty, students, families, and everyone who appreciates education as a foremost human pursuit may have the force to stop or even reverse the disease. Collectively insisting that teaching, learning, and doing should be at the heart of education structures can be a form of resistance. Programs like the General Studies Learning Community otherwise have no secure future.

The continuation of such programs requires steady assertion. Executive compensations making multimillionaires of their recipients should be brought down to earth with a jolt. Earmarking funds for educational and associated purposes (including buildings, classrooms, technologies, libraries, counselors, and full-time professors) should take precedence over lavish cosmetic improvements. Turn the college experience again into a community of relationships between and among students and instructors.

NOTES

1. Interview with Robert A. Scott, New York City, January 21, 2016.
2. Claudio Sanchez, "Is This the Beginning of the End for the SAT and ACT?" National Public Radio, July 28, 2015, http://www.npr.org/sections/ed/2015/07/28/427110042/is-this-the-beginning-of-the-end-for-the-sat-and-act. Accessed July 30, 2015.
3. Oren Pizmony-Levey and Nancy Green Saraisky, *Who Drops Out and Why? Results From a National Survey on Opting Out of Standardized Tests*, Columbia University Teachers College, August 2016.
4. Interview with Robert A. Scott, New York City, January 21, 2016.
5. Jake New, "Counseling Anytime, Anyplace," *Inside Higher Ed*, June 3, 2016, https://www.insidehighered.com/news/2016/06/03/colleges-expand-access-mental-health-services-campus?utm_source=Inside+Higher+Ed&utm_campaign=ad3ee7ecd9-DNU20160603&utm_medium=email&utm_term=0_1fcbc04421-ad3ee7ecd9-199367377#.V1Fan0E4Qls.mailto. Accessed June 3, 2016.
6. "Pre-College Program for Low-Income Students May Be at its End," *The Bristol Press*, July 30, 2016, http://m.centralctcommunications.com/bristolpress/article_3e47d8ca-56ac-11e6-9b83-9faaeb54e700.html?mode=jqm. Accessed August 24, 2016.
7. Howard Bunsis, *Analysis of the Financial Condition of Adelphi University*, AAUP, November 2015, 56, 60–65.
8. Eric Kelderman, "What Are College Governing Boards Getting from their Search Firms," *The Chronicle of Higher Education*, June 17, 2016, http://chronicle.com/article/What-Are-College-Governing/236842. Accessed August 25, 2016.
9. Office of Research, Assessment and Planning, "Fall 2011 Admissions Comparisons," June 2, 2011; Office of Research, Assessment and Planning, "Fall 2013 Admissions Comparisons," February 7, 2013; Office of Research, Assessment and Planning, "Fall 2015 Admissions Comparisons," April 16, 2015; Esther Goodcuff, associate vice president for Enrollment Management and Student Affairs, Adelphi University to author, Email, October 3, 2012.
10. Howard Bunsis, *Analysis of the Financial Condition of Adelphi University*, AAUP, November 2015, 3, 37, 38.

11. Letter from the provost to the author, January 31, 2007, GSC; General Studies Report to the Board of Trustees, Spring 2008, GSC; General Studies Report to the President and Senior Staff, February 14, 2007, GSC.

12. Notes from meeting with the provost, April 27, 2006, GSC; Letter from the provost to the author, January 31, 2007, GSC.

13. *Academic Impressions,* Measuring Academic Program Cost and Demand for Improved Resource Allocation, conference, December 9, 2015, http://www.academicimpressions.com/conference/measuring-academic-program-cost-and-demand-improved-resource-allocation-december-2015?mkt_tok=3RkMMJWWfF9wsRolvKvMZKXonjHpfsX66%2BUoWaCg38431UFwdcjKPmjr1YEFTMp0aPyQAgobGp5I5FEJQrDYULN2t6MKWQ%3D%3D#Agenda. Accessed November 27, 2015.

14. Jessica Mai, "6 Sneaky Ways Colleges Get You to Spend More Money," *Business Insider,* January 29, 2016, http://www.businessinsider.com/sneaky-ways-colleges-get-you-spend-more-2016-1. Accessed January 31, 2016.

15. Rudy Fichtenbaum, "How to Invest in Higher Education: A Financial Speculation Tax," *Campaign for the Future of Higher Ed Working Paper,* February 2013, 1, 2, 3, 6; College Board, Trends in College Pricing, 2014, 19, 24–26.

16. Henry George, Jr., *The Menace of Privilege,* New York, 1905, 286–87; C. Wright Mills, *The Power Elite,* New York, 1957, 128–29.

17. Rudy Fichtenbaum, president, American Association of University Professors, to the author, July 31, 2015; Philip Deery, *Red Apple: Communism and McCarthyism in Cold War New York,* New York, 2014, 75–111; Upton Sinclair, *The Goose-Step: A Study of American Education,* Pasadena, 1923, 28–29.

18. Interview with Robert A. Scott, New York City, January 21, 2016; Sean Salai, "The Spirituality of Money: Author Q & A with Heather King," *America: The National Catholic Review,* April 27, 2016, http://americamagazine.org/content/all-things/spirituality-money-author-qa-heather-king. Accessed May 6, 2016. Quoted by permission of Heather King; Robert A. Scott, "The Modern American University: Observations from the Field," *Oxford Magazine,* Fifth Week, Michaelmas Term, 8.

19. Benjamin Ginsberg, *The Fall of the Faculty: The Rise of the All-Administrative University and Why it Matters,* New York, 2011, 17, 65; Jeff Charis-Carlson, "University of Iowa Sanctioned by National Professor Body," *Des Moines Register,* June 18, 2016, http://www.desmoinesregister.com/story/news/education/2016/06/18/national-professor-group-sanctions-university-iowa/86085620/. Accessed August 25, 2016.

20. Dragan Plavsic, "E. P. Thompson on How to Save the University," *Counterfire,* December 1, 2016, http://www.counterfire.org/articles/analysis/18648-e-p-thompson-on-how-to-save-the-university. Accessed December 5, 2016.

21. David Schleifer, Carolin Hagelskamp, and Chloe Rinehart, *A Difficult Balance: Trustees Speak About the Challenges Facing Comprehensive Universities,* Public Agenda, December 2015, 11, 13, 14; "University of Akron President Scott Scarborough Garnering Lots of Attention, But For All the Wrong Reasons," *Cleveland Plain Dealer,* July 29, 2015, http://www.cleveland.com/metro/index.ssf/2015/07/university_of_akron_president_4.html. Accessed July 30, 2015.

22. Adelphi University Board of Trustees, http://president.adelphi.edu/university-leadership/board-of-trustees/. Accessed November 6, 2015; 11–12; Jason Furman and Peter Orzsag, *A Firm-Level Perspective on the Role of Rents in the Rise in Inequality: Presentation at "A Just Society" Centennial Event in Honor of Joseph Stiglitz,* Columbia University, October 16, 2015, 11–12; Campaign for the Future of Higher Education, *Who Needs Faculty?* A CFHE Working Paper, September 2015, 6–7; Ginsberg, *The Fall of the Faculty,* 24–25.

23. Stephanie Saul, "Salaries of Private College Presidents Continue to Rise, Chronicle Survey Finds," *New York Times,* December 7, 2015, A13; Tamar Lewin, "Many Specialists at Private Universities Earn More Than Presidents," *New York Times,* February 22, 2009; Andrea Fuller, "Salaries Rise for Senior Administrators but Lag Behind Inflation," *The Chronicle of Higher Education,* A22–A23; Howard Bunsis, *Analysis of the Financial Condition of Boston College,* AAUP, March 2012, 43, 52, 56, 69; Ron Lieber,

"Why the Cost of College Rises, Even in a Recession," *New York Times*, September 5, 2009, B1.

24. Howard Bunsis, *Update on the Financial Condition of Hofstra University*, AAUP, March 2013, 55, 57; Rudy Fichtenbaum and Howard Bunsis, *Hofstra University Financial Analysis*, AAUP, 2011, 33; Howard Bunsis, *Financial Analysis of Whittier College*, AAUP, May 2014, 56, 58; Whittier College Mission Statement, http://www.whittier.edu/about/mission. Accessed November 6, 2015.

25. Ginsberg, 9–11.

26. Interview with Robert A. Scott, New York City, January 21, 2016; Robert A. Scott, "The Modern American University: Observations from the Field," *Oxford Magazine*, Fifth Week, Michaelmas Term, 8.

27. Karl Marx, "Economic and Philosophic Manuscripts of 1844," in Karl Marx-Frederick Engels, *Collected Works*, Volume 3, New York, 1975, 272.

28. ACT-United Negro College Fund, *The Conditions of College & Career Readiness: African American Students 2014*, 2015, 11; Adelphi University Office of Admissions, Accepted Students Day, Sunday, April 10, 2016, Garden City Campus, "Attendees," GSC.

29. Rudy Fichtenbaum, president, American Association of University Professors, to the author, July 31, 2015; Martin Luther King, Jr., quoted in Yohuru Williams, "What Would Martin Say," *The Progressive*, January 16, 2015, http://www.progressive.org/news/2015/01/187969/what-would-martin-say. Accessed January 20, 2015.

30. Interview with Robert A. Scott, New York City, January 21, 2016.

31. Rudy Fichtenbaum, "The Crisis is Real," *The European*, February 27, 2015, http://www.theeuropean-magazine.com/rudy-fichtenbaum/9691-higher-education-crisis-causes-and-solutions. Accessed August 4, 2015.

Bibliography

COLLECTIONS

General Studies Collection. University Archives. Swirbul Library, Adelphi University.

INTERVIEWS

Della Hudson. Garden City: June 24, 2014.
Peter Katopes. New York City: June 26, 2013, June 20, 2014, August 13, 2015.
Robert W. Scott. New York City: January 21, 2016.
Lisa Wolf-Wendel. October 16, 2015.

PUBLISHED SOURCES

ACT. *The Condition of College & Career Readiness*. Iowa City: ACT, 2013.

ACT-United Negro College Fund. *The Conditions of College & Career Readiness: African American Students 2014*. 2015.

Addo, Fenaba R., et al. "Young, Black, and (Still) in the Red: Parental Wealth, Race, and Student Loan Debt." *Race and Social Problems*, Vol. 8 (2016): 64–76.

Allen, Gary L., et al. "Measures of Learning Rate and Scholastic Aptitude as Predictors of Performance in Training-Oriented Academic Courses." *The Journal of General Psychology*, Vol. 117, No. 3 (1990): 277–93.

"Almost No Blacks at the Top of the ACT Scoring Pyramid." *The Journal of Blacks in Higher Education*. August 30, 2007.

American Academy of Arts and Sciences. *The Heart of the Matter*. Cambridge, MA: Commission on the Humanities and Social Sciences, 2013.

American Association of University Professors. *Academic Freedom and Tenure*. National Louis University (Illinois): April 2013.

American Council of Trustees and Alumni. *Governance for a New Era: A Blueprint for Higher Education Trustees*. Washington, DC: American Council of Trustees and Alumni, 2014.

Artman, Salvia, et al. *The Role of Self-Efficacy Beliefs in College Student Performance & Persistence*. University of Utah Department of Experimental Psychology, 2015.

Au, Wayne, ed. *Rethinking Multicultural Education*. Milwaukee: Rethinking Schools, 2009.

Auguste, Byron, et al. *Closing the Talent Gap: Attracting and Retaining Top-Third Graduates to Careers in Teaching*. New York: McKinsey & Company, September 2010.

Benford, Russell, and Gess-Newsome, Julie. *Factors Affecting Student Academic Success in Gateway Courses at Northern Arizona University*. Flagstaff: Center for Science, Teaching, and Learning, 2006.

Benningfield, Margaret M., et al. "Treatment of Alcoholic Intoxication at University Health Services: Examining Clinical Characteristics, Drinking Patterns, and Adherence with Referral." *Journal of Alcohol and Drug Education*, Vol. 53 (April 2009): 54–69.

Booker, K. "Building the Connection: An Evaluation of New Student Orientation at a Women's College." *The Journal of Orientation and College Transition*, Vol. 13, No. 2: 5–9.

Boucher, Kathryn L., et al. "Forecasting the Experience of Stereotype Threat for Others." *Journal of Experimental Psychology*, Vol. 58 (2015): 56–62.

Bloom, Benjamin S. "The Search for Methods of Group Instruction as Effective as One-to-One Tutoring." *Educational Leadership*, Vol. 41, No. 8 (May 1984).

Branshaw, John, and Duneitz, Samuel. "Busting the Myths: The Annual Report on the Economic Status of the Profession, 2014–1015." *Academe*. March–April 2015, 4–19.

Bulotaite, Nijole. "University Heritage: An Institutional Tool for Branding and Marketing." *Higher Education in Europe*, Vol. 28, No. 4 (December 2003): 449–54.

Callahan, David. *The Cheating Culture: Why More Americans Are Doing Wrong to Get Ahead*. Orlando: Harcourt, 2004.

Campaign for the Future of Higher Education. *Back to School in Higher Ed: Who Needs Faculty?* September 2015.

Campaign for the Future of Higher Education. *Who Needs Faculty?* A CFHE Working Paper. September 2015.

Carnevale, Anthony, et al. *African Americans: College Majors and Earnings*. Washington, DC: Georgetown University Center on Education and the Workforce, 2016.

Cavallo, Dominick. *A Fiction of the Past: The Sixties in American History*. New York: Palgrave Macmillan, 2001.

Center on Urban and Metropolitan Policy. *The Rise of New Immigrant Gateways*. Washington, DC: The Brookings Institution, 2004.

Chapleo, Chris. "What Defines 'Successful University' Brands." *International Journal of Public Sector Management*. Vol. 23, No. 2 (2010): 169–72.

Clark, Lucy. *Beautiful Failure: How the Quest for Success is Harming Our* Kids. Melbourne: Penguin, 2016.

College Board. *The 10th Annual AP Report to the Nation*. February 11, 2014.

"College Board-Sponsored Study Claims SAT is Good Predictor of Grades, Graduation." *Black Issues in Higher Education*. Vol. 18, No. 7 (May 24, 2011), 11.

"College Freshmen Drink at Levels Well Beyond the Binge Threshold." *Brown University Digest of Addiction Theory and Application*, Vol. 26, No. 1 (January 2007), 1, 7.

Collins, Chuck, and Hoxie, John. *Billionaire Bonanza: The Forbes 400 and the Rest of Us*, Institute for Policy Studies, December 2015.

Conroy, Martin. *Faded Dreams: The Politics and Economics of Race in America*. Cambridge: Cambridge University Press, 1994.

Cooper, David, and Mishel, Lawrence. *The Erosion of Collective Bargaining Has Widened the Gap Between Productivity and Pay*. Washington, DC, Economic Policy Institute, January 5, 2015.

Curtis, John W., and Thornton, Saranna. "The Annual Report on the Economic Status of the Profession." *Academe*. March–April 2013, 4–19.

Davidson, J. Cody. "Increasing FAFSA Completion Rates: Research, Policies, and Practices." *Journal of Student Financial Aid*, Vol. 43, No. 1 (2013): Article 4.

De Angelis, Massimo, and Harvie, David. "'Cognitive Capitalism' and the Rat Race: How Capital Measures Immaterial Labour in British Universities." *Historical Materialism*, Vol. 17, No. 3 (2009): 3–30.

DeAngelo, Linda, Franke, Ray, Hurtado, Sylvia, Pryor, John H., and Tran, Serge. *Completing College: Assessing Graduation Rates at Four-Year Institutions*. Higher Education Research Institute at UCLA, 2011.

DeDonno, Michael A., and Rivera-Torres, Karla. "The Influence of Time Limit and Bilingualism on Scholastic Assessment Test Performance," *North American Journal of Psychology*, Vol. 16, No. 2 (2014), 211–24.

Democracy Now. *Part II: Leading Education Scholar Diane Ravitch on The Death and Life of the Great American School System*. March 8, 2010. http://m.democracynow.org/web_exclusives/572.

Eagan, Kevin, et al. *The American Freshman: National Norms Fall 2014*. Cooperative Institutional Research Program at the Higher Education Research Institute at UCLA, 2014.

Edelman, David C. "Branding in the Digital Age." *Harvard Business Review*, Vol. 88, No. 12 (December 2010): 62–69.

ERASE Initiative of the Long Island Community Foundation, *Racism and the Opportunity Divide on Long Island*, 2002.

Everyone Graduates Center at the School of Education at Johns Hopkins University. *Building a Grad Nation: Progress and Challenge in Ending the High School Dropout Epidemic*. Baltimore, School of Education at Johns Hopkins University, 2015.

Feistritzer, C. Emily. *Profile of Teachers in the U.S. 2011*. National Center for Educational Information. Washington, DC, 2011.

Fichtenbaum, Rudy. *Presidential Address*. American Association of University Professors, June 15, 2015.

Fichtenbaum, Rudy. "Protecting Academic Freedom for Faculty Working on Contingent Contracts: Contract Language for Full-Time Faculty at Wright State University." *Journal of Collective Bargaining in the Academy*. Vol. 0, Article 25, 1–10.

Forman, Seth. "Racial Composition of Long Island School Districts, 1991-2001: Change and Stagnation." *Opolis*. Vol. 1, No. 2 (2005): 17–31.

Fry, Richard. *Young Adults, Student Debt and Economic Well-being*. Washington, DC: Pew Research Center, 2014.

The Futures Project, *Correcting Course: How We Can Restore the Ideals of Public Higher Education in a Market-Driven Era*. San Francisco: Jossey-Bass, 2005.

Garcia, Emma, and Elaine Weiss. *Early Education Gaps by Social Class and Race Start U.S. Children out on Unequal Footing: A Summary of the Major Findings in Inequalities at the Starting Gate*. Washington, DC: Economic Policy Institute, 2015.

George, Henry, Jr. *The Menace of Privilege*. New York, 1905.

Gershenfeld, Susan, et al. "The Role of First-Semester GPA in Predicting Graduation Rates of Underrepresented Students." *Journal of College Student Retention: Research, Theory, & Practice*, Vol. 17, No. 4 (2016): 469–88.

Ginsberg, Benjamin. *The Fall of the Faculty: The Rise of the All-Administrative University and Why it Matters*. New York: Oxford University Press, 2011.

Gould, Eric. *The University in a Corporate Culture*, New Haven: Yale University Press, 2003.

Graham, Sergio Pinto, and Ruiz, Julia. *Stress, Worry, and Social Support: Inequality in America's Cities*. Washington, DC: Brookings Institution, November 5, 2015.

Greenstone, Michael, and Looney, Adam. *Is Starting College and Not Finishing Really That Bad?* Washington, DC: The Hamilton Project, June 7, 2013.

Grinstein-Weiss, Michal, et al. "Racial Disparities in Education Debt Burden Among Low-and-Moderate-Income Households." *Children and Youth Services Review*, Vol. 65 (June 2016): 166–74.

Hanley, Larry. "Academic Capitalism in the New University," *Radical Teacher*, No. 73 (August 2005): 3.

Hanover Research. *Strategies for Improving Retention*. Arlington, VA, November 2015.

Hart Research Associates, *Falling Short? College Learning and Career Success*, January 20, 2015.

Haynes, R. Michael, and Atchley, T. Wayne. "The Impact of a Camp Orientation Program on First-Year Academic Engagement and Persistence." *The Journal of College Orientation and Transition*. Vol. 20, No. 2 (Spring 2004), 78-93.

Hemphill, Clara, and Mader, Nicole. *Segregated Schools in Integrated Neighborhoods: The City's Schools Are Even More Divided Than Our Housing*. New York: New School Center for New York City Affairs, 2015. http://www.centernyc.org/segregated schools.

Higher Education Research Institute at UCLA. Research Brief, *The American Freshman: National Norms Fall 2015*. February 2016.

Hillman, Nicholas W., et al. "Evaluating the Impacts of 'New' Performance Funding in Higher Education." *Educational Evaluation and Policy Analysis*, Vol. 20, No. 10: 1–19.
Hiss, William C., and Franks, Valerie. *Defining Promise: Optional Standardized Testing Policies in American Culture and University Admissions*. February 5, 2014: Arlington, VA, National Association for College Admission Counseling.
Hoffman, Banesh. *The Tyranny of Testing*. New York: Crowell-Collier, 1962.
Hollins, Jr., Thomas. "Examining the Impact of a Comprehensive Approach to Student Orientation." *Inquiry*, Vol. 14, No. 1 (Spring 2009): 15–27.
Howlett, Chuck. "The Long Island Civil Rights Movement in the 1960s, Part Three: Militancy and Black Consciousness." *Long Island Historical Journal*, Vol. 9, No. 2 (Spring 1997): 168–88.
Hurley, Sarah, and Cole, Ann. *College Counseling for Latino and Underrepresented Students*. Arlington, VA: National Association for College Admission Counseling, 2015.
Inside Higher Ed. *The Retention Agenda*. Washington, DC: 2013.
Insler, Gayle, et al. The Committee to Save Adelphi, *Petitioners against Peter Diamandopoulos et al., Respondents, To the Board of Regents*. 1996.
Institute for Policy Studies. *The One Percent at State U: How Public University Presidents Profit From Rising Student Debt and Low-Wage Faculty Labor*. Washington, DC: Institute for Policy Studies, 2014.
The Institute of Politics. *Survey of Young Americans' Attitudes Toward Politics and Public Service: 17th Edition*. Cambridge: Harvard University, 2010.
Ivie, Rachel, and Ephraim, Arnell. "Women and the Imposter Syndrome in Astronomy." *AAS Status Report on Women in Astronomy*, Washington, DC: American Astronomical Society, January 2011.
John N. Gardner Institute. *Expert Consultation and Proven Processes: Student Learning, Success, Retention and Completion*. Brevard, NC: John N. Gardner Institute, n.d.
Jones, Janelle, and Schmitt, John. *A College Degree is No Guarantee*. Washington, DC, Center for Economic and Policy Research, May 2014.
Junco, Reynol. "Student Class Standing, Facebook Use, and Academic Performance." *Journal of Applied Developmental Psychology*, Vol. 36 (January-February 2015): 18–29.
Kantrowitz, Mark. *Who Graduates with Excessive Student Loan Debt?* Student Aid Policy Analysis Papers. December 14, 2015.
Katopes, Peter J., with Ruth Miller. "The Harlem Renaissance: Arna W. Bontemps, Countee Cullen, James Weldon Johnson, Claude McKay, and Jean Toomer," in M. Thomas Inge et al., eds. *Black American Writers: Bibliographical Essays, I: The Beginnings through the Harlem Renaissance and Langston Hughes*. New York: St. Martin's, 1978.
Katz, Michael B. *Class, Bureaucracy, and Schools: The Illusion of Educational Change in America*. New York: Praeger, 1975.
Knight, John R., et al. "Alcohol Abuse and Dependence Among U.S. College Students." *Journal of Studies on Alcohol*, Vol. 63, No. 2 (2002): 263–70.
Kucsera, John, and Orfield, Gary. *New York State's Extreme School Segregation: Inequality, Inaction, and a Damaged Future*. Los Angeles: The Civil Rights Project, 2014.
LaBare, Martha J., ed. *First-Year Engagement: Sound Foundations for College, Citizenship, and Democracy*. Columbia, SC: National Resource Center for the First-Year Experience and Students in Transition, 2008.
Lavy, Victor, and Sand, Edith. "On the Origins of Human Capital Gaps: Short and Long Term Consequences of Teachers' Stereotypical Biases." *NBER Working Paper No. 20209*. Cambridge, MA: National Bureau of Economic Research. January 2015.
Lemann, Nicholas. *The Big Test: The Secret History of the American Meritocracy*. New York: Farrar, Straus and Giroux, 1999.
Levin, Shana, and Van Laar, Colette, eds. *Stigma and Group Inequality: Social Psychological Perspectives*. Mahwah, NJ: Psychology Press, 2006.
Lewis, Lionel. *When Power Corrupts: Academic Governing Boards in the Shadow of the Adelphi Case*. Piscataway: Transaction Publishing, 2000.

Long Island Index. *At the Breaking Point? Taxation and Governance on Long Island: A Report Prepared for the Rauch Foundation*. Stony Brook, NY: Long Island Index, 2005.

Long Island Index. *Places to Grow: An Analysis of the Potential for Transit-Accessible Housing and Jobs in Long Island's Downtowns and Station Areas*. Garden City: Long Island Index, 2010.

Loveless, Tom. *How Well Are American Students Learning*. The Brookings Institution, The Brown Center Report on American Education. Vol. 3, No. 1 (February 2012).

Mabli, James, et al. *Hunger in America 2010: Local Report Prepared for Long Island Harvest and Long Island Cares*. Princeton, NJ: Mathematica Policy Research. January 2010.

Markle, Ross, and Robbins, Steve. "A Holistic View of Course Placement Decisions: Avoiding the HS GPA Trap." *Educational Testing Service*. March 2013.

Meeker, Frank, Fox, Daniel, and Whitney, Bernard. "Predictors of Academic Success in the Undergraduate Psychology Major." *Teaching of Psychology*, Vol. 21, No. 3 (December 1994): 107–13.

Morphet, Edgar L., et al. *Educational Organization and Administration*. Englewood Cliffs, NJ: Prentice-Hall, 1967.

Miller, Casey Miller, and Keivan Stassun. "A Test That Fails." *Nature*, Vol. 510 (12 June 2014): 303–4.

Mills, C. Wright. *The Power Elite*. New York: Oxford University Press, 1957.

National Association for College Admission Counseling. *Report of the Commission on the Use of Standardized Tests in Undergraduate Admissions*. Arlington, VA: National Association for College Admission Counseling, 2008.

National Center for Educational Statistics. *Institutional Retention and Graduation Rates for Undergraduate Students*. May 2015.

National Fair Housing Alliance, *Housing Segregation Background Report: Long Island, New York*. Washington, DC: 2006.

National Student Clearinghouse. *National College Progression Rates*. Herndon, VA: 2013.

National Survey of Student Engagement. *Promoting Student Learning and Institutional Improvement. Lesson from NSSE at 13*. Bloomington, IN: Indiana University Center for Post-Secondary Research, 2012.

New York State's Extreme School Segregation: Inequality, Inaction, and a Damaged Future, Long Island (Suffolk and Nassau Counties), NY Metro Summary. Los Angeles: The Civil Rights Project, March 2014.

NYU Furman Center. *CITI Report on Home Ownership & Opportunity in New York*. August 5, 2016.

Pager, Devah, and Western, Bruce. *Discrimination in Low-Wage Markets: Evidence from an Experimental Audit Study in New York City*. Submission to the Population Association of American Annual Meetings, 2005.

Palumbo, Michael, Meltzer, Tom, and Owens, Eric. *The Best Northeastern Colleges 2010: 218 Select Schools to Consider*. New York: Princeton Review, 2009.

Paterson, Jim. "Case Loaded." *The Journal of College Admissions*. No. 227 (Spring 2015): 36–39.

Pew Hispanic Center. *Hispanic High School Graduates Pass Whites in Rate of College Enrollment*. Washington, DC: May 9, 2013.

Pew Research Center, *America's Changing Religious Landscape*. Washington, DC: May 12, 2015.

Pew Research Center. *The American Middle Class is Losing Ground*. Washington, DC: December 9, 2015.

Pew Research Center. *Parenting in America*. Washington, DC: December 2015.

Porter, Michael E., and Rivkin, Jan W. *An Economy Doing Half Its Job*. Cambridge: Harvard Business School, 2014.

Public Agenda. *With Their Whole Lives Ahead of Them: Myths and Realities About Why So Many Students Fail to Finish College*. New York: Public Agenda, 2010.

Quinn, Diane, and Spencer, Steven. "The Interference of Stereotype Threat With Women's Generation of Mathematical Problem-Solving Strategies." *Journal of Social Issues*, Vol. 57, No. 1 (2001): 55–71.

"The Racial Gap in Advancement Placement Test Scores," *The Journal of Blacks in Higher Education*. November 16, 2015.

Rojstaczer, Stuart, and Healy, Christopher. "Grading in American Colleges and Universities." *Teachers College Record*. March 4, 2010.

Rojstaczer, Stuart, and Healy, Christopher. "Where A Is Ordinary: The Evolution of American College and University Grading, 1940–2009." *Teachers College Record*, Vol. 114, No. 7 (2012): 1–23.

Rosenberg, Daniel. "The Twilight of Reason: Neo-Conservatism and Corruption at Adelphi University." *Left History*, Vol. 8, No. 2 (April 2003): 71–113.

Rude, Jesse D., Wolniak, Gregory C., and Pascarella, Ernest. *Racial Attitude Change during the College Years*. Prepared for the 2012 Annual Meeting of the American Educational Research Association (AERA) in Vancouver, British Columbia. April 12, 2012.

Ruffalo Noel Levitz. *A Compendium of Successful, Innovative Retention Programs and Practices*. Coralville, IA: Ruffalo Noel Levitz, 2015.

Sadovnik, Alan R., ed., *Knowledge & Pedagogy: The Sociology of Basil Bernstein*. Norwood, NJ: Ablex, 1995.

Schleifer, David, Hagelskamp, Carolin, and Rinehart, Chloe. *A Difficult Balance: Trustees Speak About the Challenges Facing Comprehensive Universities*. New York: Public Agenda, December 2015.

Scott, Robert A. "The Modern American University: Observations from the Field." *Oxford Magazine*. Fifth Week, Michaelmas Term, 2015, 5–10.

Sheffield, Robert M., Montgomery, Rhonda J., and Moody, Patricia G. *Case Studies for the First Year*. Upper Saddle River, NJ: Pearson, 2003.

Sinclair, Upton. *The Goose-Step: A Study of American Education*. New York: Albert & Charles Boni, 1936 (1922).

Sparkman, Larry A., Mauling, Wanda S., and Roberts, Jaylynn G. "Non-Cognitive Predictors of Student Success in College." *College Student Journal*, Vol. 46, No. 3, (September 2012): 642–52.

Spencer, Harry E. "Mathematical SAT Test Scores and College Chemistry Grades." *Journal of Chemical Education*, Vol. 73, No. 12 (December 1996): 1150–53.

Sweet, Elizabeth, et al. "The High Price of Debt: Household Financial Debt and its Impact on Mental and Physical Health." *Social Science & Medicine*, Vol. 91 (August 2013): 94–100.

Tai, Robert H., Sadler, Philip M., and Loehr, John F. "Factors Influencing Success in Introductory College Chemistry." *Journal of Research in Science Teaching*, Vol. 42, No. 9 (2005): 987–1012.

Talbott, Laura L., et al. "Drinking Likelihood, Alcohol Problems, and Peer Influence Among First-Year College Students." *The American Journal of Drug and Alcohol Abuse*, Vol. 34 (2008): 433–40.

Torras, Mariano, and Skinner, Curtis. *The Economic Impact of the Hispanic Population on Long Island*. New York: Horace Hagedorn Foundation, 2004.

Understanding Retention: An Analytical Review. March 28, 2008: Scannell & Kurz, Inc.

Upcraft, M. Lee, Gardner, John. *The Freshman Year Experience*. San Francisco: Jossey-Bass, 1989.

Veblen, Thorstein. *The Higher Learning in America*, New York: Hill & Wang, 1957 (1918).

Wæraas, Arild, and Solbakk, Marianne N. "Defining the Essence of a University: Lessons from Higher Education Branding." *Higher Education: The International Journal of Higher Education and Educational Planning*, Vol. 57 (2009): 449–53.

Wai, Jonathan, and Rindermann, Heiner. "The Path and Performance of a Company Leader: A Historical Examination of the Education and Cognitive Ability of Fortune 500 CEOs." *Intelligence*, Vol. 53 (November-December 2015): 102–7.

Ward, Rose Marie, Oswald, Barbara B., and Galante, Maria. "Prescription Stimulant Misuse, Alcohol Abuse, and Disordered Eating Among College Students." *Journal of Alcohol and Drug Education*, Vol. 60, No. 1 (2016): 59–80.

Wells, Amy Stuart, et al. *Divided We Fall: The Story of Unequal Suburban Schools 60 Years After Brown v. Board of Education*. New York: The Center for Understanding, Race and Education, Teachers College, Columbia University, 2014.

Wells, Amy Stuart, et al. *Why Boundaries Matter: A Study of Five Separate and Unequal Long Island School Districts*. (Abridged). Garden City: Long Island Index, 2009.

White, Geoffrey D., and Hauck, Flannery C., eds. *Campus, Inc.: Corporate Power in the Ivory Tower*. Amherst, NY: Prometheus Books, 2000.

"The Widening Racial Scoring Gap on SAT II Subject Tests." *The Journal of Blacks in Higher Education*. December 24, 2009.

Zwick, Rebecca. *College Admission Testing*. Arlington, VA: National Association for College Admission Counseling, 2007.

Index

About the Author

Dr. Daniel Rosenberg teaches history and directs the General Studies Learning Community in the College of Arts & Sciences at Adelphi University. He obtained his doctorate from the Graduate Center of the City University of New York. His publications in American labor and social history include *Underground Communists in the McCarthy Period; Racism, Dissent, and Asian Americans from 1850 to the Present;* and *New Orleans Dockworkers: Race, Labor, and Unionism, 1892–1923*. He lives in Brooklyn, New York.

CPSIA information can be obtained
at www.ICGtesting.com
Printed in the USA
BVOW06*0532170417
481344BV00004B/6/P

9 781498 532662